DATE DUE

DEMCO 38-296

Turning Points

Essays in the History of
Cultural Expressions

Marshall Brown

Turning Points

Essays in the History of
Cultural Expressions

Stanford University Press
Stanford, California 1997

Stanford University Press
Stanford, California
© 1997 by the Board of Trustees of the
Leland Stanford Junior University
Printed in the United States of America

CIP data are at the end of the book

Stanford University Press publications are distributed
exclusively by Stanford University Press within the
United States, Canada, Mexico, and Central America;
they are distributed exclusively by Cambridge
University Press throughout
the rest of the world.

To Dorrit and Benedict

Preface

Turning Points collects both "theoretical" and "practical" essays on literature, philosophy, music, and art. "Cultural expressions" is my umbrella coinage for these various entities, whose similarities, as I argue, far outweigh their differences. The essays share a vision of cultural history rather different from those currently in favor. Our prevailing materialisms examine how cultural expressions are produced by or react to the conditions of their emergence. Texts, however important, come late, or last. In my book they come first, often rhetorically and always in importance. Whatever the massed force of circumstance, our cultures are shaped to a vast extent by the ideas, insights, and expressions of distinctive, individual minds. This book is devoted to examining and reflecting on the imprint of individual works on the history of culture.

To be sure, great works embody and express powerful cultural forces. Even anticanonists rarely escape some such implications, for it is hard to know how to recognize a culture if not at least in part through its expressions. But I want to say something different. Theories of embodiment and expression, of correspondence and mirroring, ultimately betray the history they claim to serve. That is the gist of the polemic that concludes "Why Style Matters." Instead, cultural expressions act in and on history to the extent that they are not of their time. Significant works are beyond their moment, underway toward a new age. Culture does not advance (or retreat either, for that matter) through being represented but through being escaped.

The negativity of texts is crucial to their historicity. What is deter-

mined and known is not in movement. That applies even to oppositional stances and texts: they embody one positivity facing another.
Where movement begins is where definition ends. That is why my
attention goes to the indefinite moments in all the works I study: to
the nonconceptual intuitions of style and of form, to misunderstanding, mistranslation, and disarticulation. History is made of the break-
throughs not into but out of time.

I am concerned first, then, with works in history. "Mozart and After"
serves as the model here, beginning with its very title: a new textual
intuition—a musical text in this case—becomes the vessel of a new sensibility through which new concepts and cultural shapes arise. Other
chapters trace the backgrounds rather than the aftereffects of such innovations. In "Kant's Misreading of Descartes," it is a conceptual background from which Kant swerves—and which, I suspect, could only
become coherently visible as a result of that swerve. In "Toward an
Archaeology of English Romanticism," it is a historical thrust out of
which a revolution in sensibility emerges. This essay is the earliest and
the most causal in its rhetoric; I am now inclined to explain less and
admire more. The last two chapters in this section focus on widespread
phenomena instead of individual texts, but they too are concerned with
the history made in shadows, intuitively, in acts of the mind rather than
those of the body. It may seem paradoxical that I should write about
periods when I profess such a belief in flux, but I would have periods
always understood as movements. These two essays posit a ground that
appears stable in retrospective view, but the figure only comes to rest
because the essay must stop somewhere.

Turning points thus are not just where significant works are found
but what the works are made of. They are divided and in motion, not
unified. Thomas Parnell's "Night-Piece on Death" (in "Deconstruction
and Enlightenment") is a test case, but always I am fascinated with
textual shifts and emergences. Heinrich Wölfflin is my inspiration here,
though like any great critic he must be read as a great writer, to see how
his rhetoric and critical practice escape the doctrines encumbering his
reputation. My essay on Jerome McGann argues that even a critic appearing to be a cultural historian is fundamentally motivated by the
history made in the texts themselves. Some readers have objected that

McGann is not as good a critic as I make him out to be. Perhaps by conventional standards they are right. But I make him out to be a different kind of critic, who brings texts alive by moments and who is not adequately judged by familiar criteria of coherence and completeness. For me, however, the greatest figure remains Hippolyte Taine, in whose work as in no other that I know the history stirring within texts becomes congruent with the history flowing without.

What I have called negativity also goes by the name error. Deconstruction is the most recently popular theory of error, and the opening essay might well be subtitled "From Deconstruction to History." Too often, deconstruction appears to subside into mere drift (*dérive* being the common French term). But the more Derrida and others argue with history, the more they acknowledge it as an inescapable factor. Error, deviance, vagrancy may be random in origin, but they become productive in effect; as Valéry writes: "No 'truth' without passion, without error" (*Oeuvres* 2: 641).

The agencies of the text's productivity are its style and its form. The notion of form as an inert drag upon expression depends on an identification of expression with content and on an individualist bias, both of which are at odds with the doctrines of many of the very critics who attack formalism. As my last chapter argues, form is the unheard melody that transcends the individual and releases singular thoughts into collective force. Valéry again sums up, with a pregnancy I can only envy: "*Writing*—being supposed to construct, as solidly and as exactly as possible, that language machine in which the release of the activated spirit is expended in conquering *real* resistances—demands that the writer become divided against himself" (1: 1205).

It remains only to say that the divisions celebrated by Taine, Wölfflin, and Valéry are also itineraries. My own book is divided by topics and approaches, but I would have the divisions be understood as its directions. I can identify at least four: from deconstruction to history, from style to form, from theory to practice, from expressed to concealed meanings. What I have not seen remains for others to point out.

For the present publication I have touched up the writing, corrected a handful of errors, and inserted a handful of references previously overlooked or subsequent to the original publication. (Unattributed translations are my own throughout; italics are reproduced as in the originals, except where noted.) The original publications and occasions are as follows.

"Errours Endlesse Traine" began as a lecture at the University of Washington and was published in *PMLA* 99 (1984): 9–25.

"Why Style Matters" is a new essay realizing an old dream. I first read Taine in 1976–77, when Gene Falk made me teach the history of criticism at the University of North Carolina, and an early sketch of my reading was the first conference paper I ever presented, under Don Marshall's tutelage, at the Society for Values in Higher Education in 1978. I picked the talk up again for a paper at the 1994 MLA, courtesy of David Bell, and Heather Dubrow gave me a needed critique of the pages on New Historicism. The paragraphs on Proudhon derive from a paper written in 1967 for Peter Demetz's realism course.

The essay on Wölfflin, another old passion I got to earlier, was published in *Critical Inquiry* 9 (1982): 379–404.

"What's in a Text?" was written for *Review* 12 (1990): 89–106.

"Deconstruction and Enlightenment," *The Eighteenth Century: Theory and Interpretation* 28 (1987): 259–64, was commissioned by Bob Markley before we were colleagues. The assignment, to say something about the eighteenth century and critical theory in around five printed pages, prompted the stylistic experiment.

"Mozart and After" started life as a footnote; I made it into an essay on the sly, in the basement of our house in Virginia. It was my second conference paper, for the American Society for Eighteenth-Century Studies in 1980. When I couldn't get it published, Doug Johnson told me why and showed me how. It comes from *Critical Inquiry* 7 (1981): 689–706.

"Kant's Misreading of Descartes," unpublished, started life as a digression to the book I still haven't written on Kant and the gothic novel. Early versions were presented at annual meetings of the MLA in 1983 and the International Association for Philosophy and Literature in 1992, and a full-length version—decked out as "Kant und Descartes—ein interkulterelles Mißverständnis?"—was given at Harald Weinrich's invitation in 1992 for the Institut für Deutsch als Fremdsprache of the University of Munich. At the last minute Marjorie Grene intervened to save me from the crudest of my errors.

Geoffrey Hartman suggested in 1967 that I write a course paper on Sarbiewski; one sentence from it survived into the essay that was published in *Comparative Literature* 30 (1978): 313–37. It had a tryout in Bill Oram's Renaissance colloquium at Smith around 1975. It was written long before I met Mona Modiano but was clearly destined for her.

"Romanticism and Enlightenment" was written in 1987 for Stuart Curran's *Cambridge Companion to British Romanticism* (Cambridge: Cambridge University Press, 1993). Versions were read at the MLA in 1988 (where Starry Schor and Jerry McGann asked memorable questions I only later learned how to answer) and in 1990 at the University of Florence, by invitation of Guido Fink. My memory also links David Simpson, the most enlightened romanticist I know, with the writing of it. It realizes another long-standing dream, to be able to publish an essay without footnotes.

"Origins of Modernism" was extracted by Charlie Altieri for the 1982 MLA and subsequently delivered as a lecture at Stanford and at the University of Southern California in 1984. The final version comes from a conference at Dartmouth organized by Steve Scher and Larry Kramer and appears in *Music and Text: Critical Inquiries,* ed. Steven Paul Scher (Cambridge: Cambridge University Press, 1992). Doug Johnson and Steve Hefling both commented coruscatingly and beneficially on an early version, Tom Bauman on the final draft. I owe the Billings reference to Karl Kroeger.

Finally, "Unheard Melodies" is dedicated, in code, to the musicians from whom my spirit draws sustenance. It was Lucy Shelton who sang the Strauss. Steve Hefling (musicologist as well as musician), John Rahn, and Tom Bauman all gave me musical advice, and Tom was kind enough to prepare the musical examples. Paul Fry pointed me toward Derrida's "Force et signification." Earlier versions were presented at the University of Colorado School of Music, the University of Northern Colorado, the University of Bologna (on the generous invitation of Giovanna Franci), and the University of Washington. It was published in a group of essays about performance, in *PMLA* 107 (1992): 465–81.

Mara Bundza did most of the burdensome task of creating computer files and converting them to a common reference system. The press readers—Paul Fry (a frequent inspiration) and another—saved me from error, showed me what I was about, and offered hope for the future.

Helen Tartar did nothing for three years, the kindest thing an editor can do on such occasions. A fellowship from the National Endowment for the Humanities provided the time to write the essay on Taine and to complete revisions of the entire manuscript, and a grant from the Graduate School and the Center for the Humanities of the University of Washington supported production of the index. Jane has stood by me since the beginning. Dorrit and Benedict have come and gone while the essays were a-writing; I dedicate this book to them, now that they have both reached an age where they can decide of their own accord not to read it.

Contents

xiv Contents

Turning Points

*Essays in the History of
Cultural Expressions*

PART I

Overture

Errours Endlesse Traine

All transitions are crises.
—Goethe, *Wilhelm Meisters Lehrjahre*

WHERE DO WE GO from here? is, I suspect, a question more often asked than answered. Yet put it into the past tense, and the historian has little difficulty in telling us where we went from there. Indeed, the more up-to-date or, let us say loosely, the more structure-oriented the historian's approach, the easier the question is to answer. Mentalities, epistemes, deep structures: these overviews of where things were and where they went provide a kind of knowledge rarely vouchsafed to the actual participants.

This observation prompted me to reflect on the way a transition appears from the inside. The following pages are less a line of reasoning—in fact, they ultimately turn against the whole concept of linear reasoning—than they are a meditation; their aim is not to generate knowledge but to comprehend the mood in which we desire knowledge. The inquiry cannot proceed from facts to meanings or from initiatives to consequences, for what I wish to understand is precisely the moment when meanings are obscured and consequences still withheld. I offer instead a meditation on a series of images, all of which project and reflect emergent occasions. I want to examine not what was a turning point or crisis, as seen after the dust has settled, but what is a turning point in the turbulence of its occurrence. At such a moment deformity itself may wear the radiant guise of divine beauty, as Satan does in *Paradise Lost*: "So varied hee, and of his tortuous Train / Curl'd many a wanton wreath in sight of Eve, / To lure her Eye" (9.516–18). But innocence is equally prone to show up in the garb of evil, as Dickens's Esther Summerson does in her hour of trial, "when I laboured up colossal staircases, ever striving to reach the top, and ever turned, as I have seen a worm in garden path, by some obstruction, and labouring again" (*Bleak House*, chap. 35, p. 431).[1] At the height of frenzy, who can distinguish fidelity from betrayal, rectitude from its distortion?

> Ay: you did wish that I would make her turn.
> Sir, she can turn, and turn, and yet go on,
> And turn again; and she can weep, sir, weep;
> And she's obedient, as you say, obedient.
> Very obedient.
>
> (*Othello* 4.1.263–67)

As these examples show, the turning point is a trial or, as so many languages have it, a process. But when does the judgment come? "We have put our shoulders to the wheel, Mr. Carstone, and the wheel is going round," says the repulsive lawyer Vholes (*Bleak House*, chap. 39, p. 484). What sort of conclusions, if any, can the process have? What is on trial? These are the questions I wish to consider.

The Mill and the River

Maggie Tulliver first becomes aware of her "great temptation," if such a gradually dawning emotion may be said to have a beginning, at a ball. The revival of old loves in conflict with newly restored economic hopes for the family, the resolution to "go away, and wait" (*Mill on the Floss*, 6.9, p. 467) that is suspended by the intoxications of the moment—waltzing "is rather dizzy work," says Maggie, even just "to look on"—all combine to create a state of mind whose lability is extreme even for George Eliot. Stephen Guest—that dreamily romantic outsider who steals Maggie's affections away from Philip Wakem—looks powerfully at her, and his gaze "made Maggie's face turn towards it" (6.10, p. 470) in an instant of self-contradictory and indescribable emotion: "The hovering thought that they must and would renounce each other made this moment of mute confession more intense in its rapture" (471). The ecstasy cannot endure, of course, but neither does the vise of emotions ever loosen to the point where Maggie can determine her fate: her entire seduction and return pass as if in a dream that washes over her like the flood in which she and her brother will eventually drown. Let us observe some of the twists and turns of these crucial scenes.

The "mute confession" takes place as Stephen and Maggie are walking "unsteadily" across the conservatory. It ends when they "reached the end of the conservatory, and were obliged to pause and turn. The change of movement brought a new consciousness to Maggie: she blushed deeply, turned away her head, and drew her arm from Stephen's." Her departure leaves Stephen "dizzy" in his turn, angry, confused, irresolute, indeed hardly aware of himself or of the whirling of the dance that still goes on. "Stephen turned away, and walked backwards and forwards at the other end of the room. There was the dire necessity of going back into the dancing-room again, and he was beginning to be conscious of that" (471–72). The disturbed, instinctive pacing resumes—we feel that it has never stopped—in the next chapter (6.11), four days later in the lane before Aunt Moss's house. Stephen appears; Maggie, in her embarrassment, "turned to walk towards the gate. Stephen turned too. . . . Maggie . . . turned again to walk back." It is the dance of feeling that neither character can control ("Maggie dared not speak—dared not turn her head") and that prevails over all exercise of judgment (even the horse protests "against this frequent change of direction") until, "sliding downwards into a nightmare," they turn yet again "out of the sun into a side lane," and Stephen's passion "burst[s] out impetuously" yet again. Maggie yearns to yield herself up to his direction—if only she "need no longer beat and struggle against this current, soft and yet strong as the summer stream"—but instead she flees by "turn[ing] sharp round towards home again" (476–79).

There follows a family party (6.12) to celebrate the prospects for recovering the old mill, which would restore to the Tullivers their "full-rounded splendor" (482). The euphoria leads cousin Lucy, bright with optimism, to feel that even the stubborn Tom can be bent toward accommodation with Wakem and the forces of conscious progress. "Nothing was wanted, then, but for dear Tom . . . to turn completely round . . . and declare that he, for his part, was delighted that all the old grievances should be healed" (487). But the mills of the Lord grind too fine to leave this escape route, which is really a turn back rather than a turn ahead. Instead, as if in a dream, Maggie is carried off by Stephen on "the backward-flowing tide" (6.13, p. 496), in a dream she drifts out of bounds while time "flowed over her like a soft stream" (502), and still in a dream she wakes and repents: "Maggie was not conscious of a decision as she turned away from that gloomy averted face, and walked out of the room" (6.14, p. 513).

For Maggie consciousness comes too late to avoid a life of misery. ("Too late! it was too late," she thinks, and Stephen echoes later, "It is too late" [505, 511].) Indeed, we may wonder whether it ever comes. For by the time that she decides, after a long anguished vigil, to burn the last pleading letter from Stephen, the floodwaters have already begun to swirl around her feet, and the "great calm" that ensues lies far from the resoluteness that Bob Jakin thinks she possesses: "The whole thing had been so rapid—so dreamlike—that the threads of ordinary association were broken" (7.5, p. 552).

But does consciousness ever come on time? Are those threads of association ever secure? The one extended description of the mill that Eliot vouchsafes us confirms Maggie's susceptibility to the ravishments of power. After grinding her doll's head against the wall in a fit of anger and then "whirling around like a Pythoness" with her dog in a fit of exuberance, Maggie enters the mill.

The resolute din, the unresting motion of the great stones, giving her a dim delicious awe as at the presence of an uncontrollable force—the meal forever pouring, pouring—the fine white powder softening all surfaces, and making the very spider-nets look like a faery lacework—the sweet pure scent of the meal— all helped to make Maggie feel that the mill was a little world apart from the outside every-day life. (1.4, p. 28)

The spiders are emblems of consciousness that weave their connecting filaments all through Eliot's novels. But as the mill grinds, it denatures such connections: "She wondered if [the spiders] had any relatives outside the mill, for in that case there must be a painful difficulty in their family intercourse—a fat and floury spider, accustomed to take his fly well dusted with meal, must suffer a little at a cousin's table where the fly was *au naturel*" (28). Tom, too, is ground down at the mill, and so is his father; as the novel says at one point, "it is still possible to believe that the attorney was not more guilty toward [Mr. Tulliver], than an ingenious machine, which performs its work with much regularity, is guilty towards the rash man who, venturing too near it, is caught up by some fly-wheel or other, and suddenly converted into unexpected mince-meat" (3.7, p. 265). For Tom, consciousness comes too soon, as the rashness of premature judgment, and "the mill-like monotony" (2.7,

p. 200) of penurious labor converts it into a stupid and destructive obstinacy. But whether consciousness comes too soon or too late, the obscure violence of Eliot's turns shows that it is never adequately synchronized.

Such is the nature of time that its flow escapes knowledge. Rivers never stop changing: the Rhine was not always so mellow as now, nor—in Eliot's famous contrast—was the Rhone always so prosaic. And the Floss (archetypally named for the flux of time and perhaps also the filaments of consciousness) harbors "a kind of population out of keeping with the earth on which they live" (4.1, p. 289). If St. Ogg's is out of sync—its clocks fast, its civilization slow—that is better read as a metaphysical than as a social dilemma. Time is always out of joint, either a slow "doubtful distant hope" or "a fast-approaching dread" (3.7, p. 260), either the tedium of childhood that always wants to be grown up or the dizzy speed of romance that regrets having grown up so soon. But "the future will never join on to the past again" (6.8, p. 474), and the present is only fully experienced as the turning point when we are swept off our feet. "Life at this moment," thinks Maggie at the ball as Stephen approaches her, "seemed a keen vibrating consciousness poised above pleasure or pain," but how ironically constrained by encompassing dangers is Maggie's present moment. "This one, this last night, she might expand unrestrainedly in the warmth of the present, without those chill thoughts of the past and the future" (6.10, p. 470).

Eliot's present is never so warm as it appears to poor, deluded Maggie, but it is always thoughtless. It is thoughtless precisely because the meaning of time in its turnings lies beyond all possibility of awareness. For time—and here Eliot joins forces with one of Hegel's best-known concepts—is cunning. "That same nature has the deep cunning which hides itself under the appearance of openness, so that simple people think they can see through her quite well, and all the while she is secretly preparing a refutation of their confident prophecies" (1.5, p. 32). "Time, with ever-unrelenting purpose, still hides that secret in his own mighty, slow-beating heart" (2.2, p. 163). We can, of course, cooperate with the cunning of time. But to do so we must be cunning ourselves, like the wily Bob Jakin, a sympathetic character who disappears from the narrative for long stretches while his energetic slyness amasses a patrimony and a home. Bob lives in the present, as is signaled by his opportunism, his unfailing good nature with those around him, and above all his alert, salesmanlike volubility; to his whirl of words we may contrast the silence of the bookish schoolmaster Stelling, whose insistence on the classics may be considered a repudiation of time. But not even Bob understands the presence of the present; his cunning is, rather, that he has "perceptions more perfect than his comprehension" (3.6, p. 256). The cunning of history is that history is always made without our awareness, or at least without our comprehension.[2]

Literary art is constantly literalizing the turning point when actions outstrip comprehension. Among the countless ball scenes in nineteenth-century novels it is perhaps enough to cite the crisis at Netherfield that Elizabeth Bennet spends most of *Pride and Prejudice* trying to understand. Here is the dialogue that precedes the quarrel between her and Darcy:

> "I cannot talk of books in a ball-room; my head is always full of something else."
>
> "The *present* always occupies you in such scenes—does it?" said he, with a look of doubt.
>
> "Yes, always," she replied, without knowing what she said, for her thoughts had wandered far from the subject. (chap. 18, p. 93)

At turning points our thoughts always wander, and the result is, as Darcy puts it, "I could wish, Miss Bennet, that you were not to sketch my character at the present moment" (chap. 18, p. 94).[3]

The Wheel and the Swing

At the turning point an old order is lost and a new one has yet to arrive: "things fall apart; the center cannot hold," as Yeats so famously described in "The Second Coming." Afterward, reflection begins, an image dawns, "a vast image out of *Spiritus Mundi*," and judgment becomes possible once again. But in the moment itself both thought and feeling die "into a dance, / An agony of trance" ("Byzantium," *Collected Poems* 244): the turning point is a suspension, a hiatus, the summer or winter solstice of the intellect.

Vertigo or reverie, the turning point comes as a point of disorientation "in which I had the fancy of our being almost as lost as a handful of passengers in a great drifting ship" (James, *The Turn of the Screw*, chap. 1, p. 22). "The stars ahead seemed to be gliding from right to left. And all was so still in the world that I heard the quiet remark, 'She's round,' passed in a tone of intense relief between two seamen" (Conrad, *The Secret Sharer* 143). The troubled decades before World War I are particularly prone to represent the turning point as an ongoing crisis—a screw like James's that turns relentlessly and will not relax or a story like Conrad's that refuses to let go its hold on the narrator—and thus to profile and anatomize the crisis. The turning point is, first of all, not merely vertigo or reverie, excessive speed or excessive languor, emotional heat or cold, but, confusingly, both at once, a turbulent flow whose speed is as inscrutable as its direction. Thus Mallarmé, writing in 1886 of the ballerina, that "unconscious revealer" who "delivers . . . the nudity of your concepts and will silently write your vision in the manner of a Sign, which she is," speaks in one paragraph both of the "vertiginous play of her pale satin shoes" and of a "reverie full, yet adequate: vaporous, clear and ample, or restrained" (*Oeuvres* 307). And second, it is more complicated than the mere submergence of thought and feeling or the temporary occultation of the subject while the flood of time cunningly prepares to reveal the Sign of the future. On the contrary, the subject remains, engaged yet detached, as the participant observer of his fate, "most alien spectator, Friend," as Mallarmé writes with the precision of a paradox. There is always a struggle both to know and to feel. In this moment feeling does not disappear but changes into an obscure passion to recognize itself: it grasps at knowledge. And knowledge does not disappear but gropes blindly toward a point of reference, the shred of evidence that will resolve the mystery: knowledge yearns for a feeling of orientation. The turning point, then, is a true dialectical moment, when each force of the soul turns toward its opposite to prepare for that passionate knowledge that will know how to steer into the future.

My next turning point occurs in a little-known novel, *Une Page d'amour*, by Emile Zola. From its graphological title on, this is an exceptionally self-conscious work, with five parts of five chapters each on the model of an ancient tragedy, and with a carefully measured and calculated dance of characters. The mechanism of the plot is set in motion by a scene in the fourth chapter, where Zola's femme fatale, the widowed Hélène Grandjean, falls or jumps off a swing and sprains her knee in the presence of her future lover, Dr. Deberle. The vertiginous activity of the mother who is recreating a childhood pleasure thus launches the tumultuous passions of the novel.

But it is the resonances of swinging, rather than the activity itelf, that are particularly germane to my theme. In French "swing" is *balançoire*, whose root verb also evokes the rocking of a cradle, the regulatory mechanism of a watch or clock, proportion and symmetry, and hanging and balancing. All these associations are activated at one point or another in the novel. However, Zola does not activate but instead leaves pervasively implicit the one meaning that cannot be excluded from this novel, so abstractly concerned with states of mind rather than with states of physical existence. For *balancer* is also a mental term meaning to hang in the balance, to weigh, to ponder.[4] The turning point is both a moment of balance and a moment of unbalance, of decision and of indecision, of determination (like the fatalistic mechanism of a clock) and of indeterminism. It is a regressive and metaleptic moment when the woman becomes a girl and gives birth to a monster. Finally it is the moment when falsehood begets knowledge and ignorance engenders insight. In the next chapter Hélène, still dreaming the vertiginous reverie of her passion, looks out from her sickroom one February morning over the fog enveloping Paris.

That had a great charm: not to know, to guess by halves, to yield to a slow initiation, with the obscure feeling that she was beginning her youth afresh.
    How those novels lied! (1.5, p. 1007)

The explicit reference here is to *Ivanhoe*, which Hélène has just been reading. But in so highly wrought a novel as *Une Page d'amour* an element of self-reference is inescapable. The balance and symmetry of the work are a lie calculated to yield up a recognition: the insight that to ponder, not to know, or half to know—to weigh the right answer with the wrong—is the wintry ignorance from which passionate knowledge springs.

It is not coincidental that my vocabulary has taken on a Socratic tinge here in linking ignorance with insight. For if the mill is the figure of the material dialectic of history, the swing is the figure of the dialectic of mind perfected in the Socratic dialogues. The dialogue is, as it were, a con-versation, a turning together of minds in the replies and retorts, the turns and returns of utterance. Its gentle form appears in the roundtable discussions of the Ciceronian dialogues and their Renaissance avatars.

But I prefer to concern myself with the original and more dramatic form found in Plato and then spontaneously reinvented by Dante, the pilgrim who has lost his way and must wind along an incline, turning an ear now toward, now away from all those spirits that would bend his thoughts toward them, until he finally emerges into the ecstatic truth of the rotating stars.

Plato's Greek, unlike Latin and its derivatives, does not embed its metaphors for turning in its words for utterance and response. But we may find the metaphors buried in a more typically Socratic concern, the refutations of false opinion that are sometimes called turnings back.[5] Socrates' imaginary dialogue with a slave boy in the *Meno* distills the procedure: Socrates turns the boy back from all his beginnings until, like Dante, the boy has lost his bearings and does not know where to turn. This is the Socratric ἀπορία, or perplexity (84a–d), which Socrates describes as a "dreamlike" state (85c) in which true opinions can at last be aroused. The *Meno* uses the concept of recollection (ἀνάμνησις, which suggests a kind of backward flow of the mind) to bridge the gap between error and truth, but elsewhere Plato stresses the radical alteration that ensues on the turning point when the mind is perplexed. Thus in the *Phaedrus* he seems to have coined the term "method," or following a road, as the corrective for the pathlessness of aporia. The turning, or way (τρόπος) of the medical art, says Socrates, is identical to that of the rhetorical art (270b). In both, we need a road or method—the key word is first supplied by Phaedrus (270c)—without which our merely empirical procedures might be compared to the pathfinding of a blind man (ὥσπερ τυφλοῦ πορεία, 270d). The method—not so much the path as the ability to follow the path—is found, after a period of darkness, "suddenly, like a blaze kindled by a leaping spark" (letter 7, 341d).

In another dialogue, the *Statesman*, the Stranger relates to the young Socrates the myth that governs the dialectic conversion from pathlessness to path. He tells of a time when the universe rotated in the opposite direction from its present one under the direct impulse of Zeus; of the moment when Zeus released his hold and the universe, "in perplexities" (ἐν ἀπορίαις), was "in danger of sinking into the pathless (ἄπειρον) sea of unlikeness" (273d); and of the need for a terrestrial statesman to guide things into a stable path. Just as the seventh letter offers a political as well as an epistemological psychology, so here we clearly have an epistemological as well as a political myth. The moment when we swing back from subjection—whether under a dogma or a political leader—to independence is a period of turbulence when the movement of the soul and the movement of the world are no longer in alignment, a period of blindness and floundering before the new path is illumined.[6]

> When Loie Fuller's Chinese dancers enwound
> A shining web, a floating ribbon of cloth,
> It seemed that a dragon of air
> Had fallen among dancers, had whirled them round
> Or hurried them off on its own furious path;
> So the Platonic Year
> Whirls out new right and wrong.
> Whirls in the old instead;
> All men are dancers and their tread
> Goes to the barbarous clangour of a gong.
>   (Yeats, "Nineteen Hundred and Nineteen,"
>   *Collected Poems* 205–6)

Revolution

Just as in the Marxian view revolution is dialectic writ large, so from the very beginning, as we can now see, dialectic has always been revolution writ small. The analogy helps explain at least one major puzzle that, so far as I can see, no one has adequately addressed, namely, the origin of our modern term *revolution*. Indeed, it is not that long since Melvin J. Lasky first traced in reliable detail the semantic shift that changed *revolution* from an astronomical term with gradualist and conservative political implications to a primarily political term with connotations of violent progressivism (*Utopia and Revolution*, chaps. 5–6). But why should this shift have occurred? Lasky does not attempt an explanation. Nor does Hannah Arendt, whose anatomy of revolution comprises freedom, innovation, and violence (*On Revolution*, chap. 1) but omits what I have been suggesting is the key element—namely, aporia, or confusion. And Georges Gusdorf, who has also discussed the semantic shift, merely comments laconically, "De là une équivoque" (from whence a pun; *Principes* 415). A revolution is not so much a way people act as a way things move; as Reinhardt Koselleck argues, it has a characteristic speed that takes over as individual actors lose control of events (*Futures Past* 39–54;

see also Behler, "Die Auffassung der Revolution"; Ward, "The Forging of Orc"; Blanchot, "The Main Impropriety" 58–59; and Culler, "The Uses of *Madame Bovary*" 78). All these scholars remind us that until well into the eighteenth century the term revolution tended to be contrasted to rebellion. But they fail to realize that even the most peaceful revolution is a turning point. Like the sublime movement of the spheres, it transcends human comprehension; like any dance, it has—at least for some who live through it—its moments of confusion, vertigo, aporia. Turning has always suggested disorder and violence; indeed the Greek verb ἀνατρέπω means to overthrow politically as well as to refute dialectically. Thus, I suggest, a natural development led the astronomical term revolution to become a political term, winning out over less dialectical competing terms such as renewal, change of state, and rebellion.[7]

To illustrate the dynamics—the dialectic—of revolution while maintaining my focus on acts of the mind, I want to consider Kant. In the introduction to the second edition (1787) of the *Critique of Pure Reason*, Kant compares his "transformation" (*Umänderung*) of metaphysics to various "revolutions" in the history of science. On the purely intellectual level the sense of Kant's comparisons is entirely clear. Each of his revolutions is the sudden illumination of what had been perplexing; each one is accomplished by "the happy insight of a single man in one experiment, from which point on, the path that had to be taken could no longer be missed, and the secure course of a science was initiated and designated for all times and in infinite distances" (Bxii). Thus conceived, a revolution resembles more a coup than a civil war, more the Glorious Revolution that had been than the French Revolution that was about to be. But alongside this intellectual ideal of the revolution as an abrupt and enduring break with the past, there is even in Kant, as I want to show, a psychological sense of revolution as a dark force that drives individuals and is not driven by them. At such a turning point, not even the great master of the architectonic could be entirely in control of his structures.

The decisive psychological element, or inner sense, in dialectic as in revolution is the pace. Even Kant's preface acknowledges the swiftness with which a science is transformed after a long period of groping. But that account of revolution is undialectical; Kant writes as if error is motionless, the groping of a group of deluded scientists who get nowhere, and as if it is is simply abolished by truth, which is equally motionless, since a single individual instantaneously and permanently establishes the truth.

Kant's preface is a wish fulfillment. Nothing in the history of Kant's revolution in dialectic displays the ease of his ideal models. Certainly not the book itself: the 800-odd pages of elephantine prose did not suddenly illuminate everything to early readers such as Mendelssohn, who couldn't get through it; Garve, who reviewed it without pretending to understand it; or Herder, who responded with a vitriolic book attacking his former friend and teacher. And the rebarbative style is no mere blemish that accidentally obscures the basic clarity of Kant's revolutionary insights. (For further comments on Kant's style and for references to secondary literature, see Brown, *Preromanticism* 70–73.) On the contrary, despite his yearnings for popularity Kant repeatedly warns in letters and prefaces that his discoveries cannot be clearly or easily communicated. Indeed, the first preface to the *Critique of Pure Reason* claims that too much clarity can be detrimental. This preface seems to place difficulty and confusion on the side of truth and not, as in the later preface, on the side of error. Aporia is a permanent element of dialectical discovery; it is a part of the revolution in thought and not what the revolution eliminates. This, at least, is what Kant wrote to Mendelssohn on August 16, 1783: "From thence would begin the actual pleasure of a critique, walking around with a secure guide [*Leitfaden*] in a labyrinth, where one is lost at every instant and just as often finds the exit" (*Briefwechsel* 346). What a curious Ariadne's thread this is, seeming to lead onward but never altogether out! And what about the scholastic Mandarin in which Kant chose to write: is it not simultaneously the secure guide that lays the stable foundation for the new science and yet in itself the labyrinth that has doomed readers and editors alike to incessant perplexity? This is the dialectical moment in which error and truth, confusion and clarity, labor and delivery are inseparably mixed.

On the question of pace Kant's biography is instructive. From the moment he conceived his grand project Kant refused to be hurried: "Now long experience has taught me that insight into our projected materials can by no means be forced and hastened by effort, but instead requires rather a long time" (letter to Marcus Herz, June 7, 1771, 122). The threads of the secure guide must be spun—or, to change the metaphor, the text must be woven—slowly. Yet the illumination comes with dizzying rapidity: as early as the famous letter to Herz of February 21, 1772, in which Kant announced his great breakthrough, he was promising to be done with the first critique in three months. And when he finally wrote the work, he did so in a frenzy, "for I had brought to completion the product of a period of at least twelve years of reflection within about 4 to 5 months, as if on the wing, . . . a decision that I even now do not regret, because in the contrary case and with greater delay in order to bring in popularity, the work would presumably never have been finished" (letter to Mendelssohn, August 16, 1783, 345). The revolution in metaphysics is thus the product of unnatural slowness followed by unnatural haste. Or rather, of both at once: "I receive reproaches from all sides on account of the inactivity in which I seem to have been for a long time, and yet I have really never been more systematically and persistently occupied than in the years since you last saw me" (letter to Herz, Nov. 24, 1776, 198).

Fortunately, we have a guide for diagnosing the condition of the revolutionary dialectician. In the years following publication of the *Critique of Pure Reason*, Marcus Herz was at work on a book that, as he writes (letter to Kant, Nov. 25, 1785, 427), was originally inspired by conversations with Kant. In his *Essay on Vertigo* (*Versuch über den Schwindel*, 1786), we may learn to recognize Kant's state as verging on the pathological.[8] Herz considers that the soul, in its natural condition, alternates imperceptibly between effort and relaxation (153–54). In Herz's terms, Kant's ten years of inactivity constitute a condition of "Langerweile" (boredom), which can lead either to despair or, as it did for Kant, to that "preternaturally swift progression of ideas" which Herz designates as vertigo (154–62). The second edition of the *Critique* came in the following year. Can we interpret Kant's new preface, with its idea that timeless truths instantaneously replace timeless errors, as a defensive reaction to the book on vertigo and an attempt to sanitize the notion of speed that is central to all revolutionary dialectic?

Dialectic

I have no wish to argue that logic or dialectic is diseased. Quite the contrary, I have chosen examples to show how inescapably aporia is linked to progress. Feelings of disorientation and vertigo are a normal part of the processes of discovery; they constitute the inherently revolutionary element of dialectic, the dialectical element of revolution. An allusion to the work of Thomas Kuhn seems unavoidable here, since he has argued the most forcefully that revolution is a normal component of scientific progress. Yet I do not believe that Kuhn has adequately accounted for the dialectical aspect of revolution, that is, for the ways that the new does not appear randomly but necessarily emerges out of the dissolution of the old. For genuinely dialectical theories of emergence we may turn, not surprisingly, to philosophers after Kant.

Nietzsche, using some of the worst puns in the history of philosophy, ties together the threads I have been tracing. The passage in question is the chapter "Von den Taranteln" (Of Tarantulas) in the second part of *Also Sprach Zarathustra*. The theory is outspokenly dialectical: "And because height is needful, steps are needful, and contradiction of steps and of those who climb! Life wants to climb and in climbing to overcome itself" (359). Nietzsche here professes precisely the vertiginous component of dialectic that has been with us from Eliot's floury spiders on. The poisonous tarantulas, the dark negation in the dialectic, infect the dialectician with their venom. The resulting vertigo undermines the elegant demonstrations in the "divine . . . pugilism [*Ringkampfe*]" (359) of classical reasoning. Negation, the tarantula, makes the ring that was always a part of the arena into a wheel that racks the reasoner: "now it will avenge itself and make my soul rotate [*drehend*] as well" (357). But are confusion and confutation really the work of the negative, or do they begin with the inception of dialectic? Who, in fact, is first stretched on the wheel of dialectic, the bright intellect or the dark spiders? For Zarathustra has begun this section by threatening to do to the tarantulas what they later do to him: "Thus do I speak unto ye in a parable [*Gleichnis*] that will make your souls revolve, ye preachers of *Equality* [*Gleichheit*]" (357). Who is the preacher here, who the congregation? Who amid Nietzsche's "pathless sea of unlikeness" is the apostle of similitude? And who, we may finally wonder, is good, who evil? This last question arises, surely not accidentally, because of the jingle of the tarantulas' two expressed aims, which are both good and evil, both justice (*Gerechtigkeit*) and the wish to be revenged (*gerächt*). There is no escaping from the entanglements of thought.

If the tarantulas do symbolize dialectic, then what Nietzsche conjures up is the confusion intrinsic to dialectic. It is the confusion of the dance. For the tarantulas are not just spiders; they are also dancers. They dance the spider dance, the tarantella. They are, in German, *Tarantel-Tänzer*. Is Zarathustra also a tarantula? He describes himself as a dancer from the start of the book; indeed, only in the chapter on tarantulas does he resist the impulse to dance: "Truly, Zarathustra is no tornado or whirl-wind; and if he is a dancer, still nevermore a *Tarantel-Tänzer*" (359). Yet by the end of the book his dance does become a whirlwind: "Praised be this wild good free storm spirit, which dances on swamps and afflictions as if on meadows." For the true dance is the wild dance that is the true dialectic: "Ye higher men, your worst side is: none of you has learnt to dance as one must dance—to dance over and beyond yourselves [*über euch hinweg*]" ("Vom höheren Menschen" [Of the Higher Man], part 4, sec. 20, p. 531). Dialectic is choreographed transcendence.

My discussion to this point can be considered a commentary on one of the most notorious utterances in the history of philosophy, Hegel's aphorism in the preface to the *Phenomenology of Mind*: "The true is thus the Bacchic whirl in which no member is sober." Easily forgotten, espe-cially by those who are dizzied by Hegel's prose, is that the Bacchic revelry is not the end of the line. For Hegel calculatedly revives and revises the precise terms of the Platonic dialectic. Truth, he says, is not only the Bacchic revelry but also "transparent and simple peace." The mediator between these two aspects of truth, just as in Plato, is recol-lection, anamnesis: "In the *whole* of the movement, conceived as rest, that which differentiates itself in it and gives particular existence, is preserved as something that *remembers*, whose existence is the knowl-edge of itself" (39). Vertigo is a part of dialectic; in fact, in a sense, it is present in all parts. But this is a case where the whole is greater than its parts; in Nietzsche, as in Hegel, the Dionysian "drunken song" turns into a "Rundgesang" (canon) that produces self-transcendence and self-knowledge ("Das trunkene Lied" [The Drunken Song], part 4, sec. 12, p. 558).

Such absolute knowledge at the end of the dialectic remains, of course, a utopian horizon for Nietzsche, as for Eliot and our other storytellers and I believe for Hegel as well. The end of dialectic for Plato, as we have seen, is method—literally, the discovery of a path (*hodos*) for the truth seeker to follow. Nietzsche responds that "all goods things approach their goal crookedly" ("Of the Higher Man," sec. 17, p. 529). And Hegel likewise turns from his identification of truth as revelry and recollection to a critique of method as it had been traditionally understood, namely, as a collection of principles and procedures: "It is not difficult to recognize that the fashion of proposing a theorem, presenting reasons for it and likewise refuting its opposite with reasons, is not the form in which truth can appear. The truth is its movement in itself; but that method is the knowledge that is external to its matter" (40). The wheels of history, of knowledge, of fate never cease turning; the swing never comes to rest, except in death. Truth is not a place (*topos*) but a way, and the way is not a road (*hodos*) but a turning (*tropos*) off the deadly highroad. Truth is not a place: "The meaning of Socratics is that philosophy is *everywhere* or nowhere" (Novalis, *Schriften* 2: 545). It has no place, no time, and no path, or at least none in the sense that Plato meant or was often understood to mean. "Being begins at every instant; the ball There rolls around each Here. The center is everywhere. Crooked is the path of eternity" (Nietzsche, "Der Genesende" [The Convalescent], part 3, sec. 2, p. 463; the first phrase repeats the opening of Hegel's *Science of Logic*).

A Poem on Dancing

Whether we think of Berlioz or Ravel, of *Don Giovanni, Tannhäuser*, or *Salomé*, we all know the giddy seductiveness that dance had for the Romantic sensibility. In *Can You Forgive Her?* Trollope writes: "I dared them . . . to do their worst . . . ; I waltzed with him for half an hour. . . . I don't think, even in my maddest days, I ever kept it up as long as I did then. . . . There I was, going round and round and round with the only man for whom I ever cared two straws. It seemed as though everything had been a dream since the old days" (chap. 62, 2: 223). But was turning always so dangerous? Was there not a time when the crooked path of eternity was imaged as a perfect, unblemished circle? At court did not the dancers go in perfect, balanced order to the stately strains of the minuet or pavane, just as the heavenly bodies follow their appointed rounds to the accompaniment of the music of the spheres? Such, at least we are told, was the Renaissance vision of delight in a period when turning suggested concord rather than discord.

Yet all depends on how you read the evidence. Texts are, unfortunately, less stable than truth, and though we do find an ideal of order in the Renaissance, under scrutiny the ideal often seems to turn into a mirage, as evanescent as any other promised land. Thus, while one scholar assures us that the court masque allegorically instructs the participants in virtuous discipline,[9] the next scholar is apt to find in the proceedings all the intoxications of a heady illusion:

The world is topsy-turvy or "tottering" in a condition of rocking, as on the verge of turning over; reality is unstable or illusory, like a theatrical decor. And man too is in disequilibrium, convinced that he is never entirely what he is or seems to be, concealing his face under a mask with which he acts so well that it is no longer clear where the mask is, where the face is. (Rousset, *Circé* 28)

Should we regard Ben Jonson primarily as the master of the masque or as the inventor of the antimasque? Is his fundamental impulse directed toward a "stable, if beleaguered human center," or is it "a strain of half-repressed envy for the homeless and centrifugal spirit" (Greene, "Ben Jonson" 329, 337)?[10] Too often for comfort, Jonson's spokesman is Daedalus or Proteus (*Pleasure Reconciled to Virtue, Neptune's Triumph*), the steps are "curious knots and mazes" (*The Vision of Delight*, line 211), the meaning of the whole is withheld (*The Masque of Argus*, lines 336–37: "Still, still the auspice is so good; / We wish it were but understood"), or if some magic name serves as a guarantor of order, it belongs to a king already translated to the heavens (*News from the New World Discovered in the Moon*) or to the deity presiding over a millennial "heav'n on earth" (*The Golden Age Restored*, line 214). The allegory of the dance points to a transcendent mystery, not to a human truth.

Perhaps the most familiar Renaissance vision of cosmic order has been Sir John Davies's *Orchestra: A Poem on Dancing*, ever since E. M. Tillyard used it as a touchstone in *The Elizabethan World-View*. (*Orchestra* is cited by stanza number. The received view of the poem may be found in Tillyard, *Five Poems* 30–48, to be supplemented by Major, "The Moralization of the Dance," and by Thesiger, "*Orchestra*.") For this reason, I want to reexamine the poem in some detail. The poem is—like all truths—unfinished: more precisely, if we are to believe its editor, it was originally written as a finished poem in 113 stanzas that Davies later expanded and altered "to give the appearance of being incomplete" (Davies, *Poems* 359). Known as one of the great didactic poems of the Renaissance, it is also, as Tillyard himself acknowledges, full of fantasy, exuberant, and even "impudent" (35).

Impudent the poem certainly is. The praise of dancing is uttered by Antinous, better known as the most impertinent of the suitors of Penelope, whose reasoned objections to his speech Antinous glibly overrules three times in Davies's poem. At one point Antinous even has the impudence to compare the art of dance to the martial arts:

> For after Townes and Kingdomes founded were,
> Between great States arose well-ordered *war*,
> Wherein most perfect measure doth appeare.   (87)

It is hard to know just what Davies would have thought of this argument, which he drew, like so much of the poem, from a dialogue attributed to the Greek satirist Lucian. But it is easy to know that the argument would have disgusted Penelope, on the evidence not so much of Homer—Davies's editor doubts whether Davies had read Homer, though he was a close friend of Chapman, who translated Homer—as of a more accessible poem that must have echoed in the mind of any Renaissance reader, the first of Ovid's *Heroides*. By the end of the speech Antinous has "ravished" Penelope's "mind" if not her body (122), and the stanzas added in 1622 call the court

> So rare a worke, and of such subtilty,
> As did all eyes entangle and deceive,
> And in all mindes a strange impression leave.   (130A)

I do not think that the poem lets Antinous's praise of the orderliness of the dance stand uncorrected.

According to Tillyard, the prime value attributed to dance is its combination of motion and fixity. It would be more accurate to speak of motion without instability, or motion without end. As one critic has rightly observed, what the suitor seductively invokes is an Elizabethan never-never land of mutability without decay. (See Wilkes, "The Poetry of Sir John Davies" 287–90, and also Howarth, *The Tiger's Heart* 181–82. Howarth roundly confronts Tillyard in this chapter, entitled "Put Away the World Picture.") To be sure, one stanza, quoted by Tillyard, says that "the Earth doth stand for ever still" (51), but this stanza also acknowledges the new Copernican discoveries, and earlier Antinous has derived the name "world" from "whirl'd" (34) and has told about the dance of the fixed stars ("Fixt they are nam'd, but with a name untrue," 35). One climax does speak of the firm and visible order of the dance:

> Concords true picture shineth in thys Art
> Where divers men and women ranked be,
> And every one doth daunce a severall part,
> Yet all as one, in measure doe agree,
> Observing perfect uniformitie:
> All turne together, all together trace,
> And all together honor and embrace.   (110)

Yet the end of the poem insists that love is a "Maze" where footsteps are traced by "Blindness it selfe" (116) and that Penelope's ecstatic concluding vision is a "strange-eye-dazeling-admirable sight" (122).

Antinous speaks in disguise (7); his motive is love, an emotion that he, Penelope, and the narrator all term "cunning" (6, 53, 98, 105); his oration dances teasingly around its main target, which is the capture of Penelope's heart. Given such inconsistent and unreliable praise, we cannot fairly attribute fixity to the dance.

More than either motion or fixity, the dance signifies to Antinous proportion and balance. He invokes the technical balance of music with movement, the social balance of man with woman, the allegorical balance of the dance with the virtues that dance symbolizes. We have already seen numerous times how suspect and vertiginous notions of balance can be—the swing of Zola, the flywheel of the *Statesman*, the "tottering" world of the French baroque. And here, of course, Antinous's purpose is not to convince Penelope rationally but to bowl her over with the force of his eloquence. At this he may be judged to succeed, for at the end Penelope "Faine would have praised the state and pulchritude, / But she was stroken dumbe with wonder quite" (122). Instead of leading to ordered fixity, Antinous's cunning leads to subversion that wears the guise of order. Each of the balances he evokes becomes unbalanced in its turn. Thus, the technical balance seems perfect: "Where *Time the measure of all moving is*; / And Dauncing is a moving all in measure" (23). And yet Antinous immediately stresses the difference, his purpose being to insinuate an erotic note by portraying dance as the younger and thus as a "lustie youth" (25):

> Now if you doe resemble that to this
> And think both one, I think you think amis:
> But if you judge them Twins, together got,
> And Time first borne, your judgment erreth not.   (23)[11]

The social balance likewise turns slippery, as Antinous first cites the sex-changing examples of Caeneus and Tiresias (82–83) and later hints that wives sometimes get "the upper hand" of their husbands (112). This is not merely impudent but shameless.

The poem actually describes two kinds of dance. When "men more civill grew," they learned the true dance of morality and balance:

> With such faire order and proportion trew
> And correspondence every way the same,
> That no fault finding eye did ever blame.   (65)

But Antinous slips this dance into his discourse only to slip it out again. Not only were Atlas and Prometheus unable to "find such measures in the skies" (66), but also Antinous makes this poor dance sound most unappealing: "Yet all the feete whereon these measures goe, / Are onely Spondeis, solemne, grave, and sloe" (66). "Spondeis" could plausibly be etymologized as "married" feet. They are the true twins among meters, since arsis and thesis (upbeat and downbeat) are identical in the spondee. But who wants to dance with two left feet, so to speak? This kind of dance is prosaic at best, for spondees do not conform to the rule governing poetry that "all is mard if she one foote misplace" (93). Indeed, Antinous spends the rest of the poem describing the other sort of dance, the dance of nature that love teaches, a less perfectly balanced, gayer, lustier sort of dance, composed of *"rounds* and *winding Heyes"* (64).

Need it be said that dance is a rhetoric, not a logic, of action? It is "Rhetorick whose state the clouds doth reach" (92), thus introducing the poem's cosmic element. (The next section of this chapter will pursue the clouds of rhetoric further.) For rhetoric, not the more precise art of poetry, exemplifies the richly erotic movements of the dance:

> For Rhetorick clothing speech in rich aray
> In looser numbers teacheth her to range,
> With twentie tropes, and turnings every way,
> And various figures, and licentious change.   (93)

Incessant and exuberant punning clearly marks Antinous as a rhetorician, ever alert to the body of words and eager to twin in illegitimate fashion sound with sound, making use of echo effects (which come "after time") and of the "tricks and turnings of the aire" (44–45). Love is Antinous's ultimate value, and love too is a rhetorician, that is, a speaker who throws listeners off balance.

> Then first of all, hee doth demonstrate plaine
> The motions seaven that are in nature found,
> Whereof, a thousand brawles he doth compound,
> And ever with a turne they must conclude.   (62)[12]

For the purpose of my argument it is sufficient to have shown that turning and dancing were never fully imaged as a principle of order, even at the height of the Elizabethan world view. But I would be tempted to go a step further and allegorize the poem in the punning spirit in which it is written. The question is why Davies lit on Antinous as his spokesman. At the end, as a poem on dancing ought, *Orchestra* does seem to pair up Antinous and Penelope as he ravishes her mind with the aid of a magic mirror donated by Love. Tillyard reads the episode as a true pairing, a triumph of platonic love. Yet surely this is as improper a linkage as all the other twinnings of the poem, such as the twinning of poetry and rhetoric or of civil and erotic dance. Throughout the poem Penelope is associated with mind, with thought, with "reasons eye" (26).[13] Antinous, by contrast, is always the persuader, the rhetorician. Is he not therefore to be understood as the *anti-nous*, the anti-mind? Antinous is the spirit of the flesh, the life force that compels reason to remain in motion and continually to unweave the fabric of thought the mind has woven.

According to Jean Rousset, time "is engaged and rendered sensible in the [baroque] work, whereas the classic artist tends to eliminate time" (*Circé* 232).[14] This view of classicism is an idealist illusion. Time never stops; the world never ceases turning; not even the truths of reason endure forever. In a stanza added some 25 years after the original publication, Davies compares Penelope to a silkworm (130A). The comparison is either highly artful or, more likely, highly negligent, for silkworms do not weave but spin. In truth Penelope is one more of our spiders of reason, in danger of being caught, like Maggie Tulliver, in a web of her own making.

Turn Against Turn

Where do we go from here? A purely negative conclusion can hardly satisfy, yet the sense of this whole meditation has been that every point is a turning point. There is no crisis for Maggie Tulliver, no "great temptation," at least no conventional seduction. Maggie is fallen from the start, born an outsider to her society, too dizzy even to attempt joining the dance. The Greek for judgment or decision is *krisis*. Every point of judgment is a point of peril; every moment of balance a moment of unbalance. There is no right way, no end of knowledge, no truth to be unveiled. Indeed, of the texts discussed, only the second preface to the *Critique of Pure Reason* has even claimed that truth may take the form of a revelation, and that text proved a veiling of the labyrinthine truth of the *Critique*.

Alas, we cannot even receive the consolation of having discovered this melancholy condition, for Jacques Derrida ("Facteur de la vérité," "Tympan") and others have been sending us dead letters revealing the undiscoverability of truth for some years now, pounding the message into the curved drums of our middle ear. And of course Derrida did not discover this truth—if it is a truth—either; quite the contrary, he has labored to convince us that his is the oldest news known to Western civilization. Thus, my own title comes from Spenser, who tells us at the outset of *The Faerie Queene* that there is no escape from error: "So many paths, so many turnings seene, / That which of them to take in diuerse doubt they been" (1.1.10). Must we then be content to subscribe our names to the twisted line of denouncers of the truth? Or can we convert their insights to use? Is it conceivable to turn against turn?[15]

The end of Spenser's endless poem tries to do just that and nearly succeeds. Mutability, it will be remembered, claims dominion in her great peroration.

> Then, since within this wide great *Vniuerse*
> Nothing doth firme and permanent appeare,
> But all things tost and turned by transuerse:
> What then should let, but I aloft should reare
> My Trophee, and from all, the triumph beare?   (7.7.56)

Mutability loses the battle when Nature rules against her. Things

> by their change their being doe dilate:
> And turning to themselves at length againe,
> Doe worke their own perfection so by fate:
> Then ouer them Change doth not rule and raigne;
> But they raigne ouer Change, and doe their states maintaine.

$$(7.7.58)$$

Yet, though we know that Nature wins the battle, we cannot be sure she wins the war.[16] Our uncertainty relates in part to the origin of the episode, which is obscure both extratextually (we cannot know how it was to fit into the scheme of the epic) and intratextually, since the first of its two cantos asserts the absolute stability of the legendary records, whereas the second asserts their absolute inaccessibility.[17] But above all it is the end that is not clearly in sight. In appearance the decision goes against Mutability. But in fact does not Nature's judgment—"And thee content thus to be rul'd by me" (st. 59)—grant what Mutability had claimed, namely, "the rule of all, all being rul'd by you" (st. 56)? What about Nature's exhortation—"Cease therefore daughter further to aspire" (st. 59)—does this mean that Mutability should not aspire at all or that she should not aspire beyond what she has already claimed? And what are we to make of Nature's sudden disappearance in the last line, just after she has awarded herself the rule of the universe? Nature's judgment sets "all things" over change; does this mean that she is subjecting Mutability to constancy, or does it mean that she is acceding to Mutability's demand by rearing things aloft and making them the trophy of Mutability?

"Trophy," like "universe" and "transverse," is yet another turning word; more specifically, a trophy fixes and consecrates a turn. "But time shall come that all shall changed bee, / And from thenceforth, none no more change shall see" (st. 59). These are Nature's last words against Mutability. But do they not constitute precisely a trophy of Mutability, a turn that is eternized? In equating the triumph of life with the triumph of death, Nature is endorsing the claims of Mutability. Alas, it does not prove so easy to turn against turn. In passing I note further that the scene on Arlo Hill is overcast—stanza 7 alludes to the episode on Mount Thabor in which the disciples hear a voice out of a cloud—and the obscurity of the judgment may reflect the obscurity of the weather. And since this is Spenser, who cannot resist a pun, perhaps we could suggest that Nature's declaration that things "raigne over Change" (st. 58) is no more than a passing shower that evaporates to make way for the greater light of "the great Sabbaoth God" (7.8.2). Perhaps this is reading too much naturalism into Spenser's Nature; it is true, in any event, that the outcome remains disappointingly cloudy. At the end of *The Clouds*, the child beats the parent—which is, of course, the central metaphor for revolution right through the *Communist Manifesto*—and perhaps the child does the same in the Mutability Cantos.[18]

One other sadly cloudy trophy will claim attention before my argument winds to a close. The ode tradition constitutes the most systematic literary exploration of turns. And given the critical popularity of Keats's "To Autumn," with its exaltation of steadiness and gradualism, we might remember that the poem is followed in order of publication by "Ode on Melancholy," which Keats intended for the conclusion of his 1820 *Poems*. "Melancholy" is a poem of memory and of the power of the past over the present. The final version opens with the line "No, no, go not to Lethe, neither twist"; the deletion of Keats's original first stanza has thus left the ode to begin with a fervent turn against turn. Written in May 1819, "Melancholy" is one of those spring songs so cavalierly dismissed by "Autumn," but it retorts with an even ruder treatment of the fruits of the harvest when it urges us to "burst Joy's grape." By his placement of the poem Keats reminds us that we cannot escape from spring, which means life but also, alas, the revolutions of the life cycle: the poem's figures of turning include the rainbow of new life, the "globéd peonies" of summer's perfection, and winter's "rosary of yewberries." However muted by the April shower, the poem's contents originate in the tropic zone of human passions, and even if wolfsbane is not twisted into poisonous wine, nevertheless "aching Pleasure" will turn "to Poison while the beemouth sips." Melancholy's cloudy trophies are turnings after all. (Cf. the turns and clouds of Keats's "Ode on Indolence," which Patricia Parker identifies as Spenserian motifs in *Inescapable Romance* 168–69.)

"Autumn" offered a myth of continuity; "Melancholy" now appears as but one more in our long list of deconstructions of that myth. Yet the deconstruction is performed here in the service of a different kind of permanence, of an unforgetting, an anti-Lethe, an *a-letheia*, a truth. "And be among her cloudy trophies hung," reads the last line. The verb "be hung" is a curious substitute for the normal "hang," which we find, for instance, when Shakespeare's melancholy Orlando makes an offering to his nocturnal goddess: "Hang there, my verse, in witness of my love" (*As You Like It*, 3.2.1). "*Be* . . . hung": the victory of Keats's Mutability, of "Beauty that must die," turns into a consecration of being rather than a triumph of death.

The melancholy train of error has no terminus named "truth." But as Keats shows us, the truth that does not lie ahead of us may, under a different name, lie behind, in the melancholy of recollection. If I were to offer a summary justification of the deep warmth of Keats and Eliot or the high spirits of Nietzsche and Hegel, I would do it by saying that something which we might call knowledge survives the demise of truth. The Greek word for knowing is *oida*, the perfect tense of the verb meaning to see. Knowledge results from a kind of vision, more specifically a pro-vision, a looking out. What I have seen and retained so that I still see it, that is my knowledge. Put in the simplest terms, knowledge pertains to process, truth to product. And human experience is always in process, a trajectory toward an unknown goal. That goal constitutes the truth of structural historians, but it is a reification that only exists outside of time. The melancholy fact is that our living knowledge abides in a fragile temporality, with a continuity of past and present that is always subject to being ruptured in the future. But a compensatory consolation is that such pro-visional knowledge can be faithful to the directions of real experience in a way that a timeless or structural truth cannot.[19]

The moment of disorientation, the moment of turn against turn, is also the moment of openness to real possibility. Thus it is, in the sense that I mean, the moment of knowledge. One commentator on Milton has put what he calls "the story of the tree of knowledge and of death and sin" in these terms: "The moment of turning, when motion in one direction is arrested and motion in the opposite direction is about to begin, is the still point at which the present is captured and alternatives are real" (Brisman, *Milton's Poetry* 61). To be sure, Brisman evokes only one of our figures for turning, the swing, and not the mill or the whirling dance. But in fact the dialectical sense of an ever-changing, ever-provisional, and therefore ever-present knowledge is the same in all figures. We might turn to one of Yeats's greatest poems of encounter with reality for a last reminder of the dialectical character of knowledge. It is the poem where Yeats asks, "How can we know the dancer from the dance?" (*Collected Poems* 214). The context is cosmic, and the attitude toward human acquisition of ultimate truths is correspondingly elegiac: "Among School Children" is a Keatsian poem about aging, full of the cloudy trophies of a visionary mutability, with elements of the last stanza deriving from Keats's "Ode on Melancholy," from "Ode on a Grecian Urn," and from the third stanza of "Ode to a Nightingale." Yeats's concluding question is correspondingly and profoundly dialectical, for it asks both about recognition (how is the dancer shown through the dance?) and about differentiation (how can we distinguish the dancer from the dance, body from soul?).[20] Knowledge of unity becomes one with knowledge of separation; the capture of the present makes alternatives real. Yet for Yeats the uncertainty or, rather, the negative capability of knowledge is finally not melancholy at all, but a "brightening glance," alert and forward-looking. It is the human intellect stepping westward into its destiny.[21]

Let me return to my original reflections. I want to suggest in conclusion that we can provide ourselves with history; we can give our truths that visionary and provisional character which stamps them as knowledge. We need only remember that the form of history is movement, not just at obvious flash points but, for those who experience it, at all points. History, as we know (experience) it, is under way toward the truths at which it never finally arrives. Historical actors are always, knowingly or (more usually) unknowingly, turning events and struggling against the counterturns of others. The historian's question of truth—"Where did we go?"—is asked of results, not of movement. It is, grammatically, in the wrong aspect. For to know, to have seen, is an ongoing and evolving condition, and the historian who wants to know must ask the question in the tense of evolution—or of revolution—which in English is the progressive tense: "Where were we going?" The structures or truths of history are not actualized in experience; they are that toward which experience points, tangents to the wheel of events.[22] We write a genuinely dialectical history when we remember that every event functions historically as a pointer, as a direction, and not as an embodied truth.[23]

Unterwegs zur Geschichte might be the motto of a study that takes movement rather than accomplishment as its fundamental category. The one in the middle, as Pope says, is "Sole judge of truth, in endless errour hurled"; truth is the regulative ideal, but turbulent movement is the reality. And the redemption of that turbulent movement comes neither from determinations of truth nor from deconstructive denials of truth but from a different, more provisional and humane kind of insight. Historical knowledge, as we are all too prone to forget, concerns truth in movement, a constant interplay of intentions and originations, and not mere results; it deals with impulses rather than with impacts. The remedy for the anxieties of "Errours endlesse traine" is perhaps to be found less easily in Spenser's conclusion in which nothing is concluded than in the lovely Wordsworth poem "Stepping Westward," to which I alluded in my last paragraph:

> and while my eye
> Was fixed upon the glowing Sky,
> The echo of the voice enwrought
> A human sweetness with the thought
> Of travelling through the world that lay
> Before me in my endless way.
> *(Poetical Works* 3: 76)

Escapable Romance

Parker has argued, on the basis of texts ranging from Ariosto through Stevens, that romance is inescapable. If nomen is numen, she shows us that the numinous, in turn, is not far from the nubilous.

THE PLEASURES OF MERELY CIRCULATING

> The garden flew round with the angel,
> The angel flew round with the clouds,
> And the clouds flew round and the clouds flew round
> And the clouds flew round with the clouds.
> (Stevens, *Collected Poems* 149)

But how can we convert such an experience or insight to use? The romance perspective is liable at the end merely "To have squeezed the universe into a ball / To roll it toward some overwhelming question" (T. S. Eliot, "The Love Song of J. Alfred Prufrock," lines 92–93). Is there any truth at the end of the street or at the end of time? More colloquially put, is there anything in our heads? Has there ever been, since we descended from the animals? Or is revolution the permanent dark mystery with no solution, the anguishing sound of all experience? What can we make of the uncertainty of origins, the swerve (Bloom) or turbulent flow (Serres) of descent?

> Is there any secret in skulls,
> The cattle skulls in the woods?
> Do the drummers in black hoods
> Rumble anything out of their drums?
>
> Mrs. Anderson's Swedish baby
> Might well have been German or Spanish . . .

For an expression of faith that there is more to life than these errancies and this gibberish, we may well listen to the conclusion of the Stevens poem that I have been quoting. For in a marvelously light way, free from all anxieties, Stevens urges us to turn away from the cloudy symbols of romance and toward our cultural situation and its specific processes. I could gloss Stevens's final lines with Gadamer's comment on the great philosopher of classical Athens: "It appears that it is *the* human task to constantly be limiting the measureless [i.e., the *apeiron*] with measure" (*Dialogue and Dialectic* 155).

> Yet that things go round and again go round
> Has rather a classical sound.

PART II

Critics

CHAPTER 1

Why Style Matters

The Lessons of Taine's *History of English Literature*

WITHOUT SEEKING ULTIMATES, I will open by stating my firm persuasion that Hippolyte Taine's *History of English Literature* was among the greatest works of literary criticism of its century and remains among the greatest of literary histories. Brilliant in conception, organization, and expression, it should be enjoyed as a work of art portraying the panorama of a nation. But its importance is not merely historical and aesthetic. Properly understood, it communicates a distinctive and powerful vision of the cultural function of literature, with a message perhaps more timely now than in its own day. Even a few years ago the sociological cast of his work represented an obstacle to understanding; it was then possible to write of "literary people who are angered by Taine's manner of using literature as a means of understanding an age or a nation rather than as an end in itself."[1] Most literary criticism was trying to break away from the threesome he popularized—race, moment, and milieu. Now, however, they are again objects of scrutiny; in the era of *Black Athena* and *Borderlands* it should seem natural to reexamine the European male who popularized these topics. His masterpiece has become worth not just reading, but debating.

For generations the introduction to Taine's masterpiece, the *History of English Literature*, was a touchstone, more seminal than anything by Matthew Arnold, more passionately controversial than any text of Nietzsche. Its cosmopolitan esteem for other cultures aided advanced thinkers in the nationalist years between the Franco-Prussian War and World War I; its fatalist rhetoric, abetted by the grim defeatism of Taine's later history of the French Revolution, irritated and provoked progressives in the years between the world wars. Subsequently, the cultural Darwinism with which Taine's name is linked has seemed more and more distant, and his text has dropped out of syllabi and anthologies. Like many great minds, he was traduced by his closest disciples—Zola and Brunetière above all. The slogans of a colorful writer were shorn of their contexts; the conclusions of a profoundly learned scholar lost their nuances and qualifications. Increasingly, for those who knew only his anthology pieces or digests of his writings, he fell into line, until he fell by the wayside, leaving little more than tags that no one should take seriously.

The task of resuscitating Taine, then, is threefold. My first section revives the once-familiar image. The second section scrutinizes its inadequacies, particularly with respect to the notorious triad of determinants and to the determinism that is attached to them. The third and fourth sections together concern the core of Taine's achievement, the vision of history and the role of style in propelling historical movement and cultural change. Because Taine is so little and for the most part so inaccurately read, I have written expansively in order to give a feel for his manner and to ground fully conclusions that have escaped many readers, however inescapable they appear to me. Throughout the analysis I have also made an effort to position Taine precisely in relation to thinkers he drew upon, lived among, and was succeeded by. A final section presents the case for Taine as our contemporary—a thinker capable of intervening productively in present-day disciplinary debates. He should be attended to at length and read in depth, I shall be arguing, because he is the person who gets right what New Historicists characteristically get wrong.

I

An independent writer having only occasional affiliations with institutions of higher learning, Taine (1828–93) left an astonishing body of work. Before he was 30 he had published *Voyage aux Pyrénées* (1855), featuring landscapes and legends; the prize-winning, oratorically mannered *Essai sur Tite Live* (1856); and the controversial polemic against French academic philosophy known under a later title as *Les Philosophes classiques du XIXᵉ siècle en France* (1857).[2] By 1870 Taine had published three multivolume works: his *History of English Literature* (1863, with a supplementary volume on six contemporary authors in 1867); five sets of lectures on the aesthetics of the visual arts and on the art of Italy, the Netherlands, and Greece, eventually collected as *Philosophie de l'art* (1880); and a massive and tedious psychological treatise, *De l'intelligence* (1870). Further books from this period included Taine's longest and most brilliant single-author study, *La Fontaine et ses fables* (1860, based on his 1853 French dissertation); the long *Voyage en Italie* (1866), with panoramic descriptions of the society and the art of the country; a set of sketches of Parisian life, *Notes sur Paris: Vie et opinions de Frédéric-Thomas Graindorge* (1857); and two volumes of collected essays (1858, 1865, containing important essays on Plato and Xenophon and on numerous French writers of the seventeenth and nineteenth centuries, and eventually supplemented by a third, posthumous volume). Apart from *Notes sur l'Angleterre* (1872), the rest of his life was devoted to *Les Origines de la France contemporaine*, of which the history of the Revolution in six large (or twelve moderate) volumes was completed. A fragmentary autobiographical novel, *Etienne Mayran*, was published in 1909 (in book form in 1910); a projected book on the theory of the will was never written. Never a focus for writing was Taine's intensive study of Hegel, without whom his vision of history would have been unthinkable.

So prodigious a writer must have had a system. I will begin by laying out Taine's system, before turning it over to find his genius. Taine sought out the regularities beneath the multiplicity of experience. He began at the level of the individual. A writer, artist, or thinker may produce many works throughout his career, but a single impulse gives rise to all.[3] Taine was fond of organic similes: works are like the leaves and branches of a common trunk. "The whole corpus arises from a main root; a dominant, primitive sensation sprouts and endlessly ramifies the complicated vegetation of effects" (*Philosophie de l'art* 458). Criticism, this passage continues, cannot "untangle" all the effects; it must rise above the details in order to encompass essences.

The task, then, is to characterize the fundamental impulse and to illustrate its operations. The cultural field resembles a landscape—one of Taine's landscapes, at any rate—and the critic must try to locate the central vantage from which the pattern of the whole can best be surveyed. Criticism becomes an exercise in perspective, sifting creative output for the principal, foreground works or the heartwood, the proliferating middle ground, and the inevitable profusion of trivial or ephemeral leaves at the periphery. The critic joins taste and judgment to discern what matters in a body of work—what endures, what fructifies. In the *History of English Literature*, where Taine could not confine himself to what he innately liked, he often clears deadwood away in order to find the living core. Thus, in the chapter on Joseph Addison, Taine suffers through the sterile verse, the pallid moral essays (his judgments, not mine, of course), and the conventionally prescriptive aesthetic writings, until he finds the warm humor characters and the gently radiant descriptions of visionary nature that are the "epitome of all Addison's characteristics" (2: 147/3: 419).* Except in the worst of the polemic against French philosophy, he invariably balances criticism against praise, and the best parts of a work are always judged the most characteristic. One reason Taine gives for choosing English literature as his subject is its nearly continuous strength; he may have to survive the tedious poets of the fifteenth century, "whom we only read because we must accept history from every quarter, even from imbeciles" (1: 163/ 1: 221), but even among the weeds there are always flowers. After so many Gowers you are sure to find at least a Skelton, after so many Priors a Pope.

So long as Taine focuses on individuals, his method seems tempered with imagination and predicated on a core of human sympathy and warmth. Here Taine is an impressionist before he is a systematist, a psychologist before a botanist. "Every painter, poet, novelist of unusual lucidity should be interrogated and observed in depth by a psychologist friend" (*De l'intelligence* 1: 13–14). The travel books are an essential part of his oeuvre because they let the spontaneous feelings of the man unfold. "I write down my impression just as it is and on the spot, and I do not write until I have an impression"; "since you like frank impressions, I will give you the succession and the diversity of mine" (*Italie* 1: 119, 169). In studying authors Taine regularly begins with a biography, and not infrequently (as with Pope and Wordsworth) a luridly drawn one: the man precedes and explains the work. "Faculté maîtresse" may sound dry, but Taine also calls it a passion. "If you deprive facts of the

---

* Citations from the *History of English Literature* are given in the form (2: 147/3: 419). Volume(s) and page(s) before the slash refer to the English translation, those that follow to the French. Translations are modified where necessary.

original passion that calls them forth and of the color that illuminates them to the senses, they do not enter the mind either pure or whole. Let us then change abstractions and reasoning into emotions and into images. May history, like nature, touch the heart and the senses at the same time as the intelligence. . . . Science becomes art" (*Essai sur Tite Live* 190). The side of Taine that loves the sketches of Rubens above all other painting (see *Italie* 1: 198 and *Philosophie de l'art* 244–49) is a connoisseur of vivid and immediate images. At this level his system would appear to be merely a more focused application of Sainte-Beuve's sensibility.

But Taine was never content with the individualism of pure feeling. Having begun with art, he must always be converting it back into science. Even Sainte-Beuve, in Taine's eyes, was covertly a systematizer: "He imported into moral history the procedures of natural history" ("Sainte-Beuve," *Derniers essais* 96). Psychology rarely means for Taine what it commonly means for us, the insightful understanding of the emotions of the soul. Instead, it is the queen of the sciences. "Just as at bottom astronomy is a mechanical and physiology a chemical problem, so history at bottom is a psychological problem." "When you have observed and noted in man one, two, three, then a multitude of sensations, does . . . your knowledge appear complete? Is a book of observations a psychology? It is no psychology" (1: 24, 8 / 1: xlv, xv). To be sure, Taine's treatise on psychology—the book he felt most affection for, the only major project not prompted by an occasion or a commission—does concern itself with the buried wellsprings of personality. But the unconscious for Taine proves to be a peculiarly abstract and desiccated realm: it is the "moral event" that is "signified" by the "physical world," which, in turn, "is reduced to a system of signs" (*De l'intelligence* 1: 331). The inner truth of character is the cause of the appearances of character, the law of its manifestations. Outer and inner prove equivalent; each reduces to the other in a common, generative necessity. In this mood, Taine is a genetic structuralist, but bereft of Jean Piaget's exploratory sensibility. "Given any pair whatever of any data whatever; so soon as they are effectively linked, there is a reason, a *because*, an intermediary that explains, demonstrates, and necessitates their connection" (*De l'intelligence* 2: 441). The study of individual character is merely an example of science in general; really, there are no individuals—and hence no faculties, no passions, no characters—but only data and their laws.[4]

Consequently, the study of individuals appears to be only a passing illusion. Yes, Taine wrote detailed studies of many great authors, painters, historians, and philosophers. But in truth these individuals are merely indicators of the unity and the law of much greater and more lasting collectivities. The *History of English Literature* is less a portrait of individuals than a panorama of eras and, ultimately, a depiction of the English nation as it has endured from the dawn of history. The book's second sentence already points the way: "A work of literature is not a mere play of imagination, the isolated caprice of a heated brain, but a copy of the surrounding manners and the sign of a state of mind" (1: 1 [but poorly translated] / 1: iii). Taine's novel remained a meager torso, and it is striking how bereft of identifiable figures many of his books are. Thus, while *Notes sur l'Angleterre* reports many conversations—England being the land of particular existences as well as the subject of the masterpiece I will later rescue from the picture I am now painting—in the more than 800 pages of the *Voyage en Italie* only a few puppet-like individuals flicker briefly into view at the opening of volume 2 ("Pérouse et Assise"). Otherwise, even in "La Société," there is only a "digest of fifty or sixty conversations" (1: 317), quoting but a single, stereotypical, reinvented political debate (1: 377–81). Even more striking is the history of the Revolution, a grim sociological study obviously intended to counterbalance the vivid poetry of the two great historians whom Taine admired but also warned against, Carlyle and Michelet.[5] The Revolution could hardly be written without its leaders, but they (and even Voltaire and the *philosophes*) become the impotent vehicles of positions and groups, and the greatest events themselves fade into a subordinate clause.[6] Taine calls the Terror an example of "forces devoid of intelligence" (*La Révolution* 1: 345), and the phrase could apply to virtually the entire story he tells.

Trees are rooted in soil, and the soil rests on bedrock. More resonant even than the botanical metaphors that evoke the life force of individuals are geological metaphors reflecting the impersonal workings of nature. "When we wish to construct a man, we must dig down to the man's foundation; that is, we must define to ourselves the structure of his bodily machine and the primitive gait of his mind" (1: 329 / 2: 110); "the fundamental faculty, . . . buried but present, [is] like one of those deep and primeval rocks, which, lying far inland, give to all undulations [*accidents*] of the soil a basis and a support" (2: 72 / 3: 277). Even intelligence is not so much human intelligence as abstract intelligibility.

Taine's fondness for grand landscapes (such as the Dickensian view of England that opens the first chapter of the history) bespeaks a desire not to write a history of literature or indeed of human affairs but to tell the story of the earth itself. The *History of English Literature* is a book about the English—and ultimately about the land of England.

The psychological reduction of creativity to a master passion is thus only a halfway house. Psychology gets reduced in its turn. For "the question of origins is no more mysterious than that of characters" (*De l'intelligence* 2: 440). There is no force, there are only forces. The greatest among us discover or voice them; the rest merely represent them and carry them out. As character unites the traits of an individual—as it is the substance of which they are the signs—so the many characters that constitute a nation are in turn united. The forces constituting their unifying origin are the grand trinity I have already named—race, milieu, and moment. To be sure, not every mote and speck of dust can be fully explained, but everything that matters can, and the explanation invariably lies in these three factors.

Indeed, the more salient a characteristic, the more fully and convincingly it shows its causal origin, which is its meaning, the bedrock of which it is the sign or the trace. Hence the notorious slogan (to which I shall return), "Vice and virtue are products, like vitriol and sugar" (1: 8 / 1: xv). They are products of their time, their environment, and their race. Everything that matters is determined in the same way, by the same factors, in manifestation of a common essence of the individual, of his time, of his nation, and finally of humanity, or intelligence, or nature in general. Freedom is an illusion. The cosmic perspective may be exhilarating, as in the Spinozist paean that concludes *Les Philosophes classiques*. But before the immensity of nature individuals shrink into insignificance, and after the eternal order is established, human endeavors can do little but mar it. Taine's pessimism was notorious; he had a bleak and frequently reiterated view of outcomes and endings. Ben Jonson's death appears as one among many such: "Thus almost always, sadly and miserably is dragged out and ends the last act of the human comedy. After so many years, after so many sustained efforts, amid so much glory and genius, we find a poor shattered body, drivelling and suffering between a servant and a priest" (1: 325 / 2: 103). Perhaps Taine let the *Origines de la France contemporaine* displace his projected *Traité de la volonté* because he had everything to say about origins and nothing about will.

For the moment I will leave open the meaning of the terms race, milieu, and moment. But from everything I have said about the thrust of Taine's thought, it should be clear that the three causal determinants are not equal in value. One—race—is the bedrock, fixed, general, and unchanging like the soil. The other two are local, contingent, or transient. One determines the essence, the others modify it. "In all things, there are *superficies* [des *dessus*]—more or less external, accidental and temporary, changing, consequently of lesser importance—and a *foundation* [un *dessous* fondamental]—stable and solid, hence of greater importance. . . . [The followers of Poussin] instinctively sought locales where steep mountains display the earth's skeleton, and where man feels himself not in a backyard but on a planet" ("Edouard Bertin," *Derniers essais* 347, Taine's emphasis). If we dig deep enough, we will strip away the surface layers and arrive finally at the one thing that is the root of all.

- And so, finally, the term *history* unmasks itself as a deception. Just as there is no history in the *Voyage aux Pyrénées*, but only magnificent mountains and valleys and sordid tales and legends, so there is none in the *History* and in the *Origines de la France contemporaine*. The Revolution neither established liberty nor crushed human dignity; it merely repeated all the bureaucratic follies of the old regime, with greater outbursts of violence. Historians don't write history, they paint mankind, whether like the colorfully emotive Dutch painters or like the colorlessly energetic Greek sculptors. The end of historical study is the end of history. "In advance, and without its knowledge, each generation carries within itself its future and its history; to this one, well before the end, one might have foretold its destiny" (*L'Ancien régime* 2: 315). Hence, the *History of English Literature* originally concluded with a portrait of England:

Having reached the limits of this long review, we can now embrace in one prospect the aggregate of English civilization: everything is connected there: a few powers and a few primitive circumstances have produced the rest, and we have only to pursue their continuous action in order to comprehend the nation and its history, its past and its present. At the beginning, and furthest removed in the region of causes, comes the race. . . . This is the primitive stock: of its substance and innate properties is to spring almost the whole future growth. (2: 395 / 4: 424–25)

Once you have read the *History of English Literature,* you will never need to read it again.

II

That would be a pity, because it's a wonderful book. I know no work of scholarship to equal it in the combination of visionary sweep with coherent, meticulous immersion in its subject matter.

The previous section in effect reproduces the common view of Taine, both among his followers and through subsequent generations. In one form or another it can be found in countless books, essays, anthologies, and handbooks. An important recent example is the chapter in René Wellek's *History of Modern Criticism,* which echoes all the commonplaces and says almost nothing of why Taine is more than a fossil. The elements of this picture are all true, but they are only a part of the truth. They reflect the system but ignore the critic.

There is no shortage of signs pointing beyond the picture of Taine as a scientific determinist and a philosophical pessimist. He was not slow to protest explicitly against such one-sided readings.[7] Though he had a method (amid his veneration, Zola short-sightedly complained that it was too much of a method), Taine inveighed ceaselessly against the slaves of method, Rousseau and his revolutionary followers above all.[8] If we trust him as a writer, then we should seek a counterbalancing side to his achievement. But, indeed, we shouldn't trust him as a writer—or consequently take him at his word—when he formulates doctrine. For Taine always wrote for effect. His most memorable and most widely remembered utterances are calculated exaggerations; it is a mistake to consider his prefaces and programmatic declarations as the core of his vast achievement.[9] Rather, by his own lights they should be regarded as the sprouts of an indwelling sap or the traces of a bedrock that is to be sought beneath or within the proliferating texts.

What, first of all, can be intended by the three determinants: race, milieu, and moment? More ink has been spilled over these terms than about anything else in Taine, for nothing is really simple about them.

Race appears dangerously circular—in Taine's usage as in the present day. Race, for him, is the permanent, unchanging core. It is what remains unaccounted and mysterious when everything that has a manifest origin has been removed—a kind of residual essence, contingent surface mystically transmuted into depth. If a feature has no visible cause, then it must be racial; conversely, if it is racial, then it is inherent. By such logic, race becomes a vanishing mediator that redescribes what is least understood as that which is most true, without otherwise affecting its nature. It defines without explaining.

Milieu, on first, crude approximation, looks like a middle ground; in contrast to the everchanging moment, milieu varies slowly and produces deep, abiding effects. But if that were its character, then milieu would occupy only a vague and ill-defined terrain. It would differ quantitatively from moment by virtue of its pace, and as it approaches the permanence of landscape or climate (the quintessential milieux) it would likewise differ only quantitatively from race. In the distant past, to be sure, races traveled: you can really distinguish race from milieu when you see how the Norman character was modified when it descended into Normandy or when it swept into England. But in fact *Völkerwanderung* is not otherwise Taine's subject, and it becomes increasingly difficult to distinguish the Englishman from his milieu. Hence, milieu spoils the system: race is bound to place, moment changes with time, while milieu unsteadily absorbs whatever does not quite fit.

On closer examination, however, perhaps milieu is the system. Milieu suggests harmonious, meaningful correspondence, leaving to one side the imponderable givens of race, to the other the unseizable vagaries of the moment: "If great art and its milieu are contemporaneous, it is not that they are assembled by chance, it is that the second sketches, develops, ripens, spoils and dissolves the first along with itself, amid the accidents of the grand hubbub of humanity and the unforeseen sallies of personal originality" (*Philosophie de l'art* 168). So perhaps it is race that spoils the system: locality and time provide the external causal nexus, with race as the name for internal factors lacking visible explanation. Or, finally, perhaps moment is the spoiler: race and milieu constitute internal and external influences, and the rest is made up of the fleeting and unpredictable contingencies of the moment. "Two natures, one innate, the other acquired, constitute all the springs of . . . conduct," even though "at first sight it seems as if accidents or circumstances will govern their pace, their fall, and their success" (2: 398 / 4: 429). Taine simply offers too much facility for a rigorous, uniform system.[10]

As if that were not enough, examine the psychology. Virtue and vice may in some sense be products like vitriol and sugar—but only in their "chemical" nature, not in their historical existence. In a conceptual framework such as an introduction it may be helpful to see how vice and virtue are constituted. Yet even vitriol and sugar require a confluence of circumstances—suitable growing weather, an economic framework of production and distribution, and above all a will toward a desired result—if they are actually to be produced. The causal framework is not the only perspective on human life as experienced through time. For a naturalist such as Balzac (as Taine says in his long essay on the novelist), "virtue is a product, like wine or vinegar," but it is not one for a moralist such as Corneille. Ultimately the logic of Balzac's vision makes virtue "nothing but a usurious secured loan. It is Balzac's ugliest idea" ("Balzac," Nouveaux essais 60–61). Here Taine condemns the very determinism that he flaunts in introducing the History of English Literature. Determinism is only one side of Taine's vision; it is often the side he turns outward to capture the imagination of others, but not the side that captures his own most personal vision.

Indeed, before taking any of Taine's generalizations at face value, we must acknowledge that he had more than one face. In Etienne Mayran we find the conscious portrayal of the divided personality that was Taine, at once scientist and poet, prize scholar yet, when provoked, dashing pugilist. The novel fragment alternates analytical passages with landscapes and other portrayals of exalted emotion. In his introduction to the novel Paul Bourget quotes a notebook entry from 1862 (just when Taine was hardest at work on the History of English Literature): "My fundamental idea has been to reproduce the emotion, the passion peculiar to the man being described, and beyond that to lay out one by one all the steps of logical generation: in short, to paint him in the manner of artists, and, at the same time, to reconstruct him in the manner of reasoners" (Etienne Mayran 8). Of these two options, the reasoning manner is what Taine has been known for. The reasoning, however, turns out to be simplistic, arbitrary, and chaotic—good for sloganeering and partisanship, but not enduringly persuasive as scientific explanation. To be sure, I will have more to say about Taine's analytical gifts, with a different and more sympathetic way to understand his methods. But his astonishing passion and energy came from the magic of immediate contact with other souls, not from the sovereign command of meticulously disposed information.

The entire page came back, and seeing it thus unfold in his mind without needing to strain, he *felt* it, and he seemed to be hearing, not written words, but uttered speech. The book had a voice, and this voice reached his ears. "Now it is no longer my tables that I shall be studying, it is that book there; what a remarkable book!" . . . For the first time, he was touched by a thing proportioned to his mind, and that was *alive* for him. The rigid barrier that separates the books of men and the intelligences of children had given way at one point. (*Etienne Mayran* 204–5)

Such is the climax of Taine's fictional self-portrait, in the last and longest completed chapter, "Premières idées." The ecstasy was to be followed by a renewal of discipline, but Taine's heart was not in it; the next chapter (and the book) breaks off after barely a page. There are two sides to Taine's nature, as there are two sides to vice and virtue: you can know moral qualities, or you can be possessed by them. Ultimately you cannot really separate knowledge from possession. Still, what matters most is not the timelessness of science, but the feeling contact with life.[11]

Taine the vitalist. In reading Taine's more personal writings I find myself constantly thinking of Henri Bergson.[12] Everywhere, tirelessly, what captivates this man, who was himself a force of nature, is the driving energy of life. Products that can be known—even moral products such as vice and virtue—are not the vital source:

Neither the vices nor the virtues of man are his nature. . . . Our true essence consists in the causes of our good or bad qualities, and these causes are discovered in the temperament, the species and degree of imagination, the amount and velocity of attention, the magnitude and direction of primitive passions. A character is a force, like weight or steam. . . . It is therefore to ignore man, to reduce him, as Thackeray and English literature generally do, to an aggregate of virtues and vices; it is to lose sight in him of all but the exterior and social side. (2: 511 / 5: 142–43)

We study history, above all, in order to revive the lost art of the past. For a man so often accused of imposing scientific norms on artistic works, Taine leaves no doubt of his attachment to the irreproducible human individuality that they contain: "If some words are dry, like philosophical terms and like figures, others are alive like the vibrations of a violin or the tones of a painting" (*La Fontaine* 288). In his treatment of one author after another Taine extols the character portrayal; the role of literature is to bring people to life on the page. Hence his noteworthy and influential admiration for Stendhal, whose characters "are complex, multiple, particular and original like those of living beings; . . . they draw us far from our stale habits, from our mechanical life. . . . It is the spectacle of force, and force is the source of true beauty" ("Stendhal," *Nouveaux essais* 238–39). And the same is true of painting as of writing. "To paint living flesh is the supreme difficulty of art, for life is a profound, infinite thing" (*Philosophie de l'art* 501). The *Voyage aux Pyrénées* even contains a long paean to the life of rocks and to the mountains that people the earth, changing with a pace and a force that dwarf the insignificant flutterings of humanity (226–32).

But if even stones live, it is water that fascinates Taine above all. Water is his master metaphor, flowing and circulating life in all things. The definitive version of his first book opens with a prospect on a river, where "it seems that . . . the water lives and feels" (*Pyrénées* 4). The journey to England passes through a kind of landless baptism (*Notes sur l'Angleterre* 1–3; the paragraph headings—the only ones in the book—are "June 1862, at sea," and the curious "In the Thames"). In its definitive version even the book on La Fontaine (the writer's very name must have been captivating) opens, implausibly enough, with a water journey from the North Sea up the Rhine into France. And the *History of English Literature* starts with a long eulogy of English waters (1: 29–32/1: 2–6), which the original closing chapter renews (2: 403–6/438–43). Taine's waters are remarkable for their variety: the circulation of British commerce (2: 410–11/4: 449–51), the percolating terrain where the Dutch painters lived (*Philosophie de l'art* 184–88), the miracle of Venice (*Italie* 1: 290–91), the ripples that are "the only living thing" at night on the Lago Maggiore (*Italie* 1: 433), the gushing spring of Guido Reni's talent (*Italie* 2: 198), and, overwhelming all, the torrential force of the French Revolution. Even rocks are etched by water, or are residues left by water, or channels for water, a symbiosis without which rocks would be mere geometry and not the signs of authentic life. Man "is like a water" (*Italie* 1: 335); "the human spirit flows with events like a river" ("Mme de La Fayette," *Essais* 256); in its perfection "life flows, broad and measured, like a fine river" (*Philosophie de l'art* 428). While Taine was working on his *History of English Literature*, Michelet wrote a book on the sea (*La Mer*, 1861); his waters are a cauldron, a powerful engine, with a titanic circulation, the nourishing matrix of countless fascinating creatures and phenomena. But they are not, like Taine's, alive with any life of their own except for what scientific instruments discover in the currents of the globe. They teem with life, but it is Taine's waters that live.

Consequently, we must reverse the usual picture of Taine. He is not a determinist; or rather, to use the vocabulary that Zola favored, he is a determinist but not a fatalist. Even though it is closed in the past, history is open to the future: Taine willingly identifies causes but refuses to predict effects. Even so pivotal a poem as *Paradise Lost* is "not of its century" but rather a product of situation and opportunity alike, "the chance of a revolution," "the chance of a throne preserved, then re-established," "the force of his intellect," "the force of his enthusiasm" (1: 540, 555/2: 488, 515). To be sure, in the grand retrospect of Taine's original conclusion all falls into place. But in the supplementary volume, with its six chapters on the most notable figures of the present, the introduction avers that nothing can be securely foretold about the future course of events. There will be a pattern, but it will be composed from the inventions of the great thinkers and writers, and it cannot be traced until it has happened. Not even the men can be known truly during their lifetimes: "Unfortunately Dickens is still alive, and refutes the biographies made of him" (2: 430/5: 4). Events end as knowable history, but they begin with spontaneity and originality. In his last decades Taine lost his vision of human accomplishment; what makes the *Origines de la France contemporaine* so dreary is the concentration on origins and the bleak denial of individual initiative. But in the *History of English Literature* he manages the feat of balancing historical comprehensibility with personal invention.[13]

Taine's fusion of a backward-looking necessity and a forward-looking freedom is soundly Hegelian. As Taine was often caricatured as an objective, scientific determinist, so Hegel as a subjective determinist claiming that history finds its fulfillment with Napoleon. But Hegel's teleology is no more fatalistic than Taine's. His present is indeed the culmination of history, but that is because, looking back, the present always seems to be the goal. When in his lectures on the philosophy of history Hegel concludes, teleologically, that "the present form of spirit comprehends all earlier stages in itself," he does not restrict the meaning of present to his own time, but implicitly extends it to any present that reflects on its past. In truth spirit is timeless and ever present, always capable of being revealed through historical consciousness, for "what spirit is, it has always been." But while hindsight shows the present always spiritualized—fully rational and joyously perfect—in its unfolding it is tragically vulnerable. Like the phoenix, spirit must die; like the family of Zeus, it must consume its matter and be consumed in turn in order to be reborn. This "bitter potion" of determination and indeterminacy, of an unending cycle of foretold fulfillment and unforetold change, is what we can expect in the future, however cunningly rational the past inevitably appears (*Werke* 12: 104–5). While the negative and destructive sides of free, individual force figure more prominently in Hegel, a lurking suspicion of originality surfaces at times in Taine, for instance in his grim admiration of Swift: "What truth and force! . . . His originality is entire, and his genius creative; he surpasses his classical and timid age; he tyrannizes over form, breaks it, dare[s] utter anything, spares himself no strong word" (2: 174 / 4: 49–50). The passages in Taine where everything sounds totalized and foretold in the ageless and inescapable constancies of race are not his last word. Despite the panoramic retrospects collapsing history into a spatialized simultaneity, his vitalist dialectic reconciles comprehension with the onward flow of time.[14]

Comprehension is a key term: "If it is beautiful to paint a personage, it is perhaps interesting to make him *understood*" (preface [1858], *Essais* vii). Taine explores historical causation not with the scientific aim of producing or reproducing events, but with the hermeneutic one of understanding them. He clarifies his principles in the new preface to his essays, published in 1866, while he was at work on the supplementary volume to the *History of English Literature*. Claiming for himself only a retrospective system of explanation and not a prospective method of construction, he insists that his goal is a psychological analysis to reveal the structural node of an individual personality or the spirit of an age. Those who accuse such an explanatory system of inhumanity overlook

that the fundamental aptitudes and penchants of a soul belong to it, that those that it takes from the general situation or the national character are or become first off personal, that when it acts through them, it does so according to itself, by its own force, spontaneously, with complete initiative, with entire responsibility, and that the analytical artifice by which we distinguish its principal motors and gears and the ensuing distribution of its primitive movement, does not prevent the whole, which is itself, from drawing from within its impetus and its direction, that is, its energy and its effort. (*Essais* xxiii)

The more we penetrate the forces animating societies, the more we appreciate the individuals that mobilize those forces.

Taine is misconstrued as a fatalist when his notion of causes is taken in too strong a sense. The causes he alleges are factors that promote a result rather than determinants that precipitate it. He found the distinction worked out in John Stuart Mill, and he explains it in his study of the philosopher, where he reinterprets Mill's method of induction as a system of abstraction:

A fact, or a series of facts, can always be resolved into its components. It is this decomposition that is required when we ask what is the nature of an object. It is these components we look for when we wish to penetrate into the interior of a being. These we designate under the names of forces, causes, laws, essences, primitive properties. They are not new facts added to the first, but a portion or extract from them; they are contained in the first, they have not anything different from the facts themselves. When we discover them, we do not pass from one datum to another, but from the same to the same. (2: 646/5: 398)

There is no opposition or incompatibility between freedom and necessity, any more than there is between experiment and analysis, pragmatics and speculation, or English facts and German laws. It falls to the Frenchman (Taine concludes) to combine these two perspectives in a temperate and universal vision that accommodates them both.

Taine's *History of English Literature* is one of the nineteenth century's grandest attempts to reconcile the particularism of a Hogarth, a Scott, or a Mill with the rigorism of a Luther, a Dürer, or a Kant. In its representation of historical forces, it answers Michelet's mystic populism with a differentiated narrative where group tendency and individual accomplishment operate in constant interchange. Nationality is a spirit not freighted with compulsory nationalism, a continuing process rather than a universal idea. From François Guizot, to whom the *History of English Literature* is dedicated, Taine draws the ideal of civilization, but for him civilization is itself an evolving notion quite different from Guizot's "general and definitive fact, the culmination and summary of all the others" (Guizot, *Cours* 8).[15] Even at his most pessimistic Taine is free of the disenchanted antinaturalism of his close friend Ernest Renan; Taine's account of Shakespeare's bourgeois self-sufficiency is one implicit refutation among many of Renan's maxim that civilization is a creation of the aristocracy. Whereas the *Origines de la France contemporaine* indicts one nation's well-intentioned debacle, the *History of English Literature* chronicles another's often errant successes. The arts of a nation reveal its character and genius; they forge the possibilities of what it can imagine and accomplish. In our individualist era the notion of national identity can come to seem almost oxymoronic. (That is, indeed, the unstated presupposition of Benedict Anderson's influential *Imagined Communities*.) But artistic voices raised for the people restore the balance between the centralizing lethargy of race and the unstable opportunism of the momentary. The individual imagination, in Taine's view, does not produce the community but expands it, as the community does not command but does enable the imagination. The arts are the active expression of its will not just to be but to live.

Thus, the vitalism resurfaces as the other, less familiar, half of Taine's divided sensibility. On the one hand, as we have seen, his scientific determinism drove to the solid bedrock of timeless, essential abstractions: "Nature is, in reality, a tapestry, of which we only see the reverse; this is why we try to turn it" (2: 653/5: 409). Hence, he praises Macaulay for his penetration of the logic of events. "He had a most lively consciousness of causes; and causes unite facts. By them, scattered events are assembled into a single event" (2: 540/5: 201). To know causes is to secure the comprehensive grasp that makes them comprehensible; a unified vision is what makes understanding possible. On the other hand, in their most uncompromisingly fatalist form, abstractions clash irreconcilably against the pure contingency of random facts. When we seek the ultimate truths hidden under nature's tapestry, "we are outflanked on all sides by the infinity of time and space. . . . Chance is at the end of all our knowledge" (2: 655/5: 412). The ultimate in causes is an illimitable multiplicity of causes. Taine concedes as much only two pages after praising Macaulay's power of unification. "It is not enough to see causes; we must also see many. Every event has a multitude of them. . . . An incomparable advocate, [Macaulay] pleads an infinite number of causes" (2: 542/5: 202–4). Demands that are too positive subvert themselves in the end. It is not in experimental, materialist absolutism that man will find human truths, but in the psychology of human experience.

Taine's other great philosophical master was Spinoza. Spinoza taught him many of the same divided lessons about historical evaluation that Hegel taught him about historical understanding. From Spinoza, Taine draws not only the conventional determinist clichés, but likewise the recognition of how human consciousness encounters determinism. While material forces may steer the world, our engagement with the world occurs on a different plane—not in the absolutes of science and truth, but in affect and judgment. In the fifth and final book of Spinoza's *Ethics* the mastery of emotions through their conversion into clear and distinct ideas becomes the endless task of human reason. But the reality with which we deal as conscious beings continues to lie in the vague and fluctuating terrain of the passions, which are the subject of the fourth book. Because feelings precede knowledge, they shape our conscious experience more immediately than do the ultimate truths of nature. Fundamental for Taine's Spinozism is an axiom of *Ethics*, book 4: "Whatsoever thing be given, there is something stronger whereby it can be destroyed" (*Works* 2: 191). Precisely because everything is necessarily subject to something else, we can never actually get to the bottom of anything. Consequently, the material foundations of the world lie only with its founder. "Deus sive natura": natural forces exceed our power of control, to be sure, but also lie outside the finite realm of our existence. A human science deals with the human face of things, hence with what we now would call psychology rather than ontology. Just like Taine's supposed Darwinism, Spinoza's geometrical method works with stable axioms and postulates, but its object is the unstable intermediate terrain of humanity.

Taine footnotes the axiom to *Ethics*, book 4, at a crucial moment in the fifth section of the introduction to the *History of English Literature*. Earlier, better-known sections discuss quasi-paleontological or geological excavations for fixed, original truths:

There is an inner cause. . . . This itself comes from another more general cause. . . . This second idea in its turn depends upon a third still more general. . . . That is the master idea. . . . Here we track the root of man, . . . race itself. . . . There the search is at an end; we have arrived at a primitive disposition. . . . Here lie the grand causes, for they are the universal and permanent causes, present at every moment and in every case, everywhere and always acting indestructible, and in the end infallibly supreme. (1: 8–9 / 1: xv–xvii)

The rhetorical inundation appears uncontrollable. But then the focus shifts, as the other, more tempered side of Taine comes to the fore. "The vastness of the distance lets us but half perceive—and by a doubtful light—the origin of species,"[16] he writes in the fifth section. Essences may have ultimate explanations, but the universal ocean is too immense for us. Better to look for the indications where they gather in surveyable if provisional aggregates. Taine avoids terming these aggregates causes, for—as the imagery and the footnote to Spinoza both make clear—he is no longer thinking of the unshakable first causes with which his reputation is wrongly associated. The paragraph concludes: "Such is the first and richest source of these master faculties from which historical events take their rise; and one sees at the outset that if it be powerful, it is because this is no simple spring [punning on the French "source"], but a kind of lake, a deep reservoir wherein other springs have, for a multitude of centuries, discharged their several streams" (1: 14 / 1: xxvi). Taine's compromise learns to have it both ways: his lake is a source, yet not a source (spring) but a receptacle. Such imagery is appropriate to the logic derived from Mill; the understanding and judgment that Taine seeks are collective abstractions that pool or distill general, moral verities. In one perspective virtue and vice may be natural products, but the Spinozistic challenge is to resist and correct that perspective with the aid of human reason.

History is thus Taine's alternative to science. For, as his sentence about the origin of species continues, "the events of history sufficiently illumine the events anterior to history, to explain the almost immovable steadfastness of the primordial marks [caractères]" (1: 13 / 1: xxiv–xxv). In the Darwinian perspective, even race, though "almost immovable," is not a true absolute, but rather the outer bound of historical comprehension. Indeed, the History of English Literature opens with the migrations of the tribes that shaped the English character at the dawn of history. Of all the civilizations that Taine loved, the English appealed the most to him because of the evolving continuity of its culture, fostered by its cool, damp, settled climate. England produces strong, steady, earthy characters—at one extreme the "sympathetic genius" of a Shakespeare that becomes "a sort of abstract [abrégé] of the universe" (1: 366 / 2: 178), at the other the icy firmness into which Byron congeals Goethe's all too "flowing water" (2: 305 [a remarkable page] / 4: 387). So stable an environment allows for the powerful unfolding of the essential forces of civilization. Taine developed a horror of sudden revolution, but he continued to admire change, and his book contains numerous paeans to the quietly epochal shifts that have allowed England to adapt to circumstance without either destroying or being destroyed. The steady progress of history is the vital expression of the characters that live in it. Without stability there is no character and hence only the fearsome turmoil of the Year III of the Revolution. But without history there is no life—and that would be a transcendental condition inhuman and unearthly.

III

The debates about Taine, when he has been debated, have focused on the forces driving history: the causal or (as I have argued) explanatory determinants of events and texts. To move beyond these debates, we can turn from the forces to the object itself. Through race, milieu, and moment we can comprehend history, but what is the thing we are comprehending? Here I will introduce another triad, never formalized or expressly articulated by Taine but fundamental to his motivation. As an object of study history has for Taine three elements: the past, time, and the ideal in history. I propose to move toward the substance of Taine's achievement by surveying each of these in a widening circle.

The past. The past is the not-present. The past must be recovered if it is to be studied. Since we know men through "present, personal, direct, and sensible observation," our knowledge of the past must be "always incomplete." Still, we must do what we can to compensate (suppléer) the deficiency. The "first step in history" is to "make the past present" (1: 4 / 1: 9). Without that, it remains a fossil embedded in an unexcavated rock. Taine must have seen the evocations of this aspect of history writing in the much-admired Macaulay. It is the imaginative and poetic side of history: "To make the past present, to bring the distant near, to place us in the society of a great man or on the eminence which overlooks the field of a mighty battle . . . , these parts of the duty, which properly belongs to the historian, have been appropriated by the historical novelist" ("Hallam," in Macaulay's *Essays* 1: 111–12). By the novelist or, indeed, even by the poet: "No sooner are [Milton's words] pronounced than the past is present and the distant near" ("Milton," *Essays* 1: 12). Taine himself revives the past with his colorful descriptive passages, sometimes in the present tense, with his prosopopoeias, and with the sharply etched metaphors that render phenomena from the past in familiar natural or experiential terms.[17] He peppers his studies with comparisons between earlier and later or between foreign and French authors to help reduce the differences of time and space: an Anglo-Saxon funeral song sounds like Jeremy Taylor, Caedmon speaks like Milton, John Fortescue is the fifteenth-century Locke, Shakespeare's sonnets are at times worthy of Heine (!), La Bruyère foreshadows Balzac's realism, La Fontaine's power of evocation is like Musset's. To this extent Taine's practice offers a classic instance of what Collingwood (followed by Gadamer) was to claim as the historian's duty: "The gulf of time between the historian and his object must be bridged" (*The Idea of History* 304).

But if *Horizontverschmelzung* is the start of history, it is not the end. The past that is made present is no longer the past. (Gadamer, for whom history is merely a salient example of more diffuse hermeneutic concerns, does not acknowledge this limitation.) Hence, as Macaulay called for history as picture or as sculpture to be balanced by history as map or as anatomy ("Hallam" 112–13), so Taine urges a "second step" beyond evocation into excavation and analysis (1: 4, 7 / 1: ix, xiv). It is no longer a matter of bringing the past into the present, but conversely of entering the past: the historian is now "present at the drama which was enacted" (1: 5 / 1: xi). The historian submerges his sympathetic, novelistic force beneath his scientific ambitions to know his material in its irreducible inner core.

Though articulated early in the introduction, the scientific aim of history comes to the fore only rarely in Taine's writing. There are a few moments in the *History of English Literature* where he lapses into the past tense as he confronts the genuine alienness of, say, seventeenth-century religious polemic or of Hobbesian and Restoration materialism. And the essays on seventeenth-century France occasionally defer to its remote sensibility. "This style and these sentiments are so remote from ours that we understand them with difficulty. . . . We must neither denigrate nor imitate, but invent and understand. History must be respectful and art must be original" ("Madame de la Fayette," *Essais* 255). Taine is capable of forcing himself to accept what he instinctively rejects. "I even dare to go further, and I transport myself among the habits of the seventeenth century. . . . Each art and each century cloaks truth in a form that beautifies and alters it; each century and each art have the right to cloak the truth thus" ("Racine," *Nouveaux essais* 121). But such detachment is truly exceptional in his writing—and reluctantly professed at that. Even Macaulay's passions were too rationalized for Taine's taste: "He is not a genuine artist: when he draws a picture, he is always dreaming of proving something" (2: 624 / 5: 223).

For just as the drive to ultimate sources and unifying totalities is checked by Taine's humanistic vitalism, so too a self-suppressing immersion in the past yields to the urgent desire to establish a relationship. The past should no more be left in its fossil state than conjured up as a kind of paler present. It cannot be fixed at one pole or at the other. Rather, the past is like flowing water, like the circulation of mists, like the stream-fed lakes and the lake-fed streams. Even at the very moment when Taine is professing a geological model of the past as "great rocks deep-seated in the ground," he will also speak of "the continuous development and the ever-changing succession of the emotions and conceptions out of which the text has sprung" (1: 5–6 / 1: xi). The object not of charted knowledge but of nuanced understanding, the past must neither be fixed in alienness nor allowed to lapse into repetitive familiarity. For its essence is precisely to be in movement. At the heart of the era of positivism, the first great achievement of Taine's history is to have overthrown the conception of the past as fact.

Time. It might seem self-evident to take time as the founding category of history. Surely it was not without shock value when structuralist historiography from Febvre to Braudel and the early Foucault claimed to overthrow Taine's legacy and to transcend time's explanatory mediations.[18] However, Friedrich Meinecke long ago showed how arduous a process it was before growth and change became enshrined—not so long before Taine's day—as the basic focus for history. Even then, the conception of time was not yet altogether what Taine made of it. For time functions in nineteenth-century narrative representations as a regulative ideal; it is the force that is always moving onward, beneath the surface of events. What happens, then, is not part of time, but rather an interruption of time. History consequently is riven between the poles of flow and event. "Consider it well, the Event," writes Carlyle, "is it not, in all cases, some disruption, some solution of continuity?" (*French Revolution* 23). Time in this sense is not part of history but its horizon and outer bound. "But, on the whole, does not TIME envelop this present National Convention . . . ? Time surely, and also Eternity" (*French Revolution* 530). Consequently, we are but "a Phantasm-Reality born of Time . . . ; flitting ever backwards now on the tide of Time" (*French Revolution* 387). Carlyle is extreme, to be sure, but in these matters extreme in his lucidity, and a powerful stimulus for Taine as well.

The reconciliation of duration with change was a central problem for nineteenth-century fictional and historical narrative alike. Here, for instance, is what Georges Poulet concludes concerning the "moment" in Michelet. "On the one hand, the instant that he celebrates is the creator of the future, a flash of eternity, annihilating duration. On the other, it is prepared by a confluence of forces. So that this moment is at once *ultra*- and *extra*-historical. It is an apex of history, which comes to pass in a moment where the being that sees it, sees at the same time and all of a sudden history destroyed and history rebegun" (*Mesure de l'instant* 269).[19] It was one thing to make history temporal at bottom (rather than, say, moral and exemplary); it was quite another to make time part of history.

Taine's simplest solution to the polarization of events and time is to write histories without events. Thus, there is *Les Origines de la France contemporaine*, burdened by its crowds and mass forces and, as I have said, tragically occluding events from its history. But the *History of English Literature* is lightened by its freedom from events. England was of course favored in that its revolutions—with one exception that was not productive of great writing[20]—were peaceful and mostly intellectual or (in the broad sense) social rather than political. The flow of history was steadier there than in France. But Taine does much to sustain the flow. Dates, for one, are refreshingly scarce, and the disposition of the history works to reinforce a developing continuity. The *History of English Literature* is the masterpiece of a writer, all of whose writing is unsurpassed, in my reading experience, in organizational lucidity. Time progresses, but effortlessly. Seven of the original nineteen chapters (before the supplement on modern writers) concern individual authors, with the presentation sweeping effortlessly from the dynamic historical background into the life and works of the writer who shapes and advances the movement of civilization. The other twelve concern periods but remain unobsessed with chronology as they trace influences and developments. That is to say that Taine reinterprets periods as movements. Ideas and forms of expression are in continual flux, and within his always steady outline he masters the art of transition. Ends of chapters, above all, gather energy. Consolidation in Taine is tidal, not glacial, nor, except for 1789 (concluding the chapter about 1688, called "The Revolution"), volcanic.

We must, then, return to the three determinants—race, milieu, moment. If the first, scientific and geological model for Taine's theory points toward the permanence of race as the final explanatory ground, the revised, temporal and hydrologic model seeks elsewhere. It finds time operating not just through the determinants but within them. For moment in Taine is not just circumstance; it is movement, momentum. It is called "vitesse acquise" (acquired speed) in French and given the hybrid translation "acquired momentum."[21] To race we attribute the constant factors located within the person, to milieu the factors without. What these do not fix is what changes and thus what lives, and that is moment. Moment, or momentum, or speed, in this sense, cannot be dead, passive, or reactive, because then it would be race or milieu. Rather, moment is the spontaneity of active energies generated by individuals.

Most frequently, Taine specifies moment as developmental stage, particularly in the introduction, where he so consistently works to channel his vitalism into a system. The succession of "buds, flowers, fruits, seed-vessels" seems to provide a "law" that models the birth, maturing, and decadence of a movement or an epoch (1: 16–17 / 1: xxx–xxxi). This organic model is applied throughout the history, where Taine often writes eloquently about the gathering or waning energies of civilization. In the *Philosophie de l'art* a classicizing bent tends to normalize the model, so that perfection is found in the harmonious middle: "That is the moment when an art flourishes; previously it was a seed; a little later, it has faded. At this instant, the convergence of effects is complete, and an admirable harmony internally balances the characters, the style and the action. This moment is found in Greece in the time of Sophocles" (448). In such a passage moment is indeed passive; it measures value and is left behind as the organism follows the predetermined path of its race and its milieu.

But a different and more generous spirit animates much of the best of Taine. Resisting the inclination toward systematic norms, the introduction again retreats: "The magnitude and direction cannot be valued or computed" in "moral problems" as it can in "physical ones." "This quantity is not measurable like . . . pressure or . . . weight. We cannot define it in an exact or approximative formula; we cannot have more, or give more, in respect of it, than a literary impression" (1: 17 / 1: xxxii). The true emphasis lies not on position within set coordinates but on the animation moving from one position to the next. Different moments— different stages of life—are distinguished less by different degrees of perfection than by their different speeds. Each stage has its characteristic pace, and that above all is what is meant by its moment, its *vitesse acquise.* Even in the *Philosophie de l'art* Taine says so, though with a hard, stony metaphor. "Time scratches and digs at us, like a man with a pickaxe, and thus displays our moral geology; under its efforts, our superimposed layers depart one by one, *some more swiftly, and others more slowly*" (390, my emphasis).

The truth of moment is that we carry our determinants within us; as we are moved, so we move. The speed and the momentum vary with the age and the individual; what does not vary is that side by side with race and milieu runs the ever-changing current that defines humanity. Life is not a mechanical field of levers and pulleys but a dynamic universe of velocities and impulses encountering inertial drags and resistances. Nothing can be calculated or fixed. "Change a virtue in its milieu, and it becomes a vice; change a vice in its milieu, and it becomes a virtue. . . . Our true essence consists in the causes of our good or bad qualities, and these causes are discovered in the temperament, the species and degree of imagination, the amount and velocity of attention, the magnitude and direction of primitive passions. A character is a force, like gravity, weight, or steam" (2: 510–11 / 5: 142–43). If vice and virtue are products like vitriol and sugar, so be it; but Taine's deepest interest lies in understanding the productive forces and not merely the reagents and reaction conditions—race and moment—that some celestial manufacturer can then learn how to vary or to change.

The ferment of England as milieu surmounts the inertia of England as ground and as race. England is not a classicizing civilization that culminates in perfectly poised and harmonious forms. Rather, as in any arena of vitality and flux, everything is in movement. There still are swells and troughs, but no apexes or dead points. The youthful profusion of the Elizabethan stage or the twilight exquisiteness of Pope and Tennyson have a value that might be surpassed but that cannot be replaced (1: 169; 2: 262, 660/2: 6–7; 4: 199–200; 5: 421). No single standard will hold. "The pretention to judge all styles according to a single rule is as outrageous as the intention to reduce all spirits to a single mold and to reconstruct all centuries on a single plan" ("Balzac," *Nouveaux essais* 40). For indeed civilization never rests, neither on the heights nor in the abyss. The time of history knows no events because it needs none; it is always moving forward, without depending on external impulse. There are no fixed points, only transitions.

Thus, it is not the moments of classical perfection that truly enchant Taine, but the moments of passage. And they are ubiquitous—so much so that to call them moments is a misnomer. Impressionistically throughout the *Voyage en Italie* and systematically in the *History of English Literature*, he captures the flux of careers and of eras as devotedly as any critic I know. "In all times and in all countries"—everywhere, always—"what calls forth works of art is a certain complex and mixed state that is encountered in a soul located between two epochs and divided between two orders of feeling; a taste for greatness is being replaced by a taste for the agreeable; but, in passing from one to the other, the soul unites both" (*Italie* 2: 320). The poetry and art that Taine loves above all are those located not at the height of their period, but between times, like the poet Milton: "Placed, as it happened, between two ages, he participates in their two characters, as a stream which, flowing between two different soils, is tinged by their two hues" (1: 556/2: 516). Like the Sistine Chapel, in one of Taine's great set pieces, the masterpiece of a time when "man is . . . in a state of passage and leaving the Middle Ages in order to enter the modern age; or rather the two ages are at their confluence" (*Italie* 1: 215). Like Rubens, in whose characters "the present . . . is impregnated by the past and pregnant with the future" (*Philosophie de l'art* 247—an exceptional moment in this book). Like the valedictory vision of the Simplon pass at the end of the long *Voyage en Italie*: "This is the boundary of two regions, and it seems as if it is the boundary of two worlds; the dazzling summits blend with the whiteness of the clouds, so that one no longer knows where the earth ends and where the heaven begins" (2: 437). Or, indeed, like all moments of greatness: "That is why the fleeting and precious flower is found only at the confluence of two ages, . . . at the moment in which man . . . begins to rest. . . . Sooner, it would have been too early . . . ; a bit later, it would be too late. . . . Between the two is found a unique moment . . . in which men . . . relax their outstretched will to rejoice magnificently their spirit and their senses" (*Italie* 2: 320–21). A moment? Perhaps. But there are no moments, only expanses of flowing time. So let me restore and italicize a crucial phrase omitted from the abridged quotation: "a unique moment, *longer or shorter*, according as the transformation of the soul is more or less prompt." Periods, not moments, of passage are the special times of human achievement.

How unique are these passages? Gradual, steady, quiet change is as much Taine's subject as it is George Eliot's or Trollope's. Time works within his history because there is no moment without change and consequently none that initiates change. Beginnings thrill him, as in the ecstatic pages on Nicholas of Pisa (*Italie* 2: 52–54), but they come as stealthily as the dawn, which is his invariable figure for beginnings (thus, *Italie* 2: 433). And everywhere there is quiet, unperceived change, with no manifest impulse. Taine's skill at marshaling evidence and tracing the currents is such that it is difficult to describe an instance (they don't break down into instances) and unfair to highlight an example (for how can there be an example of a uniform substance, as if a drop of water could be an example of a stream?). Still, here is one among so many, so that there can be no mistaking. "Such were the ornate and polished manners which gradually pierce through debauchery and assume the ascendant. Insensibly the current grows clearer, and marks out its course like a stream, which forcibly entering a new bed, splashes about at first in a tempest of slime, then pushes forward its still muddy waters, which are purified little by little. These debauchees try to be men of the world, and sometimes succeed in it" (1: 606 / 3: 81).

The ideal in history. Images of constant flux, however, problematize human effort. What role do men play in the insensible and irresistible stream of history? The answer of the history of the Revolution is, in effect, none. In the maelstrom of "forces devoid of intelligence" (*La Révolution* 1: 345), "the revolutionary malady"—an "epidemic and contagious" disease (2: 313)—poisons even the rare individuals who surface from the swarm of names. A Marat swims with the deluge, a Danton steers briefly to no real avail, even the great Napoleon finally drowns of his own superabundant motion. Civilization turns out to be mere costume, as the innate bestiality of man comes to the fore: "All the clothing woven for him by the centuries and placed on his shoulders by civilization, the last remnants of human apparel, falls to earth; only the primitive animal remains" (3: 267). Taine's Revolution is a zoo—a Darwinian cosmos where tigers and gorillas, dogs, sheep, locusts, and countless other species follow their instincts to the bitter end. Its lesson, as Taine drew it in writing of the great novelist of the Revolution, is that "Social history is but the prolongation of natural history" ("Balzac," *Nouveaux essais* 40).

When Taine is in this cynical mood, ideas do not seem any more effective than deeds: "A doctrine only becomes active in becoming blind" (*L'Ancien régime* 2: 12). Force and mass determine what can be done or, for the writer, what can be said: "Art varies when the audience varies. . . . No one has the right to impose his pleasure and his nature on another" ("Balzac" 39). Realism thus became a watchword for Taine, as for all the advanced writers of his time. The artist in the modern spirit reproduces reality, and his value lies in extensive variety and intensive precision. He does not actually *do* anything; rather, he serves as the vehicle for the physical world to be itself to the fullest.[22] Fixed in stone, the life of the past survives into the present: "Donatello dares to risk the whole truth, the coarse details that can seem homely [*disgracieux*] to the vulgar, the frank imitation of the real individual with his own traits and the traces of his craft, and we see . . . a fragment of living humanity which, torn alive from his century, by his originality and his energy prolongs his century's life to us" (*Italie* 2: 234). Such an art can capture and preserve life. But how can it be said to live? "If you insist on photography, you become obscure and boring" (*La Fontaine* 256). Photography can be a "useful auxiliary," but "if exact imitation were the supreme goal of art," then the highest achievement would be "a shorthand transcript of trials at the court of assizes" (*Philosophie de l'art* 26). The art that is of its time may capture its time, may reflect it, may preserve it. But no such aesthetic can satisfy a need for art (or human action in general) to make, shape, or lead its time.

At the time Taine was writing, the figure around whom debates concerning the destiny of art coalesced was the great social philosopher (and exponent of realism) Pierre-Joseph Proudhon.[23] Inevitably, any publication entitled *De l'idéal dans l'art* (as was the last part of Taine's philosophy of art) would have been seen as a riposte to Proudhon and to his realist sympathizers. Indeed, in the same year Taine satirized photographic realism as shorthand reporting, a notorious passage in Proudhon's posthumous *Du principe de l'art et de sa destination sociale* instanced a photograph of a side of beef as the first level of art (29–30). But the opposition is not simple, for Proudhon was an idealist in morality and family values, and Taine was a democrat (of sorts) with great admiration for realist art, especially in earlier periods when realism marked a historical advance.[24] One explanation for the enthusiasm of Taine's early auditors and readers may be that he made sense out of the inconsistencies in the aesthetic theories around him; at any rate a summary of Proudhon's shifting aesthetic tenets will illuminate the specificity of Taine's achievement.

Proudhon's career manifests contemporary perplexities about the value of art. He had begun by scorning art in the name of reality: "The golden age of what is called purely literature has passed for ever" (*Correspondance* 1: 182). "The interest of novels disappears before the attractions of reality" (*Carnets* 1: 379). In print such condemnations climaxed in vitriolic attacks on art in the late 1840's, both in the famous *Système des contradictions économiques, ou philosophie de la misère* of 1846 that Karl Marx attacked and in the 1848 essay, "Ce que la Révolution doit à la littérature" (collected in *Idées révolutionnaires*, 1849), which lashes out at artists as sycophants to all those with power. But the Platonic attack on artistic hypocrisy leaves room for a neo-Platonic defense of true artistic insight. Two developments in Proudhon's writing of the 1850's typify the theory of realism in the Second Empire. First, Proudhon increasingly acknowledges that art can have other bases than prettification: "The image of vice, like that of virtue, is as much part of the domain of painting as of poetry" (*Philosophie du progrès* 99). Art is not decorative beauty opposed to the real, but moral beauty within the real, so that it can legitimately aim at reaching and ennobling all the people. "All of us, so long as we live, are artists, and the job of all is to erect in our persons, in our bodies and in our souls, a statue to beauty" (98). Second, Proudhon consequently develops a radical aesthetic populism. Mere utilitarianism "would have photographs, not painters," but "an artistic, flexible, living word belongs only to a free being" (*De la justice dans la Révolution* 3: 583). Art belongs to and liberates everyone equally.

Hence, as Proudhon writes in *Du principe de l'art* not three pages after faintly praising the realist photograph of the side of beef, "Art is noth-ing except by the ideal, has value only by the ideal; if it is confined to a simple imitation of nature, it would be well advised to bow out" (32). The resounding prophet of real life turns into an equally resound-ing apostle of transvaluing reality. Proudhon's late book on copyright hymns the "all but sacred" mission of the artist to reform and redeem his society: "He is the eternal prophet of divine things, . . . working . . . toward the exaltation of humanity" (*Les Majorats littéraires* 134). The artist speaks both to and for the people; he is "the interpreter of collec-tive reason, of what is most inward in the life of the people, and of which they do not have a clear and formal awareness. . . . In a word he must be a prophet, he must speak the future, he must enlighten his contemporaries with his inspired utterance" (*De la justice dans la Révolu-tion* 3: 417). Realism has mutated into the belief that art and the artist were powerful enough to transmute even reality, and that they must not be allowed to deflect us with any less vital interests.

The constant throughout these vagaries is the opposition between the real and the ideal. Whether denigrating art for its false glitter or extol-ling it for its power to transform the prose of the world, Proudhon maintains an unyielding two-valued logic that forces a choice between them. If the artist falls to the aristocrats or the bourgeoisie, he becomes a renegade to humanity. If not, he is a savior. Either way, the artist stands outside the society whose spokesman he should be. His mode remains ecstatic; his mission a conversion of the heathen; his action an elevation beyond the plane of ordinary existence. The future that he proclaims is a utopian eternity of unchanging goodness. Absolute sympathy for puri-fied humanity must somehow join absolute judgment on social degra-dation. Yet the more fully the poet is clothed in a prophet's garb, the less suitable he seems as a mediator. He cannot both preach from without and work from within. Proudhon's exalted extremism was echoed by a generation, most famously in the well-known lines of Baudelaire:

> Viens-tu du ciel profond ou sors-tu de l'abîme,
> O Beauté! ton regard, infernal et divin,
> Verse confusément le bienfait et le crime.
> ("Hymne à la Beauté," 1860)[25]

So resounding an appeal cannot control its effects. That is a dilemma that equally confronted the Parnassian exponents of art for art's sake, the socially conscious realists, and the satanists, all of whom mingle confusingly in the cultural landscape of the period.[26] The haunted realist's godlike artist, as Flaubert envisioned him around the same time, would have no truck with his creation.

After an early flirtation with realist denigration of art, in an unpublished essay "Du style," Taine moved toward a reconciliation of realism with idealism.[27] If, as I have illustrated, he quickly became disillusioned with mimetic realism, he avoided his generation's temptations to veer to the opposite extreme. Rather, his vitalism responds to the quandaries of mid-century aestheticism. Taine's artist works on society, but from within, as a part of the social process. To be sure, he is then never perfect—neither a saint nor a prophet. On the other hand, the means of his influence become comprehensible without resort to religious or mystical enthusiasm. His effect is historical, not transcendental. The role and the possibilities of art gain in nuance: different expressions have valid functions in different societies and ages (different races and milieux), and the strength of the artistic intervention or the degree of its opposition to the social flux likewise varies according to the moment of historical inertia. In his capacity as the mediator of cultural evolution the artist can both speak for his time and advance his cause, without self-contradiction. Proudhon's artist prophesies a future that is all but eschatological; Taine's artist, along with bringing our past near to us, likewise brings the future near to his contemporaries. The representative artist lives, for Taine, between eras because he makes eras happen; the currents of time flow through him and his labor.

Consequently, the artist becomes essential not to the mystical transfiguration of society, but to its very existence. The nadir of the Revolution, grimly highlighted at the end of a long chapter, is the murder of a poet, André Chénier, by illiterate scum.

"The Republic [the judge says to the doomed Lavoisier] needs no scientists." It has equally little need for poets, and the first poet of the era, the delicate and superior artist who reopened the springs of antiquity, who opens modern ones as well, André Chénier, is guillotined; we have in the original the handwritten transcript of his interrogation, a veritable masterpiece of barbarian gibberish; it should be transcribed whole with "its turpitudes of sense and of orthography." Read it, if you want to see a man of genius delivered up to beasts, to coarse, choleric, and despotic beasts, who hear nothing, who comprehend nothing, who do not even understand ordinary words, who stumble over their own malentendus and who, in aping intelligence, wallow in asininity.—The overturn is complete: subject to the revolutionary government, France resembles a human creature who has been forced to walk on her head and to think with her feet. (*La Révolution* 3: 459–60)

No passage in Taine's writing more powerfully communicates his creed that the power of art sustains civilization. If history is the ever-flowing current passing between past and present, art is its channel. The country that murders its poets murders itself.

Striking and characteristic in Taine's narration of Chénier's murder is the association of barbarism, bestiality, and babble. Civilization, intelligence, and linguistic expression are intimately linked; what kills one kills all three. If Proudhon's artist saves humanity through the content of his message, Taine's furthers history through his form. To understand the mediations at the heart of Taine's vision, we must therefore turn to his virtually unrecognized master concept, which is that of style.[28]

IV

The artist in words, to be sure, acts directly only on words; his immediate creation is new writing. But the new writing then mediates new ways of thinking and new social constellations. He achieves a style, and the style achieves the rest. The *Philosophie de l'art* starts with the axiom that "every artist has his style" (12). When the writer is in control of his words, "the style is like a torch . . . passed in succession before each part of a large canvas. . . . By this power, imagination reproduces and replaces sight; the imagination takes the place of the object; the phrase gives presence to the thing that is not there" (*La Fontaine* 289–90). Life-preserving and life-giving, style is the vehicle through which culture enters history. "A geometer has no style" because he needs none, since he seeks the "pure light" of "universal truth" (*La Fontaine* 324). Conversely, historical degeneration correlates with a loss of style: the Revolution descends to Jacobin illiteracy (*La Révolution* 2: 264: "Social condition and degree of culture are often indicated by orthography"), to the darkness of cliché and "rude familiarity" in which "there is but one tone, one style, one language" (117), and downward to the degraded rant of Saint-Just (3: 245: "He laughs no more, he kills, but with what arguments and in what a style!" and on for three pages). To have a style is to participate in the progress of civilization; to have none is to be exempted, excluded, or corrupted.

Where Taine's interest in style is acknowledged at all, it is normally in dismissive terms such as these: "He frequently deals with style, but rarely for its own sake, his purpose usually being to illustrate through it changing modes of thought" (Weinstein, *Hippolyte Taine* 99). Indeed, Taine does repeatedly claim that human expression reflects human history: "With a sincere writer, doctrines foretell the style"; "such and such a subject demands such and such a style" (1: 521, 539 / 2: 450–51, 486). The "spirit" of an age (a very common expression in Taine), the "dominant form of thought," is at the same time "the sway of [its] style," and in return "the possession of this style [by the writers of the age] is . . . universal" (2: 246 / 4: 173–74, specifically about the classical style). Hence, at every level Taine looks for what represents the whole: "Art is the resumé of life"; "everywhere art and spirit meet; for that reason the first expresses the second and the second produces the first" (*Italie* 1: 136, 177). What applies to an age applies to an author: "Let us then look for the man, and in his style. The style explains the work; whilst showing the principal features of the genius, it proclaims the rest" (1: 370 / 2: 184). And what applies to an author applies to every line or word that he writes, at least when he is truly himself: "At every instant, in a word, in a gesture, in an imaginative sally, in an unbuttoned reflection, in a turn of phrase, a reminder and an indication that will show you the whole interior, the whole past, the whole future of a character" (Shakespeare's greatness, as summarized in *Philosophie de l'art* 440). Style does more than transmit the spirit of earlier ages and creators; it brings the past to life.

Even Taine's most routine adoptions of the language of reflection thus entail more than mere copy or illustration of the dominant present: a style that conveys the inside, past, and future of things reflects rather after the manner of a mind than after that of a mirror. Style transcribes what cannot otherwise be seen: "The principal service that literary writings render the historian is to put *extinct sentiments* before his eyes," to wit, "the spring of moral action" and "the soul" of history ("Renaud de Montauban," *Nouveaux essais* 327). And its representations arise from and serve thought: "The difference of [Xenophon's] style and of our own will mark, better than any commentary, the difference of the two civilizations" ("Xénophon," *Essais* 151).[29] Taine's countless discussions and evocations of style invariably presuppose its mission to the perceiver's present and even (as in a "presentment") to the future. "The mode of conception in a man governs the mode of thought. . . . When the mind [*l'esprit*], with rapt attention, penetrates the minute details of a precise image, joy and grief shake the whole man. . . . This impassioned style is extremely potent" (Dickens; 2: 442 / 5: 27–28). Even in his most realist utterances, Taine is capable of being seized by the power of style to govern sensibility.

As there should be no question of Taine's devotion to style, so there can be none of what he means by it. He routinely scrutinizes the characteristic sentence structure of authors, their diction, their versification and paragraphing, their imagery, their plot organization. *Explication de texte* is his métier, supported by wide reading that develops confidence in the representative nature of the passages selected. Here is one instance among countless others, giving a vivid picture even in the case of an author Taine disliked: "[Pope's Eloisa] puts ornaments in every line. . . . Now it is a happy image, filling up a whole phrase; now a series of verses, full of symmetrical contrasts; two ordinary words set in relief by strange conjunction; an imitative rhythm completing the impression of the mind by the emotion of the senses; the most elegant comparisons and the most picturesque epithets; the closest style and the most ornate" (2: 256 / 4: 189).[30] With works of visual art, similarly, Taine brings formal dimensions to the fore: "A painting is a colored surface, in which the various tones and the various degrees of light are distributed with a certain choice; there is its intimate being" (*Philosophie de l'art* 453). For these are the aspects through which artistic works communicate the spirit of their age. Typically, Taine will move from style to characters, as in the once-famous chapters on Shakespeare and Dickens. But characters themselves have for Taine a function that is more ideological than psychological, like Milton's Adam and Eve, "an English household, two reasoners of the period," who make of the epic "a political poem" (1: 541, 543 / 2: 489, 494). Indeed, "every literature," as Taine writes in summing up Thackeray's characters, "is a definition of man" (2: 509 / 5: 141). Viewed in this way, character is the apex of style, where spirit of the age and language of the text are fused.

The last chapter of the *Philosophie de l'art* relates the "force" or "expressive power" (436, 454) of a work to the cooperation of all the levels of artistic expression, in what Taine terms "the convergence of effects." Such formulations reveal the affinities between Taine and twentieth-century structuralism.[31] While he registers disparities and interferences, his primary interest lies in the higher-order regularities of a work, an author, and a period. Yet clearly he does not accord the same primacy to the synchronic as Ferdinand de Saussure or Claude Lévi-Strauss. It is not the static uniformity of unconscious conception that is envisaged, as Lévi-Strauss does in his call "to eliminate . . . historical process and . . . conscious thought" ("History and Anthropology" 23). Rather, as with the living waters of England, there is a mutual, circulating influence in which style and conception continuously regulate and shape one another. At one moment the expression will appear to be merely the surface manifestation; the true "insides" (*dessous*, italicized by Taine) consist of "the bodily temperament, the original or acquired aptitudes and tendencies, the complicated vegetation of distant or recent ideas and habits, the whole sap of human nature [which] has contributed to produce the actions and words that are its ultimate offshoot [*jet terminal*]" (*Philosophie de l'art* 441). But then Taine will reverse the valuation, making primary what seemed derivative: "There remains a last element, style. In truth, it is the only visible one; the two others [characters; situations and events] are merely its *insides*; it clothes them and is alone found on the surface.—A book is nothing but a succession of sentences that the author pronounces or has his personages pronounce. . . . This, then, is a third element of higher importance" (443–44). Here, where the imagery changes from botany to culture and where determinist natural history thus appears to yield to the vitalist history of civilization—here, where "art is higher than nature"—"each form of style determines a state of mind" (444–45). Style takes over as a force not merely expressing but guiding the inside of man in his historical expression.

Everywhere in Taine there is this dynamic of style. In bringing forth or advancing thoughts and intuitions, expression also moves them forward. By expressing, it creates possibilities for expression. It is style that performs the work of culture. The history of civilization is a history of art which is in turn a history of style for the very reason that, simply put, *style is history*. All the rest is mere events. And it is abundantly clear, from the historical passages in the *History of English Literature*—above all concerning medieval *Völkerwanderungen*—and certainly from the history of the Revolution, that events can only consolidate and affirm the ahistorical constancies of the race. To say that race and style are the two poles of human experience—the former negative, passive, determinist, the latter positive, active, and creative—is to reach the heart of Taine's vision.

Taine's first published book was a study of a historian, the *Essai sur Tite Live*. It is divided into two parts of equal length, first "History Considered as a Science," then "History Considered as an Art." One chapter of the second part concerns Livy's style in particular. But it is the culmination of its first chapter, "Of the Art in History," that forms Taine's earliest great statement of faith. "For," he writes at the climax, "in what does style consist, if not in the author's share in the narration, in the emotions that it arouses in him, in the passionate accents, the varied tones, the agitations of the soul manifested in the choice of words and expressions, the sound and the symmetry of the sentences?" The science of history, according to this book, begins with criticism of the sources and aims at reconstructing the past in its authentic pastness. But the art of history brings that pastness alive. Style gives form, order, and consequently meaning to science's raw assemblages of fact. Style is intelligence, "because the art of writing is only the art of thinking, and, in order to speak well, one need only have thought much" (193).

The *Essai sur Tite Live* is about a historian but is not really a work of history. It is still too caught up in a Spinozist exhilaration at perfect, rational orders. The ambition to capture the Academy's prize by sheer force of intellect—an ambition equivocally depicted in chapter 7 of *Etienne Mayran*, "The Test"—seduces Taine into a desire to explain and also to judge everything as the operation of unchanging laws of the intellect. In subsequent books the work of style and thought becomes more differentiated, more subtle, and thus more powerful as well. It transforms whatever it expresses. Hence the greatest creators do not just happen to fall between epochs; it is their works that make the epochal changes constituting history. Earlier I quoted the opening of the last paragraph of Taine's Milton chapter: "Placed, as it happened [*par le hasard*], between two ages . . ." But there is more than happenstance to make Milton the significant figure of the transition. He worked to fuse the two ages: "He employed the one in the service of the other, and displayed the old inspiration in the service of new subjects." And that work, as Taine describes it, seems at once severely truthful and prophetic: "This style and these ideas are monuments of history: they concentrate, recall, or anticipate the past and the future; and in the limits of a single work are found the events and the feelings of several centuries and of a whole nation" (1: 556/2: 516–17). Milton makes it possible to conceive the future, to imagine the movement of the past into the future, and thus he opens the way for the future to happen.

I have glossed the Milton passage somewhat freely. It is a striking expression of the imaginative presence of history in literature, but perhaps not so unambiguous a celebration of the historical power of literature as I have made out. However, as one of a series, its intent seems to me beyond question. In the aggregate, it is clear that style does not simply represent or participate in the progress of civilization, but in fact makes that change happen. Chaucer's artistry is another instance, at an earlier stage. He was the first writer in England to develop a self-conscious awareness of his place in history. At his best—and his inconsistency is part of Taine's story—his skill at disposing events and reflecting on them prepares the ground for the human mastery over events that constituted the Renaissance. His writing gives men power—not yet confident, controlled power, but at least the image of where that power might lie. Thus, it starts freeing men from the shackles of scholasticism. In the case of a newcomer such as Chaucer the achievement is less certain than was Milton's; more certain, on the other hand, is that his texts were responsible for what achievement there was. Here are some distinctive fragments from the center of the remarkable chapter, representing at least the generalizations, shorn of most of the fabric of observation that supports them:

Such is the reflection which begins to dawn, such the high art. . . . The poem is no longer, as in contemporary literature, a mere procession, but a painting in which the contrasts are arranged, the attitudes chosen, the *ensemble* calculated, so that life is invigorated. . . . Weigh the value of this *ensemble*. Is it a dream or not, in its maturity or infancy? The whole future is before us. . . . Here for the first time appears a superiority of mind, which at the instant of conception suddenly halts, rises above itself, passes judgment, and says to itself, "This phrase tells the same thing as the last—remove it; these two ideas are disjointed—bind them together; this description is feeble—reconsider it." When a man can speak thus he has an idea, not learned in the schools, but personal and practical, of the human mind, its process and needs, and of things also, their composition and combinations; he has a style, that is, he is capable of making everything understood and seen by the human mind. . . . He is capable, as Chaucer was, of seeking out in the old common forest of the middle ages, stories and legends, to replant them in his own soil, and make them send out new shoots. . . . At the distance of a century and a half, he has affinity with the poets of Elizabeth. . . . Affinity merely. He advanced a few steps beyond the threshold of this art, but he paused at the end of the vestibule. (1: 154–56 / 1: 214–17)

The Chaucer passage is revealing in another way: style is the form or garb of thought. The *Essai sur Tite Live* makes style sound secondary to thought, as initially does the last chapter of the *Philosophie de l'art*. But the reversal in that chapter reflects a crucial development in Taine's conception, where style becomes formative rather than formed. Thought follows the course laid out by the style or form of expression. But if it is through a style that thought becomes possible, then the style itself cannot be the product of thought, at least not in any ordinary sense. Rather, style is the threshold or dawn of thought. Primitive shapelessness is thoughtless; with style, consciousness appears, as it did in Chaucer. Hence style is the birth of consciousness, the becoming-conscious of consciousness; or, more simply put, style is equivalent to self-consciousness. One knows oneself in the manner of one's thought. Style itself is then a borderline or transition, from nature to civilization and from stupor to awareness. The border (or "end of the vestibule," as the Chaucer passage calls it) is a shadowy realm, half-awake but not yet fully conscious. As such, it is naturally the realm of art, where the inspired artist, always a historical threshold figure, sees and does more than he knows.

A new style advances civilization—gropingly at first, until successor figures explore and refine its accomplishments. Eras thus have their stages or moments: the inconspicuous yet increasingly confident young dawn of new conceptions, the striding maturity, the ornate and subtle twilight, each with its own characteristic unfolding and pace. Historical development is semi-conscious; true progress is never imposed. It creeps over the age and even over the artist who is first responsible, never sudden, always gradual. It can happen over a span of nearly anonymous creations, as it did at the birth of the Renaissance: "Insensibly the growth becomes complete, and at the end of the century all was changed. A new, strange, overloaded style has formed . . . , so suitable to the spirit of the age, that we meet with it throughout Europe" (1: 193 / 1: 277–78). It can also happen in specific, individual models, like Dryden's few poetic masterpieces. Here, surrounding a splendidly detailed synopsis and evocation of the characteristics of Dryden's style and imagery, are the generalizations that again reveal Taine's fundamental conception: "In these three poems . . . a new career is opened; man has the whole world resubjected to his thought; the change in his thought has changed all the aspects, and everything assumes a new form in his transformed mind. His task is to explain and to prove; this, in short, is the classical style, and this is the style of Dryden" (2: 47–48 / 3: 236–38). And it can even arrive in single flashes of intuition, as with Robert Burns: "Now and then, driving his plough, he lighted on genuine verses, verses such as Heine and Alfred de Musset have made in our own days. In those few words, combined after a new fashion, there was a revolution. Two hundred new verses sufficed. The human mind turned on its hinges, and so did civil society" (2: 282 / 4: 231).[32]

In portraying the accomplishments of style Taine does not even shy away from the dangerous word *revolution*; indeed, he features it repeatedly. For the curative to the kind of style-destroying revolution that occurred tragically in France is not stagnation and regression—which occur at the ends of eras and actually precipitate revolutions—but the reformed thinking that a successful new style brings with it. Not all styles succeed, to be sure. The style of the *philosophes*, notably, was so full of "multiple precautions," so "insensible" in its transitions, leading its readers to advance so "involuntarily," that it missed out on the true course. Its "excess indicates a lacuna"; "the obligation always to speak well interfered with saying everything needful"; the "personages are only half real." "There is then an original defect in the classical spirit," which might not be so bad, "if we did not know that all this ends in practical and terrible effects." For "when the Revolution comes, the retrenchment will be all the greater" (*L'Ancien régime* 1: 302–15). Revolution is the punishment for stylistic failure, for a refusal to advance or an advance so hedged in that it amounts to a blind refusal.

That, however, is France. Except during the Interregnum, England successfully negotiated its transitions, with reformations in thought that permitted it to cope conceptually and practically with changes in society.[33] Revolution in England characteristically takes place in the mind, not the body, and is progressive rather than destructive. A dozen or more noble passages in the *History of English Literature* extol this greatest historical accomplishment of English civilization. At the end of the Mill chapter there is, for instance, a lengthy vision of a rich autumn landscape whose organic growth reconciles steadfastness and innovation. Taine sees

enormous trees, four centuries old, extended in regular lines; and I found in them a new trace of that practical good sense which has accomplished revolutions without committing ravages; which, while improving everything, has overthrown nothing; which has preserved both its trees and its constitution, which has lopped off the dead branches without levelling the trunk; which alone, in our days, among all nations, is in the enjoyment not only of the present, but of the past. (2: 658 / 5: 418)

Steering between the poles of Experience and Abstraction (Taine's names in this chapter for empiricism and dogmatism), England has avoided their respective blindnesses to the future and to the past. Revolution becomes a common stylistic project, intuited, felt, conceived, shaped, and implemented first by the artists and through them by society as a whole.

English revolutions are the achievement, collective or individual, of speakers and writers; they are promulgated in public forums like the pulpit, diffused through shared practices like the art of conversation in the public culture promoted by Addison (an argument that did not have to wait on Jürgen Habermas to be made), or disseminated in the publications of the great and popular poets. The best revolutions come "slowly, by degrees," like the "moral revolution" after 1688 (2: 58 / 3: 255, the start of the chapter called "The Revolution"). Or even "by a side door," like the Reformation, "for great revolutions are not introduced by court intrigues and official sleight of hand, but by social conditions and popular instincts" (1: 483 / 2: 301). "A revolution," Taine writes at yet another moment, "is but the birth of a great sentiment" (2: 599 / 5: 313). That one, deep-seated change changes all.[34]

Because style is a cultural system and a structure of expression, style change appears in the guise of structural transformation. Alert to systematic interrelationships, Taine is partial to the image of a pivot on which the whole mechanism of society turns: "The central pivot of the vast wheel on which human affairs move must be displaced one notch, that all may move with its motion. At this moment the pivot was moved, and thus a revolution of the great wheel begins" (1: 265 / 1: 402; for another instance see the passage about Burns, four paragraphs back). Such imagery bears an important relationship to Saussure's famous comparison of language to a game of chess: "A certain move can revolutionize the whole game and even affect pieces that are not directly involved" (*Course* 89). But the differences from twentieth-century structuralism are as significant as the similarities. Change, as Saussure describes, is deeply meaningless—abrupt, disruptive, entirely external, and even antithetical to the systems through which meaning is constituted and expressed: "The change effected belongs to neither state: only states matter." Consequently, change has no past ("the route used in arriving there makes no difference") and at best a very uncertain future ("it is impossible for the player to foresee exactly the extent of the effect"). As his editors comment, change "is outside the system, for the system is never observed in its evolution" (*Course* 143, note). The motor may even be simply error (Burger, "Phonématique et diachronie" 230). Saussurian structuralism, as Piaget finely observed, deprives structure of value in depriving it of history (*Structuralism* 79–80). Taine's machine produces value—designated moral or scientific "truth"—as his trees produce limbs and fruit; Saussure's chess game produces nothing.

At the cost of some reiteration, I want to dwell for a few paragraphs on the mechanisms of history. I do so partly to create the opportunity for quoting further representative passages (though by no means all such), in the hope of persuading readers how consistent and unmistakably present are the themes I have been discussing. But I do it chiefly in order to build up the case that Taine's two-sidedness is not merely accidental. Hitherto I have written of ways in which Taine appears divided between falsity and truth—an apparent determinist who in reality is a vitalist. I now wish to show that his view makes contradiction fundamental to human experience and expression. Smooth change and quiet revolutions, yes, but not for all that without contrast and opposition.

True, history is not the product of individual volition. Not even Napoleon, though Taine calls him a towering political artist and a sculptor of living flesh, could alter civilization by design. In the period when France was suffering its cataclysm, the English romantic school "had violently broken with tradition"; its Jacobin-leaning poets "labored to destroy the great aristocratical and oratorical style" and "proposed to replace studied phrases and lofty vocabulary by natural tones and plebeian words" (2: 314–15 / 4: 286–87). The works of these writers do not much please Taine; he disapproves of the literalist exoticism of the historical poetry, of Scott's pedantry and his "pasty and emphatic style" (2: 325 / 4: 304), and of the hectoring philosophic verse.[35] Nevertheless, England works its magic even at this most dangerous passage: "Under their multiplied efforts, and by their involuntary concert, the idea of the beautiful is changed, and other ideas change by contagion. . . . The old edifice totters, and the Revolution enters, not by a sudden inundation, as in France, but by slow infiltration" (2: 341–42 / 4: 330–31). For 50 years, Taine concludes, all great writers have been "bent, some with more of eagerness, others with more of distrust, in welcoming or giving entrance to the growing tide of modern democracy and philosophy in constitution and church, without doing damage, and gradually so as to destroy nothing, and to make everything bear fruit" (2: 343 / 4: 333). The long revolution is the genuine one.

Still, history is neither willful nor random. It may be that "the circumstances that are encountered finish the natural revolution" (1: 600 / 3: 70), but they do not propel it. "Great and efficacious [ideas] do not come at will and by chance, by the effort of an individual, or by an accidental encounter" (1: 264 / 1: 401). And when it comes to the destiny of the great races, "chance has no influence over events so vast" (2: 398 / 4: 429). Even though prediction is impossible, the retrospective teleology whose law Mill formulated guarantees the meaningfulness of organic historical development.

Following Mill, Taine succeeds in having everything about history both ways. It both is and is not purposive; it both is and is not shaped by individual creativity; its transformations both are and are not radical or revolutionary; its constancies both are and are not fated. Yet whatever the impression such a summary gives, it is hard to imagine a book more masterfully controlled and less confused than Taine's, or more consistent in its unfolding and in its methods. The contradictions are fundamental to the system. For the spirit of the book is deeply if unostentatiously dialectical. That above all is missed by the vulgar view of Taine as a narrowly Darwinian dogmatist. In its systematic and explanatory character it resembles a hierarchical, Kantian dialectic, divided between the flux of empirical facts and the constant, regulatory, transcendental, or phantasmic truths of race (pseudo-material causality) and morality (pseudo-ideal purpose). The process and the hermeneutic texture, however, are more Hegelian.

Taine's history spirals ever onward, with a constant interchange of powers and directions, none of which remains for long the ground of the others; "After all, man is ever his own master and his own slave" (2: 398 / 4: 429). The original last page of the book expresses a faith in the stability of nations, but even there the faith is hedged around by the onward march of history. The English race suffered "a violent perturbation" with the Norman Conquest and subsequently "various oscillations," but we are on a more even keel "now that great historic violences . . . have become almost impracticable." (As if that proclamation of the end of history were not belied by the French Revolution and by the impending upheavals of 1870 that were to impel Taine to study the Revolution; as if the general unpredictability of the future were not one of Taine's themes.) But the book then ends on a note of fundamental change, not of stability: "We know that positive discoveries go on increasing day by day, that they will increase daily more and more, that from object to object they reach the most lofty, that their useful application and their philosophical consequences are ceaselessly unfolded; in short, that their universal encroachment will at last comprise the whole human mind." There is, it seems, a perspective even beyond race or nationality, an absolute knowledge from whose vantage any human structures appear merely historical. But that perspective is given to us only as the eternal power of the negative to resist all premature fixities, which is to say, all fixities whatsoever:

From this body of invading truths springs in addition an original conception of the good and the useful, and, moreover, a new idea of state and church, art and industry, philosophy and religion. This has its power, as the old idea had; it is scientific, if the other was national; it is supported on proved facts, if the other was upon established things. Already their opposition is being manifested; already their results begin; and we may affirm beforehand, that the proximate condition of English civilization will depend upon their divergence and their accord. (2: 425–26 / 4: 473–75)

The contradictions upon which Taine's history rests are the work of the never-ending dialectic of history. Opposition, divergence, and accord are the last words that Taine originally bequeathed to the readers of his history.[36]

From the pervasive dialectic arises the strangest and most wonderful characteristic of artistic style. Gradualist, half-conscious, diffusive, the last thing that the artist can be is imperious. The man with a new vision is not a monomaniac (like Napoleon) who imposes his will upon others. Nor, more surprisingly given his intellectual pedigree, does Taine ever portray the artist in the guise of a Kantian genius who spontaneously gives laws to nature. For laws are not where Taine's interest lies; it lies in change. In touch with the most profound nineteenth-century conception of organic life, Taine regards organisms not as beings that can reproduce themselves but as beings that can differ from themselves. They do not settle into a rock-solid unity such as "agreement" might betoken, but rather into the harmonious concord or working together of different functions. And if they are to live, they must produce further differences, which are their most genuine offspring.

No creator could consciously fashion a genuine style. For conscious fashioning proceeds according to a ruling idea. It aims at uniformity. But styles are not ideas, and they are productive of antitheses, not of agreements. This is a theme that Foucault has formulated pregnantly for our time: "Contradiction . . . functions throughout discourse, as the principle of its historicity" (*The Archaeology of Knowledge* 151). But Taine formulated it a century earlier: "When a form of mind comes to light, it . . . enters simultaneously the two opposite camps, and seems to undo with one hand what it has made with the other. If it is, as it was formerly, the oratorical style, we find it at the same time in the service of cynical misanthropy, and in that of decorous humanity, in Swift and in Addison. If it is, as now, the philosophical spirit, it produces at once conservative preachings and socialistic utopias, Wordsworth and Shelley" (2: 337/4: 322). The greatest genius of all time, Shakespeare, is ipso facto the most fertile in contradictions; that is how Taine introduces him and how he regularly praises Shakespeare's unequaled capability as a dramatist. But self-contradiction is likewise characteristic of Milton, who "refused to be a priest from the same feelings that he had wished it" (1: 502/2: 417); of Puritanism, which, by unleashing the forces of the Restoration, "brought on an orgie" (1: 559/3: 5); of the "two currents" of "modern man, impelled by two sentiments, one democratic, the other philosophic, . . . at once generous and rebellious" (2: 289/4: 242). The deepest reason why the great artists are always found between two ages is not just that their work initiates changes, but that all true change proceeds by way of contrast and contradiction. The most authentic creators are not the most unified but the most divided.

Divided, but not at war. That is the meaning of the term "accord," which is so much richer than mere agreement. The richest art of all, for Taine, is the art of accord. And that art, which he himself practiced for enjoyment throughout his life, is music. Perhaps there was in Taine something of the music teacher of chapter 5 of *Etienne Mayran*, capable of conceptualizing technique and of training fluent players, but frustratedly incapable of communicating the spirit that he feels so intensely. At any rate, on the few occasions when Taine speaks of music, he does so with a rare intensity. In one place only there is an extended, uniquely rapturous description of a Beethoven soirée (*Notes sur Paris* 322–33).[37] And a long climactic paragraph in the lectures "Of the Nature of the Work of Art" concerns music as the quintessential art of the nineteenth century. Devoid of representational features, music is free to be pure style. It is, in consequence, the ultimate in contradiction, for, "on the one hand," it is a cry from the heart, "the direct, natural, and complete expression of passion" that "instantaneously arouses our involuntary sympathy," while, "on the other hand," it is a pure formalism of "relations of sounds imitating no living form" (*Philosophie de l'art* 77).

Pure formalism—that is another scapegoat of much of the most recent aesthetic and critical thinking. But, like style, formalism does not mean to Taine what it means to its present-day detractors. It is exempt neither from significance nor from history. Rather, its formalism, its stylistic purity, frees music into—not from—the historical expression of everything that is of deepest concern to humanity.[38] Resembling "the dreams of an incorporeal soul, [music] is more fitting than any other art to express the floating thoughts, the formless dreams, the desires without an object or a limit, the painful and grandiose confusion of a troubled heart that aspires to everything and attaches itself to nothing." Intimate, yes, but why do I say historical? Because Taine concludes the peroration by invoking the public destiny of music's private dreams: "That is why, with the agitations, the discontents and the hopes of modern democracy, it has come forth from its native lands to spread all across Europe; and today you see the most complicated symphonies attract crowds, in this France where our national music was hitherto limited to the vaudeville and the chanson" (*Philosophie de l'art* 77). In music, style fulfills its mission to shape, indeed to *be* the historical destiny of civilization, private and public, with all its essential contradictions. The dialectic distills not into a static essence, but into a living spirit. The impure examples of style at work—soiled, as it were, by words or pictures—are more approachable for being more local and limited. Shakespeare is the grandest and the hardest, a man of pure imagination, "shocking to all French habits of analysis and of logic," "one of those delicate souls which, like a perfect instrument of music, vibrate of themselves at the slightest touch" (1: 357, 365 / 2: 164, 177). Yet beyond even Shakespeare lies the magical accord of music, harmonies compounded of differences, which in their unspeakable purity engage all the antithetical forces of human existence.

Style incorporates the contradictory factors that constitute the historical dialectic: it is personal and social, mental and embodied, expressive and formal, revolutionary and incremental. While an isolated action or utterance is attached to a moment without temporal depth, a work of art draws on the resources of the past and advances the interests of the future. Music, as the most rarified and stylized form of expression, is at once the most powerful and the most impalpable. All others are necessarily imperfect in comparison. Consequently, they appear at least partly willful, unpredictable, or random—though retrospective, explanatory abstraction succeeds in putting everything in its place and generating the appearance of determinism. These paradoxes of artistic achievement are essential to the destiny of race (or nation) that remains constant to the character it is always in the process of discovering. The national character is not "the caprice of an artist or the chance of the moment." A series of chances steers it: "The chance of a victorious invasion," "the chance of an insular position," "the chance of an old hostility to Rome," and the like combine to form "dispositions" that in turn are corrected when a writer (Dickens in this case) "moves his reader in the most inner depths, and becomes the master of all hearts" (2: 464–65 / 5: 65–66). Style is, in its fundamental character, a happily mixed blessing.

V

It remains now to position Taine's dynamic of style with respect to other conceptions. Before the eighteenth century style was the point of intersection of the aesthetic and the ethical. Adjusting the form of speech to the form of thought led to a fit for which the name was decorum. The choice of a style or form—high, middle, or low, Ciceronian or Senecan, and so forth—was also a choice of personal stance. Style was the individual's manner of engagement with the world.[39] Style in this older sense is descriptive, not normative. Everything has a style of one sort or another. While the value (but more often the decorum or suitability) of a particular stylistic choice could be debated, it would not be meaningful to ask whether style as such has a value. Only at the very end of the eighteenth century did the normative terms "stylish" and "styleless" enter the language, and apparently the normative uses of the noun as well.[40]

In Buffon's famous dictum that style is "l'homme même," style acquires a new status. The qualities of style evoked in Buffon's inaugural discourse for the Académie Française are numerous, but all relate to its character as a transcendental absolute. Higher than mere facility of speech, style is a mysterious, distilled, almost transcendental quality. "It is nothing but order and movement" (*Oeuvres* 500b): though the categories of *taxis* and *dynamis* could come straight out of the Renaissance, the limiting "nothing but" frees style from its earthly entanglements. Its material is ideas, not words or imitation of things; its atmosphere is "luminous" (502a) but not dazzling; its ethos is "good faith with oneself" (503a). Thus, it demands unity (the chief characteristic distinguishing men from animals, as Buffon says in "Le Lion" 378a and elsewhere) but remains indefinable; it can be taught only by example, not by precept. Buffon's examples are the great men of history, much of philosophy, poetry always. The oration concludes with praise of the king (as the source of illumination), of the Immortals in the Académie, of France, and, obligatorily, of Buffon's deceased predecessor. While itemizing many characteristics of style and numerous goals such as truth, wholeness, Being, and eternity, Buffon isolates it from all questions of substance or morality. In its unifying and ennobling force, style is constitutive of true humanity—"man himself, . . . the truth that is enduring and even eternal" (503b), to continue the normally truncated passage. But style then becomes a concept so nebulous that it vanishes into the Empyrean.

The next two centuries have insistently taken apart what Buffon so eloquently put together.[41] From his universal absolute, different thinkers absolutize various particulars. In Goethe's distinction of style from simple imitation and from mannerism (in the essay "Simple Imitation, Manner, Style"), and likewise in Nietzsche's equation of style with culture in contrast to bourgeois philistinism (*Bildungsphilistertum*, in the first of the *Untimely Meditations*), style becomes a high ideal, accessible only to the chosen few. In the nineteenth century style is equated with beauty (both Louis Juglar, *Le Style dans les arts* 89–94, and Gilles-Gaston Granger, *Essai d'une philosophie du style* 208, attribute this notion to the architect Eugène-Emmanuel Viollet-le-Duc); among symbolists and imagists such as Remy de Gourmont and J. Middleton Murry, style is exalted as contentless purity of vision. For Proust, too, "style for the writer . . . is a question not of technique but of vision. It is the revelation, which would be impossible by direct and conscious means, of the qualitative difference that there is in the manner whereby the world appears to us, a difference which, were it not for art, would remain the eternal secret of each of us. Through art alone can we go outside ourselves, know what another sees of this universe which is not the same as our own" (*A la recherche* 3: 895). Others personalize style in less exalted ways by treating it as linguistic usage (as, say, in William Wimsatt's *Prose Style of Samuel Johnson*), as ornament, or as individual quirk (as in Wolfgang Kayser, "Der Stilbegriff"). Thinkers resistant to cults of personality, on the other hand, have often condemned style as irresponsibility (Roland Barthes being a notable recent example) or exalted bad style for its rugged honesty.[42] Wanting to have it both ways, finally, Walter Pater subordinates style in the course of trying to exalt it. He links style to soul, but he is opposed to ornament, in favor of austere truth, and given to images of hardness: thus, he speaks of Flaubert's "phrase so large and so precise at the same time, hard as bronze, in service to the more perfect adaptation of words to their matter" ("Style" 33). His criticism of "surplusage" is consonant with Herbert Spencer's contemporaneous advocacy of economy, as style becomes an instrumental value in the service of ethical absolutes. For none of these thinkers is style, as it is for Taine, both representative and ideal, imaginative and historical.[43]

Inevitably, changes in taste, the growth of specialized knowledge, and the emergence of new objects and forms of attention all will lead today's readers to critical judgments different from Taine's.[44] Yet the kind of analysis and synthesis he practiced retains a value that is more than merely historical. In my concluding pages I wish to argue that a study of Taine's methods can suggest a way out of certain impasses of contemporary criticism. Indeed, in some ways Taine's contemporary relevance may be greater than his historical importance. For it is a curious fact that his admirers and his detractors alike grievously misrepresented Taine, to the point of ignoring what is expressly pivotal in his writing. They may perhaps be excused by the impression created by Taine's last, longest, and for them most recent work, the history of the Revolution. But it seems clear that his great achievement remains unassimilated. In studies of style he represents a road not only distinctive, as I have just suggested, but never again taken with his kind of commitment.[45]

What is called New Historicism has compelled reconsideration of the historical dynamic of literature. New Historicists diverge radically, of course, in their conceptions of textual individuality and textual agency. But there is general consensus that powerful currents flow into and through representative texts (and text-like artifacts and practices) and that these texts in turn powerfully further social and historical processes. After decades of avoidance, Taine's triad of race, milieu, and moment is rarely far from the surface of New Historicist writing. (Race is often replaced by nation; perhaps even more often the two are played off against one another.) Yet for all the power exerted—or exuded—by society and by social texts in these critics' descriptions, the dynamic falls short of a dialectic. In the fascination with the power of texts to shape and to express, their power to effect change is slighted. Because it replaces a one-sided progressivism with an even less fortunate, self-regarding teleology, the recent critical fashion of renaming the Renaissance as the early modern period signals the deficient historicism in much of what currently passes for materialist enquiry.[46] The limitations are encapsulated in one of Stephen Greenblatt's epigrams (highlighted by citation out of its deceptively cushioning context): "If I wanted to hear the voice of the other, I had to hear my own voice" (*Shakespearian Negotiations* 20). It will be my closing contention that New Historicists, above all, can profit much from hearing the voice of Taine.

Greenblatt's work is the best case in point, not so much on account of its originating influence as because of his self-aware fascination with individual authors. A professed dialectician, Greenblatt if anyone should be alert to interchanges between individual and social expressions. Indeed, the title of his programmatic essay (and subtitle of the book), "The Circulation of Social Energy" (*Shakespearian Negotiations* 1–20), suggests the same sort of fluid vitalism that Taine so fully develops. But Greenblatt's circulation is economic, not hydraulic, and it produces neither fruit nor (as in Marx) capital, but only "simulations" (1). Negotiation is linked with exchange, contest, conflict. It is, however, "absolute play" (a phrase used in titling the Marlow chapter in *Renaissance Self-Fashioning*), marked by repeated denials of movement: "there is no escape from contingency"; "there is no originary moment, no pure act of untrammeled creation"; "there is very little pure invention in culture," but only many "modes [that] are continually renegotiated," in "a sustained collective improvisation" (*Shakespearian Negotiations* 3, 6, 13, 8, 14). The demand for absolutes or "pure" states sets a standard for historical outcomes as definitive ends, without which no result is acknowledged: either there is victory or there is running in place. The alternatives are power and subversion, the circulation is only the mutual reinforcement of the two poles ("the subversiveness is the very product of that power and furthers its ends," 30), and self-fashioning becomes inseparable from submission (*Renaissance Self-Fashioning* 9). Such rigid categories undermine any possible self-transforming process. Dialectic turns out to be equivalent to *aporia*.[47]

Hence, I do not think it is merely coincidental that the word "style" is all but absent from Greenblatt's writing.[48] For style names the individual's differential engagement with cultural norms, or else the individual's self-transformation into a real or potential norm. Even in its simplest designations, style is an impure invention or a mongrel act of trammeled creativity—exactly the sort of complex, partial cultural action that Greenblatt's polarizations devalue. In what may be his most forthright theoretical pronouncement on the activity of the literary critic, Greenblatt has advocated a "daylight method of interpretation" ("Loudun and London" 343) that could bring to light the cultural negotiations producing the aesthetic and social construct known as the theater. If the light imagery is reminiscent of Auerbach (see note 45), so is the problematic sense of historical action. The negotiation, in this image, is all backstage. What enters the public sphere has already lost its potential and been abandoned to a role as mere product or reflector. And the interpreter, as light-bringer, remains comparably passive. If only all could be revealed. If only things could speak for themselves, without style or other such entanglements that sully their pure visibility. Greenblatt's power as a critic resides in his resourceful and relentless demonstration of the impossibility of his aims. From Taine one can learn how the shadows are not a pathology but the very process of living.[49]

When more or less closely related studies do acknowledge style, the results are not much happier. Jonathan Goldberg's *James I and the Politics of Literature*, for instance, includes a section titled "The Style of Gods" (28–54). The source for the phrase is a line by James in which style means label or title: "God gives not Kings the stile of *Gods* in vain" (26). During his discussion, Goldberg corrodes the phrase so that "style" bends toward its more common meaning, as when he calls "textual transformations into enduring Roman images," "the style of gods and of royal representation" (42). But the powerless inertness of the earlier sense hovers over the text: "The coins and medals preserve, commemorate, and memorialize the style of power and translate it into the vital economy of real life" (46). "Style here . . . is content" (47). Expression intrinsically corrupts, governed by "the sustaining contradictions by which power is represented" (5). Cultural products have an overwhelming past, an earnest present, and no future. A richer valuation of the expressive dynamic of style, inspired by Taine, could model a different lesson— that the "infinite regress" (affecting "absolute power," "real power," and "represented power" alike [12]) is not a defect to be contrasted to the real and the vital, but rather the imperfection making thought and expression human.

One of the most acute critiques of New Historicism, mounted as it were from within, is found in Richard Halpern's *The Poetics of Primitive Accumulation*. Objecting that "the new historicism dissolves [questions of epochal transition] into empiricisms or pragmatisms" (13), Halpern endeavors to recapture from Marx a historical dynamic hollowed out by Foucault and his followers. His primitive accumulation is the materialist counterpart to Taine's idealist emergence or dawning. But even Halpern, I believe, succumbs to the lure of categories too pure and demanding for instantiation. It is not just that his chapter on education, "A Mint of Phrases: Ideology and Style Production in Tudor England" (19–60), regards styles as conformations instilled by pedagogical technologies.

Nor is it even that he remains mystified by the genuinely profound problem he unearths—namely, how such an educational system could have fostered poets. It is, rather, that he acknowledges no mediation between (nor any alternates to) subjection and lawlessness. In the language of Gilles Deleuze and Félix Guattari he writes: "Style was the sign that textual decoding had ultimately been unified and reterritorialized and could now be inserted into a system of regular differences. . . . It is clear the role of style is to reunify and homogenize the text, to recode its imaginative anarchy while guarding against sudden power surges of *energeia*" (56). In irreconcilable contrast to the uniformity of style is poetic imagination, which "implied a desire whose workings were more fully opaque and unpredictable, more resistant to attempts at rational or instrumental control . . . , an outlaw factor [whose] autonomy and automatism . . . resisted instrumental control and thus threw a shadow on humanist optimism" (56–57). Halpern's imagery in these sentences intones a curious logic: they presume that a system of regular differences is likewise a homogenization, that resistance to control is outlawry, and that shadows are opaque. The later chapters on individual writers and works do not liberate expression from this bind. Signally, the concluding analysis of *King Lear*—named "*Historica Passio*" from a phrase (presumed to be a typo) that equates history with hysteria—leaves society "reconstitute[d] through destruction" (269). The conflictual logic operates throughout, on a deconstructive ground resembling that of Greenblatt and the others whom Halpern means to be revising. The interesting analysis of penmanship as both a discipline and a skill can serve as a last example: "The ideological force of writing is the specific pressure that its virtual regimes can exert . . . either to reinforce or to oppose the reproduction of the social order." No middle ground between reproduction and destruction is envisioned, even in such a case as this, where "the pressure is neither especially great nor particularly focused" (84). No wonder primitive accumulation turns out to be a myth. Studies of this sort—enormously fertile in observing, questioning, and critiquing—fall short when it comes to constructing an alternative vision. What they consign to the dustbin of history is, finally, history itself.

Even Richard Helgerson's *Forms of Nationhood*, a more dialectical and consequently more historical work than those I have just discussed, falls prey to the same polarizing tendency. Helgerson studies the passage "through self-alienation" "to an acceptable national self" (243). Yet throughout the book (and even in the opening chapter on the apparently stylistic issue of versification) agency tends to grow "depersonalize[d]" (220—and see the skittishness about agency on 215); negation is a "dark other" (212), something "powerful and powerfully disruptive" (170) that "upend[s]" authorial intentions, even Helgerson's own (9). Defining general issues requires a distanced view (72) and a "superficial regard" (54) resistant to close reading (which Helgerson sees rather as an "institutional" imperative than as a personal engagement, 311 n. 55). Hence, the decisive texts are those in which the strongest authorial resistance is conquered by the most powerful historical current. History is inherently, if abstractly, imperialist, imposing its "misnamings" through "powerfully hidden . . . material and textual forces," in a world where no true namings are conceivable (190–91). Helgerson had previously written the ironically titled *Elizabethan Prodigals* and *Self-Crowned Laureates*; in *Forms of Nationhood*, with its national self and depersonalized agents, it is not surprising that no chapter or section titles bear the name of an individual and that the word "style" appears, so far as I have noted, only once, in a quotation (35).

Halpern alludes disparagingly but not inappropriately to Hegel with a "capital H" (2). For the operational tool neglected by the works I have been discussing is indeed a Hegelian one. They all lack a concept of determinate negation.[50] A contradiction that advances an alternative rather than a conflict, a negotiation that is not primarily a contest, an other that is neither alien nor dead—positions like these remain uncharted by the critics I have discussed. At best their stark contrasts employ only the more primitive form that Hegel calls general negation. General negation is the subject of the famous chapter of the *Phänomenologie des Geistes* on master and servant; it is the moment of arrest opposing selfhood and world, or knowledge and action. Whenever we stop thinking and start doing, or confront our consciousness with an actual object, we engage in a general negation. It is a jolt of reality, accompanied by anxiety or fear, that tests, corrects, and validates what we think we know or what we think we have done. It remains general, however, because it entails a holistic movement from one plane of existence to a different plane, as being is tested by life, or form by content, and vice versa.

Determinate negation, by contrast, is the passage from the abstract "thing" (*Ding*) to the intentional object that Hegel calls "the matter itself" (*die Sache selbst*), and from consciousness to individuality. Whereas general negations teach conscious beings their limits and impose form on recalcitrant materiality, determinate negations begin with already identified things and shape them to particular purposes. They are "negativity as quality" (*Phänomenologie* 289) rather than as contradiction; they foreground facets of the thing in order to bring it into relationship with a particular will. General negation, says Hegel, imputes "absolute difference" such as good versus bad (289), whereas determinate negation modalizes things in terms of their correspondence to particularities of wish, interest, and fortune (*Mögen, Interesse, Glück*, 296). The logic of determinate negation can be wishful in its claims for the suitability of particular judgments: instinctive animal purposiveness does not really understand what it is doing, frank acknowledgment (*Ehrlichkeit*) deceives itself about the stability of matter's adjustment to mind, and hightoned moralism such as Antigone's tragic self-sacrifice condemns itself in the attempt to return the individual will to a universal destiny. But when determinate negation fails, the problem lies in a faulty adjustment of conscious intention to particular circumstances, not in general quandaries about finding stable names for unstable things or articulated categories for fluid perceptions. Lacking the appropriate category, Helgerson figures negation either as a "signifying absence" (71) or as a heuristic comparison and contrast, where "similar questions" give "interestingly different" answers, while other oppositions can generate "suddenly changing" evaluations of the same term (154). Using such logic criticism either falls back into the old view that the Renaissance self was infinitely flexible or ahead into the new one that it is a hollow shell of impersonation.[51] But no positive, stable core remains. There are no beginnings, only resistances.

What such studies lack is what Taine has to offer. *Style*, as he presents it, *is precisely the ideal form of determinate negation*. A better dialectician than any I have just cited, Fredric Jameson, in fact invokes the concept of determinate negation in his analysis of Wyndham Lewis's style (*Fables of Aggression* 30). He puts the matter most simply and effectively in his first book, on Sartre's style: "Where there is no possibility of doing something in different ways, there is no possibility of a style" (*Sartre* 41). And his general discussion of style in *Marxism and Form* comes close to the spirit of analysis for which Taine provides the finest exemplar. "To define style," he writes, "as language which deliberately calls attention to itself . . . is to reassert, as over against stylistics, the profoundly historical nature of the phenomenon" (335). It remains only to be said that if style is "profoundly" historical, that is because history is begotten within the depths of the stylistic imagination.

Style as such cannot ever be defined conceptually because it constitutes the movement between concepts. It is the personal element in a collective discourse, the public stance of private expression, the alterity within the present, and the coherence within change. We locate as style whatever remains outside of the conceptual determinants of an utterance. To be style, however, it must be identified: it is a specific inflection and a specifiable qualifier. It is not content but what relativizes content—ornament, or trope, or mode, or ethos. But to be distinguished as style, it must be regarded in a determinate relationship to content. Hence, style is "at once the writer's internalized knowledge and what in it can be captured in a formal theory" (Banfield, *Unspeakable Sentences* 14). Neither empty form nor unanchored invention, it is what Jerome J. McGann calls "the refusal of . . . refusal" and, invoking Hegel, "the negation of the negation" (*Black Riders* 34, 56).[52] In Taine's most profound insight, style generates antitheses because style is the perpetual dialectical unrest that makes works alive and productive. That construction of the experience of time is what we stand to recover in rereading Taine's grand enterprise.

CHAPTER 2

The Classic Is the Baroque

On the Principle of Wölfflin's Art History

HEINRICH WÖLFFLIN belonged to a large and distinguished generation of art historians and aestheticians.[1]* At the height of his career, he appeared to be merely *unus inter pares*, not *primus* or *unicus*. Since his time, the names of his contemporaries have mostly faded into semiobscurity or fallen into oblivion, while Wölfflin's works continue to be readily available and widely read. He has become what no one can be in his own time: a classic. Yet in the continuing stream of critical commentary, it is difficult to find any wholehearted praise except in the writings of Wölfflin's own students. And even among the students who experienced the magic of Wölfflin's presence, some dissenting voices have arisen, such as that of Frederick Antal, who wrote in 1949, "Wölfflin's very lucid, formal analyses, behind which there is an undisguised bias in favour of the classicist Cinquecento composition, reduced the wealth of historical evaluation to a few fundamental categories, a few typical schemes" (Antal, "Remarks" 49).[2] Wölfflin's classically clear and modest work often serves today as provocation rather than inspiration or else seems to be on the point of dissolving into insipidity, as E. H. Gombrich claimed in his well-known attack: "I remember the high hopes with which I went to Berlin University and the impression Wölfflin's personality made on me, the tall Swiss with beautiful blue eyes and a firm and self-assured manner of delivery that held the *auditorium*

---

* All references to Wölfflin's works will be included in the text, abbreviated as follows: CA = *Classic Art*; *Dürer* = *The Art of Albrecht Dürer*; *Ged* = *Gedanken zur Kunstgeschichte*; *KS* = *Kleine Schriften*; *PAH* = *Principles of Art History*; *RB* = *Renaissance and Baroque*; *SFA* = *The Sense of Form in Art*.

maximum spellbound. I confess that the spell did not work on me for very long" (Gombrich, *Norm and Form* 92).

Some paradoxical quality has evidently kept Wölfflin's writings alive while concealing the nature of their vitality from his commentators. In his eloquent memoir, *Zu Heinrich Wölfflin's Gedächtnis*, Fritz Strich tells us that Wölfflin was not an easy man to know, and this is just as true of his works, which are likewise animated by unsuspected conflicts and dynamisms. Far from "exclud[ing] the possibility of the coexistence of several modes of vision in a single period or an individual work," as W. Eugene Kleinbauer claims, Wölfflin's real message is that the history of art is an unremitting struggle for expression (Kleinbauer, *Modern Perspectives* 28). Those who criticize Wölfflin's apparent oversimplifications almost invariably do so in the service of convictions about the complexity and difficulty of style formation that they have unwittingly learned from him. I hope to show that the hidden power of those insights accounts for the continued importance of Wölfflin's works to contemporary critical theory.

Before analyzing Wölfflin's masterpiece, *Principles of Art History*, I would like to discuss two general issues. The first is the nature of Wölfflin's categories. It is essential to recognize that Wölfflin considered himself a morphologist and not a taxonomist of art. Morphology as Wölfflin practices it, in the spirit of his predecessor Johann Wolfgang von Goethe and his contemporary Max Weber, is not the study of forms but of forming powers. The taxonomist multiplies categories in order to establish a stable stratification of reality. Ideally, all taxonomic types are pure; deviation from type creates a new type or a monster. We denominate biological types in Latin, as if the dead language guaranteed their freedom from change, and in fact Carolus Linnaeus, who founded modern biological taxonomy, was one of the last rigid scientific "fixists." The charge of inflexibility often leveled against Wölfflin's categories properly applies only to taxonomic typologies, and a taxonomy that consisted of ony two genera and five species would be negligible indeed. But a morphologist's categories are limited by design. His universe consists not of numerous separate classes but of a continuum of individuals related through principles of formation and transformation. As Goethe says, "Here we do not inquire after causes but after conditions under which phenomena appear; we view and accept their consistent sequence, their eternal return in a thousand different circumstances, their uniformity and variability; we recognize their definiteness and redetermine it through the human spirit" (Goethe, "Erfahrung and Wissenschaft," *Werke* 18: 95–96). This sense for the pullulation of things is fundamental to Wölfflin, as to any true morphologist.

My second general consideration concerns the relationship of morphology to Wölfflin's philosophy of history. Whereas his great contemporary Alois Riegl was committed to a progressivist view of history, Wölfflin subscribed to a cyclical view derived from biological morphology, with its circular succession of seed, stalk, leaf, flower, fruit, seed. "Style unravels, fades out, or however one wishes to express it. The image of the blooming and fading of a flower presents itself as the guiding perspective of this theory" (*RB* 74). Yet this theory is weakly supported in Wölfflin's writings, which obsessively focus on a single transformation, that from the mature flowering of the classic to the late style of the baroque, which is initially seen as classicism gone to seed and in later writings as the fruit of classicism. Of the process of rebirth and renewal, Wölfflin's entire corpus contains no account more specific than this one of Albrecht Dürer: "His historic deed was to have broken through to a new attitude and a new perception. No one will be able to say where he got the strength to do so. Even if the whole network were visible and we could see what influences he came under we still would not find an answer because genius cannot be explained by an addition of influences" (*Dürer* 41–42).[3] Wölfflin's commitment to historical circularity thus seems empirically superfluous and can only be explained on an emotional level: it marks a refusal to admit the possibility of either an end point or a simple directionality in the historical process. As static as Wölfflin's view of history appears in the hands both of his critics and of imitators such as Strich and Marcel Raymond, history never stops for Wölfflin himself. Form for Wölfflin always needs to be energized, under way; his sense of the will to form is even more dynamic than that of Riegl, who coined the term *Formwollen*. It remains to be shown how this concealed Romantic vitalism governs *Principles of Art History*; like most aspects of Wölfflin's Romanticism, it is fully explicit only in his dissertation, *Prolegomena to a Psychology of Architecture*, which announces outright the maxim "Form is act" (*Form ist Tat*; *KS* 39).

A balanced, objective, or "classic" description of *Principles of Art His-*

tory might begin as follows. The book is an account of the main trends in Western art in the sixteenth and seventeenth centuries. Its purpose is to return art history "to the objects themselves" by considering them strictly as formal structures, without reference to what they represent or express. By a kind of phenomenological reduction, Wölfflin aspires to a scientific presentation freed from subjectivity, an "art history without names" (*Kunstgeschichte ohne Namen*) as he termed it in a famous slogan.[4] The resulting book is a careful and subtle interweaving of many strands. Wölfflin develops his well-known set of five paired categories to distinguish Renaissance from baroque (linear vs. painterly, plane vs. recession, closed vs. open form, multiplicity vs. unity, clearness vs. unclearness) and examines their ramifications with respect not only to periods but also to national differences and to the various genres and subgenres of the major and minor visual arts. The book is thus remarkably comprehensive, even while restrained and selective in presentation.

The aims and virtues of *Principles of Art History*, on this account, are entirely those of classicism. The book can be readily tested by its own categories. Its careful discriminations mark it as clear and linear; its comprehensiveness is that of classic closed forms; its articulation into separate units and subunits displays the multiplicity of classic structures. The overall objectivity of presentation is itself a classicizing trait, for, as Wölfflin says, classicism "represents things as they are," while the baroque represents them "as they seem to be," even though this appearance "never coincides with the form of the object" (*PAH* 20). It is true that Wölfflin intended *Principles of Art History* in part as a defense of baroque art; indeed, he takes to task those who read his predecessor Adolf von Hildebrand as a one-sided exponent of classicism. Yet Wölfflin's defense of the baroque seems curiously backhanded, for he spurns the flamboyance of mannerism and regularly praises the most restrained and orderly manifestations of seicento art. Only these latter, he insists, are the baroque in its pure form; mannerist art is actually a transitional form. In Wölfflin's hands, the true baroque becomes nothing other than a delicate variation on the classic, "indicated by very slight means," "by quite trivial projections," "the gentle flicker of a façade in which the projections are hardly noticeable" (*PAH* 112, 122, 65). This assimilation of baroque to classic might seem to be baroque trickery on Wölfflin's part, a kind of logical trompe l'oeil, were he not so astonishingly direct, so classically naive in his acknowledgment: "The word classic here denotes no judgment of value, for baroque has its classicism too" (*PAH* 14)!

Wölfflin's praise of the baroque in fact belongs to the classicizing presentational strategy; it gives the book a flexible balance, unlike the structured imbalance that characterizes the baroque. Bilateral symmetry is a classic virtue, and hence it is the classicizing historian who says, "The occidental development of modern times cannot simply be reduced to a curve with rise, height, and decline: it has two culminating points" (*PAH* 14). Like every other book, *Principles of Art History* had to be narrated in one-dimensional fashion, with a beginning, a middle, and an end, but its symmetries and interweaving of motifs are designed to cancel the temporal directionality of presentation. The book exhibits what has come to be called spatial form, a static quality that is clearly to be associated with classicism and that leads to some subtle compositional effects.

Each of the five main chapters, for instance, moves from painting to architecture. (The earlier chapters include other headings as well, but these drop out as the structural symmetries grow more evident.) And the movement within the chapters is duplicated by the book as a whole, which begins with a distinction (linear / painterly) that is native to painting and progresses toward distinctions that are naturally architectural.[5] This overall sweep from painting to architecture entails a shift in values, for painting inevitably comes to be associated with the painterly or the art of the baroque (specifically in *RB* 29), while architecture is preeminently a classic art: "The Cinquecento conceived everything *sub specie architecturae*" (*CA* 286; see also *PAH* 139 and *SFA* 87). The organization of the book thus betrays a quietly polemical intent. But what is the direction of the polemic? Are we to take the movement toward architecture as a return from the baroque back to Wölfflin's true base in classicism? Or do we perhaps read the book under the aegis of what has been termed the "primacy effect" (see Sternberg, *Temporal Modes*, chaps. 4–5), so that each chapter appears to be governed by the example of painting and thus to subsume the architectural or classic under the painterly or baroque? The most startling aspect of the book's classicizing balance is indeed that it perfectly balances praise of classicism with praise of the alternative to classicism.

It quickly becomes evident that this "classic" reading of Wölfflin is self-limiting. In the first place, the objectivity of the morphological approach is a mask. For Wölfflin as for Weber, value-freedom is itself a value and disinterestedness a polemical stance.[6] There is a forcefulness within his lucidity that Wölfflin's interpreters have tended to repress, as when Wölfflin attributes classic beauty to "figures energetically [posing] in the plane, so that the stratum of space looks uniformly living in all its parts" (*PAH* 76).[7] Moreover, the value-free value that Wölfflin inculcates is itself ambiguous, for the classicism or objectivity of the classicist impels him to admire that which is anticlassic—or, more specifically, classic forms of anticlassicism—along with classicism itself. In the current parlance of criticism, *Principles of Art History* might be termed a deconstructive machine that repeatedly entraps the impartial reader into a value system and then turns around to problematize that system. It is no wonder that most of those who write about Wölfflin express mystification, frustration, or anger. But this dilemma becomes benign once it is recognized that deconstruction is not an end in itself; it is a highly flexible mode that leads to a reorientation, not a destruction, of perspectives.[8] Wölfflin's paradoxes do not undermine classicism; rather, they redefine and reinterpret it, provided only that we are sufficiently attentive to his specific procedures.

Wölfflin begins with a principle of bilateral symmetry. But my analysis has shown an unsuspected or overlooked dimension to classic symmetry: the balance of a thing not against itself but against its opposite, right against left, classic against baroque. "There is symmetry and symmetry," writes Wölfflin. "Not until Leonardo's *Last Supper*, by the . . . contrasted handling of the groups to right and left, did the symmetrical form first become living" (*PAH* 128).[9] It is true that the distinction between the balanced unbalance of classicism and the unbalanced balance of the baroque is as minimal as all other differences between the classic proper and the classic or pure type of the baroque. "The baroque, however, consciously emphasizes one side, and thus, since the really unbalanced is no longer art, creates the relation of oscillating balance. . . . Always, *often with quite unobtrusive devices*, the balance of the picture is upset" (*PAH* 130, my italics). The troubling thought arises here that *Principles of Art History* might in fact be an example of *baroque* historiography, dedicated not to a symmetrical contrast of classic and baroque but rather to creating an oscillating balance of sympathy between them. (Michael Ann Holly has pursued this suggestion in "Wölfflin and the Imagining of the Baroque.") Where, in fact, can we draw the line between classic and baroque? Does anything ultimately distinguish the one-sidedness of the baroque—which isn't really unbalance—from that of a classic picture where "the figures are moved to one side without the balance being upset" (*PAH* 143)? Could the whole point of Wölfflin's book be that the classic and the baroque are identical?

Hardly that. The distinction between baroque and classic must be upheld if the principle of bilateral symmetry is to have any meaning. Yet Wölfflin maintains a difficult, Hegelian logic which regards contrast as a form of mutual dependence. Polar definitions of style in the tradition of Schiller were ubiquitous during Wölfflin's formative and creative years, but Wölfflin was alone in the generation after Nietzsche in understanding how each style necessarily implies the antithetical style as a negative self-image.[10] The full importance of this logic will become clear later; for now it is enough to see why the proponent of classicism who is constantly metamorphosing into a proponent of the opposite of classicism embodies the classic spirit. That spirit of self-definition through self-contradiction animates Wölfflin's account of classicism, with its "relation between energy and repose which we feel to be an enduring state," and it equally animates his account of the baroque, where "the a-tectonic always mirrors itself in the tradition of the tectonic" (*PAH* 152). The classicism of *Principles of Art History* is a form of negative capability; it has no other principle of identity than that of identity with the opposite. When the classicist looks in the mirror, he always see a reversed or mirror image. The identity of same with same, the principle of mimesis—never a positive notion in *Principles of Art History*—is invariably associated by Wölfflin with the so-called primitives of the fifteenth century. What the classicist sees in the mirror is a transformation, not a transcription; his mirrorings are speculations, detached, idealizing counterparts of the world around him. The classicist's objectivity is a reflective mode, antithetical both in its internal structuring and in its external relationship to the world.

The paradoxical logic of identity gives rise to well-known problems of definition: the troublesome overlap of the terms "painterly" and "painting" as well as the often-alleged possibility of reducing Wölfflin's five paired categories to Riegl's single pair, optic and haptic.[11] The same framework explains the numerous rhetorical excesses that seem to tarnish the classicism of *Principles of Art History*. In a classic painting by Joachim Patenir, "the tree is thoroughly felt in its relation to the picture edge, from which it draws strength just as, on the other hand, it establishes the close of the picture"; in a baroque Rembrandt, "the unity . . . lies in the absolutely compelling coherence of the movement of the whole" (*PAH* 144, 171). Such effusive writing is by no means rare in *Principles of Art History* and reflects Wölfflin's intuition that cool classicism is inseparable from its warmer opposite.

The impurity of *Principles of Art History*, on this view, is part of its strength. However, at least one major art historian, Gombrich, has expressed a decided preference for Wölfflin's earlier book, *Classic Art*, and the grounds for his preference are evident: *Classic Art* is less emotive and more consistently formalistic, as well as simpler in structure, than its successor. Gombrich's preference suggests a schematization of Wölfflin's four major surveys of Renaissance art in which *Renaissance and Baroque* (written in a staccato telegraph style) illustrates the undisciplined genius of the primitive, *Classic Art* the economy of the classic, *Principles of Art History* the intricacy of the baroque, and the effusively generalizing *Sense of Form in Art* the mechanical formalism of rococo decadence. There are two pillars in Wölfflin's achievement, and they confront us with a critical choice. Which is the true model, the analytical classicism of *Classic Art* or the expressive (baroque) classicism of *Principles of Art History*?

Wölfflin's answer to this question is unambiguous. Greatly as he was influenced by the formalistic theories of "pure visibility" found in the writings of Conrad Fiedler and Adolf von Hildebrand, he never treated them as more than a way station in formulating a true understanding of the artistic process.[12] The last sentence of *Classic Art* is perhaps sufficient evidence: "We have no desire to advocate a formalist type of art criticism: it is indeed the function of light to make the diamond sparkle" (*CA* 288)—as is the equally decisive opening sally of a review of Riegl's *Entstehung der Barockkunst in Rom*: "That art history is primarily concerned with seeing does not mean that thinking must be shunned" (356). Formalism is not the thing itself but the foil against which the thing appears. Forms as such are dead, and the mechanical production of forms is always, for Wölfflin, a sign of decadence. In order to come alive, the form must be broken, the spatial symmetry must be violated by a univocal and temporal element, the stable patterning must be marked by a moment of will or intentionality. We have already seen that classic symmetry cannot exist for Wölfflin without incorporating a contrast—at least the contrast of right and left—that prevents the symmetry from collapsing into unity. But beyond this, symmetry also cannot exist—or cannot come alive—except in the presence of asymmetry. Put in the most elementary terms, classicism cannot exist without the baroque.

The principle of contrast, in this more radical form, is one of the constants of Wölfflin's work. Where all conforms to a single code, there is compulsion, not free expression, and therefore only primitive or decadent art. "This classic plane looks quite different from the primitive plane, not only because the relation of the parts is more deeply felt [another example of the baroque or expressive prose of *Principles of Art History* that makes its predominant classicism perceptible], but because it is interspersed with contrasting motives. Only by the foreshortened motives leading into the pictures does the character of what is extended and united in the plane reach its full significance" (*PAH* 101). What applies to the intentionality of mature classicism also applies, of course, to the intentionality of mature (or classic) baroque. "The baroque arranges the figures in rows, orders them in niches: it has the greatest interest in insisting upon a spatial orientation. Only in the plane, in the negation of the plane, does recession become palpable" (*PAH* 108; see also *Dürer* 234 and *SFA* 89). The most extreme and decisive formulations of this notion, as well as many of his others, may be found in Wölfflin's dissertation; here he claims—against the authority of the source he cites—that symmetrical arrangements, as in Greek temples, always have an odd number of parts. Without an asymmetrical central element, there can be no symmetry. "We use a symmetrical articulation of uneven division for everything self-contained, since when the middle is stressed, and unlike the parts, it stands for just this inner cohesion" (*KS* 34–35; see also *SFA* 92).

The whole purpose of classic symmetries can be seen as that of concentrating the energy in the center of the work. Classicism began when the dynamism of the center was discovered, as will be seen when I restore a phrase omitted from an earlier quotation: "Not until Leonardo's *Last Supper, by the isolation of the one central figure and the contrasted* handling of the groups to right and left, did the symmetrical form first become living" (*PAH* 128, my italics). In this respect, as in all others, it must be added, the difference between classic and baroque is minimal. "It is a natural result of the facts here given that the baroque façade will tend to emphasize individual parts, at first in the sense of a dominating central motive" (*PAH* 189). Even in works of the purest (most symmetrical) classicism, Wölfflin's interpretive eye regularly gravitates toward the expressive center of the picture. "The whole picture is so planned that the central figure has no counterpart but only favourable contrasts. . . . She [Raphael's *Sistine Madonna*] is the norm, the others are variations from it which yet seem ordered by some hidden law" (*CA* 134).

Where the center is unmarked, Wölfflin can arbitrarily displace its life-giving force. He says of Barend van Orley's *Rest on the Flight*: "Naturally, much depends on the tree. It does not stand in the middle, but for all that, we perceive very clearly where the middle lies: the trunk is no mathematical vertical, but we feel that it is related to the line of the picture frame: the whole growth goes into the picture space" (*PAH* 143). The greater the displacement, the greater the violence attributed to the energizing function that must be present. For example, in Raphael's *Death of Ananias* the center retains a power of a life-denying sort, while the energy of life is wrenched into a different position. Wölfflin's emotional response to this high-classic work is nearly indistinguishable from his response to baroque art.

The people nearest him recoil in horror, and the circle of these foreground figures [who, incidentally, make Ananias into a kind of surrogate center] is so constructed that Ananias, in collapsing backward, tears a hole in the composition which is visible even at a distance, and this shows why everything else in the picture is so rigidly ordered: for this one asymmetry is the more powerfully reinforced by it. Like a thunderbolt, the judgement has torn the ranks apart and struck down its victim. . . . The eye is led directly to the centre, where St. Peter stands, a minatory arm outstretched, yet it is not an excited gesture and Peter does not fulminate: he merely pronounces the judgement of God. The Apostles themselves remain calm and unaffected by the occurrence. (*CA* 114)

Wölfflin's classicism is a structure that channels expressive energies. His categories are not taxonomies of dead or unchanging species but a morphology of living forms. His analyses, to be sure, are formalistic or objective, but his is a sophisticated objectivity rather than a primitive one: that is, in terms of the principle of contrasts, Wölfflin's objectivity is inseparable from subjectivity. He dissects not to murder but to bring to life. The three analyses from which I have just quoted all typify his procedure: he regularly allegorizes because every significant structure is also a signifying structure. Intentionality must be present; there is no mature form without a will to form. To find the expressive center of a work is to make the leap from structure into meaning, for at the center is not a mere pattern but an eloquent, unquenchable human voice.

The fundamentally baroque aspect of Wölfflin's thought is thus that his categories are anthropological and affective. They work as analytical categories because they work as human categories. This is the assumption behind the title of Wölfflin's *Prolegomena to a Psychology of Architecture*, and it is repeatedly stressed throughout that work. "We impose the image of ourselves on all appearances." "*Our bodily organization is the form in which we grasp everything corporeal*" (*KS* 16, 21). Though Wölfflin uses the term "form" here, its meaning is antithetical to the formalism of Fiedler and Hildebrand (see in particular Hildebrand's posthumously published essay "Über das Vorstellen"); the sequel shows unmistakably Wölfflin's affinity with the philosophy of "empathy" (*Einfühlung*) developed by followers of the Romantic philosopher Johann Friedrich Herbart. "Cubes are clumsy—good-natured—dumb"; windows are eyes that " 'spiritualize' the structure"; "the pillar knows exactly what it has to carry and acts accordingly." Buildings are living beings and they speak to us with the voice of their age: "What a people has on its mind it speaks out in every case" (*KS* 31, 38, 42, 47). Underneath form lies feeling, and the primacy of the body lies in its role as the medium for understanding and communicating human emotions. Or, as Theodor Lipps writes in his introduction to logic, in a sentence that might have been written by Wölfflin himself: "We do not learn the form of the human body from considering the clothed body; rather everyone knows on the contrary that the forms and folds of drapery can only become comprehensible from a knowledge of the body."[13]

Principles of Art History is far more mature and restrained than the dissertation, but the anthropological basis has only been concealed in the later work, not eliminated. Wölfflin still begins by calling himself a "psychologist of style," and the psychological dimension of the categories remains implicit in his imagery, though not always explicit in his analytical terminology. Indeed, for purely analytical purposes, the categories have often seemed dubious. The distinctions between opposing pairs only become clear when the categories are translated into their psychological equivalents, for their true function is to identify the expressivity, not the patterning, of the work of art. In recognizing that the categories are both sign and significance, we are driven back once again to that nagging question, where *is* the boundary between form and meaning, classic and baroque, north and south?

The first chapter of *Principles of Art History*, "Linear and Painterly," is preliminary to the whole; it is the longest and has the broadest coverage of genres as well as the only "general," nongeneric subchapter. Its categories, likewise, translate into the most general terms: the linear "represents things as they are," the baroque represents them "as they seem to be" (*PAH* 20). The linear style, in other words, is objective, the baroque subjective. Initially this clarification seems to give priority to the linear, for in classicism the image coincides with the form of the object, whereas the baroque is a "system of form-alienated signs" and is thus based on a negation (*PAH* 44). A second and more obviously anthropological rendition of the categories takes this apparently evaluative system and moves toward restoring its objectivity and classic balance. According to this rendition, the linear "appeals to the sense of touch" as well as to the eye, whereas the painterly "appeals only to the eye." This still seems to attribute greater breadth to the linear style, but the painterly compensates with possibilities unavailable to the linear, for "the painterly style alone knows a beauty of the incorporeal." In terms of subject matter, the linear style is more comprehensive: it can represent the sensations of both senses. But, curiously, in terms of the perceiving subject, it is the baroque or painterly experience that seems the richer: "And if we can say that in the linear style the hand has felt out the corporeal world essentially according to its plastic content, the eye in the painterly stage has become sensitive to the most various textures, and it is no contradiction if even here the visual sense seems nourished by the tactile sense— that other tactile sense which relishes the kind of surface, the different skin of things" (*PAH* 21, 27).

At the end of the chapter, Wölfflin acknowledges what is implicit in the greater sensual richness attributed to the second, baroque sense of the tactile: the anthropological pressure of these categories pushes us away from the linear and toward the painterly. "We are always prone to take things in a still more painterly way than they are meant to be taken, even to force the definitely linear, if it is at all possible, into the painterly" (*PAH* 71). The apparent reversal of evaluation in this chapter becomes comprehensible if we realize just how broadly anthropological this first pair of categories is. The linear or objective hand feels out the "plastic content" of things, while the painterly or subjective hand "relishes" their "skin": the difference in rhetorical intensity between these two descriptions shows clearly how objective and subjective become tantamount respectively to the simple absence or presence of human subjectivity. Here lies the ultimate significance of the first pair of categories: the linear, pure formalism of classicism is that which excludes us; the painterly system of "form-alienated signs" is that toward which the human subject gravitates by its very nature.

The next paired categories, plane and recession, are equivalent in psychological terms to rest and movement. Wölfflin is explicit about the significance of the baroque forms. "The beauty of recession," he says at one point, "is always combined with an impression of movement," and later he repeats that "recession speaks most intensely when it can reveal itself as movement" (*PAH* 76, 94). He is not so explicit with reference to classic art, but numerous references to "quiet plane-form" in Raphael, to the "unprecedented repose and lucidity" of Joachim Patenir's planar landscape, to the "atmosphere of quiet plane sequence" in Quentin Massys, and the like render unmistakable the association of the classic plane with a state of rest (*PAH* 79, 82, 90). Wölfflin's discussion of an interior by Pieter Janssens in the following chapter reveals the inherent subjectivity of his approach; he shows that the painting is entirely recessional and atectonic in its formal arrangement, yet he concludes by attributing a classic repose to it. "For all its intersections and discrepancies, however, the picture does not look limitless. The space enclosed apparently haphazard is still quite at rest in itself" (*PAH* 133). Here it is evident that the psychological interpretation takes precedence over the formal analysis. Closure and planar structure are ultimately feeling-states, and the decision to declare the painting closed depends on the decision about the feeling it communicates.

Wölfflin is again quite explicit about the feelings communicated by closed and open form respectively: "The a-tectonic style does not fall into lawlessness, but the order on which it is based is so much freer that we may well speak of a general contrast of law and freedom." "In the former case, the vital nerve in every effect is the inevitability of the organisation, absolute immutability. In the latter, art plays with the semblance of the lawless" (*PAH* 134, 149). Again the prevalence of affective over analytical motives is self-evident: the baroque style differs from the classic not because it *is* lawless but because it gives the effect of lawlessness.

In the chapter on multiplicity and unity, the affective or anthropological motifs are both more complex and more interesting. Wölfflin's initial distinction is between "the articulated system of forms of classic art and the (endless) flow of the baroque" (*PAH* 158). Imagery of fluidity pervades the chapter, for water, according to Wölfflin, "was the period's favourite element" (*RB* 154). "Now, and now only," he says, "the greatness of the sea could find its representation" (*PAH* 178), and as if to inculcate this affinity he places the reproduction of a baroque seascape by Jan van Goyen at the head of the introduction to the book and a riverscape by Pieter Breughel at the head of this chapter even though neither painting is discussed where it is reproduced. In fact it is worth observing that Wölfflin does not discuss any water paintings in this chapter, though of course he does so elsewhere. Where fluidity becomes the meaning of his category, it is absent from the contents of the paintings. Wölfflin's procedure, as I have argued, is both objectively analytical and subjectively interpretive, and in this chapter he seems careful to preserve the distance between the forms he describes and the significances he reveals. Were he to treat water paintings here, he would obscure the fact that his analyses are always the prelude to translations.

Though he conceals the fact, Wölfflin has here effected a translation of the baroque into itself, of water painting (and fountain architecture) into fluidity. Baroque art has declared its true meaning, which is to be an art of flux—of time and, throughout this chapter, of momentariness. Suddenly here the baroque comes into its own, with a surprising reversal in Wölfflin's categories. Until now he has associated the baroque with lawlessness and confusion, and classicism with the unifying force of symmetrical organization around a center. Unity is repose—the equation had been made explicitly in the discussion in *Classic Art* of Michelangelo's Medici *Madonna* (see 194)—and early in *Principles of Art History* Wölfflin seems to say that the unification achieved in Leonardo's *Last Supper* was later lost in Tiepolo's version.[14] As Wölfflin says in the first sentence of chapter 4, "The principle of closed form of itself presumes the conception of the picture as a unity." But as the baroque now comes into its own, it appears that the unity of classicism is an illusory, "multiple unity," whereas the true or "unified unity" actually pertains to the baroque. It is the usurping baroque, rather than the deposed classic, that now has "a dominating central motive." And so Wölfflin returns in this chapter to the two *Last Suppers* in order to rescind his earlier position. He still claims that Leonardo's painting is unified, but he offers Tiepolo's version to illustrate the "possibility of surpassing this unity" (*PAH* 189, 174). In becoming itself, baroque art has overthrown classicism.

As throughout *Principles of Art History*, the difference here between classic and baroque with respect to the question of flow is minimal; specifically, in Leonardo "a definite moment is seized for representation," while Tiepolo features "a more acute concentration on the momentary." Once again analytical categories fail us here. But that is because Wölfflin's true impulse is anthropological (or affective, or baroque), and at this point in the book voice supervenes on the motif of flux as a second and more anthropological motif. In terms of voice classic and baroque are as distinct as night and day. It is in this chapter, it will be remembered, that content and meaning coincide—as they never do in classicism, where instead form and meaning coincide—so as to reveal the true significance of the baroque as flux. The baroque at last *speaks out.* Though "it is a pity Tiepolo has no more to say to us," even he "speaks with double energy throughout the whole picture" (*PAH* 174).

The unity of classicism is an articulated unity, a rhythm or harmony, as Wölfflin constantly repeats. But anthropologically it is a silent articulation. Indeed, Wölfflin elsewhere tells us that "Leonardo was the first to venture" "to make the silence following speech the motive of the principal figure" (*CA* 27). He touches on this theme again in describing Leonardo in chapter 4 of *Principles of Art History*, where he contrasts the absence of voice in the classic with the presence of voice in the baroque, which could be described as articulate articulation or, in Wölfflin's phrase, "unified unity." (There is a clear though distant echo here of a Romantic motif, Friedrich Schlegel's oft repeated definition of Romantic—anticlassic—poetry as "the poetry of poetry.") In the baroque, "places of most speaking form emerge from a groundwork of mute or less speaking form"; "the babel of voices here rises to intelligible speech"; the older versions of the Susanna story concern how "the elders watch their victim from afar," while the baroque version concentrates on the enemy "whispering his lascivious words into her ear"— such motifs are rife in this chapter (PAH 164, 172, 175).

Particularly subtle is Wölfflin's play on the word "accent." Accent is first of all a painterly technique: "a single colour can stand out as a solitary accent." But the single-color accent is part of a whole expressional system, a "new economy of spiritual accents," accents that can, for instance, "re-echo in the 'topographical diagonal' of Van Goyen's dune landscapes." And so accent is not just a technique but a technique that for once coincides with its affective meaning, for "the liveliest expressional accent" is equivalent to "intelligible speech" (PAH 165, 171, 175, 172). Classicism gives us the background rhythm and harmony; the melodic flow and expressive accent of the leading voice are added by the baroque. Or is this not a type of presence that is demanded within the very heart of the structured absence that is classicism? For one of the glories of sixteenth-century art is Michelangelo's crowning, though alas unfinished, masterpiece, the Medici Chapel. What makes this room so splendid is the accents, the "violations of the expected," the "dissonances," the "shift of emphasis" to the side niches; as a result "there is no other room in the whole world where sculpture speaks with such force" (CA 186, 188). It seemed that chapter 4 of Principles of Art History had at last established a decisive difference between classic and baroque, but again the distinction is no more than a trick, capable of dissolving at a wave of the interpreter's wand.

Wölfflin returns in chapter 5 to a very general anthropological motif that is decisive for his reevaluation of art history. He comes back to Leonardo and Tiepolo yet once more in order to say that "the clarity of renaissance art must have seemed lifeless to this generation." And if it seemed so to them, it also seems so to us, for later on the same page, in connection with a painting by Joos van Cleve, Wölfflin drops the modal qualifier and says that the coloration "is not a homogeneous living element"—and that despite the fact that color is van Cleve's great achievement and "orders the whole" (PAH 208). Classicism is an art of the dead, to be set beside the baroque, which gives, "primarily" or in fact "only" (this is Wölfflin's self-correction), "the form of the living." In the baroque, "the body breathes" (*PAH* 232, 229).

On the one side, we have absence, rest, law, silence, death; on the other, presence, movement, freedom, voice, life. It could hardly be clearer that in affective terms Wölfflin's sympathies are entirely with the baroque; indeed, in his first book he even writes of "the affinity that our age in particular bears to the Italian baroque" (*RB* 87). Over and over again we have seen how classic works triumph by breaking out into the values of the baroque, into energy, speech, life. This subsurface energy is ever present in the masterpieces of classicism. To the baroque (read: the German spirit), "the clarity of renaissance art" (read: Italy) "must have seemed lifeless." But it is not lifeless, or at least it can be brought to life. This was Wölfflin's mission, to translate, allegorize, and humanize classicism so as to bring back to life what age and distance had rendered sterile and artificial. It is only if we treat him as an advocate not of the classic forms of baroque art but of the baroque element hidden at the heart of classicism that we can understand why he devoted two books entirely to Renaissance art—*Classic Art* and *The Art of Albrecht Dürer*—but none entirely to the seventeenth century. It was about classicism that he had something passionately new to say. The young Gombrich missed the baroque urgency in that tall, blue-eyed Swiss, but it emerges luminously throughout Strich's memoir: "When I again . . . think of the twitching and the lightning around his eyes, of his restlessness and impenetrable reserve, of his speaking style, this never overloaded, never overbalancing, measured and rhythmic style that struggled upwards toward the light out of deep shafts and layers, then do I understand that classic art indeed brought him release, but release into the very thing that he himself was not" (Strich, *Zu Heinrich Wölfflin's Gedächtnis* 34–35).

Down deep this classic taxonomist is really a baroque morphologist. His forms are never stable but always shadings and accents. "Everything is transition," he tells us early and late (*PAH* 22, 183, 227). "We should need a thousand words to denote all the transitions. It is throughout a question of relative judgments. Compared with one style, the next can be called painterly" (*PAH* 30). Such statements, prominent though they are, seem to contradict the broad canvas over which the book is articulated, but close reading has shown us how invariably the clear-cut differences dissolve in favor of a living energy that permeates the whole.

A deeply buried polemical intention can be recovered here. It is possible to recognize as Wölfflin's unnamed antagonist his revered teacher Jacob Burckhardt. In *The Civilization of the Renaissance in Italy*, Burckhardt had created an intricately composed and moving panorama of a world of spectacle that could change only to decay. History is an aesthetic pageant that turns to action at its peril, and the classical world is defined conjointly by its changeless purity and by its remoteness. This is an old tradition in German thought that acquires in Burckhardt the political dimension of a deeply felt quietism: the remoteness of history in the past is echoed by the individual's remoteness from history in the present.[15] Against this are to be placed Wölfflin's images of the growth of a remote style into a familiar one, of south into north, and of death into life. History is movement, in a constant interpenetration of forces and motifs.

The vitalism that separates Wölfflin from Burckhardt links him to two other great contemporaries. Behind his account of the birth of the baroque out of the spirit of music can be recognized the impact of his other great compatriot, Nietzsche, with his similarly shifty dialectic of the Apollonian and the Dionysian. And I think that another influence can be discerned as well. At the end of *Classic Art*, Wölfflin argues against Hippolyte Taine, but this is as deceptive as his apparent alignment with Burckhardt.[16] In fact, *Principles of Art History* is concerned with the relation of "personal style" to "the style of the school, the country, the race" (*PAH* 6), a triad of factors discernibly derived from Taine's moment, milieu, and race. Wölfflin rejected a tendency in Taine toward a mechanicalism "which attempts to interpret every style as an expression of the prevailing mood of the age" (*CA* 287). But he would also have found in the historian of English literature the century's greatest psychologist of style, concerned, precisely like Wölfflin, to show that works of art have a "double root," in form as well as in content. As the preceding chapter has shown, Taine, like Wölfflin, conceived of history as movement rather than (like Burckhardt) as spectacle, and as the source rather than the antidote of the modern. Taine also would have appealed to Wölfflin as a writer concerned to balance the traditional twin aims of the historian, the "baroque" or animating aim of making the past present and the "classic" aim of preserving the pastness of the past. This delicate balance is at the heart of Wölfflin's dialectic.

There cannot be a dialectic without differences. Yet so far, wherever we have approached Wölfflin, the line between baroque and classic has dissolved. I have just suggested that Wölfflin's thought was shaped in response to some of the great historians of the nineteenth century, but Wölfflin is still liable to seem an outright failure as a historian. Even if we discount as an aberration Wölfflin's cyclical view of development, his "history of the development of occidental seeing" appears to issue in chaos rather than system (*PAH* 12). First, he insists that there is no connection between classic and baroque and that no evaluative comparison of them is possible. "Baroque . . . is neither a rise nor a decline from classic, but a totally different art. The occidental development of modern times cannot simply be reduced to a curve with rise, height, and decline: it has two culminating points." "It is not a difference of quality if the baroque departed from the ideals of the age of Dürer and Raphael, but, as we have said, a different attitude to the world" (*PAH* 14, 16). Second, he stresses the irreversible logic of the historical curve that leads from classic to baroque and never in the other direction. "The transition from tangible, plastic, to purely visual, painterly perception follows a natural logic, and could not be reversed," a logic, be it said, that begins with a rise from the primitives and ends with a decline into the rococo (*PAH* 17). Third, from whatever conventionalities of diction or strategies of rehabilitation, a rhetoric of historical progress is often on the horizon; wittingly or unwittingly, Wölfflin often speaks of the "advancing" of art, of an "enhancement of interest" in the baroque, of the development of taste, of a "gain" that results when the baroque "avoids classic frontality" (*PAH* 196, 223). And fourth, as we have seen, Wölfflin repeatedly insists on denying the historical dualism that he has insisted on establishing: "As regards chronology, the facts cannot, of course, be mastered with two concepts" (*PAH* 67). The baroque is at once the opposite of the classic and identical to it, later and simultaneous, cancellation and fulfillment.

The explanation of this historiographical muddle—which points to the core of Wölfflin's achievement—is both unmistakably implicit and, at one key point, inescapably explicit. Classic art is absent, silent, static, or even dead; baroque is present, vocal, and alive. The difference between classic and baroque that rationalizes Wölfflin's system and that establishes at once their radical opposition and their total identity is quite simply this: that *the classic does not exist*. It never existed and can never have existed, for when the classic comes into existence or manifests itself, it does so in the form of existence, which is the baroque. The classic *is* the baroque. This is not a speculative judgment about Wölfflin. It is precisely what he says, if not about all of classic art, at least about the most classic form of classicism, the art that forms the subject of *Classic Art*. The passage from the introduction to *Classic Art* is long but worth quoting in full for its pathetic and rhetorically moving insistence on the irredeemable nonexistence of the classic.

It is not easy to obtain a general view of this period. However well-known to us from youth onwards these masterpieces may be through engravings and reproductions of every kind, only slowly does a consistent and living picture form itself of the world which bore these fruits. It is different with the Quattrocento. In Florence the fifteenth century still stands before our eyes like a living thing. True, much of it is lost, many things have been taken from their natural setting and put into the prison-like custody of museums but there still remain enough places to recreate for us a vivid impression of the life of those days. The Cinquecento is preserved more fragmentarily and, moreover, did not reach a complete development. In Florence one has the feeling that the broad substructure of the Quattrocento lacks the crown of final achievement because one cannot properly see the completion of the development. I do not mean that this is because of the export of panel pictures out of the country, so that, for example, there is practically nothing by Leonardo left in Italy, but because, from the beginning, the forces squander themselves. Leonardo's *Last Supper*, which is an essentially Florentine work, is in Milan; Michelangelo became half Roman and Raphael entirely so. Of their great Roman works, the Sistine ceiling is an absurdity, a torment to the artist and the spectator alike, and Raphael had to paint some of his Vatican pictures in sections on walls where one can never see them properly. So one is left wondering how much ever came to anything, how much out of those short, few, peak years remained only as a project or fell victim to early destruction. Leonardo's *Last Supper* itself is only a wreck; his great battle-piece, commissioned for Florence, was never finished and even the cartoon is lost. Michelangelo's *Bathing Soldiers* shared the same fate, while the Julius Tomb remained unexecuted save for a few single figures, and the facade of San Lorenzo, which was to have displayed the full splendour of Tuscan architecture and sculpture, remained no more than a project on paper. The Medici Chapel only counts as a partial substitute, for it already stands on the verge of Baroque.

Classic art has left no monument in the great style, where architecture and sculpture are blended together for the full expression of the artist's concept, and the greatest architectural commission on which all the artistic forces of the age were concentrated—St. Peter's in Rome—was, finally, not allowed to become a monument of the High Renaissance.

One can compare classic art with the ruins of a building, nearly, but never quite, finished, the original form of which must be reconstructed from far-scattered fragments and incomplete accounts, and it is perhaps not wrong to say that in the whole history of Italian art no epoch is less known than the Golden Age. (*CA* xvii–xviii)

Wölfflin's sensibility is thus dominated by a pathos of which hints can be found even in Burckhardt, who writes at one point in the *Cicerone*, "Naturally the best and grandest projects also remained unconsummated in the full flowering of the renaissance" (Burckhardt, *Gesammelte Werke* 9: 144). That classicism is a mirage—a necessary illusion or, more technically, a regulative ideal—is one of the profound discoveries of that branch of Romanticism curiously known as German classicism. For Schiller, for Goethe, for Humboldt, the classical is a figure of desire, an Arcadia well lost and never to be recaptured. It is no coincidence that Faust's road to the classical world is guarded by Sphinxes; for when the classical comes to life it always does so in a belated baroque language of turmoil and self-division:

> Exalted much and much disparaged, Helena,
> I leave behind the strand where first we came ashore,
> Still in a stupor from the nimble tilt and pitch
> Of rolling seas that brought us from the Phrygian plain.
> (Goethe, *Faust*, lines 8488–91)[17]

Wölfflin's logic is uncompromising: if art is a human expression subject to the flow of history, then it can never have been ideally pure or timeless. Yet he makes this rigorous logic seem natural and inevitable by subordinating it to the directness of ocular demonstration. His greatness thus rests, in the most literal sense, on a visionary power. Wölfflin's vision of classicism elided places him in one of the main lines of modern thought, a line whose empirical richness is in danger of being obscured when its insights are reduced to the formula, "the destruction of metaphysics."

It may seem a long way from *Principles of Art History* to proofs of the existence of God. Yet the classic serves as a god term for Wölfflin, and the secret kernel sentence of his writings, the classic is the baroque, is in a sense an assertion concerning the existence of a creative essence. To realize the implications of Wölfflin's writings, we need to understand the background and grammar of that kernel sentence. And nowhere—at least nowhere in the tradition out of which Wölfflin came—has the grammar of being been so extensively scrutinized as in connection with the ontological proof of the existence of God.

God is defined as the most perfect being; but to exist is better than not to exist, so by definition God possesses existence. So, in a simple form, runs the proof. God existing is better than and hence different from God merely imagined. One of the most famous sections of Kant's *Critique of Pure Reason* refutes this argument. Kant argues that being is not a predicate or, to be more specific, not a determinant. One hundred talers in my pocket is no greater a sum than 100 talers in my imagination, and God existing is no greater than God merely conceived. Existence does not change—and hence does not improve—the nature of the deity. God is God.

Paraphrased in this crude way, Kant's argument sounds like a denial of the distinction between essence and existence, and on this ground it has been repeatedly assailed (see, for instance, Wood, *Kant's Rational Theology* 104–9). The predicate, he seems to say, adds nothing to the subject and thus is empty. Being is no different from nonbeing. God is not God. But Kant's true contention is not that being is an empty notion but rather that being is unanalyzable. He denies only that we can know what existence entails. The refutation is concerned not with God's existence but with our conception of God's existence; hence God is mysterious, or, as Kant writes in a posthumous fragment, "Real being is the first absolute concept—completely heterogeneous (*but not even that*) with nothing: thus not o + a = a" (Kant, *Gesammelte Schriften* 28: 957). What this adds up to is an incipient recognition on Kant's part that being, identity, and truth are dialectical concepts, problems and not answers, tokens of an incalculable difference.[18]

Hegel's numerous commentaries on Kant's refutation—four in the *Science of Logic* alone and four more in various series of lectures on religion—all concern the dialectics of being. Kant's refutation, as Hegel says, only deals with the subjective stage of being-for-us, not the objective stage of being in and for itself. In itself being is changeless and therefore empty: "*Pure being* and pure *nothing* are, therefore, the same" (*Science of Logic* 82). And for us, being is pure evanescence and hence again empty:

The difficulty of finding *being* in the Notion as such and equally in the Notion of God, becomes insuperable when the being is supposed to be that which obtains *in the context of outer experience* or *in the form of sensuous perception, like the hundred* [*talers*] *in my finances*, something to be grasped with the hand, not with the mind, something visible essentially to the outer, not to the inner eye; in other words, when that being which things possess as sensuous temporal and perishable, is given the name of reality or truth. (*Science of Logic* 707)

But through the contrast between these two inessential modes of being, a third mode is generated in which being is assimilated to becoming. God is that purity in existence which points beyond pure existence, destroyer and preserver at once. Hegel is always at his most lucid when commenting on Kant, and despite his inveterate abstractness the ideas here are straightforward:

Existence, then, is not to be taken here as a *predicate* or as a *determination* of essence, the proposition of which would run: essence exists, or *has* existence; on the contrary, essence has passed over into Existence; Existence is essence's absolute emptying of itself or self-alienation, nor has it remained behind on the further side of it. The proposition should therefore run: essence is Existence; it is not distinct from its Existence. Essence has *passed over* into Existence in so far as essence as ground no longer distinguishes itself from itself as the grounded, or in so far as this ground has sublated itself. But this negation is equally essentially its position, or absolutely positive continuity with itself, its identity-with-self achieved in its negation. (483)[19]

Hegel stresses that this is the logic of the concept in general, of which the logic of the concept of God is only an important instance. Hegel's logic is precisely that of Wölfflin's art history as well. The baroque is the fulfillment of the classic. But it is a fulfillment in the sense of a crossing over—from essence into existence, from death into life—and hence the absolute negation of the classic. Finally, it is the condition of the possibility of classic being, determining the classic as the ever remote, alien ground of existence. This eternal mutation of classic into baroque, without which neither classic nor baroque could exist, is the logic of history—this, and not, in particular, some reverse pendulum swing from baroque existence toward classic essence, such as Strich argues for at the end of his memoir and tries to document in his studies of German classicism and German Romanticism.

History is also moving toward the baroque and away from the classic. This means that each age serves as the baroque to some earlier age and as the classic to some later one. The Romanesque can be viewed as the classic of the Gothic, the late-Gothic primitives as the silent ground underlying the expressivity to be found in sixteenth-century art, the Florentine cinquecento as the classic of a certain tall, blue-eyed Swiss.[20] And in turn history is recapitulated in each individual work of art, for each must have two faces if all do. We may take it as a second hidden kernel sentence of Wölfflin's writings that *every artwork is both classic and baroque*, classic in its essence and baroque in its existence, classic in its formal perfection and baroque in its expressivity. Indeed, form and expression are inseparable, if dialectical, complements. No matter how much form strikes us as permanently valid, it is also always something that has been created; it is both a mode of stability and a mode of beginning or initiation and cannot be the one without being the other. "Of course, in the strictest sense of the word, there is nothing 'finished': all historical material is subject to continual transformation; but we must make up our minds to establish the distinctions at a fruitful point, and there to let them speak as contrasts, if we are not to let the whole development slip through our fingers" (*PAH* 14).

By virtue of the very intensity of its commitment to formalism, Wölfflin's work thus becomes—or rather remains what his earliest writing most obviously is—the antithesis of a pure formalism. He is concerned with locating fruitful points within history, as if the continual flux of history were not fruitful enough for the imagination of any scholar. This is no mere typology, no impoverished study of artistic structures, but one of our most powerfully and concretely realized theories of the aesthetics of artistic production. To be sure, Wölfflin is less concerned than Riegl—though by no means unconcerned—with the material and technical conditions of production. Yet, though Louis Althusser has contended that Marxism is not a formalism, Wölfflin's formalism is still, if I may use names loosely for a moment, a rarefied or Hegelian brand of Marxism.

That an art history without names should at the same time amount to an aesthetics of production should no longer startle us. We have grown used to answering the question "What is an author?" with Michel Foucault's response, "What matter who's speaking?" "Art is a work not of man but of that which produces it (and this producer is not a subject centered in its creation, it is an element in a situation or a system)." This is not Wölfflin, of course—though it almost could be—but a contemporary Frenchman, Pierre Macherey (*Pour une théorie* 84). Nor, obviously, is this rejoinder Wölfflin, though again the sentiments move in territory that Wölfflin staked out:

A text puts texts in relation to one another and not an author and a reader assimilated to some referents: here the language-text is in such relation to the emitter of the text that his person, his life-his death, his biography, are indifferent: the emitter is present in the text by his very absence, but [here at last is the critique of Macherey] *it is not the disappearance of the subject that is manifested in the text, it is the disappearance of the nondialectical opposition subject-object*, and it is through this dialectic at work that the text performs its slippage.[21]

Finally, we have neither Wölfflin nor a French critic but Hegel, commenting once more on creators and on the Creator:

No man is satisfied with his mere selfhood; self is active, and this activity is to objectify the self, to give it reality, existence. In a further, more concrete specification, this activity of the concept is instinct. Every satisfaction is this process of suspending subjectivity and of positing this inner, this subjective quality equally as something external, objective, real, of producing the unity of the merely subjective and the merely objective, of stripping them of their onesidedness. (*Werke* 17: 526, from the 1827 revision of the *Lectures on the Philosophy of Religion*)

This is, to be sure, far from the only place where modern polemics sound like nothing more than a series of footnotes to Hegel. And that is why I should like to return to Wölfflin, whose research, lying almost precisely halfway between the abstract speculations of the philosopher and the equally abstract debates of the critics, gives these abstractions a concrete meaning.

Works of art participate in history because they make history. They make history—as Macherey also argues, using, like Wölfflin, an insistently bivalent logic—because they are intrinsically in flux. "Form is act" because artistic shaping both grows out of and reflects the labor of creation. This insight into the artistic process, and not the mere formalism of the product, is the true link between Wölfflin and the school of

Fiedler and Hildebrand, and it inspires the fascination with the physical aspects of graphic technique that so distinguishes *The Art of Albrecht Dürer*. Each work of art moves toward its center—what we feel, not necessarily what we measure, as its center (and here the debates about the vanishing point in *Las Meninas* can be reopened)[22]—where the expressive, existential force (*Kraft*) is concentrated that carries it beyond a merely inertial objectification (*Stoff*) of essence. This internal movement of the work is the "rhythm" that Wölfflin often evokes and that in appreciative art criticism so often degenerates into a merely formal category. But Wölfflin's own five paired categories of the understanding are tools for interpreting the meaning of the artistic act and never a merely formal or analytic apparatus. There is no magic about the number five; we may feel that more or fewer would be preferable. But I know of no author who endeavors so consistently and directly to explore the *work* performed by what all Western languages agree in calling the work of art.

CHAPTER 3

What's in a Text?

FOR AT LEAST a decade, from, say, 1965 to 1975, Romantic studies were the cutting edge of literary criticism in this country. The mantle has since passed to the Renaissance, and to nineteenth-century fiction. If Romanticism also continued through the 1980's to influence directions of thought generally, that was mostly due to two very different thinkers, Paul de Man and Jerome J. McGann. McGann's project of self-definition is contained in a central suite of volumes beginning with *The Romantic Ideology* (*RI*) and *A Critique of Modern Textual Criticism* (*CMTC*), both published in 1983, and continued with *The Beauty of Inflections* (*BI*, 1985), *Social Values and Poetic Acts* (*SV*, 1988), and *Towards a Literature of Knowledge* (*TLK*, 1989). (Also cited are *Black Riders* [*BR*, 1993] and the collection edited by McGann, *Textual Criticism and Literary Interpretation* [*TCLI*, 1985].) In them we can see the maturity of a Marxist critical orientation quite distinct from the cultural studies of a Fredric Jameson or an Edward Said. The following pages attempt to determine the essence of McGann's many seminal contributions.

That is not easy to do, for McGann's work resists summation. His principles of active, engaged writing demand an adjustment and response to varied situations and contexts. The centered self and the interpreter's self-analysis are not for him. Even his first book, *Fiery Dust* (1968), though a composed study of Byron's self-fashioning, "deliberately cultivate[s] a variety of critical approaches" (viii); *Swinburne* (1972) is an elegant, multiperspectival critical dialogue; *Don Juan in Context* (1976) programmatically proliferates contexts; and the subsequent critical books all have been in effect collections of essays, with increasingly frequent and resourceful recourse to dialogue forms.[1] The range in *Social Values* is particularly daunting. In support of general theoretical reflection of a kind he has seldom previously undertaken, McGann adds to his staple nineteenth-century repertoire (here represented chiefly by Blake, Kant, and Arnold) the Bible, the Greeks (Herodotus, Aeschylus, Plato), Pound and contemporary poets, and even *Ulysses*. *Social Values* and *The Beauty of Inflections* encompass extended close readings of poems in the context of contemporary history and social currents (among them a particularly impressive revaluation of *The Charge of the Light Brigade*); suggestions for new approaches to familiar poems (including the well-known essays on Keats and on the historically layered textual presentation of *The Rime of the Ancient Mariner*); career surveys of canonical and neglected authors (George Crabbe, Christina Rossetti, and a rich overview of the interpenetration of life and history in Byron's poems, followed in recent years by a series of exhilarating essays on women poets of the nineteenth and twentieth centuries); textual and bibliographical essays (including a fine one on the intellectual currents behind the format of Blake's *Book of Urizen*); a thematic essay ("Rome and Its Romantic Significance," which deals persuasively with Goethe, Mme. de Staël, and Stendhal, along with Byron); critical accounts of other theorists (Cleanth Brooks, de Man, J. Hillis Miller, Stanley Fish, M. M. Bakhtin, Jürgen Habermas); defenses of poetry; and even a brief set of aphorisms ("Theses on the Philosophy of Criticism," *BI* 343–44).

Questions and concerns overlap and diverge to project a mind ever alert to opportunities (as well as to what prior critics have said), never closed in upon itself. The doctrinal center lies in Marxism, but the spirit—the capaciousness, the generous response, the claims for the preeminence of literature as a vehicle for distilling and communicating social forces, the sense of the past as a varied resource that can guide the present toward the future, the rejection of disengaged hermeneutics, and even the love-hate relationship toward reductive proverbs and inevitably premature totalizations (see *SV* 105–6)—seems to me closer to Goethe. Militant humanists both, Goethe and Marx have much in common—as do Goethe and Byron—but not enough to make Marxist doctrine and Goethean spirit easily reconcilable.[2] McGann encourages us to seek out the identifying divisions, or "rifts," in poets and critics alike: "The entire *work* is never equal to itself—it is always 'incommensurate' "

(*TLK* x). It is the split between Marxism and Goethean humanisms that, for me, gives his work its distinctive profile and makes it hardest to sum up.

Contradictions energize. McGann values history for its contrasts: we need to salvage the past as ballast to the present. Poetry presents tensions, and does so "as a challenge . . . and not simply as a picture to be observed" (*SV* 9). Under poetic totalizations, he contends, lie the incommensurate particulars that "in fact *make* (*and/or have made*) a *difference*" (*SV* 128). Consequently, "sociohistorical criticism . . . holds that art imitates not merely the 'fact' and the 'ideal,' but also the dynamic relation which operates between the two . . . [and it] both assumes and seeks to display the *determinate* character of this dynamic relation" (*SV* 128).

McGann is too committed to change to be comfortable reducing his beliefs to formulas.[3] That is surely why he elsewhere avoids the propositional mode that prevails in much of *Social Values* and why his theorizing can seem frustrating. His energy and Byronic flexibility seem to entail a certain slippage in the terms. By lining up the right excerpts, you can make McGann seem to be chasing his own tail. "Of all forms of communication, the poetic alone entails the *whole* of what is true" (*SV* 92). That whole is not a Wordsworthian intuition, or "spot of time," but rather a Poundian compendium (*SV* 52). Totalization must not be idealized, as it is in the aesthetics of Kant and Coleridge, for "any great historical product . . . is a work of transhistorical rather than so-called universal significance" (*BI* 187). Hence McGann experiments in one essay with the notion of a "Mastercode" or "general fact" of a "political and social" nature (*SV* 75) that "define[s] the poem's communication system" and "establish[es] the poem's particular set of sociohistorical interests and engagements" (*SV* 77). A typically tactical formulation (the essay's full title is "Poetic Ideology and Nonnormative Truth: To the Marxists"), McGann's version of a Mastercode can serve as an alternative to the "master code" (a "theme or 'inner essence,' " a "hidden master narrative") that Jameson reluctantly rejects (*The Political Unconscious* 28). From totalizing or at least transhistorical, the Mastercode thus migrates toward the poem's particular situation—its spot of time— such as (here) the moment of composition of Juvenal's satires. "The *whole* of what is true" has shed its extensive, "transhistorical . . . significance" to acquire a punctual intensity.

McGann's turn from totality to particularity reproduces a discussion that finds Platonic truth to be not Ideas but "a pursuit and an eventuality" (*SV* 28). Ideology—if I set the accents right on some evasive passages—is not just the "permanent and originary meaning" that the Bible "struggle[s]" to "deploy" (*SV* 57), but also "a matrix of historical particularities" on behalf of which Tennyson undertakes "a quest and polemic" (*BI* 182), consequently a kind of "performativity" that "poetic performativity overtakes" as it "strives to thicken and realize the entire communicative field" (*SV* 91), and thus at its nether end the fugitive "illusions" and "ghostly shapes" that literature "dispel[s]" (*SV* 107). What matters throughout is not the position but the resistance to fixity. So, finally, "meaning in poetry is neither the ideology of the poem nor the ideology of the critic; it is the process in which those ideologies have found their existence and expression" (*BI* 10).

Such prose neither can nor wants to stand still. The occasional declarative passages are both inert and disorienting:

This emphasis upon the determinate *is* fundamental if "what is" *is* to stand in a natural or scientific relation to "what should be." But because knowledge *is* a project rather than a possession, it falls short of a complete grasp of its objects. The determinate relation between "what is" and "what should be" *is* what Shelley had in mind when he spoke of "something longed for, never seen." The determinate *is*—in the alternative sense of that word—what exists by acts of determination. Knowledge as a project *is* knowledge grounded in a platonic Eros, which *is* in the end both determined and determinative, in every sense of those two terms. Kant's "categorical imperative" *is* an analogous concept, though it seems to me that subsequent readers of Kant have misleadingly emphasized the categorical rather than the imperative salient in his thought.[4]

Yet even passages intended to declare settled convictions enact the slippage they are meant to propound. We see in them what McGann terms the hermeneutic pseudo-dialectic of object and subject (or of Realism and Romanticism), whose hegemony screens out the "third world" of the voiceless and the invisible (*SV* 63–64), and we are driven to intuit in "literary work (poetry and philology)" "a network constructed to maximize contradictions and incommensurability, . . . mark[ing] an antithesis to forms of normativity and dominance" (*SV* 55–56). De Man's work is for him the chief case in point: by pitting nature against mind in order to argue that the poetic is the only realm where the two fuse, de Man (in McGann's account) erects a false dichotomy, leading to a false reconciliation that hides the way literature "deploy[s] value" as "a concrete social institution" (*SV* 102–3). Standing Hegel on his feet, McGann argues against merely conceptual resolutions that subsume "facts" under "interpretations," and in favor of human experience as "*events*—specific and worlded engagements in which meaning is rendered and used" (*SV* 72). A literary work is "a dynamic event in human experience"; poems are "structures of social energy" (*BI* 108, 128).

* * *

It's a game of both ends against the middle. That doesn't always appear in the formulations as such, for not infrequently the treatment of tension or contradiction can verge on Cleanth Brooks's cohesive irony or on Coleridge's symbolic "translucence of the Special in the Individual or of the General in the Especial or of the Universal in the General" (Coleridge, *Statesman's Manual* 30). But the logic of the argument, reinforced by the slipperiness (or dynamic urgency, or temporality) of the terms, saves McGann from the placid center and underwrites his claim that literature is "performative," not "representational" (*SV* viii). "The Israel of Genesis is an island in a greater world, and the more it insists that it is the center of that world, the more it gives us glimpses of the actual, the whole, the objective truth. . . . Literary work is the art of multiplicities and minute particulars, the science of *un*buildings: one law for the lion and the ox *is* oppression" (*SV* 230). He prefers unpredictable debate to security and determination.

McGann drives, then, in two directions. One is toward a broadening reflection on what he likes to call "the meanings of the meanings." The other is toward an ever more precise account of texts, their production, and the factors that condition composition and publication. Arguing against New Critics and their poststructuralist avatars, McGann insists that a "work" is more than a "text," for he is interested both in the work that poems accomplish and in the work that goes into generating them. Ideology critique and textual criticism are convenient names for the two directions; future and past are the vectors that he wants to rescue from the stasis of momentary or eternal presence. (One section of *Social Values* is called "Literature and the Future of History." It includes the visionary teleology of "The Third World of Criticism," which contends that "in writing what amounts to an imaginative history of the present, every poem thereby constructs a past and a set of possible futures" [*SV* 229], encompassing insights into events after its composition.) The unacceptable alternative, he writes in his conclusion, would be to imagine literature "as occupying a world elsewhere, . . . a 'poetic' space redeemed from time and the agencies of loss" (*SV* 246). Even Genesis shows us— not through its doctrines, to be sure, but through the meanings of its meanings—that we must "relinquish an imperial imagination."

* * *

> Three times the concentred self takes hold, three times
> The thrice concentred self, having possessed
>
> The object, grips it in savage scrutiny,
> Once to make captive, once to subjugate
> Or yield to subjugation, once to proclaim
> The meaning of the capture, this hard prize,
> Fully made, fully apparent, fully found.
> (Wallace Stevens, *Credences of Summer*, lines 99–105)

It is suspicious that *The Beauty of Inflections* takes its title from that great visionary of the central imagination, Wallace Stevens. Decentering poetry may be harder than McGann dreams. Between meanings and the meaning of meanings, between textual criticism and the critique thereof, lies at best a very fine line. The more we scrutinize McGann's two moments, the ideological and the material, the more we realize that their core is textual after all. This is not to go back on his achievements: McGann's writings make it impossible to return to the negative idealizations of "the poem itself" or to confuse Stevens's problematic *Credences of Summer* with a positive creed. But it remains important to reaffirm the dialectical productivity of poetry in creating the possibility of the very critique that McGann undertakes.

What's in a poem? McGann argued lucidly in *A Critique of Modern Textual Criticism* that poems are not isolated products of the solitary imagination. Conditions of production and reception are both fundamental to what Habermas calls the communicative act. Scholars should abandon the notion that the author's manuscript, prior to editorial intervention, preserves the purest and truest state of a work, for "the fully authoritative text is always one that has been socially produced" (*CMTC* 75).[5] Hence "the study of texts is fundamental and primary" (*SV* 99) in order "to restore the connection . . . between 'intrinsic' and 'extrinsic' literary investigations, between hermeneutics and scholarship, *verstehen* and *erklären*" (*SV* 16). In the conjoint critique of de Man and Fish (*SV* 95–114), both are taken to propound self-enclosed systems, the former's exclusively intrinsic, the latter's exclusively extrinsic. Restoring connections means testing the poem's opening to the world. "The set of ideological formations imbedded in the poem at its historical inception will always remain part of the work's fixed dialectical pole with which the moving pole of the reader interacts" (*RI* 157).

The nature of the work's embedding needs to be interrogated here, together with the curious fixity of the dialectical pole. What puts meaning into the poem? The long Keats essay in *Social Values* relates textual variants to the specific media of publication of several poems as elements of Keats's communicative situation. It argues that to know what Keats meant we must know what was meant by those who designed and published his books and the journals where his poems appeared, and it has been rightly influential in counteracting both the intrinsic philosophical allegories of critics of consciousness such as Earl Wasserman and Geoffrey Hartman and the extrinsic social and class allegories of critics such as Walter Benjamin and Terry Eagleton. But in the case of someone like Keats, how do we distinguish significant choice from contingent opportunity? Did Keats intend the publishing options which he used? To what extent are they part of the meaning of his meaning? The essay has been emphatically attacked for neglecting to face these questions (see Paul Fry, "History, Existence, and 'To Autumn'"). But it does face them implicitly, for Donne's metaphor of fixed and moving poles suggests where McGann will be seen to stand: the energy to encompass and circumscribe its worldly engagements comes from the work, not from the world.

In a notable essay inspired and praised by McGann, Marjorie Levinson has claimed that " 'Tintern Abbey' finally represents mind . . . as a barricade to resist the violence of historical change and contradiction" (*Wordsworth's Great Period Poems* 53). How does the moving, extrinsic, worldly pole get attached to the fixed dialectical pole (the resistive barricade) of the text? To a large degree by conjectural inference: Levinson's essay bristles with such formulations as "to a man of Wordsworth's experience and inclination, Tintern Abbey would have represented"

(32), "a poet given to historical perspectives could not but remark" (32), "he must have felt" (34), "the spoiled ruin would have figured" (35), and "surely" (36). The moving pole of the reader, indeed. Yet Levinson shows the spirit of McGann when she rescues the argument from circularity by means of a textual sensitivity that, from within the poems, "bring[s] out . . . the aura of the enclosure in Wordsworth's authorial ideology" (33). The meanings of the meanings are the authorial ideology as its aura reaches out beyond the letter of the text.

The fixed pole of authorial ideology is the firm foot of McGann's readings, as of Levinson's. As "a social event," "every poem" may well entail a "dialectical relation" between intention ("the author's expressed decisions and purposes") and reception ("the critical reactions of the poem's various readers") (*BI* 24). Yet our access to "the aesthetic domain which Cockney verse attempted to conquer" is "not merely the abstract *characteristics*, but the felt *qualities* of its poetic structure" (*BI* 28). The word that really should have been emphasized here is "felt." Textual intuitions govern our adjustments of text to context—ours and even McGann's. Thus, in the midst of contending that we need to consider the different publication formats of *Don Juan* in order to appreciate the poem's significance, he says, "The fact that Byron's *Don Juan* should have called out these two sorts of edition is one sign of its creative power" (*BI* 121). The text's power, in other words, precedes the editions and channels their impact.

In the Mastercodes essay, McGann insists that reception defines the crucial extrinsic code, which must not be neglected: "That initial documentary situation highlights, by its concrete and positive differentials, the fact that later texts are equally marked, at the level of production, by specific ideological interests" (*SV* 83). Yet it turns out that the "horizon of critical values" is never out of sight; "In fact, *of course*, the poem *always has* been read within that context" (*SV* 85; McGann emphasizes only "has"). In repeatedly denouncing "the modern fashion of referring to poems as 'texts' " (*BI* 121), precisely in order to draw attention to their "many different textual constitutions" (*BI* 121), McGann commits a telltale terminological contamination. Much as he would like to pit intrinsic factors against extrinsic ones, the crucial dialectic remains intratextual.[6] What's in the poem is what's in the text, either as meaning, or as implication, aura, the meaning of the meaning. Reception history paves the way toward "a 'close' linguistic reading" through which "the poem's more localized and particular details might be reimagined" ("Literary History" 232). Situations may exist where the textual constitutions and the reception history of a poem contribute essential meanings at odds with the text, but I don't think that McGann ever exhibits any. Indeed, I don't think that, deep down, he even *wants* to.[7]

The fate of polarities in McGann is to be undermined. That's what gives them (like his prose) their flux and their energy. By his own yardstick, he becomes a critical thinker at the moment when his categories suspect themselves. I will examine a strong essay where the reversal is explicit, and then, approaching my conclusion, a weak essay where it is shunned. (The weaker, by the way, is the more self-revealing.) Explicit dialectic guards appearances, and the polarized categories that are transcended nevertheless remain as apparitional—the term is McGann's—structures with an illusion of substance. Hence the strong essay is incomplete, whereas the tottering categories of the weak essay provoke more forthright response. McGann is an artist of what the Italian philosopher Gianni Vattimo has come to call "weak thought." Like some of the authors he most admires, such as Herodotus and Montaigne, his writing is more than the sum of its parts, more suggestive by moments than rhetorically complete. And its true character lies in the confrontations that it evades. Thus it will take me back, at the last, to Stevens and to Goethe—and to Wordsworth.

* * *

"Some Forms of Critical Discourse" (*SV* 132–51) embodies McGann's yearnings for discontinuity. Taking off from an essay by Hayden White, McGann proposes some alternatives to the essay form that prevails among literary critics. (McGann characterizes the form he is questioning—since the text matters here—"as a lecture or, more normatively, as an essay or monograph" [*SV* 135]. His book in fact contains six lectures—the first five numbered chapters and the last—surrounding five "more detailed and scholastically rigorous" chapters that "execute shifts in the formal continuities of the book" [*SV* ix].) Essays are narrative and hermeneutic, and hence discourage "true criticism," which "entails a self-conscious response to certain social and historical factors" (*SV* 149). By disrupting the link of mind to mind, we can rupture the illusory timelessness of poetic truth so as to gain a fuller appreciation of poetic acts.

Here we have to undertake some textual criticism. When the essay
(and it is an essay) was originally published, McGann identified four
"nonnarrative forms." These are the hypothetical, the practical or in-
junctive, the array, and the dialectic, and they are exemplified respectively by the scientific paper, by "a book like Euclid's *Elements*, or any
cookbook," by the bibliography (McGann's substitute for the historical
annals that White discusses), and by Montaigne's—yes—essays.[8] Now,
it is virtually a reflex of modern critical rhetoric that any of these forms
actually ought to be decoded narratively.[9] I suspect that is the reason
why McGann drops reference to the first two forms in the *Social Values*
text. Deep down, he knows that what matters is the internal workings
of the particular text, not the external format. Formal nonnarrativity is
merely an appearance; what really counts is the spirit within: "The
apparition of such forms is not, however, a guarantee that the discourse
will in fact be critical, only that it will exhibit the form of criticism."[10]
Almost at the end, then, McGann adduces an "essay" of Hartman's,
"The Interpreter: A Self-Analysis," as an almost successful critical and
dialogic project. The essay's failure may be that it is "formally narrativized" as McGann claims (*SV* 150), but more likely the failure is
rhetorical, as his footnoted evidence demonstrates (*SV* 262 n. 16). After
all, the same "fundamental question . . . must [be] put to every form of
ideological discourse," namely, "How much genuine self-criticism does
a scholar's or an ideologue's work seek after and encourage?" (*SV* 150).
First and last, it is the spirit and the "scholarly climate" (*SV* 151) that
matter, and the forms are at most only conducive to the true aims.
Formalism is not ideological criticism, and the revised version that appears in *Social Values* retreats in full self-awareness from the formalist
illusion that seems to have prompted the essay initially.[11]

"Some Forms of Critical Discourse" ends by "speculat[ing] on the possibility that a critical edition . . . is now being assembled somewhere
which will induce a major shift in scholarly understanding" (*SV* 151).
Two essays later comes the opportunity which that conclusion had
seemed to forecast. "*Ulysses* as a Postmodern Work" (*SV* 173–94) reviews the new critical edition of Joyce's novel by Hans Walter Gabler.
Here McGann erects the editor into a hero much as earlier textual critics
idealize the author. The modernist *Ulysses*, he tells us, was a private and
elitist work, "finished and monumental," "a limited edition and supported by subscriptions of the literati."[12] The postmodern *Ulysses* is a

technological book and a process text. The editor's job is to lay bare the productive forces by determining the various layers of the text. Following several Continental precedents—McGann mentions editions of Friedrich Hölderlin, Kafka, Flaubert, Friedrich Klopstock, and Proust—Gabler has produced the first such edition in English.

To my mind this is the weakest of all McGann's essays, partly because the information is defective. The notion of Klopstock—the archsentimental author of the mid-eighteenth century biblical epic, *Der Messias*—as postmodernist poet is untenable. And the prescription for *Ulysses* combines two ideals, (hydrologic) flux and (geologic) layering, whose compatibility is open to serious question. In particular, the notorious Frankfurt edition of Hölderlin, which aroused a storm of public debate on the politics of editing, is precisely an attempt to produce an image of continual change in order to counter the layered text (based on a notion of determinate compositional process in stages) in the monumental Stuttgart edition that preceded it. Elsewhere McGann says that we live amid "an indeterminate flux of conflicted and competing possibilities" (*SV* 246). Here, by contrast, he claims that the number of forms of a given text "will always be a small number *in actual fact*" (*SV* 182) and that "unstable 'texts'—texts that are 'in process' or 'indeterminate'— always appear in material forms that are as determinate as the most 'stable' text one might want or imagine" (*SV* 186). Popular ballads are a counterinstance to the first claim, Verdi's operas to the second.[13] As so often in McGann, the polarities—modern versus postmodern, stable versus indeterminate—won't work. Where poetic movement is the concern, textual fixation comes to seem a regression, or a bulwark.

A bulwark against what? I find it curious that in listing Continental predecessors and in calling Gabler's *Ulysses* "the first English-language work to illustrate these new European lines" (*SV* 186), McGann neglects a well-established project closer to home, the Cornell Wordsworth edition. The omission is not in itself a statement, since McGann is a known admirer of the Cornell text. But it calls attention to his general slighting of Wordsworth, and that is significant. Chapter 8 of *The Romantic Ideology* presents Wordsworth as a representative of Romantic evasion and false consciousness. "Wordsworth's poetry elides history," he writes, as if the three poems discussed (*The Ruined Cottage, Tintern Abbey*, and the Immortality Ode) represented all that Wordsworth had to say (*RI* 91).[14]

Wordsworth also figures in the conclusion to *The Beauty of Inflections* as the exemplar of Romantic displacement (McGann's term for sublimation, viewed negatively), to be admired for the "resistances . . . dissatisfactions and yearnings" (*BI* 337) that hedge in his utopian individualism and psychologism. Another essay depreciates Wordsworth in order to praise Crabbe. Quantitatively, McGann's selections display an overwhelming preference for narrative poetry—for ballads or ballad-like lyrics. Lyric and reflective moments—the Wordsworthian inwardness—are kept on the margins or out of sight.

To read Wordsworthian displacement "as an invitation to substitute interiorized spiritual values for social ones is, in my view, a travesty of Wordsworth's work" (*BI* 340). I agree with the judgment here, but not with the terms. How does one distinguish interiorized spiritual values from social ones? Is not the lesson that we should draw from McGann's searchingly honest investigations that social values *are* spiritual, that the interior and the exterior are connected, that interpretation *is* critique, that reaction is a form of action, that thinkers are laborers, and that works work? The maker of the phrase, "the beauty of inflections," made other phrases that link up with it: "There is nothing beautiful in life except life." "It is life that we are trying to get at in poetry." "Art, broadly, is the form of life or the sound or color of life. Considered as form (in the abstract) it is often indistinguishable from life itself" (Stevens, "Adagia," 162, 158). McGann likes to present himself in an antithetical or polemical Blakean stance. But the separation of life from thought, or of the narrative from the reflective, is an unreflected abstraction. It is the ideological moment exposed through McGann's endeavors.[15]

Stanley Fish and others have argued that theories have no consequences.[16] That holds for abstract theories and intended consequences. A case in point would be "The Anachronism of George Crabbe" in *The Beauty of Inflections* 294–312. Here McGann describes the formal characteristics of Crabbe's poetry, which is additive, nontotalizing, nonredemptive, empiricist, and scientific—thereby, he contends, challenging idealist illusions that the Romantics share with the Augustans. To see that the conclusions do not follow simply from the abstract pattern, you need only consider John Clare, to whom all of these terms apply equally well, but who was an extreme Wordsworthian individualist.

Forms indeed do not have a life of their own, apart from the spirit that lives in their concrete embodiments. While consequences are all about us, they arise from complex insights, not from mere categories or denominations. In a writer such as Blake, absence "rises up before us . . . as objectivity and otherness" (*TLK* 36); without confidently knowing what we see, we can still advance toward knowledge through imagining what we do not see. The projected equivalence of literature and knowledge arises from literature's special power to subvert theories. Texts retain a richness always in advance of our invariably partial truths.

Despite itself, and through its failure to confront adequately the Romantic poet who should be central to it, McGann's work reveals the binding of form and content, substance and style, (hermeneutic) meaning and (ideological) meaning of meaning. Those interpenetrations are the Goethean essence of the totalizing ideal that McGann can never bring himself to renounce. He presents it in Lukácsian-sounding formulations such as "the critical ideal must be a totalizing one, for literary 'works' *continue* to live and move and have their being" (*SV* 125). But the polemical "must be" proves in practice to be an empathic "is"—a universal fact of our relation to the world:

For merely eyeing a thing is no help. Every look turns into a consideration, every consideration into a contemplation, every contemplation into a connection, and so it can be said that we always theorize with every attentive glance at the world. But to do and undertake this with consciousness, with self-knowledge, with freedom, and, to use a daring expression, with irony requires such a skill, if the abstraction that we fear is to become harmless and the desired result is to be alive and useful. (Goethe, *Zur Farbenlehre*, "Vorwort," *Werke* 21: 15)

Scratch the dialectician and you find the harmonizer. In Hugh Kenner's *The Pound Era*, "expository form . . . rhyme[s] with the complexities of its subjects" (*SV* ix). Arnold's "Sohrab and Rustum" is "a polyglottal text moaning round with many voices" (*SV* 89), but the effect is more a polyphony than a cacophony: "Arnold's book [*Poems* 1853] says one thing *and* (not *but*) means another" (*SV* 86). There is a "consonance between [Allen Tate's] interpretation of the Dickinson poem and his ignorance of its textual problems" (*BI* 130). "Tennyson's verse style and form exhibit a genuine congruence and symmetry with his methods of production" (*BI* 178). It is not by chance that one of the most brilliant of the essays demonstrates homologies among Don Juan's life, Byron's life, and the history of the French Revolution. Like the Kant whom he criticizes, McGann finally has a correspondence notion of truth: "That the poem should have been transmitted and finally published in this way is in perfect keeping with every other aspect of its text and context" (*BI* 101).

And in practice, the text remains *primus inter pares*. For, scratch the ideologist and you find the stylistician. If for McGann "the poem is a social act" (*BI* 21), it acts *as* a *poem*, and that means verbally, or, in the most extended of McGann's notions of the terms, as a text. That isn't always what McGann says, but I don't think he speaks clearly, consistently, or in his own best interest when he asserts that "it is not 'texts' which act in the world, it is the men and women who formulate and deploy those texts and who have assented to the textualization of their lives" (*SV* 16). For many of his greatest triumphs as a commentator are actually with words. His mastery lies in both the knowledge of and the feeling for words, inseparably mixed: the knowledge that Dickinson's plural "Horses Heads" indicates a funeral procession, not a bridal journey; the feel for the resonance of the word "world-wind" in a variant text of Keats's Paolo and Francesca sonnet; the knowing grasp of iconographic connotation in the wonderful reading of *The Charge of the Light Brigade*; the stylistic intuition to recognize that "bassoon" and "lighthouse" are anachronistically modern terms in *The Rime of the Ancient Mariner*—the crucial detail in McGann's historicizing account of that poem. Because he knows how saturated our languages are with meanings, with social values, and with history, McGann regularly and powerfully makes the totality of poetic acts depend on such punctual responses.

Like virtually all the poets with whom he has identified himself particularly, McGann is a connoisseur. His admiration goes out to the living world of incommensurates that are found on the textured surface of things. He is a great connoisseur because his tact is controlled by vast and exact knowledge and empowered by ideological sophistication. He knows how to make the precise details that act on him count for us as well. As editor and as critic, he takes his mission to be saving the past. Distinctions and recognitions go hand in hand as we channel past energies toward the future. "Thus," concludes the most theoretical of the essays in the earlier book, "in our differences do we learn about, and create, a community" (*BI* 132). On the one hand, as McGann has written more recently, the contexts in which we operate are entailed on us historically: "For human beings, to enter the world is to enter language—a world that is always-changing but ever-determinate and concrete, and a world no *one* ever made or could have made" (*BR* 140). Yet on the other hand the life world is one crucially begotten by our poets: "It is a (social) world made by (and discovered as) language, through unceasing acts of textual intercourse" (*BR* 140). Unlike the Renaissance New Historicists whom I discuss at the end of my chapter on Taine, McGann (together with Levinson, David Simpson, and a host of younger Romanticists) finds the resources to save the power of the word. What's in a text is the social activism of its temporality.

PART III

Texts and Periods

CHAPTER 4

Deconstruction and Enlightenment

Whither wander you?
—Shakespeare, *A Midsummer Night's Dream*
Whither wander we (*Kuda zh nam plyt'*)?
—Pushkin, *Osen'*

ROMANTICISTS HAVE BEEN the main disseminators of the various French theoretical modes in this country. American scholars consequently tend to link the two, as Jerome Christensen has done with deconstruction in an essay subtitled "The Apostasy of Criticism": "The deconstructive method makes a neat fit with the Coleridgean text—a fit so neat as to suggest a propriety for deconstruction in Coleridge" (771). This Romantic-deconstructive organism is our apostasy: "The critic is always the author of the text he reads . . . : this state of affairs is not necessarily so, but it has ever been so since Coleridge." Christensen, the critic, authored this text (781); Coleridge as the arch-deconstructor is a typically American rewriting of history.

First, a reminder. Jacques Derrida made his reputation with a book on Rousseau. Gilles Deleuze began with books on Kant, Hume, and Spinoza. Michel Foucault's thesis was on Kant, Michel Serres's on Leibniz. Roland Barthes's renown dates from his book on Racine—a neoclassicist, marginally an Enlightenment figure, certainly no Romantic. One could go back, to Claude Lévi-Strauss's debt to Rousseau, to Gaston Bachelard's beginnings as a critic of eighteenth-century science. And one could extend the list: Kant is seminal for Jacques Lacan and Jean-François Lyotard, Casanova for François Roustang. Kant and Rousseau straddle the eras but hardly the centuries; the impulse for all these theorists comes from Enlightenment and eighteenth-century authors.

Second, a reflection. To apply an Enlightenment model to a Romantic text is hard work. Most American deconstructionists—Geoffrey Hartman is the notable exception—work hard, even laboriously, at disrupting their exemplary texts. A favorite term is aporia, the pathlessness of a self-canceling argument. Reason against reason. Serious business; exhilarating, heady, even dizzy stuff.[1]

Eighteenth-century texts, large or small, are loose and baggy. They meander of their own accord, succeeding at picaresque expansiveness, failing at tragic concentration. Deconstruction comes naturally to them. Too easily, in fact. Many areas of eighteenth-century criticism are still caught up in the hard task of trying to structure them, logically, organically. I propose that we unbend. We may remember some things about the eighteenth century that we had forgotten, and learn some things about critical theory at the same time.

Third, an example. One doesn't prove anything, but it's all I have space for. Not even for one: there's so much to say about how Thomas Parnell's *A Night-Piece on Death* undoes its premises. Illogic is ubiquitous—if we are taken in by Pope's "Whatever is, is right," we are destined to be taken aback by another, equally memorable locus, "What's wrong is wrong, wherever it be done" (Pope, *Sober Advice from Horace* 78)—the trick is to find what is born of reason's collapse. *A Night-Piece on Death*, like so many texts, "is a falling away from itself that is a reading of itself, falling to know its constitution, falling to know the course of its descent—a narcissism providentially flawed by the apostasis that motivates a theoretically endless tracking." Christensen says this of the margins that unravel the *Biographia Literaria* (777), but Parnell says it too, plain as day, at the climax of *A Hymn on Contentment:*

> Go search among your idle Dreams [narcissism],
> Your busie or your vain Extreams [falling away from itself];
> And find a *Life* of equal Bliss [providentially flawed apostasis,
>   unless you can live up to your dreams],
> Or own the *next* begun in *this* [theoretically endless tracking].

Not convincing? You think celestial wisdom calms Parnell's mind too easily?

Easy does it. Tetrameters jog so nicely. That "or own" could be a consequence (own = acknowledge), or it could be a threat (own = confess). Not to worry. Tetrameters offer "a readier Path" (*Night-Piece*, like all unidentified quotes), a fallen wisdom ("Where Wisdom's surely taught *below*"— "surely," is that for certain?), adapted to night's dim vision, a "blinded insight" (Christensen 778; Parnell has, "That Steeple guides thy doubtful sight"). Colloquy leads to conviction, with the tune called by internal and external voices, bells, even croaks. But salvation can't be colloquial. The style can't free itself from quiet tropes, figures, sound effects, heightenings (note the Latinism "aspire"). The "deep . . . Sky," the "nether Crescent," "the spangled Show [that] / Descends to meet our Eyes below"—everything heaves and swells with a bad faith that looks up indirectly or with a pretense of looking down. Fuzzy is about the best you could say of Parnell's dialectic. The first two paragraphs contrast as indoors to outdoors, sky to earth, artificial to natural illumination. But what's the difference? One is "blue," the other "Azure." One light trembles, the other gleams lividly. One is "endless View," the other "from the View retire[s]." Surely, "surely," treading the path of death is not the clearest road to go. Is it, indeed, the path of death, or "the path of death"—the experience of death itself ("Death's but a Path that must be trod"—but is this utterance, or imaginary utterance, the content of the wisdom, or just the way to get there?), or a guided tour of the premises ("And think, as softly-sad you tread / Above the venerable Dead")? Confusion heaped on confusion. A "crumbled Ground" for "glancing Thought," if ever there was. Revelation comes—is that really how Parnell thinks "Wisdom's . . . taught *below*"?—but it doesn't help much. "The bursting earth unveils"—what?—"the Shades." "I hear a *Voice*," he says . . . "Methinks." Surely, "surely," this hesitancy isn't how wisdom teaches, even "from among the Bones."

So you get nowhere? Not quite. Not at all. By the end, Parnell is standing on his head, looking up at the earth ("tow'r away") instead of down at the sky. From the scholastic prison he turned to nightlife; now from the earthly prison (whose "Lamps" are stars, both like and unlike the beginning) he turns to "the Blaze of Day." Those sour scholastic books "widely stray," but, now, "See the glad Scene unfolding wide." How did we get here?

How did we get here? That's the question to be asked by a speculative criticism. Logic abandons us, but something takes us along. Parnell's flow starts punningly, with "pore" and "dies" (i.e., dyes), gingerly with "glide," but soon water is all about him. Flow is an advantage tetrameters possess over pentameters, so much more inclined to turn back on themselves. But then flow swells into a tempest vexing Parnell's decreation, "the rough Rage of swelling Seas." Flux becomes the realm of death, "flowing sable Stoles, / Deep pendant Cypress." And of release: "Spring forth to greet the glitt'ring Sun."

The image washes out the conceptual ground until "earth" seems a waste ("A few, and evil Years"). Yet isn't that natural for a cemetery, a "Charnel House" bathed "with Dew"? *Night-Thoughts* will do, so will *The Grave*, but *A Night-Piece on Death* is too much of a bad thing, one darkness canceling out the other. So, from out the logical collapse, the image takes charge, transforming itself as it goes. Self-identity, Johann Gottlieb Fichte's *A = A*, is the enabling fiction of Romanticism; from Parnell, by contrast, we get a moving picture. To "mingle with the Blaze of Day" is to experience aporia as consolation—none too easy a liberation after all. Deconstruction and the other poststructuralisms—for us modes melt together, mingling in the blaze from the East, that at a nearer, Parisian view, seems irreconcilable—are change, flow, overthrow. Deconstruction is death, is life, is history. It is the most natural, colloquial substratum of thought, not to be wondered at, though the Romantics bravely tried to face it down, packing history away in their spots of time and their Grecian urns. Theirs is the apostasy from, not of, deconstruction, and deconstruction takes its revenge on them in American criticism, appearing as a *Triumph of Life* that is also an *Arrêt de mort*. (Those are the joint pre-texts for Derrida's 1979 American essay, only belatedly [1986] published in French, "Living On: Border Lines.")

Living on is Derrida's one great theme, together with the diverse images that make living on possible when logic is dethroned. And death is the ground of living on: "It is thus the relation to *my death* (to my disappearance in general) which is hidden in this determination of being as presence, ideality, absolute possibility of repetition. The possibility of the sign is this relation to death. . . . *I am* thus means at the origin *I am mortal*" (*La Voix* 60–61, and see 44, 108, 114). Derrida says it thus early; he reiterates it in *Glas*; he bases his nuclear criticism on it, and much else besides (92b).[2] "They pierce my thickets, through my grot they glide" (Pope): here already deconstruction is joined to flow, with the heavy and complex dose of sexuality that the French teach us to recognize. That looks like the enemy, but it's all part of "this long disease, my life." It's not a cavalier acceptance of mortality that Derrida is after, but still it's less traumatic than the presumed Romantic timelessness, "the trance of literature" (Christensen, 784). Foucault talks more about death than

Derrida, and not all that differently at the moments when he remembers that discourse is discursive, flow and not stasis.

The issue, at the last, is the Enlightenment of death. That's an ambiguous phrase, one way of specifying the end of Enlightenment, but not in any event its undoing, which comes later, with the Romantic death of Enlightenment. For Romanticists deconstruction is a spiritual pugilism that topples claims of authority.

> Die abgestorbne Eiche steht im Sturm
> Doch die gesunde stürzt er schmetternd nieder,
> Weil er in ihre Krone greifen kann.
>
> (Kleist, *Penthesilea* 3041–43)

Less imperious, enlightened deconstruction takes the part of the uncrowned oak. Its activity is hermeneutic rather than critical: it uncovers and teaches the ruses by means of which death survives after all.[3] Let us not encounter as an adversary what should come to us in a spirit of consolation. The same knell tolls in Derrida as in the enlightened graveyard, calling to reckoning the currents that link death and life, the past and the present. Indulge me if I dub their affinity with the exemplary appellation of . . . par-knell.

A Night-Piece on Death

By the blue Tapers trembling Light,
No more I waste the wakeful Night,
Intent with endless view to pore
The Schoolmen and the Sages o'er:
Their Books from Wisdom widely stray,
Or point at best the longest Way.
I'll seek a readier Path, and go
Where Wisdom's surely taught *below*.

How deep yon Azure dies the Sky!
Where Orbs of Gold unnumber'd lye,
While thro' their Ranks in silver pride
The nether Crescent seems to glide.
The slumb'ring Breeze forgets to breathe,
The Lake is smooth and clear beneath,
Where once again the spangled Show
Descends to meet our Eyes below.
The Grounds which on the right aspire,
In dimness from the View retire:
The Left presents a Place of Graves,
Whose Wall the silent Water laves.
That Steeple guides thy doubtful sight
Among the livid gleams of Night.
There pass with melancholy State,
By all the solemn Heaps of Fate,
And think, as softly-sad you tread
Above the venerable Dead,
Time was, like thee they Life possest,
And Time shall be, that thou shalt Rest.

Those Graves, with bending Osier bound,
That nameless heave the crumbled Ground,
Quick to the glancing Thought disclose
Where *Toil* and *Poverty* repose.

The flat smooth Stones that bear a Name,
The Chissels slender help to Fame,
(Which e'er our Sett of Friends decay
Their frequent Steps may wear away.)
A *middle Race* of Mortals own,
Men, half ambitious, all unknown.

The Marble Tombs that rise on high,
Whose Dead in vaulted Arches lye,
Whose Pillars swell with sculptur'd Stones,
Arms, Angels, Epitaphs and Bones,
These (all the poor Remains of State)
Adorn the *Rich*, or praise the *Great*;
Who while on Earth in Fame they live,
Are sensless of the Fame they give.

Ha! while I gaze, pale *Cynthia* fades,
The bursting Earth unveils the Shades!
All slow, and wan, and wrap'd with Shrouds,
They rise in visionary Crouds,
And all with sober Accent cry,
Think, Mortal, what it is to dye.

Now from yon black and fun'ral Yew,
That bathes the Charnel House with Dew,
Methinks I hear a *Voice* begin;
(Ye Ravens, cease your croaking Din,
Ye tolling Clocks, no Time resound
O'er the long Lake and midnight Ground)
It sends a Peal of hollow Groans,
Thus speaking from among the Bones.

When Men my Scythe and Darts supply,
How great a *King* of *Fears* am I!
They view me like the last of Things:
They make, and then they dread, my Stings.
Fools! if you less provok'd your Fears,
No more my Spectre-Form appears.
Death's but a Path that must be trod,
If Man wou'd ever pass to God:
A Port of Calms, a State of Ease
From the rough Rage of swelling Seas.

Why then thy flowing sable Stoles,
Deep pendent Cypress, mourning Poles,
Loose Scarfs to fall athwart thy Weeds,
Long Palls, drawn Herses, cover'd Steeds,
And Plumes of black, that as they tread,
Nod o'er the 'Scutcheons of the Dead?

Nor can the parted Body know,
Nor wants the Soul, these Forms of Woe:
As men who long in Prison dwell,
With Lamps that glimmer round the Cell,
When e'er their suffering Years are run,
Spring forth to greet the glitt'ring Sun:
Such Joy, tho' far transcending Sense,
Have pious Souls at parting hence.
On Earth, and in the Body plac't,
A few, and evil Years, they wast:
But when their Chains are cast aside,
See the glad Scene unfolding wide,
Clap the glad Wing and tow'r away,
And mingle with the Blaze of Day.

CHAPTER 5

Mozart and After

The Revolution in Musical Consciousness

THE 1780'S WERE MARKED not only by political revolution but also by Kant's "second Copernican revolution" in philosophy and by the beginnings of a revolutionary change in literary style.[1] In at least one characteristic aspect, the origins of the musical style that we know as Romantic are to be found in the same decade and can be analyzed in exactly the same terms.

Kant's revolution was initiated by a new concept of the nature of consciousness. As the first readers of the *Critique of Pure Reason* (1781) immediately appreciated, Kant's starting point was a reversal of priorities. In the then-dominant tradition of Locke, consciousness was held to follow on perception. The mind begins empty, as a tabula rasa; it fills itself by attending to sensations which reach it from the external world. Consciousness, for Locke, is not awareness of self; instead, it is taking cognizance of what lies outside the mind. Indeed, before the 1780's it was not even possible to say, simply, "I am conscious" but only, "I am conscious of *x*." Kant began by exchanging the positions of consciousness and sensation. In his system consciousness precedes sensation, and he argues that meaningful sensations are possible only if a well-defined consciousness already exists to perceive them. Logically speaking, we must be aware of ourselves before we can become aware of anything outside us; we must be conscious in general before we become conscious of anything in particular; we must be conscious of ourselves internally—and for Kant that means in time—before we can become conscious of any objects or orientations in space. The details of this part of Kant's system are, of course, vastly more complex, but for the present analysis these elements suffice: Kant posits an indefinite, infolded, temporal self-consciousness which determines the forms (or "categories") of perception prior to any particular, structured, external acts of perception.

Literary Romanticism likewise began by isolating or discovering a state of pure undifferentiated self-consciousness. Certain well-known texts from the 1780's, often imitated and enormously influential, depict an unformed sense of self, cut off from external perceptions and entirely comparable to Kantian self-consciousness. Kant considers such a state merely a logical possibility, but these texts and their later offshoots treat it as an empirical state that can be really experienced and therefore concretely described. The fifth of Rousseau's *Reveries of a Solitary Wanderer* (1782) contains perhaps the most famous early description of the experiential origin of this "feeling of existence stripped of any other sentiment":

The noise of the waves and the agitation of the water fastening my senses and chasing all other agitation from my soul plunged it into a delicious reverie where night often surprised me without my being aware of it. The ebb and flow of this water, its noise, continuous but swelling by intervals, striking without respite my ear and my eyes substituted for the internal movements which the reverie extinguished in me and sufficed to make me feel my existence with pleasure, without taking the trouble to think. (*Oeuvres* 1: 1045)

Nothing is heard or seen in this state except an ongoing rhythmic pulse, flickering in intensity and lacking any more definite shape. Time is felt but not measured, and no effort of thought imposes an order, a center, or a meaning on the flow of sensations. Such is a general picture of a state of mind that may be called by various names: pure or primitive consciousness, preconsciousness, reverie, daydream, or ecstasy. With some variation, such states were also described, for the most part independently and without mutual influence, by a number of other leading writers of the decade, including the philosopher Thomas Reid and the poet William Cowper in England, the novelist Jacques-Henri Bernardin de Saint-Pierre in France, and the prose writer Wilhelm Heinse and the young poet Goethe in Germany.

What emerges in both the literature and the music of the 1780's is not only a new type of experience but also a new conception of form. No longer does consciousness begin with external perception or artistic form with inherited convention; now the basic structural orientation is generated from within, from the flow of time. As we read in an early review of Beethoven's Choral Fantasia, such a form is "the monologue of the artist, the pure expression of his own, personal feelings, whereas his relation to set forms—opera, oratorio, etc.—is a dialogue in which he can only deliver what is occasioned by the given forms."[2] Rather than beginning with an unmistakable tonic chord or a forthright statement of the principal theme or subject, musical reveries of this type proceed gradually from dark confusion to clarity and reason. Normally characterized by an audible pulse but no clearly articulated meter, and often characterized by an absence of clear tonal focus as well, they generate the fundamental organizing categories of the piece while seeming to lack a clear organization of their own. The opening bars of Beethoven's Ninth Symphony are a classic example. Some further excerpts from the review of the Choral Fantasia will illustrate how this principle of structure was perceived after it had become somewhat familiar:

This Fantasia opens . . . not without chaotic confusion which causes the listener at first to fear that the spirit [der Geist] might lose itself in self-absorption and, wholly dissipated, never emerge into daylight. This can be imagined as the preface to the career of the artist's life. Pictures and dreams chase and pursue one another, lose themselves in the tightly woven choreography, and the development remains latent—self-consciousness still seems to be lacking. . . . A brief allegro, destined merely as a cadence and transition to the succeeding chorus, closes the Fantasia, which now proceeds to actual words—as the genius which has now arrived at self-consciousness hastens to display itself in the utmost clarity. (78–79)

Reveries such as I have been describing are rare and pioneering innovations in the 1780's and become increasingly common thereafter. Furthermore, the condition of reverie came more and more to be described for its own sake rather than as the prelude to some ordinary, waking consciousness. By the middle of the nineteenth century, many independent "moodpieces" were written which were not subordinated to any larger structure. In literature the prose poems of Thomas de Quincey, Charles Baudelaire, and Louis Bertrand come to mind, the poems of Eduard Mörike and Annette von Droste-Hülshoff, or the dream sequences in the fiction of Emily Brontë, Nathaniel Hawthorne, and Charles Dickens. In music the moodpiece first reaches independent status in Beethoven's

Bagatelles and in Schubert's late songs, and after Schumann and Chopin it is ubiquitous. Before turning to Mozart and the origins of this phenomenon, I would like to review some later examples in order to ascertain the technical musical equivalents of the preconscious reverie and to illustrate the various means available to reach definably similar effects.

Since the presence of a text helps to validate the correspondence of musical and literary forms, I begin my characterization of musical reverie with a song, Schumann's setting of Lynkeus's song from Goethe's *Faust* (Example 1). Lynkeus is a dreamlike character in a dream vision, an alien survivor from antiquity in the medieval world. Though in theory a watchman, in practice he is completely self-involved, seeing (as the text tells us) only what he wishes to see and what is eternal and not the destructive events actually occurring around him while he sings. Since he sings offstage, the song may well be called the disembodied reverie of a timeless, "pure" consciousness. The musical expression corresponding to Lynkeus's text is marked by the following devices, among others. The first half of the melody is a repeated phrase played without harmonization. The piano plays the melody in treble and bass, two octaves apart, its hollow sonorities underlining the absence of harmonic definition. In addition, every note of the scale is sounded before the middle of bar 3 except the leading tone A, which is the crucial note for defining the key. The continuation of the melody is harmonized but cadences strongly in the wrong key, F instead of B-flat. The song also cadences in G minor and C minor and crashes into a deceptive cadence on the first inversion of the D-minor triad. Finally the vocal line comes to rest on the tonic, and the piano postlude has two further cadences that also reach the tonic but by plagal progressions so weak they undermine the tonic effect. What this amounts to, in less technical language, is that Schumann characterizes the dreamlike Lynkeus by means of notably drifting tonality. The rhythmic impulse is likewise weak: the dominant rhythm is a monotonously lilting dotted figure, with the piano initially reinforcing the offbeats with extra notes (and thus weakening the impulse). Thus the rhythm, like the harmonization, is unsettled, constantly in motion, and shapeless, a flowing duration without direction or dramatic intensity.

Schumann is not alone in furnishing a programmatic text to accompany his musical reverie. A more famous and almost equally decisive example is the prelude to Wagner's *Rheingold*. For 136 bars Wagner

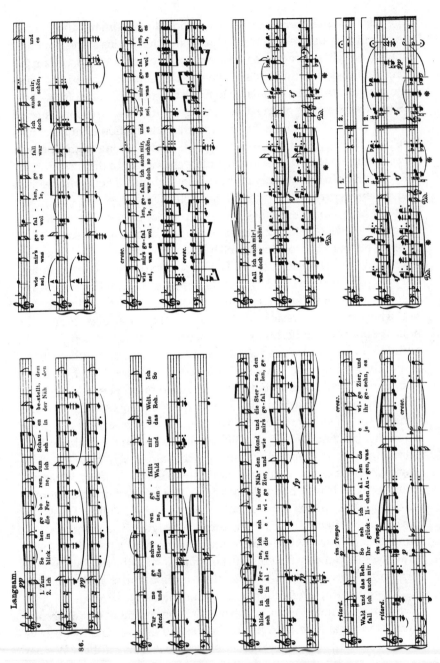

Example 1. Lied Lynkeus des Türmers, by Robert Schumann.

sustains an unvaried E-flat-major chord, devoid of either harmonic or melodic development. The tonality and meter are determinate, but only passively; there is nothing external to the central root chord and simple rhythmic pulsation. One critic has described this moment of fluid inwardness before the action begins as "timeless" music, an "account of the origins of consciousness" (Donington, Wagner's "Ring" 38, 36). But Wagner's own well-known description of the inspiration for the prelude is, if possible, even more to the point.

I sank into a kind of somnambulistic state in which I suddenly received the sensation of submerging under a powerful current of water. I soon imagined the rustling of the water in the musical sound of an E-flat-major chord breaking in waves of continual arpeggios; these appeared as melodic figurations of increasing importance, but with no change in the pure E-flat-major triad, whose endurance seemed to attribute an infinite significance to the element in which I was submerged. . . . I quickly comprehended just what my situation was: the current of life should flow toward me from within, not from without. (*Mein Leben, Schriften* 15: 68)

Throughout the nineteenth century, harmonic and rhythmic vagueness reflect the generation of form from within rather than its imposition from without. And where a program can be attributed to these musical techniques, it is associated with dreamy or abnormal states of mind. It can be the "wave of passions" pouring over the opium dreamer at the opening of Berlioz's *Symphonie fantastique*. It can be the momentary anxiety—marked *beklemmt* ("anxious" or "short of breath")—when the first violin finds itself playing in a different key and meter from the other instruments in the cavatina of Beethoven's Quartet, opus 130. Alternatively, it can be the pure ethereal bliss of the "holy song of thanksgiving of one recovered from illness" in his A-Minor Quartet, opus 132. In this quartet extreme slowness renders the beat almost inaudible, and the unusual Lydian mode (whose scale is that of C major but whose tonic is F) frustrates the ordinary sense of key, until the convalescent moves toward normal activity in the harmonically clear and metrically forceful sections marked *neue Kraft fühlend* ("feeling new force").

Such explicit programmatic associations justify attributing to other works equally specific but implicit correspondences of musical and psychological structures. Thus Edward Cone has associated the tantalizing

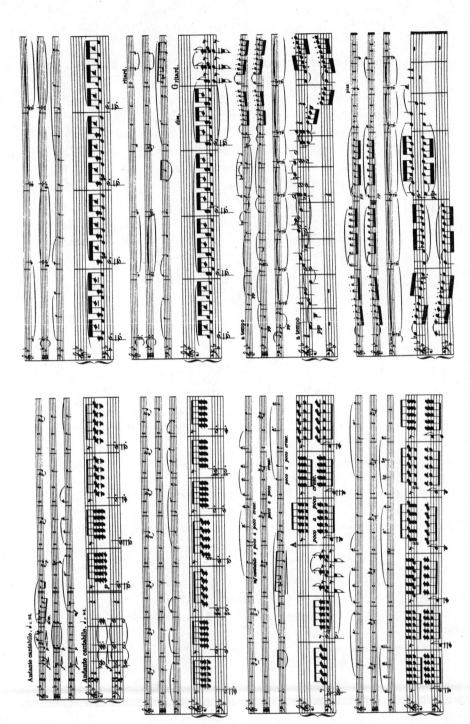

Example 2. Schumann Piano Quartet, Andante, beginning (left) and end (right).

harmonic mysteries of Brahms's Intermezzo, opus 118, no. 1, with the characteristic atmosphere of detective stories ("Three Ways of Reading"). By late in the century, the spontaneous, inward, and variable pulse of reverie becomes the norm rather than the exception, just as the three-volume novel comes to be an art of natural time in authors as disparate as Adalbert Stifter and Anthony Trollope, just as a self-absorbed timelessness becomes the characteristic stance in painting from Courbet onward, and, finally, just as the inner sense which is the ground of consciousness for Kant is generalized into the all-embracing *temps vécu* of Henri Bergson.

Before returning to the sources of these musical gestures in Mozart, I would like to discuss one final Romantic reverie, the exquisite slow movement of Schumann's Piano Quartet, which distills many of the elements I have been describing (Example 2). The key, B-flat major, is unambiguous, but the mood remains dreamy because of the unceasing yet unemphatic rhythmic pulse. The instruments enter in midtheme, as if discovering a subsisting flow, and the unbroken quarter-note pulse is maintained by dovetailing: each statement of the theme begins before the previous statement has concluded. The overlapping is reinforced for most of the movement (including the middle section) by canonic treatment of the theme. The theme itself proceeds by stepwise motion, but its simple directionality is undermined by displacements in register: up a seventh in the middle of descents, down a seventh in the middle of ascents. The opening also features a subtle rhythmic effect. The violin and viola play accompaniment notes on the third beat of each bar. The viola plays a quarter note, the violin a quarter preceded by a grace note. The violin's grace note is the same pitch as the viola's note. The result is that the note is heard twice, an instant apart, in slightly differing timbres. There is a minute eddy in the pulse; the meter is regular, continuous, yet not rigidly rationalized.

These are some of the devices that give the movement its dreamy quality. The movement is especially noteworthy, however, for the clarification at the end, as if a preconscious state were yielding to a conscious one. The canon is over, and the final statement of the theme is simple, without overlapping. The rhythmic eddy gives way early in the movement to syncopations, a more measurable kind of turbulence; at the end only a residual swaying remains in the notes, two bars long, which the violin and viola shift in turn, one instrument at the beginning of each bar. Alternation is now made to work in support of the meter rather than against it. Then, suddenly, the last eight bars of the movement replace the archaic arioso mode by rapid scales in contrary motion in the style of Beethoven: music history has come alive along with the unexpected animation. And under the whole, as the ground above which this clarification and awakening occur, the cello holds a tonic pedal tone, B-flat, for thirteen measures. This note is remarkable, for it requires tuning the lowest string down from C to B-flat just before entering. Thus the cellist plays a note which, ordinarily, does not exist, an ethereal fundamental whose entry into musical reality initiates the striking *prise de conscience* with which the reverie concludes.

Customarily only small, independent musical forms are identified as reveries, but this obscures both their function and their origins. There is a tendency to see in these small pieces only a negative or ironic import—a denial of classical norms—and to trace them back to Beethoven's Bagatelles, relatively minor pieces whose small notoriety in no way corresponds to the impact claimed for them.[3] Such a view renders a positive account of the musical reverie unfeasible: it becomes impossible to say convincingly what composers of reveries were trying to do or what models they were trying to implement. The historical picture immediately becomes clearer if we view the reverie as a musical gesture rather than as a form: a harmonic and metric uncertainty or openness which may occur in a passing episode, introduce a movement, or shape a whole piece. The function of the reverie is not simply to loosen classical bonds but to explore a whole range of formal possibilities unknown to classical experience. Historically the reverie emerged from within classical form and only gradually emancipated itself. I chose the slow movement of the Schumann Piano Quartet for analysis partly because it shows the reverie at a moment of transition. A typical extended Schumann *Träumerei* closed off by a classicizing conclusion, it is a nearly independent reverie that demonstrates the emergence of Romantic small forms out of the late-classical introduction.

Versions of the metric and harmonic inwardness of the Romantic reverie can be found in many classical-period introductions. Even a relatively simple introduction like that to Beethoven's First Symphony illustrates the form: it begins in the wrong key, juxtaposing long-held wind chords with the instantaneous sound of string pizzicatos, and only gradually works around to the C-major tonic key and develops an audible metric definition. It was Mozart, however, who composed the introductory reverie that had by far the greatest influence and renown: the introduction to the so-called *Dissonance* Quartet in C Major (K. 465) of 1785 (Example 3). An object of controversy almost from its composition, so puzzling harmonically and metrically that the powerful academician François-Joseph Fétis was led to propose a notorious correction in 1829, this piece exhibits the precise preromantic characteristics of the gradual emergence of form out of the preconscious, indistinct, throbbing pulse of time. Indeed, the authoritative Mozart biographer, Hermann Abert, has compared the quartet to "the picture of a mind weighed down by gloomy forebodings and striving to master its spiritual oppression." "In the introduction," he continues, "this process does not leave the stage of unconsciousness. Only in the allegro does the composer open his eyes, so to speak, and pursue the battle consciously" (*Mozart* 2: 145–46).[4] Among the numerous compositions directly inspired by this quartet was the musical depiction of chaos at the beginning of Haydn's *Creation*. I would now like to describe the gradual emergence of conscious form out of chaos in the *Dissonance* Quartet itself by examining in closer detail the meter, tonality, sonority, and genre of its introduction.

Meter. The introduction opens quietly, with an eighth-note pulse in the cello alone. The other instruments enter in canonical imitation on different beats. Thus, no beat is established as the principal one; there is a sense of time but no definite audible organization of the bar.[5] The ongoing regular pulse is subject to a further, almost painful disorientation in the middle of the introduction (bars 13–15). Here the two violins and the cello have imitative descending chromatic runs; the metric values are highly irregular, with each part showing a different distribution of long, medium, and short notes, an aural confusion compounded by uncomfortable harmonic intervals (seconds and parallel fourths). At the end (bars 19–22), rhythmic irregularity is systematized and thus brought a step closer to regularity: the violins play in ¾ meter, with an accent marked at the bar line, while the lower instruments play in what sounds like a displaced ⁶⁄₈, with an accent marked in the middle of the written bar and no note coinciding with the bar line. Thus, the stages leading to

Example 3. Mozart Dissonance Quartet, introduction.

the allegro are (1) empty pulse, (2) confused meter, and (3) polyrhythm, with two distinct meters in conflict. The common time of the allegro at last resolves the conflict: it divides both bar and beat into two parts and sublimates the asymmetrical triple rhythms into the three-note upbeats which are prominent throughout the first subject.

Tonality. The irregular harmonies and cross-relations that give the quartet its name are so obvious as not to need analysis here. I would point only to the gradual clarification of the tonality. Charles Rosen has claimed that features such as the Neapolitan D-flat in bar 5 and the E-naturals of bars 7–9 render the C-major tonality unambiguous almost from the very beginning of the piece (*Classical Style* 186, amplified in conversation). But the implicit tonality only becomes fully explicit from bar 13, where the dominant-seventh chord prevails. And throughout the middle of the introduction, the mode grows less certain: in bars 9–18 no less than fourteen E-flats are heard as opposed to only three passing Es. Only in the closing bars (19–22) does E-flat give way to E-natural (accented in the viola part). In addition, C-sharps are now heard in both violin parts and repeatedly, with accents, in the cello part; the sharps give these bars a strongly dominant coloration and a predominantly rising movement, correcting the subdominant coloration and downward movement of the middle section.[6] To be sure, minor episodes are not uncommon in classical-period introductions, but most often they fall between clearly demarcated, harmonically stable major-key areas. The introduction to the *Dissonance* Quartet is innovative in that it moves from harmonic obscurity through the harmonic instability of the C-minor episode and establishes the ultimate C-major tonality only after a struggle (the emphatic repetitions in bars 19–22).

Sonority. The opening cello note is unprecedented and cannily chosen. It is the C below middle C, the first harmonic on the cello's lowest string. The note may be played as a harmonic on the C string (a fingering given in some editions) or as a stopped note on the G string; in the latter case, the harmonic will still be present, vibrating sympathetically. Either alternative yields approximately the same effect: the continuous resonance of the C string helps attenuate the softly pulsating rhythm, while a "hollow" sound results from the harmonic whose fundamental tone is lacking. Thus, the quartet opens with an absent foundation, an ethereal effect symmetrical to that of the Schumann Piano Quartet, where a normally unheard fundamental becomes audible at the end.[7] The allegro supplies what is lacking in the sonority, just as it does in the meter and the tonality. The first compensation is indirect: the cello is silent during the first statement of the opening theme while the bass is supplied by repeated middle Cs on the viola. This note is analogous to the opening cello note since it is an octave above the viola's lowest string, but on a different instrument and at a different speed the articulation sounds precise and well supported rather than ethereal. The cello's fundamental open C is heard six times later in the movement at key points: as the very first note in the cello part and twice when the recapitulation begins; accented at the start of the bridge passage to the second subject (that is, as a send-off to the tonic before the customary modulation into the dominant); at the beginning of the dramatic bridge to the coda; and as the very last note in the part.

Genre. The gradual awakening that opens the Dissonance Quartet is all the more striking for being found in a string quartet, for this had become the most intimate of the musical genres. Whereas introductory fanfares and (slightly later) slow introductions were common in symphonic music as a means of alerting the audience and publicly announcing the tonality, they were rare in quartets, where the key signature is the only announcement needed. A slow introduction in a quartet thus would tend to have the opposite expressive function from one in a symphony: in the symphony the introduction makes a declaration (to the audience); in the quartet it serves to suspend or question a declaration which has already been made (to the players). The symphonic introduction is extroverted; the quartet introduction introverted. These are only generalizations, of course, and need to be tested in each individual case, but in fact no other quartet by Mozart has a comparable slow introduction (the early K. 171 has a slow-fast-slow overture form in the first movement), only one later Haydn quartet has such an introduction, and among Beethoven's quartets none has it before the ninth (opus 59, no. 3), a work in C major whose form derives in this respect from Mozart's example.[8] Thus, Mozart's unique slow introduction calls the genre into question, just as it does the tonality. The form is not given from without by conventional fiat but is engendered uniquely from within. And if this change first occurs in the most intimate of musical forms, it corresponds precisely to the revolutionary innovations of Rousseau's political theory and of Kant's philosophy, according to which social cohesion and universal truths likewise must be regenerated on the basis of the priority of the individual. The welding of four throbbing adagio voices into a harmonious allegro is Mozart's social contract.

The other essentially private musical genre is the solo keyboard sonata. None of Mozart's piano sonatas was written with a slow introduction. But a few months after the C-Major Quartet, as an afterthought, Mozart wrote a long Fantasia (K. 475) to preface the C-Minor Sonata (K. 457): this Fantasia is the other famous Mozartean example of the structural revolution I have been analyzing (Example 4). It is, as Rosen writes, "truly abnormal by classical standards," not lacking in large-scale tonal patterns but so restless that it frustrates the desire for audible tonal focus at almost every point (*Classical Style* 92). The opening four bars, indeed, are almost note for note a simplified (and hence even more ambiguous) harmonic sketch of the opening four bars of the quartet. In the remainder of the piece, the sustained harmonic turbulence is generally associated with falling movements (as is also the case in the *Dissonance* Quartet). The Fantasia develops increasingly into a combat of rising and falling movements, until at the end the tonal clarification is accompanied by the final triumph of ascending figures, as the left hand plays the only two measured ascending chromatic scales in the piece (bars 3–4 from the end) and then (rather as in the Schumann Piano Quartet) the tonic scale is heard, a loud, three-octave C-minor scale in the right hand, in the very last bar.[9]

Ambiguity or uncertainty is common in the opening of major compositions of the 1780's and even more so in Haydn's introductions in the 1790's. The two works I have discussed are, in one sense, different only in degree, not in kind. The intensification of a common gesture does, however, ultimately amount to a difference in kind: instead of confiding wit, there is a feeling of disembodied distance; instead of dramatic expectancy, there is the self-sufficiency of a slow, seemingly directionless flow.[10] The hypothesis that these two works were felt to have initiated something new is corroborated by the fact that for a long time the preponderance of compositions opening with a chaotic or dreamlike introduction were also in the key of C: the list includes Haydn's *Creation*; Beethoven's First and Fifth Symphonies, *Coriolanus* Overture, Choral Fantasia, Quartet, opus 59, no. 3, and Piano Sonata, opus 111;

FANTASIA.

Example 4. Mozart Fantasia (K. 475).

Schubert's Fourth Symphony and his song "Die Stadt"; and Berlioz's *Symphonie fantastique*.[11] The series of avatars and variants ends, perhaps, with Brahms's First Symphony. Like Mozart's *Dissonance* Quartet (and Berlioz's *Symphonie fantastique*), Brahms's work opens with an eighth-note pulse on a single tone. But unlike Mozart's ghostly solo cello, the pulse (three octaves, forte and pesante, simultaneously in contrabassoon, string bass, and tympany) gives a powerful foundation to a crashing four-octave C sustained by the rest of the orchestra and then to predominantly rising progressions, somewhat chromatic but completely unambiguous in key. Brahms's symphony is a refutation of Mozart's budding Romanticism, a return to an uncompromisingly classic stance.

We do not ordinarily think of Mozart as a revolutionary composer but rather as a "pure" classical genius, affiliated stylistically with Haydn. In the later nineteenth century, he was often compared with Raphael or with the "naive" Goethe.[12] But in his own day—when he was sometimes compared with Friedrich Klopstock, the first titanic innovator in modern German letters—and for almost two generations thereafter, the standard view was quite the reverse. Until the time of Schumann or even until Otto Jahn's standard biography (1856), Mozart was viewed as a dark and demonic figure. He was often assimilated to his own Don Giovanni, as in Hoffmann's famous "Don Juan," or else associated with the dark specter of the *Requiem* in contrast to the clear brightness of Papa Haydn, as may be seen in Hoffmann's essay "Beethovens Instrumentalmusik" and Pushkin's marvelous playlet *Mozart and Salieri*. Yet at the same time, the early biographical materials all portray him as withdrawn, innocent, childlike, and helpless in worldly matters.[13] This aspect of his image also needs to be taken seriously, for the Mozartean revolution did not proceed with the flamboyance of a Beethoven. It was a quiet, inward revolution, a new way of thinking or, yet, of dreaming in musical forms, a mood of intense self-absorption that is favored even in the operas—in lyrical pauses such as Tamino's "Dies Bildnis ist bezaubernd schön" in *The Magic Flute* or Cherubino's "Non so più cosa son, cosa faccio" in *The Marriage of Figaro*—but that is particularly developed in the more private musical genres. With this revolutionary self-absorption, we have moved again into the sphere of the hermit of the Ile de Saint-Pierre and the hermit of Königsberg.

There can be no question, of course, of any "influence" of Rousseau's or Kant's ideas on Mozart's musical structures. While I have used various loosely synonymous nonmusical terms—reverie, dream, unconscious, ethereal, and so on—the analysis could proceed on a nonmetaphorical, strictly technical basis. Indeed, much of it has. I should therefore clarify why I have superimposed a philosophical and literary layer on the musical analysis, even at the risk of giving the false impression that I wished to make the history of music dependent upon the history of ideas.

My answer lies, first of all, in the contention—in which I follow chiefly Michel Foucault, though with qualifications—that at every period in history a subterranean network of constraints governs the organization of human thought. Different fields develop and change in parallel not because they affect one another but because the infrastructures of mental activity affect all of them. In this respect, the relationship of music and philosophy is no different from the relationship of literature and philosophy. The infrastructure is the precondition of thought and is by definition unconscious and unarticulated. Because it lies outside the limits of the individual disciplines, it cannot really be formulated within any of them. Hence arises the necessity of comparative study. The infrastructure comes to light at the juncture of independent fields. In the present case, it is accurate to say that music and philosophy mutually illuminate one another precisely because they are such different media; where they coincide lie the true invariants of eighteenth-century thought.

Beyond these general considerations, applicable to all comparisons, is the special challenge of understanding a nonverbal medium such as music. Here the problem, so insistently raised in the work of Leonard Meyer, is the expressivity of musical gestures: what they mean, what their purpose is, or what they communicate. The relationship of musical (or literary or philosophical) forms to the intuitive presuppositions of thought is that of a manifest superstructure to a concealed depth: we may conceive the surface forms as representations or signs of their hidden presuppositions. The concrete manifestations *express* their latent presuppositions; they *signify* the unconscious systems in which they are rooted. To *understand* expressive forms in this sense is thus to describe the mediations between conscious superstructure and unconscious infrastructure; hence, as Claude Lévi-Strauss has said in an important justification of his own structuralist enterprise, this kind of understanding "is first of all psychology" (*Savage Mind* 131). The explanatory process leads from the musical surface to that aspect of the mental system (that "state of mind") which it represents, in this case the reverie of nascent, disembodied self-consciousness.

The Marxian terminology of infra- and superstructures seems unwieldy, but its very remoteness from the objects of study is actually an advantage: it calls our attention to the fact that all of our processes of understanding involve a movement out of one system into another. Explanation is always an abstraction or, what amounts to the same thing, a metaphor. This is just as true of the explanation of verbal media (poetry or philosophy) as of nonverbal media. It is equally daring to assign a reason for a development in the history of ideas or to declare what a poem expresses as to attribute a meaning to musical forms. The only difference is that in the earlier cases the process of abstraction is easily concealed, since words are being substituted for other words, whereas the abstraction in explanations of music is patent.

The special challenge of analyzing a nonverbal medium, then, is to recognize that no special challenge is involved. All explanation is transference or metaphor (nothing much different is meant when certain literary critics contend that all reading is misreading), for understanding depends on finding a convincing mediation between what is actually present in the text and something that, in an important sense, is not so present. Explanation never remains within the charmed circle of what is to be explained; the essential thing is to find mediations that are sufficiently precise and well articulated. Whether mine are, I leave to my examples to show; but I would repeat that my analysis has not been an application of philosophical terms to musical problems. On the contrary, the guiding terms of the analysis, disorientation and undirected pulse, surface only in Rousseau's *Reveries*, a "marginal" text by an "interdisciplinary" author who was as seriously involved in the study of music as in the study of philosophy. Indeed, it would be more accurate to say that the present essay applies musical terms to the clarification of a philosophical problem. Perhaps it would be even better to remain close to Lévi-Strauss's view and say that if music is fundamentally an expression of emotions, then my analysis may contribute toward laying bare the emotional and psychological foundations of the Romantic consciousness.

CHAPTER 6

Kant's Misreading of Descartes

KANT'S TREATMENT OF Descartes in the *Critique of Pure Reason* is notably obtuse. Descartes's systematic doubt is a kind of spiritual exercise establishing the *cogito* as a theoretical and a practical maxim. In response, Kant contends that both thought (*cogito*) and personal identity (*ego*) should be taken in some sort of intuitive and transcendental sense as entities that precede experience. Empirical reality is reduced to secondary status as the mere "condition of the application" of a dictum whose truth is "pure[ly] intellectual," with an immediacy that does not even require an act of reasoning to ground it. At one stroke, both empiricism and rationalism, as Descartes combined them, are swept under the rug, in a forbiddingly abstract dismissal. (The entire paragraph in question is quoted below.)

Short of ignoring the difficulty, we must try to account for the confusion. Steven C. Patten argues that Descartes is at fault: he singles out inconsistent statements about whether perceptions are always self-conscious. Kant's dismissal then appears as a mere reflection of Descartes's inadequacies. Alberto Rouges and Vicente Quintero both maintain that the problem is Kant's. The former claims that Kant mistook Descartes's pure consciousness for an empirical consciousness, as if Descartes were truly a Kantian all along; the latter claims that Kant mistook his own idealism for an empirical realism and was, in effect, a failed Cartesian. Ferdinand Alquié exonerates both Descartes and Kant from blame. In his view, Leibniz is the true villain, and "Kant contends only with a deformed Cartesianism" (Alquié, "Lecture cartésienne" 151). Or maybe neither philosopher can be credited with a true grasp of the issues: "Kant and Descartes alike committed the error of failing to see the relation in which the initial 'cogito'—or its more precise form as a synthesis a priori in the *Ich denke*—stood with the eternal problem of being" (Barié, "Du 'cogito' cartésien" 217). But perhaps, as I shall be arguing, such confusions about where the confusion lies point to a deeper difficulty of comprehension. We don't know who is at fault because language will not formulate what needs to be said.

My thesis in this essay will be double. First, Kant's misreading of Descartes is not a mistake but a swerve in the history of thought. It registers a change in the way problems can be formulated. Second, Descartes offers the proper subject for communicating this transformation because Kant in truth is responding to a swerve of Descartes's own. Descartes's writing matters precisely because it reflects a struggle to advance beyond his conceptions. The issue is not that Descartes had thoughts he would not or could not write, but that he wrote things that he could not yet think and that Kant's new language finally enabled Kant to think for him. Similarly, the brevity of Kant's critique foregrounds the impossibility of his ever communicating with Descartes. It is more direct and more honest than any attempt to bridge the gap between them. Heidegger says that "Nietzsche's misunderstanding of the Cartesian sentence [*Satz*—the translators write "principle"] is even necessary, for a number of metaphysical reasons" (*Nietzsche* 4: 104), and I shall be arguing the same about Kant. My analysis is directed at showing why Kant and Descartes could say no more on the very subjects they have in common.

A weaker version of my argument maintains that Descartes's ideas were in advance of the late scholastic language to which he resorted. The view that Descartes meant more than he said is perhaps best known from Heidegger: "Through his many efforts to make what was new in his grounding of metaphysics intelligible to his contemporaries by responding to their doubts, Descartes was forced to discourse at the already prevailing level and so to explain his fundamental position superficially, that is, always inappropriately, a contingency that threatens *every essential thinking*" (*Nietzsche* 4: 118).[1] Zeno Vendler argues along similar lines with an eye to Kant: "[Descartes] really speaks, or *should* speak, not of the will but of the self. . . . Yet, for obvious religious reasons, he never had the courage to . . . abandon the doctrine of the soul as a 'substance' interacting with other substances in the world. That final step remained for Kant to take" (Vendler, "Descartes' Res Cogitans" 170, his italics). Arguments such as these presuppose our ability to seize thoughts that lie beyond language—beyond the language of the philosopher whose thoughts they should have been, or else beyond all language. The philosopher's inability to complete his system becomes a mark of its pregnancy.

The notion of a truth that transcends its particular formulations accords with the tendency of most philosophical scholarship at present, and especially in English, namely, to rework and reorder a philosopher's arguments so as to uncover their fundamental logic. Oriented toward philosophical problems rather than philosophical writing, such an approach presupposes common issues discussable in a common vocabulary. It honors one of the traditional canons of hermeneutics—to understand authors better than they understand themselves—at the expense of another: to understand authors at their own level, or, as Friedrich Schlegel phrases it, to be just as smart, and just as dumb as the author.[2] As if philosophers might communicate despite themselves, those who expand Descartes's retrograde formulations or Kant's cryptic utterances about him often obscure essential differences by failing to investigate the force of the writing.[3]

More "literary" studies typically take the opposite tack by positing the equivalence of language and idea. One knows philosophers by knowing their language: "Philosophy does not preexist speech, but exists in and through it. The one does not transcend the other, and the philosophical signified and its textual signifier are one and the same" (Romanowski, L'Illusion chez Descartes 176). In its attention to systems and their expression, however, the equation of utterance with thought obscures the dynamism of struggle and advance. Even if it is difficult to accept the notion that thoughts can somehow be superior to the words that clothe them, there remains a force (at least the force of tradition) to the historical commonplace that the great philosophers were in advance of their times. Logical reconstruction of systems of ideas and hermeneutic reconstruction of textual systems represent alternative structuralisms; the stylistic approach does not so much refute the logical approach as confront it in an unresolved standoff.

An enduring legacy of deconstruction is its critique of such structuralisms. Texts can no more be tailored to the implicit thoughts than can thoughts to the explicit texts. What both approaches lack is a sufficiently rich concept of intentionality. Derrida's first book, *La Voix et le phénomène* (Speech and Phenomenon), critiques the psychologized intentionalism in Husserl that covertly reassimilates language to thought and thus impoverishes both. Derrida's theory here and his practice throughout his career show the persistence of intentions that outpace formation. The point of breakthrough does occur where language and thought are out of alignment, but not because the thoughts are somehow better formed than the words. Rather, philosophers enter history when they simultaneously say more than they can think and mean more than they can say. The strength of a philosophical system resides in its passionate desire or longing for a new idea, a kind of nostalgia for the future of the intellectual world. My essay, consequently, speculates on the Cartesian beyond.

The issue, then, is an epochal change in philosophical language. Just approaching the threshold of the new, and torn between an immature French and an overripe Latin, Descartes's language forecasts intuitions that he is not prepared to conceive. Three kinds of philological analysis form the kernel of my exposition. The first two are concrete: textual observations concerning Descartes's *ego* and semantic ones concerning the meaning of the verb *cogito*. The third is speculative and stylistic, concerning the imaginative valence of the wax that Descartes takes for an example of corporeal substance in the second part of the *Meditations*. The first two kinds fix Descartes in his roots, the third frees him into his dreams.

However much I may attempt to hedge the kernels around with supporting evidence, there will seem to be a radical discontinuity in my argument, as indeed there always is between past and future. Nevertheless, it is important to acknowledge the fundamental kinship of the apparently disparate kinds of philology—the determinate and the intuitive, the grammatical and the stylistic, the scholarly and the critical. For, on the one hand, the determination of the meaning of a word such as *ego* or *cogito* must depend on our ability to imagine how potential nuances of tone might liberate it under the influence of a second language, a resource of thought, or a stray inspiration. And, on the other hand, the identification of an imagistic resonance must equally depend on our ability to situate that resonance firmly within the thrust of the author's thinking (or, in an impersonal formulation, within the dimensions of the textual practice). In between, where meaning is free and style controlled, one can speak of choices, decisions, opportunities, experiments, successes and mistakes, felicities and infelicities. But at the ends of the spectrum with which this essay is concerned, a kind of linguistic fatalism operates. There, authors cannot help but betray themselves, violating conscious thoughts while revealing the swerves or errancies of their true inspiration. Better than any hermeneutic aids to reflection, Kant's helplessness captures the nuances of such self-betrayal in Descartes.

* * *

The most imposing and least intelligible of Kant's comments on Descartes is contained in a note to the second version of the paralogisms of pure reason (*Kritik der reinen Vernunft* B422–23). It reads as follows.

Das Ich denke ist, wie schon gesagt, ein empirischer Satz, und hält den Satz, Ich existiere, in sich. Ich kann aber nicht sagen: alles, was denkt, existiert; denn da würde die Eigenschaft des Denkens alle Wesen, die sie besitzen, zu notwendigen Wesen machen. Daher kann meine Existenz auch nicht aus dem Satze, Ich denke, als gefolgert angesehen werden, wie Cartesius dafür hielt (weil sonst der Obersatz: alles, was denkt, existiert, vorausgehen müßte), sondern ist mit ihm identisch. Er drückt eine unbestimmte empirische Anschauung, d. i. Wahrnehmung, aus (mithin beweiset er doch, daß schon Empfindung, die folglich zur Sinnlichkeit gehört, diesem Existenzialsatz zum Grunde liege), geht aber vor der Erfahrung vorher, die das Objekt der Wahrnehmung durch die Kategorie in Ansehung der Zeit bestimmen soll, und die Existenz ist hier noch keine Kategorie, als welche nicht auf ein unbestimmt gegebenes Objekt, sondern nur ein solches, davon man einen Begriff hat, und wovon man wissen will, ob es auch außer diesem Begriffe gesetzt sei, oder nicht, Beziehung hat. Eine unbestimmte Wahrnehmung bedeutet hier nur etwas Reales, das gegeben worden, und zwar nur zum Denken überhaupt, also nicht als Erscheinung, auch nicht als Sache an sich selbst (Noumenon), sondern als etwas, was in der Tat existiert, und in dem Satze, ich denke, als ein solches bezeichnet wird. Denn es ist zu merken, daß, wenn ich den Satz: ich denke, einen empirischen Satz genannt habe, ich dadurch nicht sagen will, das I c h in diesem Satze sei empirische Vorstellung; vielmehr ist sie rein intellektuell, weil sie zum Denken überhaupt gehört. Allein ohne irgend eine empirische Vorstellung, die den Stoff zum Denken abgibt, würde der Actus, Ich denke, doch nicht stattfinden, und das Empirische ist nur die Bedingung der Anwendung, oder des Gebrauchs des reinen intellektuellen Vermögens.

The "I think" is, as already stated, an empirical sentence, and contains within itself the sentence "I exist." But I cannot say "everything which thinks, exists." For in that case the property of thought would render all beings which possess it necessary beings. My existence cannot, therefore, be regarded as inferred from the sentence "I think," as Descartes contended—because otherwise it would have to be preceded by the major premise "Everything which thinks, exists"— but is identical with it. The "I think" expresses an indeterminate empirical intuition, *i.e.* perception (and thus shows that sensation, which as such belongs to sensibility, lies at the basis of this existential sentence). But the "I think" precedes the experience which is required to determine the object of perception through the category in respect of time; and existence here [referred to] is not a category. The category as such does not apply to an indeterminately given object but only to one of which we have a concept and about which we seek to know whether it does or does not exist [*gesetzt sei*] outside the concept. An indeterminate perception here signifies only something real that is given, given indeed to thought in general, and so not as appearance, nor as thing in itself (*noumenon*), but as something which actually exists, and which in the sentence, "I think," is denoted as such. For it must be observed, that when I have called the sentence, "I think," an empirical sentence, I do not mean to say thereby, that the "I" in this sentence is an empirical representation. On the contrary, it is purely intellectual, because belonging to thought in general. Without some empirical representation to supply the material for thought, the *actus*, "I think," would not, indeeed, take place; but the empirical is only the condition of the application, or of the employment, of the pure intellectual faculty.[4]

Ego

The confusions in this passage begin at Descartes's name, which appears at the point where Kant challenges the status of the *cogito*. It is uncertain which verb the "because" clause modifies and consequently it is unclear whether Kant thinks Descartes believed in an implied major premise. If so, Kant was wrong, since Descartes's discussions in the *Meditations* repeatedly deny the presupposition of a distinct major premise. It could also be wrong to claim that Descartes regarded the *cogito* as a deduction, though here the uncertainty lies in Descartes's texts: it remains a matter of debate whether his *therefore* (*ergo, donc*) is meant to signal a consequence or a clarification. (For a good analysis, see Bernard Williams, *Descartes* 88–90.) Textual confusions in both authors thus lie behind Kant's description of "an indeterminate empirical intuition, *i.e.* perception": whatever the psychology of the *cogito* may be, its logic is vague.

Too much cannot depend on it; consequently Kant concludes his note by relegating the *cogito* to an accessory status, as he had done even more decisively in the first version of the paralogisms, where he called the *cogito* "the form of apperception, which *attaches to* [*anhängt*; Kemp Smith translates "belongs to"] and precedes every experience" (A354, my emphasis). Kant acknowledges the *cogito* as a first principle, but a principle of something else, namely of experience. It is obscurely there, but Kant refrains from saying that we must be conscious of our consciousness. Rather: "It must be *possible* for the 'I think' to accompany all my representations" (B131, Kant's emphasis, omitted by Kemp Smith). Descartes, of course, had explicitly identified "I think" as the shiningly clear and distinct idea that grounds the possibilities of knowledge. Even as he aims to be faithful to the obscure truth of the Cartesian *cogito*, Kant thus deviates massively from Descartes's stated intentions. I shall be arguing that his instincts in doing so are better than either he or Descartes could have recognized.

Kant's note starts by calling "ich denke" a "Satz," which derives from the verb *setzen* and connotes something settled, either a sentence or a theorem. But he concludes unsettlingly by calling the *cogito* an "act." Descartes's *Discourse* calls the *cogito* a "vérité." The Latin translation, whose departure from the French is surely authorized, calls it a pronouncement (*pronuntiatum*), and that word reappears to designate the statement "ego sum, ego existo," in the Second Meditation, where it is translated with the French term *proposition*. No word available to Kant (neither *Satz* nor *Äußerung* nor *Behauptung* nor *Verkündigung*) could quite capture the existential, here-and-now quality of *pronuntiatum*; nor for that matter could any French word. Yet, paradoxically, its spontaneity is lost in being conceptually captured and thus better preserved in Kant's terminological fluctuations. Rather than an eternal truth, it is a living gesture, not stable, but forever repeated and renewed: "Statuendum [est] hoc pronuntiatum, *Ego sum, ego existo*, quoties a me profertur, vel mente concipitur, necessario esse verum" (It is to be taken as settled that this pronouncement, "I am, I exist," every time it is uttered by me or conceived in my mind, is necessarily true; *Oeuvres* 7: 25).[5]

Cogito and its correlatives in other deductions (*dubito, sum*) are not the true founding moment of Cartesianism. Descartes's truth lies in the exact wording of his Latin. Though *"Cogito ergo sum"* (thus, in quotes) is the title of Hartmut Brands's valuable but tendentious collection of materials on my topic, I do not believe that it is, in this form, an authentically Cartesian phrase. Descartes seems to have written it only once, in a letter (Jan. 1642 to Regius; *Correspondance* 5: 133), where he quotes it from an attack on him. The phrase "cogito ergo sum" appears in two other passages in Descartes's works, in the conversations recorded by Burman and again in the posthumous Latin translation of the *Recherche de la vérité*. But the phrase apparently never occurs as Descartes's own. Rather, in the second Responses to the *Meditations* and the *Principles of Philosophy*, as well as in the authorized Latin translation of the *Discourse on Method*, the phrase that appears is this: "Ego cogito, ergo sum." The *I* comes first, not just in French, where it is grammatically required, but equally in Latin, where it is optional. It initiates Descartes's statements of principle.

A pronouncement must be pronounced. Before Descartes could say "think," or "doubt," or "am," he had to say "I." That word, or that intuition of self, is his true starting point. In the first version of the paralogisms Kant reduces "I think" to "*I simply am*" and finally to "this representation, 'I'" (A354–55).[6] Descartes never acknowledges such a reduction. Yet that concealed self-assertion is the true origin of Cartesianism—true as assertion, and equally true in the concealment whose veil Kant lifts—an assertion that Descartes did not know how to assert, a pronouncement masquerading as a truth.

What is Descartes's *I*? Kant rightly calls it indistinct, even though Descartes insists that the *cogito* is a clear and evident pronouncement. And, echoed by Heidegger, Kant calls it an intuition, a representation, and simple being, all of which it would be if Descartes knew how to imagine it so. Heidegger turns the *cogito* into Kant's implicit, intuitive "ich denke" when he writes, "We can most pointedly express what the *ergo* is supposed to say if we leave it aside, and furthermore if we remove the emphasis on "I" in the word *ego*, because the first-person pronoun [*das Ichhafte*] is not essential here" (*Nietzsche* 4: 113). But Descartes lacks the kind of implicit, essential ground, the subjacent "subject in the subject" (4: 114) that would free him from saying *I*. He designates himself in lieu of feeling or knowing himself inwardly.

By saying that Descartes lacks a substantive subjectivity, I both do and do not mean to accuse him of a deficiency that Kant cures. It is all too easy to write the history of philosophy on the Whig system, as a series of errors righted and ignorances satisfied. Yet for Descartes the absence of a notion of personal essence constitutes the strength and solidity of his system. By comparing French and Latin texts we can see that Cartesianism regularly equates "who I am" with "what I am," that is, the personal being with the knowable quantity.[7] To this extent there is not even a problem of personal identity in Descartes, as Locke was to formulate it, because there is no possibility of conceiving the subsistence of a personal essence beneath experience. To designate such a subsistence he had a name both grander and more mysterious, in which he firmly believed and which he refused to quarrel with or to doubt. That name was, of course, God. Nevertheless, at an unconscious level, Descartes is driven toward yearning for a terrestrial essence, something that might resemble a thinking stone.[8] That yearning, though it acknowledges a lack, is the opposite of a weakness; it marks the point where his philosophy imagines a future.

All Descartes scholars know the philosopher's self-portraits. One is the polysemous motto that he reports in a letter to Mersenne of April 1634, "Bene vixit, bene qui latuit" (most literally: "He has lived well who has remained well hidden"). Another is the early notebook jotting, "Vt comoedi, moniti ne in fronte appareat pudor, personam induunt: sic ego, hoc mundi theatrum conscensurus, in quo hactenus spectator extiti, larvatus prodeo" (As actors, wary lest shame appear on their face, put on a mask: thus I, preparing to ascend the theater of the world, where I have hitherto been a spectator, step forth masked; 10: 213). It appears that, having something to hide, Descartes hid himself, for, says another letter to Mersenne, "I am ashamed to speak of myself" (Jan. 1630; *Correspondance* 1: 112). Yet his voluminous discussions of his own ideas and his sometimes testy, occasionally even violent responses to others do not evidence any genuine bashfulness, and in the last part of the *Discourse on Method* (which was, to be sure, published anonymously), he tells us that "I have never sought to hide my actions like crimes, nor have I used many precautions to be unknown" (*Oeuvres* 6: 76). The conflicting evidence suggests that no uniform decoding of Descartes's fugitive personality will be satisfactory.[9]

Descartes's essence remains hidden and difficult to talk about because it doesn't exist. In the motto it is possible to emphasize the adverbs that are syntactically foregrounded: "Effective hiding makes a good life."[10] In the notebook passage it is customary to infer negative connotations from "larvatus," but it is at least equally possible to infer positive ones from mounting a stage. Putting on a *persona* may be hiding, but it may also imply becoming a person: until you put on a mask, you are not a real, living creature but only an external spectator. Another passage in the same notebook unquestionably denigrates masks, but it refers to masked objects of knowledge ("Larvatae nunc scientiae sunt: quae, larvis sublatis, pulcherrimae apparerent" [The sciences are now masked: which, with the masks removed, will appear most beauteous]; 10: 215). The situation is, at the least, less clear with respect to masked persons. The biographer Adrien Baillet reports that Descartes, on a journey perhaps a year or two after the notebook entry, heard some bandits talking in Dutch to plan a murderous attack. He saved himself, we are told, by brave theatrics.[11] In a dangerous situation, energetic deception is the only possible salvation for the ego. But indeed, no clear line can be drawn between concealment, deception, self-fashioning, and self-presentation. Both *Satz* and *actus*, the self is posited through its actions and its pronouncements. Nothing distinct precedes and grounds them, or needs to.

The absence of a substantial self makes Descartes conducive to fine deconstructive readings, such as those of Derrida, of Bernard Bass and Armand Zaloszyc, and, best of all, of Jean-Luc Nancy. Yet all except the first of these ultimately err, as does Heidegger, by treating the absence of self as a deprivation (madness, vertigo, or spasm). For a deprivation would presuppose a possible presence—some residual ideal of self that undermines deconstructive skepticism.[12] But Descartes can imagine no other self than the person saying "I" at this very moment.[13] There is perhaps no philosopher who repeats himself so much as Descartes, and none who says "I" so often. The self exists precisely as its momentary acts of consciousness. Descartes's philosophy is his identity; there is no other.

Cogito

It might seem factitious to wonder what Descartes was thinking when he said "ego cogito."[14] He provides, after all, numerous lists of the modalities of consciousness that are comprised under the rubric "thought," including doubting, willing, and feeling. Descartes might, it seems, have been thinking almost anything. Nevertheless, there is a limit to the *cogito*. The very proliferation of the faculties of mind shows us at least that Descartes was surely thinking *something*. His thought was always underway somewhere, directed toward an object. Descartes even coins the phrase "cogitative acts" as a periphrastic definition of thought (7: 176; *Responses to Objections* 3.2). Thought is Descartes's bridge to action. As he says in the second sentence of the *Meditations*, "I have delayed so long that henceforth I should be at fault if I were to consume in deliberation what time remains for acting" (7: 17).

As a generalization, then, it may be said that Descartes's thought and even his doubt formed part of a system of clear, fundamentally confident affirmation.[15] In all its modalities Cartesian thought is an assertion; it brings him into contact with the world.[16] Descartes was incapable of staying home and daydreaming. Not even his nighttime dreams exhibit the blurred obscurity of romantic reverie: "For whence do we know that the thoughts that come in dreams are more false than others, seeing that often they are no less lifelike and definite?" (*Discourse* 4; *Oeuvres* 6: 38). Let us give its full significance to the last word in the Latin formulation: "Ego cogito, ergo sum, sive existo." Thinking is being in the form of ex-isting, standing forth. Descartes's vocation, just the reverse of Kant's, led out into worldly activity.[17]

We can be sure of one thing about the contents of Descartes's thought: when he said "ego cogito," he was not merely apprehending himself in a gesture of simple self-consciousness. The verb *cogito* derives from *cogo* and refers to a bringing together of ideas in the mind; its object is always a judgment or else a thing mentally constructed, never that less than a thing which is the self. By this I do not mean to exclude the possibility that he might single out for attention some part or aspect of himself, or else, as Robert Champigny intriguingly argues, the category of "selfness." But Cartesian thought is transitive as well as active. It cannot be taken as a reflexive middle voice or an action with a purely internal object. Thus, it cannot bear any resemblance to Kant's pure consciousness.[18] The scholar who paraphrases the Second Meditation in these terms—"But even if I thinking should reach no object, if I grow uncertain and just merely think, still *I* think"[19]—is importing an alien conception into the Cartesian world.

The structure of the pronouncement "ego cogito, ergo sum" likewise forbids any interpretation that refers *cogito* to pure self-consciousness. Descartes tells us that the pronouncement is not a syllogism. He is not deriving existence from thought; he is deriving the knowledge that I exist from the knowledge that I think. It is a confirmation, not a discovery: "I exist" draws out the meaning of "I think." This seems to me clear from the Latin, which is not two independent clauses as the French necessarily is. "Ego . . . cogito, ergo sum"; we might translate, "I think, thus am," "I think, therefore, in other words, I am (namely, a thinking thing)." *Sum* explains or generalizes *cogito*; the first term of the judgment is contained within the second term. But if being encompasses thinking, then thinking cannot encompass being; "I think my being (or: I think that I am, or I think that I think), therefore I am" contains the one complement for *cogito* that for Descartes is not possible.[20] And this is precisely the possibility that Kant finally liberates.

We need to ask why thought enjoys a privileged position in Descartes's classification of mental activities. To be sure, he does explain both in the responses to Gassendi and in the *Principles* why philosophy cannot begin with a physical formula such as "I walk, therefore I am." But no such logic prevented him from arguing "ego sentio, ergo sum"— "I feel, therefore I am (a sentient being)." An underlying anthropology is presupposed that puts thought over sensation.[21] The psychological hierarchy begins to break down in the school of sensibility, and Kant (along with other writers of the 1780's) finally though silently overthrows it.[22] I could formulate my thesis about the relationship of Kant to Descartes in these terms: Kant represses thought as cogitation in order to open up a space for thought as intuitive self-presence.[23] But in order to understand this thesis, which in itself is hardly more than a slogan, we have to consider further the temporality of thought in Descartes.

Strictly speaking, Descartes's arguments do not privilege thought, but thought and doubt together: the pronouncement "ego dubito, ergo sum" is at least as important for him as the pronouncement "ego cogito, ergo sum." This fact has no influence on his anthropology; the anthropological implication of "ego dubito, ergo sum" remains "sum res cogitans," not "sum res dubitans" (see *Recherche de la vérité*; 10: 521–22). But in return the addition of the argument from doubt should remind us of a crucial aspect of Descartes's ontology, an aspect that is well known but seemingly not often enough related to the *cogito*. For what distinguishes *cogito* and *dubito* from all other types of mental activity that Descartes itemizes is their grammatical form: both are iterative verbs.[24] (A third iterative verb, *pensitare*, appears at the climax of the Second Meditation: "Adeo ut, omnibus satis superque pensitatis, denique statuendum sit hoc pronuntiatum, *Ego sum, ego existo*, quoties a me profertur, vel mente concipitur, necessario esse verum"; 7: 25). Mental life, for Descartes, exists primarily in the mode of repetition, not that of duration. What Kant makes us forget is that Cartesian thought is a worldly activity and subject to the same temporal fragmentation as corporeal existence. The continuity of mind is just as problematic as the continuity of body, except to the extent that it is sustained by God's continuous creation; as Wahl suggests (in a rhetorical question), "this continuous creation is a sort of myth maintained by Descartes in the center of his philosophy in order to signify the omnipotence of God and the independence of instants" (*Du rôle de l'idée de l'instant* 19). A thought is an act, not a substance; it lasts but an instant.[25]

Remanet Cera

Where in experience is substance to be found? Does it have no more body than a piece of wax in the sun? Being, for Descartes, remains the incomprehensible mystery of an essential existence outside of time. *Sum* functions as an empty predicate; it requires a complement or a clarification in order to have meaning: "sum, sive existo," "sum res cogitans." Even when reasoning of God, Descartes is concerned with His existence rather than His being. Even God "est ou existe" (*Discourse* 4; 6: 36) not outside of time, but in the fullness of time, as the sum of all its moments: necessary existence is the same as existing always (*Meditations* 5; 7: 65: "ut semper existat").[26] Descartes's fundamental intuition, then, is an instinctive nominalism. Though the *cogito* functions logically as an analytical truth to be unfolded, psychologically it is implicitly couched in the mode of limitation: not that thought is sufficient to ground being but that being is in truth no more than its thoughts. Nothing transcends the moment of its conception.

This reduction has evident advantages for science. All things become countable, measurable, comparable, and thus knowable in the medium of thought. But what about the costs? To us they are evident in the pathos of *L'Homme*, where man is all too easily reduced to a knowable machine. The doctrine of continuous creation precludes any doctrine of Creation, that is, of a beginning or boundary of time (see on this Gilson's commentary, pp. 390–92). The primitive or original of things is a chaos, not in the Greek sense of a "yawning void" or abyss of nonbeing, nor in the deconstructive sense of Nancy's vertiginous chaogito, but rather in the sense of a congeries of the not yet organized building blocks of our universe. That chaos, which is discussed in chapter 6 of *Le Monde* (11: 34–35), is evoked in the famous passage of the Second Meditation where Descartes looks out the window and sees not "men crossing in the street," but only "hats and coats under which automata might be hiding." Creation here requires no more than the conscious recognition of the order and meaning of our perceptions: things are constituted by the judgments (or thoughts) inseparably attached to sensation.

Can we not, however, sense a worry that the thoughts might be dreams and the reality mere hallucination? *Bene vixit, bene qui latuit.* But suppose that what hides is not alive. The translator is explicit in his fear of ghosts: "Que vois-je de cette fenêtre sinon des chapeaux et des manteaux, qui peuvent couvrir des spectres ou des hommes feints qui ne se remuent que par ressorts, mais je juge que ce sont de vrais hommes" (9: 25). Still, in some respects Descartes's own text is the more worrisome: "Quid autem video praeter pileos & vestes, sub quibus latere possent automata? Sed judico homines esse" (7: 32). The translator makes the men true and emphasizes the unreality of the primitive perceptions, though conceivably the clothes can be covering ghosts. But for Descartes himself the men are merely inferential, and automata—the subjects of the verb, rather than the objects as in the French—can indeed lurk under them. Science benefits from the *cogito*, but what becomes of soul and of substance? The best things in life are the best hidden.

The unstated question haunting the Second Meditation is this: if being is no more than thought, then what is a thing? The problem of substances becomes, at a subliminal level, a nostalgia for what, in a world of reiterated thoughts, lies beyond repetition and therefore beyond thought, or in short, for a being outside of existence. Stanley Cavell puts it this way : "The hyperbolical [doubt] is a turn to emptiness (sometimes I say a craving for nothingness), a wish to exist outside language games—not so much as it were beyond language, perhaps, as before it. Both excess and emptiness express the human wish to escape the human—the desire for the inhuman, or the demonic" ("Naughty Orators" 363–64). The true thing ("res vera," 7: 27) is, in truth ("revera," 7: 32) but an object of thought (cf. *reor*, I think), a creature of reason (*ratio* comes from the past participle of *reor*). You may repeat your search for the real thing, the substratum of thought forever, but you seek the thing in vain ("frustra re-petere," 7: 27). The example of the wax reminds us that some unaccounted residue remains of the thing itself, distinct from all its perceived metamorphoses. "Remanetne adhuc eadem cera? Remanere fatendum est. . . . Remanet cera" (7: 30). Yet the example moves toward showing that the thing itself, "nude," the mere thing, is in truth less than the mind that conceives it (7: 32). It exists only in the domain of error ("quamvis adhuc error in judicio meo esse possit," 7: 32): for Descartes, as opposed to Kant, the naked is not the pure.

Indeed, when Descartes chooses a bodily "thing" to be his example proving that the mind is a thinking thing, the example also reflects the mind's propensity to "wander" beyond "the limits of truth" ("gaudet aberrare mens mea, necdum se patitur intra veritatis limites cohiberi," 7: 29).[27] No wonder, then, that the same nominalism that reduces thought to the sum of thoughts also reduces substance to a shadowy thing. And no wonder if the thing that surfaces from the wandering error of the mind is further reduced to a syllable wandering through a text. On a single page (7: 30) we can find as traces of the subsisting thing the hope for a reduction to order ("*reductis*," "*regi*") and the search ("*requiri*") for some residue ("*reliquiae*") that might be retained ("*retinet*"). The very insubstantial substance that provides Descartes's erroneous example of a real thing has a name (*cera*) that in the French pronunciation (/ sera /) is little more than an anagram for the thing (*res*) that it would be and an echo of the cipher (*zero*) that it is. Here, in the depths of one of Descartes's most crucial and most obscure passages, we can hear his language subliminally protesting against the limits of his power of formulation, reaching out toward a reality that might become more than an assemblage of discrete thoughts.[28]

As early as his dissertation (1770), Kant criticized reductions of time and space to moments and points: "Each portion of time whatsoever is thus time, and the simples that are in time, namely *moments*, are not parts of it, but boundaries, between which time lies" (*De mundi sensibilis*

A15).[29] Objects and actions, insofar as they are bounded and particular, *occupy* a space and time of which they are not actually part. Outside these particular sensations and experiences lie a space and time without internal boundaries or demarcations. The mind or consciousness is cognate with these pure, unbounded forms of perception. In particular, the time of thought or consciousness is not a moment but an indefinite extent. Time becomes a correlative of space, long before the refutation of Berkeley in the second edition of the *Critique of Pure Reason*; it is the inner space in which our experiences become continuous and therefore comparable with one another. What matters is expanse and flow, not measure.

When we say that Kant's system is transcendental, we mean that it circumscribes the limits that constitute empirical reality. In their transcendental use words such as *time* or *consciousness* suppress the discrete, quantitative connotations of prior usage and acquire new, qualitative meanings. They become an indistinct feeling (say, of orientation or of personal identity) that precedes any possible, limited application. In these terms Kant's obscure critique of Descartes becomes comprehensible as the creation of a new conception through the willful suppression of the old.

Kant misunderstands Descartes—he *must* misunderstand Descartes—by misreading an empirical intuition as a transcendental syllogism: "The 'I think' is, as already stated, an empirical sentence, and contains within itself the sentence, 'I exist.'" But Descartes never said, "Cogito, ergo existo," but rather "Ego cogito, ergo sum (sive existo)." Kant's criticism is only possible if the difference between particular existence at this moment or these moments and existence in general (being, or necessary existence) has been effaced. He wanders furthest from Descartes not in the contents of his critique but in the vocabulary that gives it its transcendental coloration. The words *indefinite, pure, in general*, with which Kant strews his note, are, to Descartes, neither thinkable nor writable. Though Descartes inhabits "shadows" (*Discourse* 2; 6: 16: "dans les ténèbres"; Latin 6: 547: "noctu et in tenebris"), the shadows presume at least a little light, perhaps from his stove, and he marches, however circumspectly, toward the brightness. There are no fundamentally hidden recesses, no inscrutable labyrinths, no prudential authorial reserves.[30]

The Kantian self consists of a collection of pure, transcendental intuitions, such as time, that lie between, around, outside of all its empirical experiences. The problem of personal identity has been circumvented. Selfhood is not subject to the whims of empirical memory, as in Locke; our dreams are part of our self because they exist in temporal continuity with our waking existence, even though in our dreams we may not remember who we are. Selfhood is also not the fiction of a subsisting intelligence as in Hume; consequently, we remain the same person even when we go mad and lose the power to shape our life. But what this "something" is, this third thing (neither phenomenon nor noumenon) designated by the sentence, "I think"—that we cannot further say. It is an abstract existence, a space of possibility, beyond any conceivable specification. The purity of the transcendental ego depends on its intangibility. Both Descartes and Kant utter the sentence *ego sum* (or "ich bin einfach") as a founding gesture, but for the former it is the predicate, for the latter the subject that remains empty, opening onto mysterious potentialities.

Elaborating those potentialities must be the task of other accounts of Descartes's materialism and Kant's idealism. This chapter is directed toward their origins. Concepts and systems take their rise from the places where the language fails in clarity and in comprehension. Even Kant and Descartes, two of the least graceful writers of philosophical prose, elicit the conceptual power of their language from out of its nodes of silence. Kant misunderstands Descartes in virtue of a precise grasp of what Descartes would have had to say if he spoke Kant's language. The precision of the misunderstanding is reflected in the many commentators who assimilate the two philosophers to one another. Such affinities will always be felt where doctrine responds to doctrine, even in correction or disagreement. But the greatest thinkers, like the greatest poets, find their imaginations rooted in the mysteries of their language. Mind calls out to mind, but from the solitude of words, migrating through the vacancy of the ages.

CHAPTER 7

Toward an Archaeology of English Romanticism
Coleridge and Sarbiewski

GREAT WORKS OF literature conceal their origins: they are great because they solve stylistic problems, not because they raise them. Often, therefore, vital poetic issues surface not in the mature works of major authors but in less polished and more truly problematic minor works. The historical dialectic of styles is most directly expressed in such partial successes, rather than in masterpieces or in outright failures. If it is true of history, as Michel Foucault has said of discourse, that it is "the path from one contradiction to another," then these works are the points of articulation. And if to analyze history (Foucault again says discourse) is "to hide and reveal contradictions," then the historian's task is clearly indicated: to study them against the receding background to which they respond and in the light of the nascent works toward which they point (*Archaeology of Knowledge* 151). They will be the historian's poetic crossings, the signposts of literary history.

The poem at the center of the present chapter, Coleridge's "Ad Lyram," is translated from a Latin ode by Matthew Casimir Sarbiewski, among the most widely read of all neo-Latin poets and then still famous as the "divine Casimire" and the "Polish Horace." As a translation Coleridge's poem conveniently defines the specific context from which it emerges. The works of Sarbiewski present the problems and the prior English translations anticipate the Romantic solution whose stylistic intention is most clearly visible in Coleridge's exploratory translation.

IMITATION

The solemn-breathing air is ended—
Cease, O Lyre! thy kindred lay!

From the Poplar branch suspended,
    Glitter to the eye of Day!
On thy wires hov'ring, dying,
    Softly sighs the summer wind:
I will slumber, careless lying,
    By yon *waterfall* reclin'd.

In the forest hollow-roaring,
    Hark! I hear a deep'ning sound—
Clouds rise thick with heavy louring!
    See! th'horizon blackens round!

Parent of the soothing measure,
    Let me seize thy wetted string!
Swiftly flies the flatterer, Pleasure,
    Headlong, ever on the wing.

The following advertisement was prefixed to the original publication, and the Latin text was added.

If we except Lucretius and Statius, I know not of any Latin poet, ancient or modern, who has equalled Casimir in boldness of conception, opulence of fancy, or beauty of versification. The ODES of this illustrious Jesuit were translated into English about one hundred and fifty years ago, by a Thomas Hill, I think. I never saw the translation. A few of the ODES have been translated in a very animated manner by Watts. I have subjoined the third ode of the second book, which, with the exception of the first line, is an effusion of exquisite elegance. In the imitation attempted, I am sensible that I have destroyed the *effect of suddenness*, by translating into two stanzas what is one in the original.

AD LYRAM

Sonora buxi Filia sutilis,
Pendebis alta, Barbite, populo,
    Dum ridet aer, et supinas
        Solicitat levis aura frondes:

Te sibilantis lenior halitus
Perflabit Euri: me juvet interim
    Collum reclinasse, et virenti
        Sic temere jacuisse ripa.

Eheu! serenum quae nebulae tegunt
Repente caelum! quis sonus imbrium!
    Surgamus! heu semper fugaci
        Gaudia praeteritura passu.[1]

Sonorous daughter of sewn boxwood, o Lyre, thou wilt hang from the tall poplar, so long as the air smiles and a gentle breeze stirs the reclining boughs: through thee the gentler breath of the whistling east wind will blow: meanwhile I shall enjoy having reclined my head, and thus perchance having lain on the green bank. Alas! what clouds suddenly cover the clear sky! what a sound of showers! Let us rise! alas joys will always pass by with a fleeting step.

"The influence of [the Aeolian harp] upon the heart is truly pleasing," wrote one Charles Bucke around 1808: "it disposes the mind to solemn, tender and pathetic emotion, and, winning upon the imagination, strikes the heart with its simplicity, and leaves it resting in all the pure delights of a pleasing melancholy" (quoted in Bloomfield, *Remains* 1: 126–27). Coleridge's poem certainly aspires to a wistful Aeolian simplicity, and for that very reason it remains difficult to analyze. But we can take his advertisement as an initial guide to the hidden and revealed contradictions in the translation and to the necessary preparations and conditions for Coleridge's achievement. Three signal departures from Sarbiewski can be identified; in each case the English retains a trace of the original orientation as a token of the change in perspective and as a link to the past. First, there is the "opulence" and "exquisite elegance" of the Latin—such as its precious refinement of temporal and modal relationships—from which Coleridge derives only one hint of jewel-like "glitter" and one elegantly metaphorical usage, the delicate "wires" of the lyre. Second, where Sarbiewski, in the first stanza, portrays the lyre as a "daughter" of nature, Coleridge's last stanza views it as the "parent" of a humanized "measure." Gone is the natural filiation of art, though even Coleridge's lyre remains mysteriously "akin" to the air. Finally, Coleridge claims to have suppressed the original "effect of suddenness," though again the conventionally epiphanic "hark" and "see" preserve a residue of that "crash of onset" ("Fears in Solitude," line 37) with which Coleridge's poems so often flirt.

Each of these changes identifies and responds to a significant contradiction in the tradition and thus defines an element of the poem's originality. Coleridge's reservations about Sarbiewski's opening line help to pinpoint two of the contradictions. To begin with, elegant, elaborately decorative language is liable to be mere show, tinsel masquerading as substance. The first line in particular, with its all too prominent phonetic patterning and its empty mythological display, is "sonorous" and flamboyant rather than exquisite. Moreover, the dangers of excess display are not only stylistic. Sarbiewski's moral, with its shift from "I" to "we" ("surgamus"), claims to be universal. But his language is too well-knit ("sutilis"), his setting too artfully contrived, his casual "thus perchance" ("sic temere") too coyly casual—and his Latin too learned—for this to seem anything but a fashionable *bergerade*, a spoiled picnic of no general moral significance. Coleridge's simplicity, then, is an attempt to replace the false subtlety of overelaboration with a true subtlety of implication.

The second problem is that of art and nature. As the "daughter of boxwood," the lyre is a natural object. Yet even for Sarbiewski the lyre is a human artifact: it is *his* lyre ("Ad suam testudinem" is the title in the editions), and it regularly appears as a symbol for his poetry (cf. esp. *Odes* 3.32 and 4.26). Poetry is a product of human language, not of nature. Indeed, poetry is an especially artificial type of language: it uses the learned Latin instead of Sarbiewski's native Polish, the learned word "barbitos" instead of the natural "lyra" (Coleridge significantly substitutes "lyra" in the title for the original, figurative "testudo" [literally a tortoise-shell]), the learned feminine gender of "barbitos" instead of the "natural" masculine (*Od.* 4.26.11–12), the circumlocution "daughter of the box" instead of the natural "lyre," and so forth. Moreover, the artifice is inevitable. If art is to read a human significance in a natural occurrence, then it must see nature in human terms; if Sarbiewski wishes to have nature minister a moral lesson, then he must personify nature as the minister. From the romantic perspective, the language of art—indeed all language, though that is not the issue here—is not inherently natural, but rather human and, so to speak, artificial.[2] Coleridge's simplicity is an attempt to replace a histrionic pretense of naturalism with a true directness of refined human speech.

But what about the third problem? Why suppress the effect of suddenness? And what replaces—or rather transcends—it in Coleridge's poem? This is the most fundamental and difficult question. To approach it, I should like to examine Sarbiewski's poetry in more detail and in particular to study the problem of the continuity of his poetic voice.

* * *

Compounded of precious gems, flashing lights, sparkling waters, and surprising conceits, Sarbiewski's odes are anything but reticent.[3] Their poet seeks rare words ("illimis," "regemo"), coins resonant phrases ("formidolosos quadrupedantum onagrorum hiatus"), and competes with his poetic antecedents (as with the more than sesquipedalian word "superstitiosioris"). It is undoubtedly such vocal pyrotechnics which led Edward Young to praise Sarbiewski for his "ready wit and happy fire" ("An Essay on Lyric Poetry," *Works* 332). Yet the odes are wooden and without music. Extremely derivative—virtually a Horatian cento— and written in a foreign language, they are mechanical in their treatment of a limited repertoire of stanza forms, with an arbitrary placement of pauses and no regard for normal stress patterns.[4] Showy but graceless, the Latin of the odes is strictly a learned and written language.

The odes thus embody a contradiction: a will to vocal display combined with a failure of the voice. Sarbiewski's primary commitments were, indeed, not to poetry, but to the service of God, the glory of his countrymen, and the defeat of the infidels. He views poetry as imitation, a fundamentally redundant and empty activity regularly associated with the vocabulary of repetition: "iterare," "geminare," and a whole series of "re-" compounds. Properly, the poet's voice is merely a preparation for the warrior's silent action: "Many are we who can speak great things; arduous enterprises call on few."[5] Though a spokesman and a prophet, Sarbiewski's poet calls for an end to the lazy luxury of speech, notably in the last ode in book 3, a farewell to poetry which concludes the first edition of the odes and which stands in polemical contrast to Horace's similarly placed, proud, "Exegi monumentum aere perennius." Hence, a conflict arises between religious and national allegiance and poetic calling, between duty and reflection, conscience and voice.

Poetic narrative is weak and effeminate, a mere surrogate for true life: "In vain by the November hearth do we tell of the wars fought beneath the Rhaetian Alps; in vain do we recount the Gelonian standards carried backwards in retreat: unless we ourselves dare to grasp Norican swords."[6] Though the odes refer rather often to narration, they contain little actual narrative, and most of it is "concealed" in some fashion by being purely imaginary, for instance, or by encapsulation in a simile or a fictional inserted story ("fabula": *Odes* 2.17.21). At its worst—as in the following excerpt from an extended imaginary narration describing the future recovery of the lush, pastoral Greek landscape—narrative degenerates into a flamboyant play with sound effects:

Est, quem comantûm gratia montium,
Aut floridorum tangit amoenior
Vultus Viretorum?
(*Odes* 1.12.41–43)

At best, the achievement of narrative is not a creation, but a mere recreation,[7] a bad luxury purchased at a mortal cost. An exception is made only for those actions which cannot be suspected of indulgence and sloth: unconcealed narrative in the odes concerns chiefly heroic action, death, and natural catastrophe. Thus, the only conceivable modes of being are stasis (absence of narrative, pastoral reduced to gemlike hardness) and disruption,[8] and the only people are those with whom we live in harmony and the bellicose Others (Protestants and Muslims) whose very existence presents a dire threat. Predictably, this threat predominates over the illusion of peaceful harmony, just as action predominates over hollow leisure and silence over the tinkle of verse. The whole complex of values is illustrated by Sarbiewski's idiosyncratic version of the mutability theme: in his poetry time completely effaces the inauthentic, vocal, poetic order of nature, and mutability consequently is a silent and exclusively human spectacle: "Whatever a human hand has joined a human hand will tear asunder." "And I, who yesterday was beheld by many peoples not without silent joy, tomorrow shall behold the substitute tragedy from among the crowd."[9]

In order to make the ode speak, Coleridge must attempt first of all to find a compromise between the irreconcilable poles of narrative: immobility and destruction. If the language of poetry is not to be as dead as Sarbiewski's Latin, it must produce a model for a kind of change which is not destructive. It must, in sum, learn to trace a development while suppressing the shock—the "effect of suddenness"—that always accompanies development in Sarbiewski.

But the problem of voice in Sarbiewski is even more complex, for he spurns natural space along with the natural temporal continuum. The "golden profusion" of "pleasant meadows" is a deceitful illusion, and one ode reminds us that Jason had to "wound" the land "with the iron teeth of the Chalybes" before he could harvest "the deciduous manes of gold."[10] Never more than a place for temporary recuperation and dissipation of sorrow (*Odes* 3.5, "Si quae juvabit dicere saucium," again associating natural peace with a wound), nature appears more characteristically as the place in which God is silent and hidden from man: "O what region detains you in silent repose, O Jesus? What spot begrudges you to me with blind shadows or thick foliage?"[11] Indeed, Sarbiewski rarely turns his attention to nature, and then never as a real object of description but always as an unreal allegorical construct or typological prefiguration (as in *Odes* 2.13, the night sky as a figure of the absent Virgin).

There is, in effect, no world for him to describe; his speech is invariably either reflexive or empty. Where description is in order, as in *Odes* 2.12, whose subtitle is "Describit pacis commoda" [describes the comforts of peace], the incantatory excitement of the verse attempts to compensate for the absence of true vision and significant description. Instead of actually portraying the advantages of a future state of peace, the poem gives only a feeble and derivative evocation of the ceremony of triumph by the victors, with a false urgency of repetition and a false luxuriance of sound.

> Ite, Rhaetaeis sociae triumphis,
> Ite delectos religate flores,
> Ite, Virtutes: iterate nexis
>   Serta tropaeis.
>
> Te Ceres flavis redimita culmis,
> Magne pacati Moderator orbis,
> Te Jovis quercus, & Apollinaris
>   Umbra corymbi,
>
> Te volunt lauri.[12]

The emptiness of such an external world casts doubt on the authenticity of vision. The poet is a prophet, but does he see the things of which he speaks?[13] The answer is clearly no; prophecy remains intransitive. All the odes, for example, have an addressee, save one: "The Prophecy of Noah" (4.27) is the most self-consciously prophetic but also the least transitive. The omission of the addressee here indicates a general plight: Sarbiewski everywhere mistrusts his vision: "And, *Lycus*, is there anything which we discern? Or does our sight err (through the foolish lids) and the glass of the eye lie? Or is it the tale of a long sleep which is being drawn out?"[14] The odes are full of prophecies, but it is significant that the prophetic formulae are always the most cautious imaginable: "videor videre," "videor audire," "aut vidi, aut vidisse putavi" (I seem to see, I seem to hear, either I saw or I thought I saw).

Again there is a fundamental contradiction, a will to vision combined with a failure of vision. The odes contain an abundance of introspective moral reflection, but there is no revelation of an outside reality, no epiphany. Even the formulae of epiphany are absent: the Christian "ecce" does not appear significantly in the odes, and "en" (the Latin equivalent of "lo") does not appear at all.[15] Only in the *Silviludia*, a set of beautifully active hunting eclogues wrongly attributed to Sarbiewski, do we find the word "en," and the context is instructive: "Lo the many-colored flower with the painted lips of its leaves *silently* proclaims the divine graces."[16] Epiphany—the recognition of the outside world—is silent revelation. There is no revelation in Sarbiewski because there is too much noise.

Once more we return to Coleridge. First, because he installs the epiphanic appearance of an outside event; his "hark" and "see" replace Sarbiewski's theatrical "effect of suddenness" with a better prepared and more deliberate influx from outside. And second, because he corrects the imbalance between voice and eye with a perfect correlation between the sound and sight of the storm, between the music and the "glitter" of the lyre.

But the recovery in Coleridge's poem is almost too complete. His simplicity masks the complexity both of the problem and of its solution. On the one hand, he attempts to recover a temporal continuum. On the other, he attempts to restore the possibility of description, that is, of expressing the Other, the discontinuity between the self and the world. Epiphany functions, in other words, as a *discontinuous continuity*. In order to clarify its structure, we need to see it gradually emerge in response to the challenge implicit in Sarbiewski's poetry. Coleridge's poem will then find its place as the culmination of a long series of efforts to translate and assimilate Sarbiewski's odes.

* * *

Given the prominence of military imagery in Sarbiewski, one could describe the failure of his poetry as the result of a lack of discipline. Correspondingly, the one universal characteristic of the English translations is an increased formal discipline. In the couplet versions both line and couplet tend to function as units of sense, and even the freest Pindaric imitations are divided on the page into numbered stanzas that force the translator to organize his material more clearly and distinctly than do Sarbiewski's continuous stanzas. Similarly, the frequent aphorisms in the Latin can be of any length; in the translations they usually fill out one or two lines.[17]

Among the many choices to be made by the conscientious translator is that between fidelity to sound and fidelity to sense. The rare telltale Latinisms or punning translations show that it was possible to prefer sound, but the English prefer overwhelmingly to preserve the sense and simplify the rhetoric; they neglect the intricate Latin harmonies and eliminate much of the exotic paganism and many merely decorative sensuous topoi.[18] In one sense such choices impoverish the original, but in return the translations are often more general and more widely applicable than the Latin poems. Henry Vaughan, for instance, omits most mythological and geographical references, titles, direct address, and other particularizing features so as to transform poems about specific historical conflicts into utterances concerning "all" peoples.[19]

Though none simplifies so radically as Coleridge, all who discipline the excessive flamboyance of the originals endeavor to compensate for what has been sacrificed, "to supply the lost Excellencies of another *language* with new ones of their own" (Cowley, *Poems* 156). Therefore the translators countless times replace pagan, classical, or foreign details with Christian, modern, or (most often) English ones.[20] But nationalizing forms only a part of the overall endeavor of the translators, which might better be described as naturalizing. Faced with poems as dislocated in time and place as are Sarbiewski's revivals of an obsolete form, the translator attempts to place the text with respect to himself and his culture.[21] An examination of the ways in which the earlier translators attempted to localize the poems in a real time and a real space will illustrate the intentions which are more fully realized in Coleridge's version.

I will begin with a few examples of temporal placement that aims to clarify the narrative structure or point of view of the odes. Both translators of the lines "Stat tacitus cinis, / Cui serus inscribat viator: / *Cum populo jacet hic et ipso / Cum rege Regnum*" (2.5.54–57) felt the need to make the role of the "late traveler" more precise. Hils turns him into a pilgrim and emphasizes his temporal relationship to the destruction: "The silent dust remaines, to let / The weary Pilgrim this Inscription set / (In after times, as hee goes by)" (23). Hughes insists on the extent of the destruction, specifies where the inscription will be placed, and leaves no doubt that the traveler is a fictive personage: "nought remains / But dust above and desert plains, / Unless some stone this sad inscription wear, / Rais'd by some future traveller" (lines 83–86). Isaac Watts's versions are the most thoroughgoing in this regard; he strengthens or eliminates indirect constructions, simplifies complicated subordinations or turns them into independent clauses, changes rhetorical questions into exclamations, adds finite verbs, often in lieu of infinitives and participles, and supplies many vivid narrative details. The result is a complete transformation of the originals; as Coleridge says, "A few of the Odes have been translated in a very animated manner by Watts." Here is a sample:

> Vobis fugaces vidi ego Bistonum
> Errare lunas, signaque barbaris
> Derepta vesillis, et actam
> Retro equitum peditumque nubem.
>
> (4.4.65–68)

I saw Thracian crescents fleeing you, and banners torn from barbarian standards, and a cloud of horse and infantry driven back.

> Then the *Turkish* Moons
> Wander'd in Disarray. A dark Eclipse
> Hung on the Silver Crescent, boding Night,
> Long Night, to all her Sons; at length disrob'd
> The Standards fell; the barbarous Ensigns torn
> Fled in the Wind, the Sport of angry Heav'n:
> And a large Cloud of Infantry and Horse
> Scattering in wild Disorder, spread the Plain.[22]

Watts's strongly visualized, painterly landscape illustrates how narrative depends on a feeling for movement and therefore on a sense of space. Even in poems with less narrative interest the translations regularly define an absent spatial perspective or clarify an existing one. Thus, Vaughan converts Sarbiewski's baroque lament on the universal weary homelessness of mankind (*Odes* 4.15) into a Horatian satire directed against those who displace themselves by traveling abroad. The feeling of belonging to a place pervades Vaughan's version down to the smallest detail. Sarbiewski's traveler, for instance, departs from "patriis . . . arvis" (paternal fields); Vaughan expands this bare phrase in order to human-ize and localize it: "those *hills* our *fathers* walkt on here" (line 12). When Sarbiewski's traveler becomes ill, he takes his disease with him even if he returns home—home or nature is associated with illness, as elsewhere with a wound: "Frustra fideles si dominum retro / Morbi sequuntur" (in vain if faithful diseases follow their lord home; lines 17–18). Vaughan's traveler, on the other hand, takes his illness as a sign to return to where he, like all men, belongs: "And then (too late with *home* Content,) / They leave this *willful banishment*" (lines 25–26). For Sarbiewski, in fact, there is no home or place of rest on earth: "Tandemque nobis exsulibus pla-cent / Relicta" (and at length what exiles have left behind delights them; lines 21–22). The good place is not a real place but heaven. And nature is not a place but an absence, the place where I am not, the place where God is not, the place of the wound.

The emergence of a concept of real place can best be observed in the translations from the most popular of the odes, the fifth of book 2. The poem is one of many heavenly ascents in Sarbiewski; he leaves the natural world, sees the earth "vanish into a point" ("vanescit in punc-tum," line 83), and is submerged in a vast, ineffable sea of light. Though the poem is long, only one phrase has anything resembling a descrip-tive function: "hic mite coelum" (here the sky [is] mild). And this phrase belongs to an anaphoric series of clauses in which "hic" shifts con-fusingly in meaning between "here on earth" and "here in heaven"; Johann Nikolaus Götz, the most literal of the translators, can only make sense of the passage by rendering "hic . . . hic . . . hic" (lines 13–16) with "hier . . . doch anderwärts . . . dort" (here . . . but elsewhere . . . there; Götz, 2: 39). There is no real definition of place but only a polarity between absence and mysterious presence, the nothingness of earth and the indescribably transcendent heaven.

In the first of the translations, Cowley's "Exstasie," this is already changed. Cowley's heaven is not a mystical state of being, but a sublime version of the familiar sky of earth; far from overwhelming the speak-er's consciousness, it adapts itself to his capacities.

> Without *affright* or *wonder*
> I meet *Clouds* charg'd with *Thunder*,
> And *Lightnings* in my way
> Like harmless *Lambent Fiers* about my Temples play.
>   (stanza 3)

In subsequent translations the distant earth increasingly assumes its own descriptive characteristics. Two sentences out of many are particularly revealing: "Oh! Object well deserving tears!" in John Hughes's "Ecstasy" (line 17) and, in Aaron Hill's "The Transport,"

> Oh! thou dim speck!
> Thou dusky earth! farewel,
> From height, like this, I see thee, plainly now!
> Thou art, at best, a kind of hope-cool'd hell.
>
> (*Works* 3: 232)

The translations develop a new polarization, not between presence and absence but between the world of the perceiving subject and the distant world of objects, between the warm, animated world here and the world out there which is also real (otherwise it could not be addressed) but cold and inanimate. The individual's possibilities are divided not between the irreconcilable poles of life and death, but between the world in which he is now participating and the world beyond his horizon, in which he is not now a participant, though he might be at some other time.

From these observations we can begin to understand the epiphanies with which English odes abound—all those "lo"s and "see"s and "hark"s, and indeed most of the innumerable references to seeing which the translators add. They are the gesture which opens up the world to the poet. The world has always been there—objectively—but now he chooses to make it part of *his* world.[23] The term "epiphany" is unfortunate and misleading. There is no sudden change in the world, no startling self-revelation of a mystery which was formerly hidden. Rather, it is the poet who suddenly opens his eyes and looks out; he casts his light on the world and enters into a living bond with it. The English ode is not a poetry of the observing eye; it is a poetry of the illuminating eye, shedding its light on the universe.[24]

This explains the possibility of a discontinuous continuity. The objective world remains what it was. Suddenly something startling *seems* to happen: suddenly something *seems* to stream in at the poet. But nothing sudden has happened out there—*natura non facit saltus*—rather, he has suddenly blinked, turned his gaze, let the light of his countenance shine upon it.

The theological coloring which I have given this definition derives from an important fragment by the German Romantic Novalis.[25] To the sublime poets of the eighteenth century, epiphany is not yet a divine act but only the imitation of one. God remains the prime source of illumination, "one immense and ever-flowing light," as Norris's version of 2.5 has it ("The Elevation," st. 6). But the incessant epiphanizing of the eighteenth-century Pindarics is the very reverse of the continual illumination which it is designed to echo: it is bombast and completely unable to establish the desired temporal continuum bridging a spatial discontinuity. What began as a potentially expressive gesture rapidly declined into mere gesticulation. Cowley, for one, could commemorate the *middle* of his journey heavenward with, "And lo! I mount."[26] And of Aaron Hill it has been said that "perhaps no poet of his century penned a noisier page" (Aubin, *Topographical Poetry* 98).

Poetry should be continual illumination, but the poet's inspiration is both flickering and overbearing. The eye of the poet, in other words, is antithetical to the eye of poetry. The pathos of this dilemma is evoked in Hughes's "Ecstasy." "The Wond'ring Muse transported sees," in this poem, "groves of trees" on the moon. What she thought were spots were instead the result of the steady light which appears "no more in shadowy spots." Almost immediately the poet interrupts her with his "when lo!" In contrast to the Muse, the poet sees the earth, now *with* spots and with intermittent light: "And to her Sister-Moon by turns gives light" (lines 130–38). The Muse is pure imagination; at another point in the poem she looks into the future and conjures up a nostalgic world of uniform pastoral harmony. But the poet rudely interrupts with his intermittent epiphany ("and lo!") and sees, instead, present death and devastation.

> Around the space of earth I turn my eye;
>   But where's the region free from woe?
> Where shall the Muse one little spot descry
>   The seat of happiness below?
>   Here peace wou'd all its joys dispense,
> The vines and olives unmolested grow;
>   But, lo! a purple pestilence
>   Unpeoples cities, sweeps the plains,
>   Whilst vainly thro' deserted fields
>   Her unreap'd harvest Ceres yields
> And at the noon of day a midnight silence reigns.
>
>   (lines 42–52)

In the reversals of Hughes's poem we can detect the incipient stage of that troubled Wordsworthian dialectic where the light of the poetic imagination finally supersedes and disrupts the poet's "light of sense" ("the eye and progress of my Song").[27] The earlier translators imposed a discipline on Sarbiewski—in order to illuminate his fundamental message for them—but they failed to discipline themselves. The excessively emphatic eighteenth-century translations do not so much recover a foreign tradition as appropriate a foreign authority for their own poetic conventions. In translation and in its homologue, epiphanic discovery, in the confrontation both with tradition and with nature, the poet-observer illuminates the outside world, but the act of illumination is properly a passive act of participation in a common experience. The task of the Romantics in this connection is clear: epiphany must be purged of its hubris. We seem, indeed, to look beyond Coleridge toward Keats's Mnemosyne-Moneta, the goddess who links past and future and whose blank eyes "beam'd like the mild moon" (*The Fall of Hyperion*, line 269).

* * *

But for now I remain with the "eye of Day." As a response to the contradictions outlined here, Coleridge's poem shows its originality in its consistency and stylistic decorum. New-Critical immanent interpretation cannot take proper account of the poem's continuities, for immanent interpretation rests on distinctions that "open" the work, using what has been called a "hermeneutic wedge," such as a verbal or structural irony, as an initial foothold.[28] An immanent approach will not necessarily "falsify" the poem, but it will inevitably slight what is undoubtedly the poem's greatest asset, the smooth, simple flow of its verse.

What then are the continuities of the poem? Note, first, some possible ironies (that is, possible discontinuities) which are avoided. "Clouds rise thick with heavy louring." There is a possible irony of personification; the clouds seem to stare at the poet. I will return to this. There is a possible irony in the treatment of substance: the clouds are thick, filmy matter is seen as dense. And this irony, barely hinted, is virtually absorbed in a third possible irony of motion: the clouds rise heavy. In another context there would appear to be a conflict of directions, but in this poem there is a perfect merging of directions. The light emanates upward from the glittering lyre and is watched by the eye of day. The lyre hangs down but shines up. The wind seems simultaneously to rise and fall—to hover and die. A generalized diffusion of energy—energy simultaneously of sight, of sound, and of motion—replaces a limited directionality.[29] Only the lines devoted to the poet gently—and as will be seen, significantly— emphasize the downward direction: "lying," "waterfall," "reclin'd."

A related diffusion of semantic energy results in the avoidance of a number of possible puns. Puns depend on a concentration of meaning; they split one word into two meanings or else yoke two words into one. But Coleridge presents us with a paronomastic spectrum that overthrows the whole notion of a plurality of distinct meanings. The lyre glitters "to" the sun: does the word mean "toward" or "in response to"? Which is the source of light, which the recipient? The "air" is ended. This "pun" occurs repeatedly in early Coleridge. The air is the atmosphere, Sarbiewski's "aer." Can the atmosphere end? Or is this the tune? Surely Coleridge perceives the end of the musical air. But a tune does not breathe except figuratively; literally the air breathes: the wind, as the poem says, "sighs." Or is "sighs" a figurative expression, a metonymy applying to the wind what really belongs to the harp? Can the wind be "solemn" or does that word really apply to the music? It becomes impossible to speak of two meanings, literal and figurative, proper and metonymic; there is one air, not two, a generalized diffusion of music informing both the atmosphere and the lyre.[30] What about "lay"? There is another possible pun. The lyre—or the air—sings its "lay" and the poet lies down. Does the poet imitate the lyre? Does he imitate metaphorically (he wants to be like it) or metonymically (it charms him to sleep)? Dare one say that the lyre makes him a lie-er? Surely not; at least, the text shuns any such semantic outrage. There is a generalized participation by the poet in the music but no definable yoking together of distinct meanings, no pun. What about "louring"? Again there is a possible pun, suggested by the editions which print the word as "lowering" (Shedd) or "low'ring" (E. H. Coleridge). Could "louring" mean "sinking lower"?[31] That would perhaps rhyme better with "roaring" than the primary meaning does. It would also make nonsense of the line: "clouds rise sinking lower." Clearly, there is no pun here either. Still, the suppressed second meaning ("sinking") does have a function: it deflects attention away from the witty personification which yokes the cloud to a glaring human face and thus it further relaxes the tone. These are all examples of what William Empson would call emotive language: they are simple words, with a fluid range of meaning.[32] Coleridge's artfulness thus restores the native emotional force of language.

Astonishingly, the diffusion of power affects the event. Even an attentive reading must miss the significance of the third stanza unless the historical substructure has first been revealed: we must know that we are to look for an epiphany which is a streaming out, directed by mind, and not a streaming in directed by matter. While Sarbiewski first sees clouds then hears the actual sound of rain, Coleridge hears distant sounds then sees gathering clouds. We presume that in Coleridge's version a storm looms, breaks in on the poet's slumber, wets the instrument. This natural inference in fact is made explicit in Johann Gottfried Herder's version of the ode ("Die flüchtige Freude," *Werke* 3: 339). But Coleridge does not sleep; he only expresses an intention to sleep. We infer that Coleridge goes to sleep after stanza 2, as we infer that it rains after stanza 3, but the poem, like "A Slumber Did My Spirit Seal," does not report the external occurrences.[33] Even the epiphanic moments in stanza 3 do not designate external actions; they mark the instant when consciousness is directed to ongoing processes. Coleridge's poem concerns itself above all with states of mind. Indeed, it is not certain that anything forceful, abrupt, or discontinuous actually happens outside. For in a beautiful displacement, Coleridge has added a waterfall to the ode. Somewhere water is already falling, in a natural anticipation of the storm. Coleridge *may* leave, in melancholy, after the rain. But he may leave out of prudence, his attention called to the anticipated effect of the rain by the spray which has already collected on the lyre. Such is the diffusion in Coleridge's poem that ultimately we do not know what occurs when.

Is the poem just an elaborate pun, a deceitful action by nature (by the waterfall) imitating a true epiphanic interruption (the fall of rain) and warning Coleridge, with a kind of comic catharsis, not to mistake the real sources of natural power? Is there, behind the sublime exclamations of the third stanza, an implied theology, however vague? No, the concept of power and of action is too diffuse even for that. It cannot confidently be said that anything in nature makes the lyre wet. The rainstorm is never explicitly described. The waterfall is present but only out there in the distance ("*yon* waterfall"). And even before the waterfall is mentioned, the lyre appears, by a further anticipation, *already wet*. For what glitters in Coleridge is always water.[34] Thus, in "The Eolian Harp," "Through my half-clos'd eyelids I behold / The sunbeams dance, like diamonds, on the main" (lines 36–37); in "Religious Musings," "dewy glitter" (line 101); and in "Separation," "Wealth's glittering fairy-dome of ice" (line 11). *The Aeolian harp, for Coleridge, is that thing which is always already wet*, always ecstatically out there in the world, even when it is here. As a bright and glittering object, it is always the focus of attention, always monitory, always epiphanic. It is continual illumination. And it is poetry.[35]

What does this mean? It means that poetic, "Aeolian" simplicity mediates a radically new conception of events. An event is no longer merely an "occurrence," something that "runs into" one. Instead, an event is a diffusion of power. An event is an occurrence (for example, a rainstorm) that the observer takes into his or her world. Its effect is not highly localized—in a particular moment of time and a particular word of the poem—but it spreads out, coloring the future and also the past. An event is the interpretation of an occurrence; more specifically, it is the reevaluation of the observer's position, as it is, as it was, and as it will be. The cardinal event in Coleridge's poem, an event described in the text and not merely implied between the stanzas, is a change of mind, the replacement of one intention ("I will slumber") by another ("Let me seize thy wetted string").

An event colors the past and future as well as the present. No longer is time divided into two exclusive categories, the *now* and the *not-now*, the quick and the dead. Instead, the past, to the extent that it is capable of being thought at all, is still in some sense with us, affecting our behavior and capable of being affected by it. And the future, to the extent that it can be imagined at all, is already in some sense with us, influencing our intentions and influenced by them.

The poem's verb tenses flesh out this conception of experience. From the present perfect of the first line[36] through the imperative, the abundance of present participles, and the varieties of present indicative—the iterative "sighs," the momentary "hark," the incipient or durative "rise" and "blackens"—to the future-directed intentional present of "let me seize" and the gnomic, generalized present of the moral, there is a sense of continued presence, continually changing. (Herder's translation, by contrast, gives the reader a jolt with one past tense: "Dunkle Wolken umhülleten / Den heitern Himmel" [dark clouds have covered o'er the cheerful sky; *Werke* 3: 339].) The experience possesses an extraordinary ductility; there is not one single occurrence but a constellation of a dozen different ones, each with its own impetus, which combine to make the rainstorm. The sources of action are many and widely diffused.

Yet it would not be accurate to call this simply a subjectivization of the concepts of time and experience, for the observing subject is suppressed to the same extent as the rainstorm. The approach of the storm seems sudden primarily because Coleridge is slumbering; he, the subject, has decided to absent himself from the occurrence. The crucial lines in this connection are the pair which forms something of an exception to the general pattern of the poem: "I will slumber, careless lying, / By yon waterfall reclin'd." Here is the one verb not in the present tense, the one element of apparently unfettered choice, and the one passage in which a single direction of movement predominates. But the direction is downward, a movement of inertia, toward the object earth and away from the principle of life. Paradoxically, free choice—the act of subjectivity—has as its goal this gravitational movement, absence of will, slumber.

Experience is participation in the "life of things," "identifying the Percipient & the Perceived," as Coleridge comments on Wordsworth's phrase (*Notebooks* 921). More accurately, in view of the repeated anticipations and the crucial future tense in the poem, one could say that experience is an anticipatory self-projection into the world.[37] It is active— you bring things into your life. It is also passive—you enter into the life of things. Really, it is active and passive at once and indivisibly, for "self-experience . . . is not possible without an intermediate faculty"—the imagination, and above all the poetic imagination—"which is at once both active and passive" (*Biographia Literaria* 72).[38] It demands a will to enter in, somewhere: a partial submergence of things (you cannot attend to everything at once) and also a partial submergence of self. Full active presence of mind is unthinkable (though entry 2026 in the *Notebooks* does attribute to poetic geniuses the power of "*pure Action*, defecated of all that is material & passive"); it would mean that everything passed in review as an indifferent spectacle, without once casting the mind into a state of passive receptivity and affecting it. Coleridge's will to indolence in this poem, as a translation of Sarbiewski, is a form of discipline; it is the proper disciplining of egotism.[39]

* * *

Such is the nature of Coleridge's response to the problems of vision and temporality in Sarbiewski's baroque odes. Yet Coleridge's imitation, though a fine poem, is not a great one, and its shortcomings help to identify one of the fundamental ambitions of the Romantic poets.

It seems evident that the weakest lines are the somewhat top-heavy moral. Having established a continuous flow, Coleridge cannot close it off without breaking it. A similarly broken progression toward a moral is found throughout Coleridge, in "The Eolian Harp," in "The Rime of the Ancient Mariner," in "Christabel," in "Dejection," as indeed in Coleridge's life.[40] Yet it is difficult to pinpoint the nature of the break. In the version by Coleridge's friend Joseph Hucks a new, reflective speaking voice supervenes and draws the moral by rational analogy; the outcome is a false identification of the fleeing man with the figure of pleasure: "O my harp, my companion, my treasure, / Let us rise, let us *hasten away*: / 'Tis thus flies the phantom of pleasure, / With quick step ever *hasting away*" (182, my italics). But Coleridge grafts on his moral in a more subtle, seemingly less arbitrary fashion. He links it phonically ("swiftly flies"—"softly sighs") and rhetorically ("on the wing"—"on thy wires hov'ring") to the wind. Furthermore, he links it as a personification to the earlier personifications—to the personification of the wind, to the subdued but paradoxically threatening personification of the clouds, and especially, by rhyme and similarity of function, to the personification of the lyre ("parent of the *soothing* measure"—"the *flatterer*, Pleasure"). Coleridge thus aims at a generalized diffusion of relationships between the event and the moral. The moral appears to arise not out of a posterior reflection but rather as a musical echo, a sympathetic vibration in the mind.

Still, there is an evident break in tone, and it colors our sense not so much of the last two lines as of the first fourteen. In contrast to Sarbiewski's eroticism, Coleridge's poem is cool, almost inert, with its soothing parental figure, for instance, replacing what Coleridge's punning ear must have taken to be a "buxom" daughter. But abruptly "the flatterer, Pleasure," emerges as a new character for whom nothing in the earlier lines has prepared the reader. Instead of an interpenetration of human awareness and natural process, an external agency now seems to frustrate Coleridge's desires. In particular, we are reminded of another concealed flatterer, Sarbiewski's "whistling Eurus," hidden behind the sibilants of Coleridge's sixth line. In the light of the closing lines, we are led to see the wind as a seducer, playing on the harp in order to attract the poet; Coleridge's slumber in the distance then appears as a rejection of nature's advances and the scowling storm clouds as the lover's angry reaction. Thus, despite Coleridge's efforts to link the moral to what precedes, it is a new event that affects, as events often do, what seems already past. The language has seemed completely compact, with no distinction of levels, of literal and figurative, of sense and significance. But from the later perspective the event is seen merely as a literal level on which an allegorical interpretation can be imposed. The event seemed rich; it now seems less completely rich. It seemed eloquent, but now it seems to need a spokesman. The precarious continuity has been broken.

As a summary indication of the subsequent course of development I should like to juxtapose Coleridge's poem with the work of a major post-Romantic poet, Stéphane Mallarmé. Needless to say, there is even less occasion to speak of Coleridge's "influence" on Mallarmé than of Sarbiewski's on Coleridge. Nevertheless, in both cases the later poet's solution sheds light on the problems of the earlier poet: Mallarmé's poetry, that is, helps to show what was needed in order to complete the project begun in works such as "Ad Lyram."

Even in the absence of a direct line of historical influence, Coleridge and Mallarmé share important concerns. What Hugo Friedrich has identified as "the three fundamental forces of [Mallarmé's] poetry and of his thought" are named in a line of the poem "Salut" which introduces the collected poems: "solitude, récif, étoile" (*Struktur* 90). The two poles of experience are thus virtually identical for the two poets: on the one hand, the isolated consciousness, on the other, the distant star (the "eye of Day" in "Ad Lyram," "the star of eve" in "The Eolian Harp"). What is more striking is that the mediating objects also correspond, since both Coleridge's Aeolian harp and Mallarmé's reef are always already immersed in the spray of the world. This implies, as we have seen, that for both poets the unity of experience is provided by an existential projection.

But there remains a crucial difference. Coleridge's Aeolian harp is the pure poetic voice of the world, corresponding to the sound of waters in Wordsworth or (more precariously) in Joseph von Eichendorff; it is the goal of a profound, though sometimes ambivalent desire. Mallarmé's reef, by contrast, is a place of shipwreck and destruction; it is "time, the cape," whose sinking ship reflects "night, despair, and precious stones" ("Au seul souci de voyager"). The shipwreck, unlike the harp, is "silent," and its instrument—not a lyre, of course, but a (fog)horn—is "without virtue" and "enslaved even to echoes" ("A la nue accablante tu"). Throughout Mallarmé's poetry runs the yearning for an echoing song that is the reverse of the voice of the harp, not protected and edenic but destructive; he likens poetry to a swan that remains whole even when it dies and that causes more pain to the human poet than to itself ("Petit air II"). If Coleridge's harp is the pure voice of poetry, then Mallarmé's reef answers with an elusive siren voice that destroys the poetic voice.[41] Mallarmé's poetry calls for a destruction of the poetic image.

The obstacle in Coleridge's poetry is the dependence on a symbolic image, an object or occurrence which is not really literal, which does not mean itself but something else: "My heart plays an incessant music / for which I need an outward Interpreter" (*Notebooks* 2035).[42] This is the residual discontinuity in his work. Some 25 years later Shelley was still struggling to achieve a musical fusion with nature in a fully organic language, though he experienced the struggle with the greater anguish of a generation-long ambition still unfulfilled: "Make me thy lyre, even as the forest is . . . Be thou, Spirit fierce, / My spirit! Be thou me!" ("Ode to the West Wind"). In Mallarmé, subject, object, and language are all absorbed into pure, unbroken relationships—what Derrida has called an "irreducible excess of the syntactic over the semantic"[43]—into "an extraordinary appropriation of structure, limpid, from the primitive fires of logic" ("Le Mystère dans les lettres"). Two works name their primitive structure in the title—*Igitur* (therefore) and "Or" (now); in others it forms the obvious backbone of the text—"comme si" in "Petit air I" and in part of the *Coup de dés*, for instance—and always there is an attempt to abolish objects. The book itself is no longer an object; it effervesces into a "spiritual instrument."[44]

The Romantics continue to need an instrument, a symbol around which to organize their experience. For them, to return to the theme of

Coleridge's poem, an event is a re-placement of the self *by means of something*. In Mallarmé, an event is pure placement: "RIEN N'AURA EU LIEU QUE LE LIEU" (*Un Coup de dés*, *Oeuvres* 474–75).

The task the Romantics face in their great works is the submergence of the symbol. This task itself is symbolized in their abiding fascination with dangerous vessels[45] and (above all in Wordsworth and Goethe) with floods and drowning. In Coleridge himself the effort to repress or submerge the symbolizing activity of the mind is perhaps the strongest of all. It is for this reason, for example, that his odes never summon but rather dismiss the powers of the imagination: one thinks of the titles "Ode to the Departing Year" and "The Recantation: an Ode" (later retitled "France: an Ode"), of the apostrophe in "Dejection: an Ode," "Hence, viper thoughts, that coil around my mind," and of the inevitable refrain of "An Ode to the Rain," "Do go, dear Rain! do go away!" From this perspective the poem that should form the center of a future study is not a conversation poem or a poem of imagination (though the symbolic albatross sinks "like lead into the sea") but rather a poem that lies somewhere in between—a song whose title, incidentally, is a phonetic elaboration of the word "lute"—the strange love chant, "Lewti": "Nay, treacherous image! Leave my mind— / For Lewti never will be kind."

CHAPTER 8

Romanticism and Enlightenment

The new age proclaims itself fleet-footed, sole-winged; the dawn
has put on seven-league boots.—Long has lightning flashed on the
horizon of poetry; all heaven's stormy force was compressed into
a mighty cloud; now it thundered mightily, now it seemed to retreat
and flashed only from afar, soon to return all the more fearsomely:
soon there will be no more talk of a single storm, but all the heavens
will burn with one flame, and then all your petty lightning rods will
avail no longer. Then the nineteenth century begins in earnest. . . .
Then there will be readers who can read.
             —Schlegel, "Über die Unverständlichkeit"

Romanticisms and Enlightenments

ARTHUR O. LOVEJOY'S famous essay "On the Discrimination of
Romanticisms" showed the problem decades ago: Romanticism cannot
be defined. To write an essay called "Romanticism and Enlightenment"
seems, then, to be an impossibility compounded. In any reasonably
comprehensive view, the eighteenth century was not dramatically more
uniform than the early nineteenth. Indeed, in one crucial respect it was
less so, for no fact so inescapably galvanized the Enlightenment mind as
that of revolution did the mind of Romanticism. There are many versions of Enlightenment—aristocratic and bourgeois, rationalist and empiricist, modernist and classicist, mercantilist and laissez-faire, urban
and pastoral, religious and secular. Properly speaking, this chapter
should be entitled "Enlightenments and Romanticisms," a multiplicity
that leaves no hook except the little word "and" to hang a hat on.

That is what I propose to do. Though we may not be able to define
either Enlightenment or Romanticism, we may succeed better at defining their relationship. The historical sensibility was more fully developed in the Romantic period than earlier, and this means that how the
present relates to the past can be more important than what that past
was. We may be able to understand the "and" that connects Enlighten-

ments with Romanticisms without needing to fix either period as an entity. It is clear that such an approach—focusing on the process rather than the materials or the product—will not give us objective determinations. The "and" of the title is a vector without a precise location. I shall not ask what Enlightenment and Romanticism were in their essence, for they are each too manifold. Moreover, I shall compound the turn away from a goal of "objectivity" by asking how the Romantics sensed their relationship to the preceding generations rather than by attempting to ascertain the external facts.

For the truth is that the facts are contradictory. It is a truism, on the one hand, that the Romantics rebelled against their predecessors. The typical Romantic—so conventional wisdom runs—went to extremes. He was a godless revolutionary in his youth and, if he lived long enough, an orthodox traditionalist in his age but in neither case an Enlightened progressive. Somewhere along the line, the humanist tolerance best typified by Voltaire, Lessing, and Johnson (see Barnouw, "Erziehung des Menschengeschlechts") lost its appeal, giving way on the one hand to the libertinism of a Shelley or a Byron, on the other to the bigoted Catholicism of several of the older German Romantics. A common intellectual enemy was Newtonian rationalism, whose desiccated narrowness was attacked by Blake, by Keats (in *Lamia*), and, with otherwise uncharacteristic savagery, by Goethe in his vast *Theory of Color*. Romanticism, on this view, attacked Enlightened, classicizing, conformist rationalism in recognition of unstated emotions and unconscious instincts.

The evidence for the Romantic attack on Enlightenment lies everywhere at hand. The antirationalism of a De Quincey comes late enough that one might hesitate to identify it as an original impulse of Romanticism. But already among the first generation of Romantics one finds the geologist and poet Novalis (Friedrich von Hardenberg, 1772–1801) who, before his early death, composed the *Hymns to the Night*, the dream-dominated medievalizing romance *Heinrich von Ofterdingen*, the mystical, orientalizing story "The Apprentices at Sais," and the aphorisms collected under the titles *Pollen* and *Belief and Love*, most famous among them being the utterance "The secret way goes inward." Novalis was the subject of influential early essays by Carlyle: he was widely admired in mid-nineteenth-century France (see Besset, *Novalis et la pensée mystique*); and he has been taken (by Hugo Friedrich) to be, like Poe, a fountainhead of symbolist and expressionist poetry. If there had been one Romanticism confronting one Enlightenment in all of Europe, dark against light, Novalis would have been it. Were that the case, our story would be quickly told.

That simple story, finally, is easily corroborated in the English context. Blake assaulted all the canons of eighteenth-century art along with all the preconceptions of Lockean empiricism; Wordsworth vilified the diction of eighteenth-century poetry; supernatural sensationalism, such as Fielding reduces to ridicule in *Tom Jones* (8.11; 16.5), became the norm in the Romantic novel in England, France, Germany, and America; and Enlightened cosmopolitanism gave way to nationalism and the revival of indigenous mythologies. The eighteenth century wrote satire in heroic couplets, moral odes, local poetry, and extended didactic poems in Miltonic blank verse; the Romantics wrote sonnets, blank verse meditative lyrics, ballads, mythological or metaphysical odes, and first-person epics. Eighteenth-century novels were picaresque or epistolary; Romantic novelists satirized the picaresque or else wrote social, historical, or Gothic fictions. Eighteenth-century philosophy was empiricist and materialist; Romantic philosophy, after passing through the inhuman rigors of neo-Spinozism, became transcendental and idealist (see McFarland, *Coleridge and the Pantheist Tradition*).

Much in that conventional account is true. But inevitably a closer look complicates the picture. Writers such as Morse Peckham (*The Triumph of Romanticism*) and Virgil Nemoianu (*The Taming of Romanticism* 34) have shown the degree to which Enlightenment values persist despite the changed atmosphere of the nineteenth century. Formal philosophy, which became transcendental in Germany, remained rationalist with a tinge of mysticism in the French ideologues, rationalist with a tinge of metaphysics both in the English tradition that leads from David Hartley to William Godwin and Jeremy Bentham and in the later Scottish school of Thomas Reid, Dugald Stewart, and William Hamilton. Wordsworth's aesthetics, through the influence of Archibald Alison, remained strongly in the associationist tradition. Voltaire's ideal of tolerance continued in the writings of Schlegel, Shelley, and French Revolutionary thinkers—contemporaries often more different from one another than from their common ancestor. The "and" hinging Romanticism to Enlightenment links as much as it separates.

Literary developments are similarly complex. Neoclassicism, which was a formative element in the Enlightenment, remained a powerful if variable current in Goethe (who translated two of Voltaire's tragedies), Schiller, the later Schlegels, the artists of the French Revolution, Shelley, Keats, and the later Wordsworth ("Laodamia"). The mythological works of Keats, Shelley, and Friedrich Hölderlin in many respects remained faithful to the syncretic and euhemerist traditions of the Enlightenment, partly because they drew on many now forgotten seventeenth- and eighteenth-century mythographic compendia (see Hungerford, *Shores of Darkness*). In verse, Popean satire was not only reborn in Byron but also strongly colored Blake's prophecies and left traces in some of Shelley's works and even a few of Keats's. The development of stage drama is at once too complicated and (in Britain at least) too uninteresting to examine in detail here, but broadly it may be said that both in England and in France the main forms of Romantic drama (melodramatic tragedy, domestic comedy, and opera) grew continuously out of the eighteenth-century traditions, while in Germany the marked shift in style beginning around 1760 was more a turn from French to English models than an advance from Enlightenment to Romanticism. Nor did the Romantic novel simply reject earlier forms: Austen modeled her moralism and her meticulous prose on Johnson, while the epistolary novel survived, largely through the mediation of Goethe's *Werther*, in Hölderlin's *Hyperion*, Ugo Foscolo's *Jacopo Ortis*, Scott's *Redgauntlet*, and numerous others. These manifestations added up to a great deal of important writing in the Romantic period that prolonged Enlightenment paradigms, even while the mainstream—Romantic lyric, mythological closet drama (*Manfred, Prometheus Unbound, Faust*), and the familiar essays of Lamb and Hazlitt—differed profoundly from Enlightenment norms. Hence, writers like Marilyn Butler (*Romantics, Rebels and Reactionaries* 1– 10), Jerome J. McGann ("The Anachronism of George Crabbe," *Beauty of Inflections* 294–312), and Anne K. Mellor (*Romanticism and Gender* 209– 12, where the term *post-Enlightenment* is even briefly proposed) have increasingly objected that the simple view of Romanticism as a rejection of Enlightenment delivers a woefully impoverished picture of what was actually written by major figures in the decades after 1800.

A converse objection, long familiar, is that many elements of Romanticism are present in writers of earlier generations. Romantic nature feeling—affectionate dwelling on particulars, along with dreaming or daydreaming in dark grottoes, amid vast wildernesses, or on high mountains—is widespread in the writing of the second half of the eighteenth century, and it can easily be traced further back, to James Thomson and Edward Young, to moments in Pope's *Windsor Forest* and *Eloïsa to Abelard*, or, on the Continent, to such works as the precise descriptive poems of Thomson's German translator, Barthold Heinrich Brockes (1680–1747). The ballad revival, the Spenserian revival, the Gothic novel, the cult of sentiment, all date from the middle of the eighteenth century. Blank verse lyric really begins not with Wordsworth and Coleridge but with Akenside and his circle. Wordsworth's attack on poetic diction is foreshadowed in Oliver Goldsmith's *Life of Parnell* and again in chapter 8 of *The Vicar of Wakefield*, with its criticism of the "false taste" of the period that admires "a string of epithets that improve the sound without carrying on the sense." Countercurrents of Enlightenment culture, on this view, become main currents of Romantic thought: Swedenborg and Young lead to Blake (who illustrated Young's *Night Thoughts*), with the nine parts of *The Four Zoas* and of Shelley's *Queen Mab* modeled on Young's nine (see Curran, *Shelley's Annus Mirabilis*, chap. 1); Berkeley funnels into Coleridge, Friedrich Klopstock's Biblical dramas into Byron's, and Rousseau and Diderot (virtually exact contemporaries of Johnson, Gray, and Hume) into everybody. These countercurrents, it often used to be said (best by Henri Monglond in *Le Préromantisme*), constituted a preromanticism that coexisted with the official Enlightenment.

To be sure, few scholars still use the term *preromanticism*. Dislodging individual themes and motifs from the contexts where they occur gives a distorted picture of their significance: however steadily Brockes and Thomson may look at their subjects, devotional descriptions of birds and flowers do not greatly resemble Wordsworth's personal memory poems. And isolated and imperfect anticipations, such as Mark Akenside's *Inscriptions* or Horace Walpole's *Castle of Otranto* (written in 1764 but, as K. K. Mehrotra's *Horace Walpole and the English Novel* showed, not really influential until about the time of Ann Radcliffe), or even the handful of nature sonnets written by William Lisle Bowles in the years around 1790, do not equate with the prolific and controlled achievements of the Romantics. "Preromanticism," though widely diffused, turns out to be an unwitting and accidental by-product of other impulses, and hence radically different from the consciously worked out aims of the various Romantic writers, richly elaborated in a coherent body of works.

Nevertheless, accounts of an eighteenth-century preromanticism and of a Romantic post-Enlightenment conjointly remain valuable. What they lack in a spurious coherence they make up in a genuine complexity. They have taught us that many and often clashing forces were at play in both periods. We have been taught to view our traditional period concepts, as McGann says, more "critically." From Arnold to Yeats and beyond, Wordsworth and Shelley alike (let alone Keats and Blake) had been treated as elite, essentially private poets. A scholarly counterwave in the 1950's and 1960's stressed the fashionable, popular or populist dimensions of their writing. Yet the most recent criticism—partially returning to and contextualizing some Arnoldian themes (such as that poetry is the criticism of life)—has recognized that fashions respond to countervailing fashions. (This has always been evident in the German case, where the "Romanticism" of Novalis and the Schlegels encountered the simultaneous "Classicism" of Goethe, Schiller, and Wilhelm von Humboldt in a sometimes loyal, sometimes embittered opposition.) Recognizing "post-Enlightenment" values has meant learning again to highlight the oppositional elements in Romantic poetry. Wordsworth praising peasants, Shelley free love, Blake intellectual warfare, Byron libertine heroism, or Austen the traditional virtues of agrarian society— these all mean something different in the abstract from what they mean in a world of growing industrialism and antirevolutionary turmoil and repression.

Whatever one's assessment of individual arguments, critical and ideological readings of Romantic works have greatly increased our perception of covert and implicit meanings embodied within them. But they have also greatly complicated the task of the literary historian. It was all too easy to take Romantic values as the new and Enlightenment values as the old—or, worse, as the waves of the future and the past respectively in a world perpetually lacking a present. But if writing is oppositional (designed, one might simply say, to persuade someone of something), then we are dealing with a clash of contemporaneous values whose historical dimension remains to be investigated. The same considerations apply to the now outmoded accounts of preromanticism. Preromantic traits are undoubtedly present throughout the eighteenth century, and we owe a debt of gratitude to the scholars who have pointed them out. But these traits are oppositional features of the Enlightenment itself, not glimmerings of a new dawn; they need to be referred to their contemporary context in order to be understood. The Enlightenment can no more be limited to the *Essay on Man* than Romanticism to the cuckoo-and-daffodil vein.

And that is just as well. The traditional historical picture suffered from the illusion that we could simplify our task by assigning some features of a period to some other period. But the procedure is obviously circular. We need to know which values are Romantic in order to disentangle Romantic writing from post-Enlightenment writing, or preromantic from Enlightenment. But we need first to have disentangled them in order to know which values are Romantic. And the separation, could it be performed, is inimical to historical understanding. It tells us, at most, the difference between Enlightenment and Romanticism, but it does not explain the relationship between the two. Suppose we say that Enlightenment, to use Abrams's terms, is the mirror of wit, Romanticism the lamp of genius; that Enlightenment is collective and social and Romanticism private and individual (or, in accounts by Theodor Adorno and some others, the reverse); that Enlightenment is universalizing, Romanticism historicizing—any such characterizations obscure the processes by which Romanticism emerges out of Enlightenment. A taxonomic approach to periodization denies the rights of history. For all these reasons, we need to develop a more dialectical account than has hitherto been customary. Using an antithetical idiom, we can say that Romanticism *grows out* of Enlightenment. The new turns against the old, but it does so from a historical logic already inscribed in the old and still preserved in the new. The historical thrust of Enlightenment and the historical memory of Romanticism must alike be recognized if their succession is to be comprehended. Romanticism and Enlightenment differ from one another in consequence of the ways in which each differs internally from itself—in which Enlightenment is driven toward its opposite and in which Romanticism incorporates its antithesis.

The Darkness of Enlightenment

From a certain perspective it appears natural to pit the optimism or elation of the post-Restoration decades against the satiric impulse that dominated in the early eighteenth century. While the party of faith reacted to the Restoration with the resignation of the blind Milton, typified by the gloomy classicism of *Samson Agonistes*, or else with the bitterness of Marvell's "Last Instructions to a Painter," the party of Enlightenment welcomed what we call the "Glorious Revolution" in a mood of exalted panegyric. Dryden served as its spokesman, for despite the ever-popular *MacFlecknoe* and *Absalom and Achitophel*, he was only occasionally a satirist. It can easily be made to seem, then, as if the radiant fabric of Enlightenment gradually unraveled, with didacticism steadily giving way, for better or worse, before satire. With *The Rape of the Lock* leading to *The Dunciad*, Pope to Johnson, and the bright Augustan Age to the gloom of sensibility, the pattern seems to continue. From this scheme derives the oversimplified account, discussed in the first section of my chapter, which treats Romanticism as the rejection of Enlightenment and as the embrace of darkness.

By recognizing that darkness lies at the heart of Enlightenment, we can rearrange and clarify the received historical picture. If Dryden is at all representative, the mood of elation preceded the facts that were to justify it, for he celebrated Cromwell as a bringer of peace in the "Heroic Stanzas" before celebrating Charles in the same role in "Astraea Redux." Enlightenment rationalism, in other words, existed as an anticipatory cast of mind, even before it had any genuine reason to celebrate. And the hopes proved to be excessive, as genuine hope must always be. In that excess already lay the seed of the self-division that characterizes Enlightenment and that eventually destroyed it.

Here, from Dryden's "Annus Mirabilis," his greatest poem of the 1660's, are some euphoric stanzas that portray the Royal Society:

> This I fore-tel, from your auspicious care,
>   Who great in search of God and Nature grow:
> Who best your wise Creator's praise declare,
>   Since best to praise his works is best to know.
>
> O truly Royal! who behold the Law,
>   And rule of beings in your Makers mind,
> And thence, like Limbecks, rich Idea's draw,
>   To fit the levell'd use of humane kind. (657–64)

The bravado of this mood lies in its ready linkages of the divine and the human. The explosive formula of Spinozistic pantheism, *deus sive natura* ("God, i.e., nature," as it might be rendered), lurks close at hand. Milton's Adam, a year later, was to seek what the Archangel Raphael calls "knowledge within bounds" (*Paradise Lost* 7.120). His aim closely resembles Dryden's; he desires revelation in order, as he says, "the more / To magnifie his works, the more we know" (7.96–97). Yet Adam's priorities are clear: knowledge exists to further praise. Dryden's *ands*, by contrast, obscure the priority of God and nature, praise and knowledge, the rationality of law and the authority of rule. Likewise, the "is" in line 660—an uncommon and pointedly vague usage in Dryden's early style—obscures the relationship between present accomplishment and future potential: reason prevails at the expense of any clear ordering of values. And the last two lines run further risks in their implicit correlation of science with commerce, speculation with profit. "Reasoning I oft admire," Adam was soon to say, "How Nature wise and frugal could commit / Such disproportions, with superfluous hand / So many nobler Bodies to create, / Greater so manifold, to this one use" (*Paradise Lost* 8.25–29). Raphael immediately corrects Adam's rationalism with the injunction to "be lowlie wise" (8.173); there are many mysteries, he says, and the lights of heaven do not exist solely to enlighten man's mind. Reason reduces all things to man's measure.

Dryden in 1666 was no Leveller. The specious humility of his word "levell'd" betrays reason's dangerous reductions. Immediately, the perils of conflict arise to haunt the smooth progress of mind: "But first the toils of war we must endure" (665). Reason's alchemy promises to put all things on an even keel, but its anticipated glorious dawn is irremediably shadowed by the unpredictable terrain of experience. (The mixed metaphors are implied by Dryden's text and combine with the willed simplicity of the diction to constitute the complex strength of his style and of his insight.) Enlightenment begets self-scrutiny: the greater the aspirations of reason, the more difficult it is for humans to realize them. Thus does the elation of the 1660's prepare the way for the "unpolish'd, rugged Verse" (*Religio Laici* 453) of Dryden's doctrinal poems and of his fables.

> Dim as the borrow'd beams of Moon and Stars
> To lonely, weary, wandring Travellers,
> Is Reason to the Soul: And as on high,
> Those rowling Fires discover but the Sky
> Not light us here; So Reason's glimmering Ray

> Was lent, not to assure our doubtfull way,
> But guide us upward to a better Day.
> And as those nightly Tapers disappear
> When Day's bright Lord ascends our Hemisphere;
> So pale grows Reason at Religions sight;
> So dyes, and so dissolves in Supernatural Light.
>
> (*Religio Laici* 1–11)

Whether in religion or in politics, the Enlightenment yearned for the splendor of the sun. But it never forgot that light is born out of darkness. Charles II, Dryden says, began subject to a "black Star," and the "thaw" in 1660—so Dryden wishfully writes—came as but a heightening of the palette of experience.

> Yet as wise Artists mix their colours so
> That by degrees they from each other go,
> Black steals unheeded from the neighb'ring white
> Without offending the well cous'ned sight:
> So on us stole our blessed change; while we
> Th' effect did feel but scarce the manner see.
>
> ("Astraea Redux" 113, 134, 125–30)

The Enlightenment never basked in light; it was a world groping its way out of the darkness or seeing feelingly.

> The Gods are just;
> But how can finite measure infinite?
> Reason! alas, it does not know itself! . . .
> Whatever is, is in its causes just,
> Since all things are by fate. But purblind man
> Sees but a part o'the chain; the nearest links;
> His eyes not carrying to that equal beam,
> That poises all above.—
>
> (Dryden, *Oedipus* 3.1, in *Works*,
> ed. Scott 6: 174)

These lines, anticipating *Religio Laici* by some three years, typify the "Romantic" Enlightenment; in introducing the play, Dryden's Romantic editor Walter Scott calls them "excellent poetry, [which] expresses more sound truth, than a whole shelf of philosophers" (6: 123). If only the play were not so gruesome, Scott thinks the "complete management of light and shade" on the modern stage would let it "be represented with striking effect" (6: 120). We are not used to thinking of the Enlightenment as too extreme in its passions for the Romantics, but it could be. (For Wordsworth's complex response to *Religio Laici* and to Pope see Sanford Budick's brilliant essay "Chiasmus and the Making of Literary Tradition.")

The great philosophical image of the age was that of Descartes, sitting in the wintry darkness of Germany and seeking out reason by the light of his stove, "like a man who walks alone and in the shadows" (*Discourse on Method*, part 2). Like Dryden some decades later, Descartes was writing out of an experience of religious warfare with one claimant to sovereignty pitted against another (opening sentences of *Discourse*, part 2), but he acknowledges the violence and the homelessness that Dryden conceals. He will not, he tells us, preach a revolution that would overthrow the foundations of the state, but he will thrown down the house of his own experience in order to build it afresh. Locke, to be sure, never talks this way, but he too is very unsure of his ground in the "vast Ocean of Being" (*Essay Concerning Human Understanding* 1.1.7), and his famed cautiousness, as Leo Strauss beautifully put it, "is a kind of noble fear" (*Natural Right and History* 206).

Part of the oversimplification that neglects the dark side of Enlightenment results from concentrating on one or at most two genres at a time. While Dryden was writing poems in praise of reason, the nation, art, and science, comic playwrights—Dryden prominent among them—were excoriating the dissoluteness of the age. After 1700, the comic stage grew more sentimental and polite, and the Addisonian manner made the harsh polemics of a Jeremy Collier or a John Dennis unfashionable in essays. But in the verse satire of Swift, Pope, and, later, Churchill (see Lockwood, *Post-Augustan Satire*), the Juvenalian mode increased in importance (even—as Howard Weinbrot has shown—in imitations of Horace), becoming ever more personal and even vulgar in its attacks on vice and on vulgarity. Yet, on a comprehensive view, overlap between satire and sentimentality remains great: Pope and Thomson are the leading masters of eighteenth-century poetic diction; Pope and his older contemporary Young were closely associated in the popular mind; and it is not even difficult to find cases of the same poem appearing in both couplet and Pindaric dress (John Dyer's *Grongar Hill*) or in ironic and sentimental styles (William Shenstone's Spenserian imitation, *The Schoolmistress*). As the end of the century approaches, the temptation to compartmentalize grows ever greater. Vulgar spoofing seems to have been claimed by Fielding for the novel (*Humphrey Clinker, Tristram Shandy*). The heritage of Richardson goes its own separate way to fuel the explosive emotionalism of writers like Frances Burney and Elizabeth Inchbald. Satire, in Johnson and Goldsmith, turns increasingly toward an exaltation of feeling in recognition of what *Rasselas* calls "the uncertain continuance of reason." Yet stage comedy enjoys a revival noted for its decorousness of language and situation and its traditional values.

A less insular perspective can show us that these disparate phenomena must all belong to a single complex of values. In Germany, for instance, Klopstock's emotional religion and nationalism combined with Lessing's liberalism to beget the violent antics of storm and stress drama; in France, Diderot was at once the century's most extravagant admirer of both Richardson and Sterne, the responsible editor of the *Encyclopédie*, which was the great summa of Enlightenment thought, and the founder of a theatrical tradition that led to the protorevolutionary farces of Beaumarchais (the French Sheridan, who was formally even more conservative than his British counterpart but politically far more dangerous). The various literary traditions of the later eighteenth century in Britain will continue to look like the frayed ends of the Enlightenment until we decide to regard them as various positions in a continuum of values that, without ever being fully articulated, regulated the thought processes of the entire period.

Historically, the bright sides of Enlightenment dominated at first, and the dark sides—satire and then sentiment—prevailed later, especially after 1740. But the ideological and emotional precedence goes the other way. Before Charles entered the limelight, he was under a "black Star." That star—as Dryden's text makes extraordinarily plain underneath its decorative obscurity—was as much his personal dissoluteness as his political destitution.

> Such is not Charles his too too active age,
> Which govern'd by the wild distemper'd rage
> Of some black Star infecting all the Skies,
> Made him at his own cost like Adam wise.
>   ("Astraea Redux" 111–14)

The more fully elaborated sequence of "Alexander's Feast" (1697) leads music through rape, drunkenness, "joyless" military victory, the "pain" of erotic desire, nightmare, and madness, before Cecilia brings harmony to earth. The melancholy overview in Dryden's last poem, *A Secular Masque* (1700), images the completed century as a succession of bestial revelry, pointless war, and faithless love. Dryden begins his career by claiming or implying that a new age has dawned:

> Some lazy Ages lost in sleep and ease
> No action leave to busie Chronicles;
> Such whose supine felicity but makes
> In story chasmes, in Epoche's mistakes;
> O're whom Time gently shakes his wings of Down
> Till with his silent sickle they are mown:
> Such is not Charles his too too active age.
>   ("Astraea Redux" 105–11)

He ends, literally on his deathbed, by wishing for that new age, in the gloomy recognition that "supine felicity" has been the best of man's experiences hitherto: " 'Tis well an old age is out, / And time to begin a new" (*Secular Masque* 90–91).

Given the consistent pattern and the regression of confidence, I think we can use the "black Star" passage of 1660 to interpret the stage comedies of the Restoration in relationship to the ideals of Enlightenment. Even though many of the leading playwrights were also elevated poets (Dryden, William Congreve, William Wycherley) or respected statesmen (George Etherege, Sir John Vanbrugh), our impulse is to take the comedies as an outlet that vented energies antithetical to Enlightened rationalism. Such readings underrate the integrity of the age and the comprehensiveness of its vision. The plays generate happy endings out of immoral, foolish, and chaotic actions. There is little logic in this progression, but I think that we can take it as literally as the equally illogical yet psychologically compelling progressions of Dryden's poems. "Apollo's . . . drunk ev'ry Night," sings Sir Wilfull Witwoud in Congreve's *The Way of the World* (1700), "and that makes him so bright." "The Sun's a good Pimple, an honest Soaker, he has a Cellar at your Antipodes" (4.10). That is Dryden's black star all over again, and as willful and wishful as *The Secular Masque* of the same year. Mirabell, a more thoughtful spokesman, especially in soliloquy, has this to say of the force of reason and of its habitation:

To think of a Whirlwind, tho' 'twere in a Whirlwind, were a Case of more steady Contemplation; a very Tranquility of Mind and Mansion. A Fellow that lives in a

Windmill, has not a more whimsical Dwelling than the Heart of a Man that is lodg'd in a Woman. There is no Point of the Compass to which they cannot turn, and by which they are not turn'd; and by one as well as another; for Motion not Method is their Occupation. To know this, and yet continue to be in Love, is to be made wise from the Dictates of Reason, and yet persevere to play the Fool by the force of Instinct. (2.6)

The lesson of stage comedy, which is also the lesson of the greatest poetry of the age, is that reason and instinct, wisdom and passion, must coexist and that their dwelling place is a frantic bosom or a turbulent windmill.

What we see in the exemplary cases of Dryden and the comic playwrights we can learn to recognize throughout the age. In his meager refuge from the Northern cold, Descartes has to tear down before he rebuilds; that is, he is a satirist before he is a rationalist. The contents of Hume's philosophy are different, but the founding gesture is the same: he must tear down the house of epistemology before he can build those of sociability and morality. What Norman O. Brown called Swift's "excremental vision" (*Life Against Death* 179–201) haunts even so complacent-seeming a work as Goldsmith's *She Stoops to Conquer*. The disorderly house with its unruly servants here may seem too tame to count as prefigurations of Beaumarchais's riotous *Marriage of Figaro*. But when Kate possesses herself of her hereditary jewels stolen from the locked casket of Aunt Hardcastle, in a sequence that leads to a wild night-time ride ending, for the Aunt, in the horse-pond at the bottom of the garden, the dark passions at the perimeter of human rationality are unmistakably acknowledged.

"Wherefore," Walter Shandy asks at the conclusion of Sterne's masterpiece, "when we go about to make and plant a man, do we put out the candle?" (9.33). *Tristram Shandy* is arguably the century's profoundest response to Locke. Historically, readers have argued whether it is an application, a commentary, or a critique of Locke. I do not think the question has as much importance as has sometimes been thought because Locke's *Essay*, like any great book, undertakes a self-critique of its own illuminations. We will not properly understand the relationship of Romanticism to Enlightenment if we see only the light of the eighteenth century and ignore the generative darkness in the background.

Tristram Shandy includes various pages that contain no text but are eloquent in their silence. The first is the black page that covers the dead

Yorick (1.12). Much later comes the white page belonging neither to perceptivity nor to reason, but to the imagination that is left free to represent its own desire as a picture of the Widow Wadman (6.38). Whiteness likewise represents vacancy in the omitted chapters 9.18–19. When these chapters are later incorporated at 9.25, they prove to contain Toby's abortive proposal to the Widow, with its confusion of discourse with "the Real Presence," in the belief, "That talking of love, is making it." A whole century, we realize, talked of reason too, without necessarily making it. Between the black and white pages comes the mottled page of 3.36: "Without much reading, by which your reverence knows, I mean much knowledge, you will no more be able to penetrate the moral of the next marbled page (motly emblem of my work!) than the world with all its sagacity has been able to unravel the many opinions, transactions and truths which still lie mystically hid under the dark veil of the black one." It was Wordsworth who wrote that, "mid all this mighty sum / Of things forever speaking," "The eye it cannot choose but see" and that one should not fear "That nothing of itself will come" ("Expostulation and Reply"). The Enlightenment was less confidently open and took the marbled page as its motley emblem. In modern reprints that page is black and white and looks like an image produced and reproduced. (The marbled page is reproduced in color in the Florida Edition of *Tristram Shandy*, but not successfully.) But in the first edition it is an actual piece of beautifully marbled paper, seamlessly inlaid. It is an emblem, but it is also the thing itself, a real presence that brings the self-image of the age bodily into our chamber. For once, in a way perhaps only possible in a book, the image is at one with the object, in ambiguous fulfillment of age-old yearnings for a self-begetting clear and distinct idea.

The images that I have been tracing regulate the fundamental impulses of epistemology, psychology, and politics alike in the Age of Reason. Yet they are rarely acknowledged in their full extent—perhaps only in Hume and Sterne, which may be what makes those the two most disturbing authors of the age. The story I have told is one of the concealment of darkness under a utopian optimism and of the gradual and reluctant acknowledgment of the darkness—let me now call it the Romantic darkness—at the origin of life. It is the story of an age coming to know itself. The knowledge, at last, burst upon it in ways that were never entirely comfortable. That self-knowledge of Enlightenment is what we know as Romanticism.

The Great Awakening

My first section demonstrated how both the Enlightenment and Romanticism contain similar contradictions within them. The second section discusses the genealogy of reason in the Enlightenment. That genealogy is implicit in Enlightenment texts but recognized only in incomplete or fragmentary ways. Far from being a repudiation of Enlightenment, Romanticism was its summation. Of all Enlightenment authors, Hume comes closest to an overview of the dialectic of Enlightenment, and Kant says (in the introduction to the *Critique of Pure Reason*) it was Hume who awakened him from his dogmatic slumbers. Romanticism, I will suggest, is the fulfillment and awakening of Enlightenment.

To see what this formula entails, I begin with the early Wordsworth poem I have just quoted. We need first to reconstruct the situation. Matthew, the aged schoolmaster who is Wordsworth's interlocutor in the poem, represents the wisdom of an earlier generation. In the companion poem, "The Tables Turned," Wordsworth disparages his "meddling intellect," his "science," and his "art." Both poems are bantering in tone; these lines do not state settled doctrines or reflect a fundamental antipathy between the two friends, but they do associate Matthew—who appears throughout the poems devoted to him as a figure of light—with the Enlightenment. What, then, does Wordsworth mean by telling Matthew, "The eye it cannot choose but see"? The eye, after all, is the one sense organ that can be closed off. Indeed, Wordsworth's eyes in this poem must be either closed or at least vacant, for he is "dream[ing] my time away." His reverie is devoid of cause and effect or of what Keats was to call "consequitive reasoning" ("You look round on your mother earth, / As if she for no purpose bore you"), and it appears to be thoughtless ("When life was sweet I knew not why"). Yet he says it is full, not empty.

The debate between Wordsworth and Matthew—that is, I believe, between Romanticism and Enlightenment—is rooted not in alienation or incomprehension but in a common ground. For it is Enlightenment doctrine that Wordsworth turns against his teacher. Ever since Descartes, the principle that the soul always thinks had been espoused by Enlightenment rationalists and empiricists alike. As applied to the sense of sight, that principle was interpreted to mean that the eye is always on the watch, whether the lid is open or shut. Even when nothing registers, as Gottfried Wilhelm Leibniz had said in the preface to his *New Essays on Human Understanding*, we still have an unending stream of "little perceptions," though we may be unaware of them. "This mighty sum / Of things forever speaking" is the full, punctual world of empiricism, a world without empty space. "Methinks, it should have been impossible / Not to love all things in a world so fill'd," Coleridge wrote in 1817, in the lines added to "The Eolian Harp" as a reflective summing up. In "Expostulation and Reply" Wordsworth does not think (he only "deem[s]" and "dream[s]"), but he enjoins Matthew to "think" in order to accede to the totality of Enlightened experience. That is the message addressed by Romanticism to its forebears.

One mistake often made is to link Romanticism too closely with the world of dreams. *L'Ame romantique et le rêve*—Albert Béguin's title is virtually a cliché. Yet the French tradition in which he wrote traces Romanticism well back before the generation of '98. Reverie—empty dreaming or daydreaming—was at its most fashionable around the 1780's, with writers such as Rousseau and William Cowper. The writers whom we know as Romantics are distinguished from this earlier generation by virtue of the fact that they tell their dreams, and, indeed, the more haunted they are (as with De Quincey), the more they try to share and illuminate their hauntings. It is not dreaming that is the distinctive emblem of Romanticism—for even Dryden had his "black Star"—but the moment of awakening in which the dream is preserved.

Such moments are ubiquitous in Romantic poetry. There are the literal awakenings like the Arab Dream in book 5 of *The Prelude*, "Kubla Khan," Lambro's awakening of Haidée and Don Juan in canto 4 of Byron's poem, the apocalyptic moments that conclude Blake's major epics, or the image of Adam's dream in Keats's letter of November 22, 1827. Equally prevalent, especially in the younger poets, are failed or uncertain awakenings like those in "The Idiot Boy," "Christabel," the "Ode to Psyche," the "Ode to a Nightingale," Keats's *Hyperion*, and "The Triumph of Life." Moneta, the warner in *The Fall of Hyperion*, admonishes Keats that "The poet and the dreamer are distinct, / Diverse, sheer opposite, antipodes" (1.199–200); most of Keats's narratives involve struggles to awaken, and the earliest, "Sleep and Poetry," contrasts the good imaginative sleep that leads to the dawn with the self-deluding imaginative death of neoclassical "handicraftsmen" who work in "The name of one Boileau" (200, 206). Just in the weeks when he was avidly attending Hazlitt's lectures on the eighteenth-century poets, Keats penned a blank-verse sonnet ("O Thou Whose Face") that ends with the line, "And he's awake who thinks himself asleep." The full scope of mind necessarily encompasses an alertness to dreams. The Enlightenment's limitation came when it thought itself awake.

The schema of awakening or of failure or struggle to awaken is repeated even more often by analogy and metaphor. Before further considering the implications of this schema, I will present two familiar examples at somewhat greater length. The first is Wordsworth's "Tintern Abbey." The earliest experiences described in this poem are "The coarser pleasures of my boyish days / And their glad animal movements." The earliest stage of genuine humanity is Wordsworth's interpretation of empiricism: it is all elementary perceptions ("Their colours and their forms") and generically classified objects ("The sounding cataract," "the tall rock," and so forth). Pope—from whose poetry Wordsworth knew thousands of lines by heart—uses the phrase "the language of the heart," and Wordsworth, nostalgically, speaks of "the language of my former heart" as he attributes to Dorothy the "shooting lights" and the natural eyes associated with Enlightenment. (See also Griffin, "Wordsworth's Pope.") Beyond mere empiricism comes—and here Wordsworth quotes and acknowledges Young—"the mighty world / Of eye and ear, both what they half-create, / And what perceive." Half-creation is not pure imaginary guess-work, "as is a landscape to a blind man's eye," but rather a dream-world that recomposes the perceived world, when "we are laid asleep / In body, and become a living soul: / While with an eye made quiet by the power / Of harmony, and the deep power of joy, / We see into the life of things." The dark world is at once memory, dream, and imagination. Through it Wordsworth passes beyond the mechanistic and empiricist psychology of "An appetite: a feeling and a love, / That had no need of . . . any interest, / Unborrowed from the eye," toward the revived humanism of the active mind.

In the fourth paragraph of "Tintern Abbey," as Wordsworth recomposes the genesis of his current maturity, "thought" is introduced as the key term, and reasoning processes begin to govern the poem's rhetoric (paragraph 4 has "And so," "For," "Therefore," whereas the "If" in paragraph 3 lacks its consequent "then"). Yet the earlier stages of feeling, the "gleams / Of past existence," are preserved and honored, not rejected. "Day-light" is "joyless," and so Wordsworth wishes the light of the moon on his sister, yet the development leads to a renewal of vision (as the verbs of sensation in the first paragraph proceed from "hear" to "behold," "view," and finally "see") and a return to the now tamed "light of setting suns." Romanticism comes into its own by recapitulating its prehistory. "Tintern Abbey" means a great many things, and in pointing out these elements of structure I have not begun to interpret the poem. Even from the purely epistemological perspective an interpretation would need to account for the various elements in Wordsworth's assessment of empiricism: why, for instance, does he link elementary perception with such eagerly appetitive feelings? The coming-to-consciousness of Romanticism is not itself the content of Romantic belief; rather, it is the ground on which Romantics arrived at their often conflicting assessments of the world they experienced. It is the grammar rather than the text of their thinking.

Shelley's *Prometheus Unbound* depends on a more abstract version of the same grammar of consciousness. It alludes chiefly to political history (the French Revolution and the Ancien Régime) rather than to intellectual history, and its judgments of past eras differ from those of "Tintern Abbey." But it too portrays—indeed repeatedly—the dawning of a new age and the awakening of a new humanity. The necessitarian tyrant Jupiter is resisted darkly by Prometheus. Yet Prometheus is unable to free himself: mere denial is servitude, not liberation. It is, of course, a grave simplification of Shelley's multiple perspectives to identify Jupiter with light and Prometheus with night and consequently even a graver one to present the play as the triumph of the Romantic imagination (or of Revolutionary freedom) over Enlightenment reason (or aristocratic tyranny). For the victory of one power would merely perpetuate a cycle, whereas Shelley's concluding vision is of an everlasting day (4.14: "We bear Time to his tomb in eternity"), modeled on the dance of lights in Dante's *Paradiso*. It is not the evil past that is vanquished by present good, but rather the entire Miltonic conflict of evil and good that is transcended. Critics often treat the play as a lyrical effusion whose dramatic conflict ends in the very opening speech, when Prometheus says, "Disdain? Ah no! I pity thee" (1.53). Could the authority of the past be so easily put down, the force of history would be very weak indeed. But the pity is in fact both mutual (Mercury, Jupiter's messenger, twice says, "I pity thee," 1.356 and 428) and ineffective: Jupiter moans in his only appearance that Demogorgon, who eventually has the last word in the play, has "No pity" (3.1.64). Both Prometheus and Jupiter live in the post-Saturnian world where time appears as a shadow (2.4.33–34) that opposes past to present, necessity to desire. Asia's long narration in 2.4 (the center of the play, as Stuart Curran points out in *Shelley's Annus Mirabilis* 221) describes how Promethean invention mastered time and how Jovian law then mastered invention. But neither did away with the temporal cycle of negation and domination that is Shelley's real concern.

The psycho-historical dynamic issues in a characteristically Shellyan punning ambivalence. Immediately after expressing his pity, Prometheus says, "The Curse / Once breathed on thee I would recall" (1.58–59). Prometheus's recall, like his pity, is inferior because it remains oppositional. Though masked as a retraction, it is really a negation. As in Freud's account of negation, it serves as a pretext to recollect what he has forgotten. Prometheus wishes to deny power to Jupiter, but not to eliminate the whole idea of power (e.g., 1.272–73). In the process he shows his likeness to Jupiter in many ways, such as in the exultation that he condemns yet often seems to express, as well as in his victory over the Furies ("Methinks I grow like what I contemplate / And laugh and stare in loathsome sympathy / . . . . Yet am I king over myself, and rule / The torturing and conflicting throngs within / As Jove rules you"; 1.450–51, 492–94). Reminded of the curse at last, he repents (1.303: "It doth repent me"); falteringly, he asks to change his state. In all these ways he is wrong, even as he pities Jupiter. In the closing speech Demogorgon preaches a forgiving retraction or else an enduring resistance before which oppressive evil merely vanishes:

> To forgive wrongs darker than Death or Night;
> To defy Power which seems Omnipotent;
> To love, and bear; to hope, till Hope creates
> From its own wreck the thing it contemplates.
>
> (4.571–74)

Far from terminating with Prometheus's expression of pity, the play's dramatic action only begins there; its dramatic action is a complex process of development leading to Demogorgon's corrective concluding injunction, "Neither to change nor falter nor repent" (4.575).

If that process is Prometheus's way of dealing with his past, it is also symptomatic of Romanticism's way of dealing with its past. Repudiation and triumph are its most visible gestures, which have led to conventional accounts of the war of Romanticism against Enlightenment reason. Pitying condescension is another gesture that is not infrequent in writings about Enlightenment figures by second-generation Romantics. But all these gestures are surface signs of a yet more complex process that was the Romantic working-through of its roots. What was to be overcome had to be thoroughly remembered. And if the chain of necessity is overthrown, the Promethean rebellion too must give way to the eternal day of rectified Reason.

In her narration Asia speaks as if all value derived from Prometheus: "He gave man speech, and speech created thought, / Which is the measure of the Universe" (2.4.72–73). But Earth speaks differently in the closing scene—more impersonally as well as with a reformed priority that puts thoughts before an ordering language rather than after a creative language. His is the play's considered judgment of the birth of consciousness. "Language is a perpetual Orphic song, / Which rules with Dædal harmony a throng / Of thoughts and forms, which else senseless and shapeless were" (4.415–17). The "Godlike," "divine" (2.4.79, 82), creative ambitions of a Promethean Romanticism give way in the play to the synthetic and syncretic dance of all forms, thoughts, and eras with one another in the coadunative imagination. Much in Asia's praise of music replays Dryden's various shadowed panegyrics on the celestial mission of the arts, whereas Earth reminds us of their grounding and paves the way for Demogorgon to "waken Oblivion" (4.543).

The deluded "all-prophetic song" (2.4.76) that Asia recounts is really a denial of the past. The destiny of Romanticism was to proceed beyond this immature or premature stage toward a reconciliatory recollection. English provides us with the fortunate puns re-collect and re-member. The Enlightenment, as we have seen, aimed at masking and forgetting the itinerary by which it arrived at reason. Its self-knowledge was therefore only partial. Romanticism, with the same goal, undertook a synthetic itinerary. Collecting the members of the path of reason, it aimed at knowing the light through knowing the dark and the present by means of the past. Locke and Kant, for instance, shared the desire to clarify the mechanisms of consciousness. But Locke begins with perception, that is, with the bright or visible part of the process, without studying the faculties that precede and empower perception. Kant's theory of knowledge, by contrast, focuses specifically on the preexisting, imperceptible structures that beget conscious perception. And philosophy beyond Kant concentrated increasingly on the paths leading from the predisposing structures toward fully developed cognition—on what Hegel called the history of consciousness—as well as on analogously idealized histories of society and of nature. The heroines of Austen, the heroes of Scott, and the great Romantic poets all know themselves by remembering what they have experienced. That distinguishes the novels even from picaresques like those of Defoe, whose narrators recount their errors in order to segregate the renegade past from the reformed present. And it distinguishes poems of return like "Tintern Abbey" or Eduard Mörike's "Besuch in Urach" even from Gray's "Ode on a Distant Prospect of Eton College," which masks childhood recollections in an allegorical vision of future woe, an "all-prophetic song."

Consider William Hazlitt's judgment on Jeremy Bentham, a transitional figure and the eldest of the notables portrayed in *The Spirit of the Age*:

Mr. Bentham's method of reasoning, though comprehensive and exact, labours under the defect of most systems—it is too topical. It includes every thing; but it includes everything alike. It is rather like an inventory, than a valuation of different arguments. Every possible suggestion finds a place, so that the mind is distracted as much as enlightened by this perplexing accuracy. The exceptions seem as important as the rule. By attending to the minute, we overlook the great; and in summing up an account, it will not do merely to insist on the number of items without considering their amount. (Hazlitt, *Works* 11.14)

Bentham forgets nothing and hides nothing, but he also synthesizes nothing. Such indiscriminate visibility, says the great Romantic portraitist, is not true Enlightenment. "By attending to the minute we overlook the great": that is the charge leveled by Romanticism at even the most inclusive minds of the eighteenth century. Hogarth was another such. Though a notorious hater, Hazlitt treasured Hogarth. Yet even Hogarth failed to satisfy the hunger for imagination of even the most empirically minded of the great Romantics:

He had an intense feeling and command over the impressions of sense, of habit, of character, and passion, the serious and the comic, in a word, of nature, as it fell within his own observation, or came within the sphere of his actual experience; but he had little power beyond that sphere . . . [to] make the dark abyss pregnant, . . . making all things like not what we know and feel in ourselves, in this "ignorant present" time, but like what they must be in themselves, or in our noblest idea of them, and stamping that idea with reality . . . : this is the ideal in art, in poetry, and in painting. (*Works* 6.146)

In the long passage from which these phrases are excerpted, Hazlitt challenges Hogarth to bring the dark abyss to light, to lift the world around us into "the empyrean," and to give ideas reality by raising them "above the ordinary world of reality." The best of the Enlightenment, as Hazlitt saw it, was striving toward a Romantic potential.

There is no way to reduce the diffuse prose and the incommensurate ambitions of Hazlitt's critique of Enlightenment to a formula or a common denominator. Its virtue, rather, lies in its comprehensiveness. Thus does Romanticism claim not to reject but to refine, subsume, and transcend its predecessors.

Revolution

Richard Brinsley Sheridan was the great Georgian playwright who then became a leading Romantic politician. His politics looked forward, whereas his dramaturgy looked backward to the comic playwrights of the Restoration. Yet when he became manager of Drury Lane Theater in 1776, his most important reform was to increase the number of new plays produced. So representative a figure looks backward and ahead at once.

Lamb, in his permanent nostalgia, seems to me less representative of his age. Still, his comments on the comedies he saw in his youth are telling. Utterly unreal because utterly amoral, they were (as he says in "On the Artificial Comedies of the Last Century") a dream-world to which audiences repaired "to escape from the pressure of reality." They were relaxing because they were aggregates without a synthesis:

For what is Ben [in Congreve's *Love for Love*] . . . but . . . a dreamy combination of all the accidents of a sailor's character. . . . But when an actor comes, and instead of the delightful phantom . . . displays before our eyes a downright concretion of a Wapping sailor— . . . when . . . he gives to it a downright daylight understanding, and a full consciousness of its actions . . . we feel the discord of the thing; the scene is disturbed; a real man has got in among the dramatis personae, and puts them out. ("On Some of the Old Actors," *Works* 2.140)

Let us call that real man Romanticism. It was an awakening from the comic dreams of Enlightenment. Yet that awakening entailed (to Lamb's regret) a "full consciousness" of what had been superseded. You cannot look ahead if you do not know which road lies behind you.

And let us call the process of awakening, revolution. Lamb's language for the artificial comedy of the last century bears a remarkable resemblance to Carlyle's language for the artificial society of old France: "Such visual spectra flit across this Earth, if the Thespian Stage be rudely interfered with: but much more, when, as it was said, Pit jumps on Stage, then is it verily, as in Herr Tieck's Drama, a *Verkehrte Welt*, or World topsy-turvied" (*The French Revolution* 2.1.10). In the first paragraph of this chapter, I said that all the Romantics shared a consciousness of revolution. By that I did not mean only of the French Revolution. For one thing, the Revolution itself—as Carlyle's masterpiece shows—was many different things at different times, in different places, to different people. And, for another, the course of political revolutions was and is often guided by revolutions in ideas, feelings, behavior, the Industrial Revolution, Kant's Copernican Revolution in philosophy, revolutions in life style, even in poetic style. For much of Wordsworth's life the revolution in Cumberland mores preoccupied him far more than did events abroad. Even Carlyle, in the midst of proclaiming the French Revolution "the crowning Phenomenon of our Modern Time," recognized that revolution is permanent and ubiquitous:

All things are in revolution; in change from moment to moment, which becomes sensible from epoch to epoch: in this Time-World of ours there is properly nothing else but revolution and mutation, and even nothing else conceivable. Revolution, you answer, means speedier change. Whereupon one still has to ask: How speedy? At what degree of speed; in what particular points of this variable course, which varies in velocity, but can never stop till time itself stops, does revolution begin and end; cease to be ordinary mutation, and again become such? It is a thing that will depend on definition more or less arbitrary. (1.6.1)

But if we say that Romanticism was the revolutionary reawakening of Enlightenment, we need to recognize that revolution meant something different in 1800 from now. The word meant a turning back before it meant a turning away. In the seventeenth century revolution was the opposite, not the consequence of rebellion, and it retained some of these connotations even into the nineteenth century. When Hazlitt wrote that Horne Tooke "had none of the grand whirling movements of the French Revolution, nor of the tumultuous glow of rebellion in his head or in his heart" (*Works* 9.53), he continued to reflect a sense that revolution is greater and more embracing than rebellion. Even Carlyle, for whom "Time is rich in wonders, in monstrosities most rich; and is observed never to repeat himself, or any of his Gospels" (2.5.1), projects an affinity of the whirling of the Revolution with the great cycles of nature. His monumental book of memory, perhaps the first historical essay to treat modern times as a receding experience that must be reconstructed archeologically, was prompted by a passion to return to what Wordsworth's Intimations Ode had called "the fountain light of all our day."

Understand it well, the Thing thou beholdest, that Thing is an Action, the product and expression of exerted Force: the All of Things is an infinite conjugation of the verb to do. Shoreless Fountain-Ocean of Force, of power to do; wherein Force rolls and circles, billowing, many-streamed, harmonious; wide as Immensity, deep as Eternity; beautiful and terrible, not to be comprehended: this is what man names Existence and Universe; this thousand-tinted Flame-image, at once veil and revelation, reflex such as he, in his poor brain and heart, can paint, of One Unnameable, dwelling in inaccessible light! From beyond the Star-galaxies, from before the Beginning of Days, it billows and rolls,—round thee, nay thyself art of it, in this point of Space where thou now standest, in this moment which thy clock measures. (2.3.1)

Such is the sense in which Romanticism was revolutionary. It had its moments of rebellion, yet it was not fundamentally a rebellion against its predecessors. Rather, it was revolutionary in that older and more encompassing sense (discussed by Reinhart Koselleck in " 'Neuzeit': Remarks on the Semantics of the Modern Concepts of Movement," *Futures Past* 231–66) in which a revolution gathers up and recollects, as it sweeps all with it toward the future.

CHAPTER 9

Origins of Modernism

Musical Structures and Narrative Forms

COMPARISON OF LITERATURE and the visual arts is much more common than comparison of literature and music. For, as Roland Barthes wrote in a late essay that in part exemplifies the problem, "It is . . . very difficult to speak about music. Many writers have spoken well about painting; none, I believe, has spoken well about music, not even Proust. The reason is that it is very difficult to link language, which is of the order of the general, and music, which is of the order of difference." Music, as Barthes says in another essay, is "inactual," or, as I should put it, abstract.[1] Nonspecialists often feel that they can look at a painting and discern what it represents; and even those who know nothing about painting techniques are liable to have imbibed a few useful elementary notions of pictorial form. Far fewer stare at a musical score with anything but discomfort. Music suffers doubly: first from being nonrepresentational, and second from being written in a script that is arduous to learn. Even the most avid listeners would no sooner write about a piece of music than about a poem in a language they cannot read.

Yet despite Barthes's engagement on behalf of a purely affective approach, the analysis of music holds great potential. For what music lacks in external referentiality, it gains in the distinctness of internal relationships. If it is the most abstract art, it is also the most highly formalized. Or, to put this in yet a third way, while the *meaning* or denotation of a piece of music is far less explicit than that of a work of verbal or pictorial art, the *structure* is far more explicit.

The contrast among the arts can be described in semiotic terms. Language has what is known as a double articulation: a limited system of discrete sounds out of which is composed an essentially unlimited and unsystematic lexicon of discrete words. While literature intermittently exploits the phonetic system, it primarily communicates through the much more fluid lexical register. Painting, of course, has at its disposal only the lexical or conceptual articulation. A painting may represent discrete objects or actions, but its material basis is an unarticulated continuum of colors, brushstrokes, and the like. No general system of "huemes" and "valuemes" corresponds to the phonemes of language. Music, finally, has in general only the lower or systematic articulation. The elements of a musical composition are pitches, rhythms, instruments, dynamic levels, and types of articulation: more elements, in other words, than there are phonemes in any natural language but a finite number nevertheless. That is why music can be notated. The extensive writing on musical semiotics rarely seems to acknowledge the basic fact that music does not, in general, have words.[2] More specifically, since music sporadically has symbolic motifs, one should say that music does not distinguish words from sentences. Music has its own identity because it is not like language, and the manipulations of its building blocks can be described far more concretely than the manipulations of words, whose meanings and formal properties are by nature complex and overlapping.[3]

Therefore, if we are interested in the formal sense of a period or a movement, we may well look to its music for the clearest, most easily describable examples. By formal sense I mean such characteristics as the types of closure that are permitted, the nature of segmentation and transition (relationship between adjacent parts), the relative importance of local and long-distance relationships, and the types of hierarchy or equivalence that are recognized. Geoffrey Tillotson's *Augustan Studies* contains a well-known essay on the "manner of proceeding" in eighteenth-century poetry, and his phrase conveniently sums up what I mean by style. In all the arts there are characteristic manners of proceeding or formal principles by which we recognize the style of a creator, a group, or a period. In literary works the principles take the form of norms, often only loosely defined and frequently unrecognized in analysis. In music, on the other hand, the formal outlines of a piece can generally be described with a high degree of precision (or a low degree of ambiguity), and the generalizations based on a group of such formal descriptions appear much more like laws than like the flexible norms of literary form.

A preliminary example of structuring principles can usefully precede the main exposition in this chapter. One norm of plot structure in the nineteenth century is surely that there must be a satisfactory resolution. Vladimir Propp has shown that this norm has the force of an invariable law in the case of fairy tales—or at least of those collected during that epoch. But the resolutions in novels and short stories do not always take the canonical forms of marriage or death; it is not easy to define the limited number of plot functions and thereby to specify acceptable outcomes. With music, on the other hand, we are on firm ground. A precise, inflexible law that everyone acknowledges governs most music of this period, even though few bother to state something so obvious: every piece must end with a cadence in the same key in which it began.

To be sure, even the firmest laws sometimes get tested. Schumann and Chopin experimented with what Charles Rosen has called "tonal unity" without a focused "central tonality" (*Sonata Forms* 295), but only under carefully controlled conditions: in "Romantic" forms, but not in sonatas, and with the prevailing keys a third apart, usually a major and its relative minor. More radical departures—in a couple of iconoclastic forays by Beethoven and in programmatic gestures by Schubert, in songs exclusively—remain even more isolated. Such departures, furthermore, acknowledge the law of resolution through their attempt either to amend it or to motivate a repeal. Even these few works, that is, have determinate not suspended or cyclical endings.[4] In the absence of obviously Shandean characteristics (as in "Variety Without Method," a late eighteenth-century setting in various keys and meters of the psalm, "O God thou hast been displeased," by the American hymnist William Billings), should one meet a nineteenth-century piece where the first movement ends in F major while the last movement ends in D major, one would have no recourse but to conclude that the composer was terminally syphilitic. Indeed, in this particular instance—the Second String Quartet of Bedřich Smetana—the contributors to the earlier editions of *Grove's Dictionary of Music and Musicians* were unable to face the music; J. A. Fuller Maitland, the general editor of the second edition, put the piece in C major (vol. 4, p. 486), while Rosa Newmarch in the third edition put it in C minor (vol. 4, p. 789).

Now it is not difficult to see how a closely related norm of closure likewise applies to the nineteenth-century novel. Flamboyant exceptions like Charlotte Brontë's *Villette* and Melville's *The Confidence-Man*, of course, confirm the norm by the self-conscious way they reject it. But we might risk losing our critical nerve with what seems like half-cadences or half-hearted conventionality in the works of Flaubert, Eliot, or Hardy—indeed an increasingly long list of major writers. Here the musical parallel should encourage us to view the endings as adequate resolutions of problems to be critically identified. It teaches us the principle of reading the novels in the light of their conclusions, just as we analyze a symphony from the perspective of its tonal resolution rather than, say, in the light of prevailing textures or of organizational symmetries.[5]

In the spirit of this example, then, I will take up a central paradigm in nineteenth-century music, its parallel in literary form, and its fate in the twentieth century. What follows is an experiment at compactly surveying the prehistory of modernism. The intention is to show how the patterns of music history can help to organize our understanding of the more fluid patterns of literary history.

The language of nineteenth-century music was based on a series of polar oppositions that had gradually crystallized from the musical practice of the preceding centuries: the contrast of consonance with dissonance, tonic with dominant (or other nontonic) harmonies, symmetrical with asymmetrical phrasing, melodic outline with rhythmic configuration, treble with bass, strong with weak beats, solo with accompaniment, string with wind sonorities. Each such polarity functions somewhat differently from the others, and their complex interplay defines the inner form of any given piece. But all have in common that one term is the normal, neutral, stable, or principal one, while the other is abnormal, expressive, unstable, or subordinate.

String sound, to expand on one of the oppositions, is neutral. Winds characteristically gain prominence in the more excited or colorful inner sections of a movement or a piece, and they are lavishly used in ballet and opera to accompany visual spectacles.[6] Yet wind-band music virtually disappears from mainstream composition, since it would have the effect of being all message and no code: it is a sign of unreality when Mendelssohn's Overture to *A Midsummer Night's Dream* opens with wind chords and an obvious archaism when the theme of Brahms's *Variations on a Theme of Haydn* is stated by winds alone over no more string stability than is offered by cello and bass pizzicato. The string quartet, on the other hand, is the most neutral or purest medium, used only for fully structured abstract pieces and never for short character pieces or for program music. A list of exceptions shows how rare they are: apart from two or three quartet movements by Beethoven, Hugo Wolf's *Intermezzo* and *Italian Serenade,* and Tchaikovsky's sextet, "Souvenirs de Florence," you have to descend to the level of Nikolai Afanasiev's quartet "The Volga" or return to the hapless Smetana's quartet "From My Life" to find programmatic or evocative string music. And it could be argued that Schoenberg's first decisive attack on nineteenth-century musical language came with his writing a full-scale symphonic poem for string sextet, *Verklärte Nacht.*

Taken as a whole, the various oppositions define a manner of proceeding that every listener recognizes as the nineteenth-century norm: most simply, pieces oscillate between stability or resolution and excitement or expressivity, and, in particular, pieces begin in normality (in the tonic key) and move through areas of greater or lesser tension in the middle until they arrive at a concluding resolution. These patterns of what linguists call markedness are obvious; just as obviously they do not structure much of the most characteristic music of our century, and they apply only in a partial and weaker way to music of the baroque era, which depends more heavily on symmetrical balance than on pointed contrast.

The formal structures of nineteenth-century fiction are likewise defined by oppositions between tension and relaxation, complication and resolution, colorful dissonance and restored harmony. The categories for analyzing these structures are, to be sure, more flexible and imprecise than the musical categories, but they were acknowledged at the time, they remain discernible now, and, however approximate they may be, I believe that they are nevertheless essential to an understanding of nineteenth-century fiction.

The structural oppositions in nineteenth-century fiction can only be illustrated here; a full description must be left for another occasion. The terms that we most often find in nineteenth-century discussions are the true or the real and the interesting or the romantic. The struggle of the nineteenth-century writer is to accommodate both the true and the interesting or—to borrow the musical terms—both consonance and dissonance, tonic and dominant. Trollope, for instance, objects to the designation of himself as realistic and Wilkie Collins as sensationalistic: "A good novel should be both, and both in the highest degree" (*Autobiography* 194). Hardy says, "The writer's problem is, how to strike the balance between the uncommon and the ordinary so as on the one hand to give interest, on the other to give reality" (*Life and Work* 154); *Bleak House* (according to Dickens's preface) was intended to portray "the romantic side of familiar things"; and Henry James is employing only a superficially different vocabulary when he writes, "Every good story is of course both a picture and an idea, and the more they are interfused the better the problem is solved" ("Guy de Maupassant," *Partial Portraits* 269).

Just as certain composers lay bare the skeleton of the period's formal sense by simplifying and rigidifying the polarizations in harmony and rhythm,[7] so certain authors and works likewise render the polarizations of literary form in a purified and thus unmistakable way. *Bleak House* experiments with juxtaposing a pitiless, objective, foggy narrator with a romantic and sunny one and moves toward reconciling the two at the end. Stevenson's best-known work pits the real scientist Dr. Jekyll against the nightmarish romantic villain Mr. Hyde. And detective stories in the mold of Arthur Conan Doyle regularly fall into two main parts: the recital of the actual situation in the present tense with all the scattered clues of the crime, and the recital in the past tense of the romantic and exciting history of the criminal and the crime.

At the end of the nineteenth century these polarized forms become formulaic. Their interest slips, and eventually they lose their coherence. The artist who preserves the traditional forms becomes an artisan, often a miniaturist, like many of the nationalist composers or the numerous superb short story writers native to almost every country except imperial England. The grand formal problems all but vanish and hitherto subordinate resources of nuance and tone color are featured, such as piquant chords and dialect words. Increasing formal ease and virtuosity mean that a whole piece may be generated out of a kernel phrase, as in the famous Maupassant story "The Necklace," about a string of diamonds ("rivière de diamants") that is lost near the river, making martyrs out of the poor bourgeois of the nearby Rue des Martyrs.

Finally, as the charisma of the dialectic is routinized, all that matter are color and atmosphere—tone-painting or word-painting. From the other side of the great stylistic divide Schoenberg made merry over the minimal character of a language based on color: "When songs from the southern portion of West-Farinoxia," he writes in an essay on "Symphonies from Folksongs," "show Lydian tendencies in a prevailing Phrygian, whereas dances from the neighboring northern part of Franquimonia show the opposite, namely traces of Phrygian in decidedly Lydian melodies, such differences may, to a specialist in the region, indicate signs of autochthonous originality."[8] But late in the nineteenth century such minimal originality was often a composer's or a short story writer's primary resource. The character piece is a distillate, the passion without the story of the passion, "not the tale, but the sketch of a tale," "only the point of departure and that of arrival," as Giovanni Verga says in the programmatic introduction to "Gramigna's Lover" (1880; *Tutte le novelle* 1: 167–68), or, in other words, a contrasting beginning and end that virtually dispenses with the mediating middle. This type of colorful sketch, popular in both literature and music toward the end of the century—and the inspiration for verismo opera—ultimately became in its turn a commonplace convention.

When normal coherence of the old sort is abandoned in favor of such fragmentary evocation, larger structures become problematic, as most obviously in the monstrously episodic works of Bruckner, Mahler, and Zola. In longer works one solution—particularly associated with Wagner and his followers and, in literature, with Flaubert—was to sustain interest by refusing to come to rest: perpetual unresolved dissonance, a middle with very little end. This is, of course, signally the mode of Henry James's *The Turn of the Screw*, which seeks to turn the screws of intensity higher in each of its twenty-four chapters so as to maintain a constant frenzy of excitement, so different from the carefully paced, intermittent horror of romantic gothic. Alternatively, by the end of the century, impressionists such as Debussy and Chekhov (exact contemporaries, though Chekhov wrote more quickly and died younger) preserve compositional depth by melancholy or ironic reminiscences of traditional motifs and forms, the sunken cathedrals of the past: think of all the unsent letters, untold stories, and unnoticed crimes and cruelties of Chekhov's early tales.

Creators like these can now construct larger forms only as a patchwork based on recognizable motifs but lacking a prevailing tonality. Chekhov's first longer story, "The Steppe," is a degenerate picaresque. The indifferent plain (the two words pun in Chekhov's text) through which Egorushka passes decomposes into contrasting story types, the idealized princess Dranitskaya and the mysterious Varlamov, but Egorushka remains equally untouched by the tonic stability of the one and the dominant excitement of the other: "Egorushka felt that, with these people disappeared for him, eternally, like smoke, all that had been lived through until now" (*Izbrannye Sochinenia* 1: 134).[9] Such halting, uncertain cadences mark endings that are not culminations but dissolutions. Debussy's composites are games ("Jeux"); for the gloomier Chekhov they constitute "A Dull Story," but for both the climactic, structuring elements of traditional forms remain but a hollow shell. The bang of excitement may resound, as it does, almost at the end of "A Dull Story"—"There are terrible nights with thunder, lightning, rain, and wind, that among the people are called sparrow's nights. One such sparrow's night occurred in my personal life . . ." (1: 420, Chekhov's suspension points)—but the end is at best a gloomy thud. The organization, though not the texture, of "A Dull Story" resembles that of Debussy's later Cello Sonata, where an excited climax of plucked dominant seventh chords on G, instead of resolving, is followed by a return of an earlier melancholy, wailing recitative and then by a series of D minor chords, loud, to be sure, but ending low and abruptly muffled, with the marking "dry." Point and line come unglued, leaving structures that are heaps of fragments, not well shored up against ruin.[10]

By the early years of this century, post-Wagnerian continual modulation combined with the dissonant expressive leaps of Mahler's melodies and the rhythmic freedom of what Schoenberg called "the progressive Brahms" to undermine totally the stability of the tonic, of the octave, and of the beat. If tension never relaxes, then tension also never builds and the internal dramatic shape of the work is lost. There is no longer a progress from tonic to dominant, consonance to dissonance, the true to the interesting, and back again. Hence, a work like Schoenberg's *Erwartung* becomes an extended, slow rhapsody of unfulfilled expectation, its texture pervaded by the disembodied sonority of the celesta, its epiphanic moment utterly subdued (see measure 390, text "Liebster, der Morgen kommt" [Beloved, the morning comes], marked

"Ruhig, fast freundlich! ohne Leidenschaft!" [Calm, almost friendly! without passion!]).

In the absence of an audible internal structure, music for a short period predominantly seeks its coherence from some external principle of reference. Ballet, program music, and song become the norm. (The omission of ballet is an uncharacteristic blind spot in Carl Dahlhaus's magisterial *Nineteenth-Century Music*.) Out of the heart of darkness there must emerge a voice, without which pure form retains only the briefest sustaining power: it is not by chance that Kurtz ("short") is the name of the mysterious central figure in the story that climaxes with the anguished cry, "A voice! a voice!" Or else music seeks a symbolic meaning, a fugitive vision that lies beyond words, the song of the nightingale perhaps. In some posthumously published program notes to his *Orchesterlieder*, opus 22 (1915), Schoenberg speaks of this striving. Conventional program music, he says, had attempted to bring the represented object directly into the music; in semiotic terms, it had assimilated the musical sign to the verbal signified. But Schoenberg envisioned a new music that could function like enactments, not like designations, and that would ultimately circumvent or surpass language in its meaningfulness. "If an actor will speak in a different cadence of a rough sea and of a calm one, my music will be no different: . . . the music will not become agitated like the sea, but *differently*, like the actor. . . . A word describes the object and its condition; . . . music . . . *carries* the thing and its essence *up before the eye of the mind*" (*Gesammelte Schriften* 290).[11] A new semiosis is born that overcomes the disjunction between signifier and signified; the nature of meaning changes.

To illustrate the transition from the literary side, I quote from the well-known "Letter to Lord Chandos" of 1902 by Hugo von Hofmannsthal: "Everything fell apart into pieces around me; they coagulated into eyes which stared at me and into which I had to stare back: they are whirlpools into which I gaze in giddiness, which revolve incessantly and through which one reaches the void. . . . Since then I have led a life which you, I fear, can hardly grasp, so spiritlessly, so thoughtlessly does it flow by. . . . A watering-can, a harrow left in the field, a dog in the sun, a poor churchyard, a cripple, a small farmhouse, any of these can become the vessel of my revelation. . . . It is all a kind of feverish thought, but a thought in a material which is more immediate, more fluid, more glowing than words" ("Ein Brief," *Ausgewählte Werke* 2: 342–43, 347–48). Literature was striving toward the condition of music, just as music was striving toward the condition of language, and these apparently opposite strivings arose out of a single impulse, to substitute embodiment for denotation in order to restore expressivity where formal control had been lost.[12]

The limit case of the polarized forms of the nineteenth century is thus a fragmentation of form. A curious passage in *Dr. Jekyll and Mr. Hyde* seems to predict this development from polarized form to fragmented form. It comes early in the concluding section of the story, which contains Dr. Jekyll's coherent explanation of the mystery, just before he loses all control over his identity:

I thus drew steadily nearer to that truth, by whose partial discovery I have been doomed to such a dreadful shipwreck: that man is not truly one, but truly two. I say two, because the state of my own knowledge does not pass beyond that point. Others will follow, others will outstrip me on the same lines; and I hazard a guess that man will be ultimately known for a mere polity of multifarious, incongruous, and independent denizens. (*Complete Short Stories* 520)

Those who outstrip nineteenth-century form arrive at the incoherence of what might well be called atonal literature. A reference to Stéphane Mallarmé's "Un Coup de dés" would seem to be called for at this point, and that randomized flotsam of interwoven motifs is surely one type of literary atonality, following a shipwreck like Dr. Jekyll's. But even more revealing, because less flamboyant, examples of what Schoenberg was to call the emancipation of dissonance, may be found in the meandering inarticulacy of Hardy's *Jude the Obscure* and the coolly dissonant, "uglified" Romanticism of his later poetry. "So Various" is the programmatic title of a poem from the volume *Winter Words* that concerns the fragmentation of identity. Here is its discordant conclusion:

> Now . . . All these specimens of man,
> So various in their pith and plan
>   Curious to say
>   Were *one* man. Yea
>   I was all they.

Through the preceding twelve stanzas of contradictory self-portraits and all the way to the final harshly fragmenting plural pronoun, the poem shows Hardy as precisely what Dr. Jekyll had predicted, "a mere polity of multifarious, incongruous, and independent denizens."[13]

Before the turn of the century, of course, large-scale dramatic structure was already often tending to yield to motivic consistency as a shaping force, as in Tchaikovsky's *Symphonie Pathétique*, an episodic work that is almost entirely generated by the four-note motif heard at the very start. And many works of the period seem to enact the struggle between opposing forms of organization. Thus in the last song of Mahler's *Das Lied von der Erde* the dissonant final chord, C-E-G-A, synopsizes one of the two leading motifs of the movement while refusing to come to rest harmonically and while the text likewise refuses closure through its repetitions of the word, "ewig" (eternal). James's *Turn of the Screw* is a work similarly in transition; a few years ago we were treated to the spectacle of an elegant, intricately knit essay concerning the fragmentation of identity in the story, published simultaneously with an equally brilliant if disheveled structuralist reading that demonstrated how it is permeated by a systematic symmetry of motivic relationships.[14]

Ultimately Schoenberg developed the twelve-tone system as a means for integrating larger works. He systematically subordinated dramatic modulations of intensity to the continuous fabric of intervallic relationships dispersed throughout the work. The local intelligibility of a melodic curve is replaced by long-range relationships that confer a meaning on each interval only in terms of its place in the tone-row and its employment elsewhere in the piece. The ecstatic semiosis of atonality thus eventually leads to a style where meaning is felt to arise from outside the local phrase.[15] Musical expression no longer seems natural and immediate. Stravinsky, Bartók, and even to a considerable extent the greatest of the traditionalists, such as Ravel and Prokofiev, are less schematic in their procedures, but fundamentally they share the same formal sensibility. The manner of proceeding common to all these composers derives from the breakdown of the polarizations that had structured music for the preceding 150 years.

Whereas each subsystem of nineteenth-century musical language (harmony, rhythm, and so forth) is divided into an unmarked and one or more marked components, in twentieth-century musical style these internal subdivisions no longer exist or—in more traditional composers who partially preserve them—their force is reduced. As Schoenberg says in the essay "Composition with Twelve Tones," "In this space . . . there is no absolute down, no right or left, no forward or backward" (*Style and Idea* 223). Thus, for instance, dissonance is no longer expressively marked with respect to consonance. The dominant, similarly, is no longer marked with respect to the tonic, so that even when polytonal music continues to use triads, movement away from a given triad loses its significance. And melody loses its primacy through being fragmented in early twelve-tone music, demonized by pulsing ostinatos in Bartók, skeletonized by rhythmic displacement and pointillist instrumentation in Stravinsky.

As a result of such changes, formal unity and totality can no longer be generated "organically" through tension (internal division) and relaxation (reconciliation). The work is no longer an organism, self-defining and self-limiting. Instead, most often composers adopted historical forms to impose an arbitrary recognizable shape on their works. The forms of music in this period were therefore not a product of the musical langauge, as they had been earlier; the language generates only fragments, and the larger forms actually employed are alien to the language.[16] And this contradiction between form and language leads in turn to the second main result of the stylistic transformation, namely that a division between internal and external components replaces a series of internal divisions as the semiotic foundation of musical expression. The style has no internal limits—anything goes, so to speak—and only the bounded forms of the past that lie outside the modern style carry any special charge. Where dissonance is the norm, for instance, consonance becomes an expressive device, but always, in music of this type, as an untimely sonority, forbidden by some composers, archaic for the others.[17] Consequently, expressivity is always attached to devices that break the stylistic conventions of the form. And these devices— semiotically marked, expressive, and disruptive—are precisely those features of melody, harmony, form, and so forth that are the familiar elements of the older style.

Thus, we arrive at the law for music of this period, which is that the familiar is always destabilizing, while the stable elements are always estranged. Coherence and shape are at odds: the former, the unity of the piece, comes from the modern style, most often from the dense texture of microscopic motifs that permeate the whole, while the latter, the expressive totality, comes from the larger units such as melody and structure that are borrowed wholesale from the past. From this permanent division arises the unstably ironic or elegiac character that seems inescapable in the period: the music always seems to be saying one thing and meaning another or to be pointing toward a position it does not occupy. Yet the irony rarely seems to arise from the kind of firm ground that supports the puns of Haydn or the parody so frequent in late Beethoven. Indeed, the very key migrations that signal abnormality in Schubert or Chopin and madness in Smetana become unremarkable after 1900, and can be found in works like Zoltan Kodály's Cello Sonata, opus 4, Ravel's Sonata for Violin and Cello, and the first of Richard Strauss's *Four Last Songs*. The great music of the twenties seems not to take a position; it rarely has the pronounced and unmistakable ideological character found in the music of powerful revolutionary composers such as Mozart, Beethoven, and Wagner or of powerful consolidators such as Haydn and Brahms. It has no home base: even composers who preserve the notion of tonality use devices such as a confusion of major and minor modes or oblique tonal relations in order to undermine the stability of the tonal system.

Music is not a referential art, and the homelessness of musical style in this period is a structural necessity, not a biographical or sociological one. This realization may offer us one way of understanding what Hardy once called "the ache of modernism" (*Tess of the D'Urbervilles* 105)—the condition of homelessness or exile that besets the literature of the period. The happy ending and the tragic but redemptive one have become equally obsolete; the inability of the citizens of Joyce's Dublin to get along with one another is an aesthetic precondition for the energy and movement required of a narrative. Thus, Joyce's *Exiles* ends with Richard's confession of a wound "which can never be healed," consisting of the "restless living wounding doubt" that makes love possible (112).

What is a law of musical form is merely a norm of literary expression. When Joyce spoke, for instance, of the "scrupulous meanness" of his writing,[18] he did not mean that every sentence must be discordant, but he still wanted to emancipate dissonance; in consequence, catachresis or category error becomes one of his most frequent and characteristic stylistic devices: "A bell clanged upon her heart" ("Eveline," *Dubliners* 41); and "A light began to tremble on the horizon of his mind" ("A Little Cloud," *Dubliners* 73). The old organic forms are reduced to a fragmentary residue; where there is a conflict and resolution, as in "The Boarding House," the climactic scene is omitted; where there is a plot, like the friends' scheme in "Grace" to get Kernan on the wagon, it seems to turn into a raucous imposition, parodied for instance by a millinery redemption in lieu of a genuine millenary one: "His hat, which had been rehabilitated by his wife, rested upon his knees" (*Dubliners* 173). Consistency comes from the web of motivic connections. There is no law, such as in the dodecaphonic system, requiring every note to be derived from the tone-row, but there is a principle of economy; literally, "scrupulous meanness" proclaims concentration on a narrow repertoire of motifs. Totality or closure, on the other hand, comes from the archetypal patterns of aging, of the progression of the seasons, of the growth of social organization, that pervade the collection as a whole and that are entirely disjunct from the shape of the individual stories. And whereas tonal music is selective—some notes are in the scale, others are out—twelve-tone music substitutes what Rosen calls the saturation of the musical space: all notes must be represented equally (*Schoenberg* 69–70). Likewise, Joyce's encyclopedic impulse saturates the narrative space: all walks of life are represented, as are all ages of man, and the absence of spring from the cycle of seasons is the one significant structural irony in the collection: there is no pastoral and no regeneration.

At the very least, such parallels can confirm one's sense of what is truly general in the artistic culture of a period. No influence is in question here, no common heritage, no particular shared problematic, not even necessarily the same public—only a common sensibility. And I think, as well, that these parallels can aid those of us on the literary side with some of our interpretive problems and judgments. For the "laws" of musical structure offer firmer guidelines to interpretation than the more approximate principles of verbal expression. They can help guide our interpretive tact by clarifying for us what constitutes a message and what belongs to a cultural code and thus by indicating which features of the work we should decide to rely on or to stress.

In Joyce's case the musical parallels can help us with the peculiar tonelessness of *Dubliners*, that deadpan succession of declarative sentences, poor in connectives, that characterizes his prose. There is a temptation to regard this feature as a savage irony, an Irishman's pitiless exposé of Dublin, as if Joyce might have written differently of London, Paris, or Trieste. But, of course, the great artists of this period hardly wrote differently of these other cities: "scrupulous meanness" could well describe the tone of Italo Svevo's Trieste, Proust's Paris, or to a considerable degree even Woolf's London. Svevo even makes one of the apparent villains in *The Confessions of Zeno* a musician, the sort of violinist who plays Bach's Chaconne smoothly and sweetly. According to the title character, by contrast, "mistuning is the path to unison" (*La Coscienza di Zeno* 101). Yet Zeno's paradox reminds us that unison—the point of rest or the perspective point—can never be reached but only approached through the increasing acuteness of permanent mistuning. Thus does the modernist sense of structure differ radically from the nineteenth-century principle that dissonance is the road to consonance—or in the Hegelian language of dialectical musical aesthetics, "in the suspension [*Aufhebung*] of equilibrium lies the tendency to return to a condition of equilibrium."[19] There is no implied superior position, ideological or utopian, from which the creator looks down on his creations; the disjunctions in the works are not a judgment but the very form of modernism.

* * *

What are the consequences of the formalist history that the preceding pages sketch out? On one reading, they entail a fatalism or a Foucauldian power play. I have invoked Debussy, Schoenberg, Stevenson, Hardy, Chekhov, and Hofmannsthal to suggest how the European spirit was Balkanized alongside the European polity. The fate of *Realpolitik*, this account would claim, was merely one expression of the fate of *Realismus*. A terrible beauty was born, with all the violence that we have come to associate with the term revolution. It happened to Hofmannsthal in 1902, to Schoenberg in 1911, and eventually to Europe in 1914.

There is a second reading of my argument that is closer to what I would like to believe. The second reading, like the first, claims a linkage between matters of the spirit and matters of history, for I hope that any reader of this chapter feels that music matters to life. But the second reading would equate what I have called form not with fate but with what others would call ideology. A Marxist such as Fredric Jameson has drawn powerful inspiration from the formalists Northrop Frye and Algirdas Greimas as well as from Adorno's musical writings. Students of music almost invariably regard form (as literary critics also normally do) as an abstraction from meaningful substance. Yet those who oppose an empty formalism often do so, mostly without acknowledgment, in the service of an enriched one. Edward T. Cone's concluding words in *The Composer's Voice* sound the watchword: "The formalist is justified in demanding a purely musical context for music only if he recognizes that . . . the musical context and the human context are inseparably intertwined" (175). To the extent that form subconsciously regulates the possibilities of articulate thought, then I would like to think that formal analysis is the vehicle of self-reflexive ideology critique. A case in point would be Ruth Solie's essay on Schumann's *Frauenliebe und Leben*; contesting formalism ("or what," she says, "we might more pointedly call autonomism," 240), she in fact brings the resources of formal analysis to bear in an ideologically aware defense of the seemingly indefensible. Or one could invoke that other Marxist *malgré lui*, Charles Rosen, for his commitment—implicit throughout *The Classical Style*—to the view that music is the essential or inescapable carrier of our cultural determinants, precisely because it is free of the corrupting—or deconstructive—entanglements of words. On this second reading of my argument, we could say that formal analysis unveils the birth of ideology out of the spirit of music.

PART IV

Finale

Unheard Melodies

The Force of Form

for MHP

> If you have any music that may not be heard, to't again.
> —Shakespeare, *Othello*

PRELIMINARY POSTSCRIPT. Readers may wonder how an essay on silence finds its way (as this one originally did) into a collection on performance. The match was made at the last minute, not by author or coordinator of the issue where it appeared but at the suggestion of the editor and the editorial board. Perhaps they wanted to frame a debate? No incidental comments on orchestral seating will disguise the Shelleyanism of an argument for which, as Joel Fineman intimates of *Othello*, sound appears to stain the white radiance of sense. "Rome's azure sky, / Flowers, ruins, states, music, words, are weak / The glory they transfuse with fitting truth to speak" (Shelley, *Adonais* 464–66). To the committed idealist, the best artist lacks hands.

Still, if the ideal is to convey a truth without corrupting it in the utterance, perhaps music may come closer to adequacy than more denotative expressions. Free from specific markers, it might tap the empyrean. In this spirit Shelley writes in one of his lyrics "To Jane":

> Though the sound overpowers
> Sing again, with your dear voice revealing
> A tone
> Of some world far from ours,
> Where music and moonlight and feeling
> Are one.

A tone is better than a word and all the more so in the nocturnal somnolence of Shelley's dream world. If it enters into activity, it suffers corruption: in *Adonais* music is discredited by its association with the daytime azure sky and with the productions of nature and of man. But released from consciousness, music becomes redemptive. So it is in the minimalist world of "To Jane"; where the guitar is "tinkling," the moon "soft," the light "faint," and the voice "most tender," the aim clearly is to evoke the lower threshold of awareness. When Shelley wrote that "the sound overpowers," he was not thinking of Guns 'n Roses; he intended, certainly, a lullaby that hypnotizes or anesthetizes. Music transfigures to the degree that it escapes perceptual fixation. Gabriel Conroy in Joyce's "The Dead," "strain[ing] his ear to listen" in the "stillness" after a song, captures the symbolic perfection that Joyce called an epiphany: "*Distant Music* he would call the picture if he were a painter" (*Dubliners* 209–10). Joyce and Shelley join Shakespeare's clown in adhering to the credo that the perfection of music is silence.

Yet Shelley's idealism was committed to paper. And *Othello* ends not with Gratiano's despondent last line—"All that's spoke is marr'd" (5.2.358)—but with the active emissary Lodovico, promising a performance allied in spirit to what the audience has just seen: "Myself will straight aboard, and to the state / This heavy act with heavy heart relate" (5.2.371–72). Even as we teeter at the edge of the intense inane, the mission to communicate—to inform and to reform—warps us home again. There will be no show without a tell.

In what sense this counts as performance remains to be seen. For the senses of performance are multiple. For every thinker who pits form against matter or against body, there is one who ranks it against soul or spirit. Form is the visible and the invisible, the measured and the felt, the analytic and the radiant. And whether it casts forms or casts scripts into form, performance, caught between ideals of fidelity and release, lists to every wind. By implication even if not by original intent, this chapter can, I hope, contribute to a reconciliation of the energetics of performance with the contemplative repose of the creative imagination—or else of the impulsive imagination with the disciplined body of the interpreter. "For of the soule the bodie forme doth take: / For soule is forme, and doth the bodie make" (Spenser, *An Hymne in Honour of Beautie* 132–33).

* * *

Early formalism, we know, was embarrassed enough of the historical subject or Spirit . . . to transform poems into artifacts as seemingly emptied of historical subject as a Grecian Urn. (Liu, "The Power of Formalism" 740)

What does a work of art contain? The question stumps all reflection theories, however complex their mediations. For them the contents lie outside the work or on its surface. A mirror traveling down a road has no inside; on its uncertain glass lie only shadows, a Platonic cavern turned inside out. Its transcendent Ideas repose in the looking-glass world beyond the mirror, within the warp that it pretends not to have. So much do the revelations of literature or painting conceal. What then of an art that, deep down, does not reflect or denote? Even for Plato—for Aristotle even—mimesis belonged preeminently to music and to the passions of the soul. What does the musician of the *Politics* convey? What do the Sirens sing? Utterance and its cognate gestures—externalization, outreach—are at best the outer limits of expression. Art's secrets lurk within.

Within the urn. Keats's passionate music leaves his surfaces troubled and confused. Questions proliferate in "a kind of 'wild ecstasy' of syntax" (Wolfson, "The Language of Interpretation" 40). What are these, gods or men? What men, or what gods? The speaker's mind wanders, beyond and outward, to a world unknown, unfindable. Abruptly, passions fall silent, to no end. A catharsis both overwrought and cold stills life. Does it slake desire? What kind of doom, or what kind of consolation, is proclaimed to those "on earth"? It's hard to know what an ode says.

What the ode doesn't say is easier to discern. In the first stanza Keats tries to overhear the "tale" or "legend" haunting "about thy shape," but by the last stanza his meditations have redirected him to the "shape" itself, the "attitude," the "silent form." For a "silent" urn speaks ("thou say'st") through ellipsis. Its beauty and truth stem from an ancient triad. Notable for its absence is the triad's third member: between the truth of pure reason and the beauty of aesthetic judgment, the poem voids the goodness of practical reason. Its action supplants Action.[1] Whatever the tonality of Keats's coda, "on earth" means in the forest or the wilds ("trodden weed"), not in the "little town, . . . little town," to which the fourth stanza bids its lingering adieu. From Auburn to urn: desert the village and let the earth figure the ground of being.[2] Beneath the hot pipes, themselves unheard, the urn's cold bass will not be seduced by the passions on its surface. What would its quietism deny? What reject? And what enable?

"Shape," "attitude," "form." The well-wrought urn, beloved of for-

malists, sings an allied song. Donne's "hymns" ("The Canonization" 34)
link mimesis to contradiction and death. But here, too, the emptying out
of sense and the ironic reduction of three dimensions to two ("the glasses
of your eyes") prove a mysterious and sacred askesis. The contradiction
that is at once a lessening, an infecting, and a betrothing looks ahead to
resurrection and divine reward. Could Donne's "pattern" too be a mystic equation—the truth of beauty and the beauty of truth—secured by the
privitude of his music?

The path I have chosen for investigating these questions lies through
some dry, even abstruse empirics. It has the virtue of taking my topic as
literally as possible, over a restricted domain. In real music—real, non-
existent music—I will look for the key to the urns. But first I want to
dwell with beauty a few paragraphs longer, fleshing out this particular
Keatsian swoon.

*   *   *

> Heard melodies are sweet, but those unheard
>   Are sweeter; therefore, ye soft pipes, play on;
> Not to the sensual ear, but, more endear'd,
>   Pipe to the spirit ditties of no tone.

For a poem so well studied as the "Ode on a Grecian Urn," these lines
have elicited remarkably little commentary. What could they mean? The
"unheard melodies" above or within the urn are the secrets of art. First,
Keats suggests that art is like life, only more so. What we hear is sweet;
what's on the urn is even sweeter. It is endeared to more than just our
earthly ears. To be sure, "endear'd" is an odd word, a bastard cross
between endearing and endowed, and a bad pun to boot. Keats strains
here, trying to make a comparison between art and life that won't stand
scrutiny. For there is a second layer in the lines that contrasts art to life.
Unheard melodies are the opposite of heard melodies. The urn pipes *not*
to the ear *but* to the spirit. Life is "sensual"—rich and full—whereas art
is toneless. By the end of the sentence Keats seems to have reversed
himself; he began by saying that art is more than life—precisely, that it is
"sweeter," that is, more sensual—whereas by the end he says that it's
less than life, with "ditties of no tone." The sounds of the word "note"
lurk in this richly musical phrase, shadowing its denial with an unheard
antiphon. (See Garrett Stewart, *Reading Voices* 156–60, a section entitled

"Unheard Melodies," for other such "graphonics" in Keats.) But the status of sound remains undetermined. On the one hand, we have comparison between art and life, on the other hand, contrast. Art is life intensified, or it is life denied.

The awkward combination of comparison and contrast reappears in the word "soft": "Therefore, ye soft pipes, play on." Obviously, Keats doesn't mean "soft" here. The pipes are not just soft but silent, that is, ultra-soft, softer than soft; an unstated superlative or absolute comparative is implied. Yet really those pipes aren't soft at all; they are solidest marble. If we take soft materially, it is the opposite of the truth. It's another litotes—an understatement, message unspecified. The comparative reading points to the spiritual story the pipes should be ever so softly telling, the contrastive reading to the physical art object. Comparison, contrast; story, picture. The one thing absent is the tune. Music gets lost in the shuffle.

The strangely casual-sounding word "ditties" heightens the paradox. A ditty is a ballad, and etymologically it comes from the old French word for speaking or dictating. "Ditties of no tone" are, precisely, the words without the music, appropriately piped to the spirit and not to the ear, sentiment rather than sensation. Curiously, the other well-known place where Keats uses the word "ditty" also has an aura of silence: "He play'd an ancient ditty, long since mute, / In Provence call'd, 'La belle dame sans mercy'" ("The Eve of St. Agnes" 291–92). Revived in romance, as here, the ditty proves a dangerous charm. Better the toneless ditty than the opiates of Provençal song, with their life-denying, hypnotic incantation. Music is bad for the soul. In the ode Keats first mentions the pipes in connection with danger, "What pipes and timbrels? What wild ecstasy?" He says nice things to the pipes to flatter them—"Therefore ye soft pipes, play on"—knowing full well that they aren't playing at all and that he wouldn't want them to. "Therefore" is the most devious word of all. Logically, Keats should have said, "Heard melodies are sweet, but those unheard / Are sweeter; therefore, ye soft pipes, shut up." Indeed, what he does say amounts to much the same thing, more tactfully worded.[3]

A crisis, then, haunts these lines. The unheard melodies really aren't there because they have always already turned into something else. Words or pictures, more or less, comparable or contrasting: the poem gives us everything but the thing we are looking for, the music—or the muse—itself. No wonder that Keats says near the end, playfully but sadly, "Thou silent form dost tease us out of thought."

* * *

Dans cette métaphysique héliocentrique, la force cédant la place à l'eidos (c'est-à-dire à la forme visible pour l'oeil métaphorique), a déjà été séparée de *son sens* de force, comme la qualité de la musique est séparée de soi dans l'acoustique.

In this heliocentric metaphysic, force, yielding its place to eidos (i.e., to form that is visible to the metaphoric eye), has already been separated from *its sense* of force, as the quality of music is separated from itself in hearing. (Derrida, "Force et signification" 45)

Composers didn't need Keats to imagine unheard melodies. The idea is as old as the famous and widespread mystical notion of the music of the spheres and as new as John Cage's 4 minutes and 33 seconds of silence. When the bustle of daily existence falls silent, you hear the universe or else, as Cage says (13), the nervous system and the circulation of the blood—the world or else the self. Keats wasn't inventing in his ode but rethinking a long-familiar conception, as we might see from his word "spirit," which means both something transcendental and something internal, world or self. He is in tune with tradition here, and hence it makes sense to juxtapose his ode with musical passages that may have something related in view.

There is no more outspoken example of an unheard melody than that in Schumann's *Humoresque*, opus 20, so blatant a case of secrecy that it's almost funny and certainly more outrageously teasing than Keats's urn (see Example 5). The middle line in the score is a melody published with the explicit direction not to play it. Quite soberly, we can say that the "inner voice" line orients the performer's thoughts. The melody is also outlined and, indeed, discreetly highlighted in the treble part. The "inner voice" reminds the performer to think about it and to emphasize those notes in performance. Yet the inner voice also differs from the treble notes: it's written an octave down, with a rest in one bar where the right hand plays, and with dynamic indications—unplayed dynamics!—that in some cases vary from those in either the treble or bass parts. We can retain from this curiosity the simple yet vital notion that the piece is composed of two levels, outer and inner voice, sounds and thoughts. The sounds are directed at what Keats calls "the sensual ear." But the

*) Diese innere Stimme soll nicht mitgespielt werden. Der Spieler soll hier gleichsam „zwischen den Zeilen" lesen.
This inner part is not to be played. The player is to "read between the lines" here, as it were.
Cette partie intermédiaire ne doit pas être jouée. Ici, l'exécutant doit savoir „lire entre les lignes".

Example 5. *Humoresque*, by Robert Schumann. Reproduced from *Complete Works for Piano Solo in Six Volumes*, vol. 4, Melville: Belwin Mills, n.d., a reprint of a nineteenth-century edition of Schumann's works.

performer must think about the sounds in order to shape the performance: that shaping thought is the inner voice, a ditty of no tone that is
piped to the spirit. There's nothing very startling about this, yet it remains quietly perplexing to feel that the thought is somehow different
from the music or that the sense or quality of the notes is not exactly in
what you hear. Schumann, too, wants music to be "eerie"—for the spirit
and not, or not just, for the ear.[4]

Now this Schumann passage is obviously eccentric. We need to ask
whether he is doing here something that has never been done, or, on the
contrary, something that we always do and therefore rarely bother to
think about. I will rest my case that it is the latter on a series of other
examples that range gradually from the odd to the normal.

Tchaikovsky, one of the most underrated of the great masters, is distinctly odd. His unheard melody is the theme of the last movement of
the *Symphonie Pathétique*. Example 6 shows its guise on first appearance,
Example 7 a reprise later in the movement. In the reprise the first violins
play the tune. But initially it is broken between the first and second
violins. The lines they play are never heard individually, and no one
plays the melody that audiences have always heard and analysts always analyzed. Why Tchaikovsky did that is a mystery. But clearly he
had a reason. The mystery, then, is a controlling design. Something is
heard, and something, whatever it may be, is thought, beneath what is
heard. To be sure, in Tchaikovsky's day the second violins sat opposite
the firsts rather than behind them, and attentive listeners might have
caught a delicate stereophonic effect (Porter, *Music of Three Seasons* 451).
But for my purposes it doesn't even matter, finally, whether the unheard

Example 6. Symphony no. 6 (*Pathétique*), by Pyotr Ilich Tchaikovsky. Finale,
opening.

Example 7. *Pathétique* Symphony. Finale.

melody is really unheard or almost unheard. What matters is that the scoring conveys an attitude toward the melody or a thought about it. There is an undersense of strain, later relieved, that the performers must feel and that should be communicated through the intangibles of interpretation.

By interpretation musicians (and actors) normally mean expressive performance, whereas critics normally mean the elucidation of thought, design, or ideology. Unheard melodies bring the two meanings together. The undersense of strain belongs to an overall structure of feeling, expression, and import that pervades the whole symphony. From the murky vastness of its low bassoon and bass opening onward, the symphony is an epic work, the tale of a world at risk. It breaks precedent by ending with a slow movement—Mahler followed suit a few years later—and the fragmented theme is but one sign among many of an impending doom. The whole story would be too long to tell here, but some such undersense must be what led Tchaikovsky's brother to give the name *Pathétique* to the symphony. As the unheard melody in the bars that I have reproduced lies in the way the voices are fitted together, so the larger unheard melody lies in the adjustment of voices and parts in the whole symphony. Donne's "legend," epitome, and "pattern," Keats's "attitude" and "silent form"—those are what a fuller analysis could unfold and what Modeste Tchaikovsky named for us in his title.

Musical Romanticism's last gasp came some 50 years later, with the *Four Last Songs* of Richard Strauss. The last song, in the usual ordering, is called *Der Abschied* (The Farewell). The unheard melody that I single out here is found in the horn parts in the last bars, the end of the end of the end (see Example 8). From amid the whole orchestra, playing its

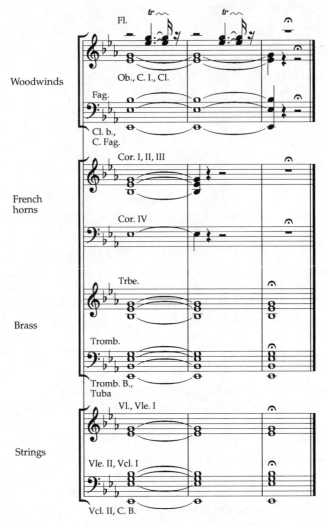

Example 8. "Der Abschied," from Four Last Songs, by Richard Strauss. Conclusion.

softest, the horns fall silent. Those horns were Strauss's father's instrument, his own favorite and that of the Romantic poets, particularly Eichendorff, who wrote the poem that Strauss set here. Strauss keeps his own counsel as to why he allows the horns to die out before everyone else. Perhaps the reasons are partly acoustical, but the silence is unmistakably an expressive gesture as well. It can be read, I think, as Strauss's secret farewell to Romanticism. More to the purpose here, however, is simply the assertion that the silence ought to be read somehow, as a commentary on the piece.[5]

In short, there is more to a piece of music than meets the ear. We can call that something more an attitude, a conception, or a thought. In the odd examples given so far the something leaves an unheard trace in the score, and they do offer glimmerings at least of what is at stake, of what really matters to the composer. More typically, of course, what really matters is also audible. But in any piece some things are more audible than others. You don't notice all the melodies that are hearable but the subliminal effect remains. The difference between a good and a bad listener is that the good listener knows how things fit together, hears the inner voices, and makes the connections. And often the composer helps things along.

In the song from *Pierrot Lunaire* called *The Pale Washerwoman*, Schoenberg silently guides the listener by printing a piano reduction in the score even though the piano doesn't perform in this piece. Amid all the "ugly" music reflecting an ugly world, the conventional minor chords of bar 4 sound pale and washed out. It's another adieu to Romanticism, shaded differently from Strauss's. But the piano reduction doesn't tell all, nor is even a careful listener of these quick moments likely to realize why the pale chords sound so very odd and out of place. What matters is less the harmonies that show up in the piano reduction than the distribution of the voices that, perhaps, only the performers can really hear (see Example 9). Three instruments play three notes each. But a different voice is on top each time, and each sounds the notes of a different chord. The violin plays an A-major arpeggio, the clarinet a dominant seventh on E, the flute a C-sharp-major arpeggio. While the chords are innocuous, the lines are polytonal. Only preternaturally swift ears could hear the counterpoint consciously, yet the sequence sounds alien. Heard melodies, in this case, are sweet, but unheard ones are acid.

Example 9. "Eine blasse Wäscherin," from *Pierrot lunaire*, by Arnold Schoenberg. Opening. Used by permission of Belmont Music Publishers, Pacific Pal-
isades, CA 90272.

You can hear sounds, but you can't hear patterns or attitudes; those
you have to think or hear with the mind. For to know what constitutes a
pattern you have to know what belongs together, what feels right or
wrong, tense or relaxed, complete or incomplete. The feelings and emotions come through the patterns that project the attitudes. Satisfaction
means making full, filling up the pattern, rounding off; emotion means
moving, changing, altering or breaking the form, making it expressive
by pressing something out of it. In an important sense, melodies are
never heard. Only notes are heard. What E. H. Gombrich has ceaselessly argued about art applies with a vengeance to music: the meaning
lies in the mind's apprehension of conventions that are being manipu-
lated.

I will therefore conclude my music section with a mainstream example that is free of the idiosyncrasies of the other examples yet still features an unheard melody. All music does—all art does—so long as you
stretch the meaning of the word melody to include any type of pattern.
But this example has an unheard melody that's really a melody, and
because it isn't there, any good listener will have to listen for the pattern
instead (see Example 10). This, following eleven tumultuous introduc-

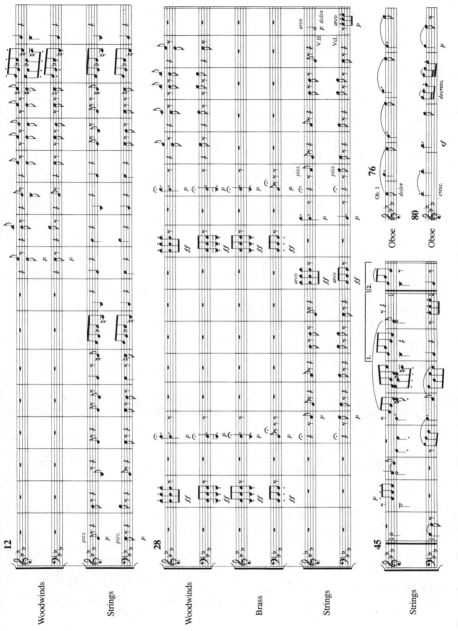

Example 10. Symphony no. 3 (*Eroica*), by Ludwig van Beethoven. Finale, bars 12–52 and 76–83.

tory bars, is the opening of the last movement of Beethoven's *Eroica* Symphony, much the most ambitious symphony yet composed by anyone. What must Beethoven's first listeners have thought, coming so far—musically speaking—in order to arrive at the puny excuse for a theme that is plunked out in the bass? Something is missing. There's not much to listen to here. Where is the tune?

A really sophisticated listener would know where the tune is, because Beethoven had already written it, in the finale of his ballet, *The Creatures of Prometheus*. If you know enough you can hear the unheard melody. But if you aren't one of the favored few, about the best you can do is think. You could think about the weather while waiting for something pretty to happen, but more likely Beethoven wanted you to think back over the symphony.

Starting on the tonic—or key—note of E-flat, the tune stretches an octave between high and low B-flat (the fifth, or dominant, note of the scale), stretching an extra note to low A at one point. It might call to mind the opening theme of the first movement, which is also a bass line covering an octave between B-flats (see Example 11). The first theme of the slow movement covers an octave between the dominant tones, G in this case, stretching an extra note to high A-flat at one point (see Exam-

Example 11. *Eroica* Symphony. First movement, opening.

Example 12. *Eroica* Symphony. Second movement, opening.

Example 13. *Eroica* Symphony. Third movement, opening.

Example 14. *Eroica* Symphony. Trio section of the third movement, opening.

ple 12). The first theme of the third movement covers an octave between B-flats, stretching an extra note to high C at one point (see Example 13). Even the theme of the trio section of this movement begins by covering an octave between B-flats (see Example 14). Altogether, the absence of a melody at the opening of the finale leaves room for reflection and helps call attention to the unity of the symphony. The skin is stripped away leaving the bones; or the decoration, leaving the framework. The unheard melody is the structural coherence of the whole.

In the *Eroica* Symphony the summing up is simultaneously a redemption of the earlier movements. The first movement theme begins with the notes of an E-flat-major triad, sinks to D, and then sinks further to a note that doesn't belong, C-sharp. Musical training is not requisite to hear the effect because the music changes character at this point, with the agitated entry of the syncopated violins (Example 11, bar 7). In the last movement, the bass line also sinks to D, but then returns to E-flat (Example 10, bars 16–17). The last movement begins, in other words, by correcting a disruption in the first movement. It also echoes in a brighter vein the tragic second movement, with rising pairs of notes (E–F, D–E-flat, A–B-flat; Example 10, bars 17–19) replacing the heavy descents of the earlier theme.

There are no such problems with the third movement. But that movement does raise another problem perhaps overlooked earlier on. The most distinctive characteristic of the third movement theme is the repeated notes. The trio is also built up of repeated notes. Repeated notes also form the introductory flourish in the slow movement theme. Even earlier they constitute the accompaniment to the first movement theme (Example 11, third staff). In other words, repetition is present from the start, adjacent to the themes, and the symphony gradually makes repetition a part of its thematic material. Now, in the last movement we also find repeated notes, and again they don't seem to be really part of the theme. They are, first, the echo effect as the winds repeat the string notes (Example 10, bars 20–25), and then, second, the loud flourish on B-flat where the motion pauses (bars 28–31). That sort of pause on the dominant was a common feature of variation themes at the time, but Beethoven seems in desperate straits when he does it so baldly. This isn't part of the tune but a crude structural device. How is he going to pull it all together? What is going to happen next?

What happens next is truly extraordinary. Beethoven does not simply fashion a unifying motif but instead stages the gesture of producing that unity. For, before the unheard Prometheus melody is at last sounded, Beethoven writes variations on the bass line. By holding off the melody, Beethoven lets us hear the motivation for it. Repetition occurs first as the interrupting element, then as echo, next as an accompaniment figure (bars 44 and 46), and at last, when the Prometheus theme appears, as part of the melody itself (bars 80–81). All the parts contribute to the whole that has grown organically. Consequently—to mention just one other effect among a large number that a full analysis might disclose—the very opening of the symphony may now be heard differently. For it opens with another flourish. Before the agitated first-violin syncopations, even before the ostinato eighth-note accompaniment in second violins and violas, come two—repeated—opening chords. Listeners may treat them as an empty gesture, and I suspect that analysts never attach them to the first theme. But in hindsight they should be reckoned with. At first sounding like a vestigial introduction, these too subsequently prove to be an integral building block of the structural whole.[6]

So let me repeat my equation. Unheard melodies are structure, skeleton, attitude, feeling: they are the inside of the piece, or of the urn. Though my examples have been a little out of the ordinary, it's really an ordinary point, worth taking a little less for granted than is often done. It's a commonplace, for instance, that themes for variation often aren't very pretty; you don't listen to them for their own sake. You listen in anticipation of the unheard elaborations to come later. And during the variations you listen back to the theme that is no longer being played. Even for a relatively naive listener the pleasure of the form lies in comparison and contrast: the invariant substructure and the potential that unfolds from it. Keats was right after all to tell the soft pipes to play on rather than to shut up. The unheard melodies aren't unplayed; they are the undertone that make their presence felt through their persistence.

The point is equally applicable to the other arts. Keats's urn, after all, features a painting, not a tone poem. His interest is excited by what can't be known about the urn or by what can't be seen on it. "What men or gods are these?" he wants to know, "What maidens loth?" "To what green altar, O mysterious priest, / Lead'st thou that heifer lowing at the skies?" The first questions ask for information that isn't forthcoming, the last for a scene that isn't painted. We hardly ever look at a painting without wanting information: who or what is portrayed, what is the story, what is the conventional or personal significance of the details? Not everything that we need to know to look at a work of art is contained within it. The iconographic quest may not concern unseen pictures in the strict sense, but it certainly concerns things unseen within the picture that are essential for a proper understanding of it.

Even more to my point, however, is the formalist quest. Looking at a painting is not the same as looking at an object, just as listening to a musical composition is not the same as listening to the tunes. Poussin's self-portrait (Figure 1) is full of unseen pictures, canvases viewed from the back or in part. The man stands behind his works, and you haven't

Figure 1. *Self-Portrait*, by Nicolas Poussin, 1650. Oil on canvas, 38½ × 29 in. (98 × 74 cm). Musée du Louvre, Paris. © Photo R.M.N.

seen everything if you have just looked at them. Yet more famous is Velázquez's *Las Meninas* (Figure 2), whose giant concealed canvas captured the imagination of painters throughout the ages (Kronik, "The Web, the Hive, and the Looking Glass"), as it has captured the imagination of critics of all stripes. But it doesn't take much to remind us of the unseen picture behind the canvas (Figure 3). A little spot of white at the center, something as chancy as a playing card facing the other way can be the signal that the world in the painting isn't our world but a self-contained, imaginary, fictive world. The boy in Chardin's *Card Castle* doesn't care about us or relate to us in any way; he is absorbed in his

Figure 2. *Las Meninas*, by Diego Velázquez, c. 1656. Oil on canvas, 125 ×
108⅔ in. (318 × 276 cm). Museo del Prado, Madrid. Photo: Alinari / Art Resource, New York.

own thoughts (Fried, *Absorption* 46–51). Chardin loved to paint a world
of thoughts, a world beyond pure visibility, or beyond the eye, so typically down-turned in this magical portrait.

Thought—reflection. Isn't that what every serious painting is—not a
copy of reality but a thoughtful reflection that composes the usual surface into something more deeply meaningful? Painters love mirrors
(Cook, "The Wilderness of Mirrors"). They love them for painterly reasons, because of the fascinating softening of contours in the painted
mirror image that seems to idealize the scene. Remember the royal cou-

Figure 3. *The Card Castle*, by Jean-Baptiste-Siméon Chardin, c. 1735. Oil on canvas, 32⅜ × 26 in. (82 × 66 cm). National Gallery of Art, Washington; Andrew W. Mellon Collection.

ple in Velázquez's mirror, miniaturized but still conceptually dominant, at the visual center of the picture. Manet's *Bar at the Folies-Bergères* (Figure 4) is another famous and fascinating mirror, which doesn't reflect the scene in front of it but some other skewed version in the painter's imagination. Enacting Manet's "attitude toward the Folies-Bergère," as a Marxist critic has written, the mirror turns the scene into something "almost real" in order to communicate "a form of explana-

Figure 4. *The Bar at the Folies-Bergère*, by Edouard Manet, 1882. Oil on canvas, 37¾ × 51¼ in. (96 × 130 cm). Courtauld Institute of Art, London.

tion" for the "social circumstances" it depicts (Clark, *The Painting of Modern Life* 253–54). Reflection isn't copying but thinking; that's what painters do and what Monet paints in this remarkable canvas that might be called a visualization of an unseen picture.

It wouldn't be hard to come up with more paintings of hidden pictures, or of mirrors reflecting scenes that aren't there, let alone of the unpainted areas of canvas that from Cézanne to Jackson Pollock and beyond have increasingly been part of the painter's repertory. (Kenneth Noland, for instance—according to Fried, *Three American Painters* 27—"make[s] the raw canvas itself work as optical space with unprecedented intensity.") But let me move on to at least one "ordinary" painting that seems to be a painting of the world rather than of the painter's activity in transforming the world. But has any of us ever seen what the world "really" looks like? Don't we always think as we see, connecting the dots on our retina, in order to turn pure visual sensations into visual pictures? We see green and black splotches but we perceive grass and

Figure 5. Detail from *Regatta at Argenteuil.*

shadows: the splotches are unperceived by us, the forms perceived, but in a literal sense unseen. Music is composed of sounds and sound shapes, and there is only noise if we don't hear the forms within the sounds—as sometimes happens to us with music from an alien culture. The same is true of visual things; unless the unseen shadows the seen, the world is no better than a hallucination.

That was the lesson of the Impressionists. Figure 5 is a detail from Monet's *Regatta at Argenteuil.* Is it possible to see the picture in the splotches? In context, however (Figure 6), their identity as a tree and a

Figure 6. *Regatta at Argenteuil*, by Claude Monet, 1871. Oil on canvas, 19 × 28¾ in. (48 × 73 cm). Musée d'Orsay, Paris. © Photo R.M.N.

house is beyond question. Yet there is more to the painting than mere linear decipherment.

The semantic relation between top and bottom, evidently works in both directions. First, the top names the bottom: this aggregate of spots that means nothing to you, presto! it's a tree, it's a house, it's a boat. Second, the bottom reveals the top: this boat, this house that you find drab in fact secretly contain these color harmonies, those elementary figures, such expressive possibilities.

In a painting like this one, what is above corresponds to what we recognize, to the reality we are accustomed to; the lower part, which conveys these houses or these boats toward us, corresponds to the painter's activity. Thus the water becomes a metaphor for painting. The broad strokes that make up these reflections vigorously affirm the material and the tools used by the artist. The liquid surface gives us an example in nature of this activity. (Butor, "Claude Monet," 285)

By separating form from visual content, the reflective surface within Monet's paintings becomes the figure of the unseen limit where mind and matter, the known and the felt, meet. Some of my examples are especially dramatic, self-conscious expressions of the reflective character of art, but my message is that all art is reflective. To a thoughtful audience art reveals the buried inside of things: the moving patterns that make sense of the world's surface, of sounds, of sights, of words.

* * *

Of words? I have talked about music and about pictures but not yet about my own field. Where are the unread poems?

That's an easy one. One example is the passage I quoted early on from Keats's *Eve of St. Agnes*: "He play'd an ancient ditty, long since mute, / In Provence call'd, 'La belle dame sans mercy.'" Keats wrote a ballad called *La Belle Dame sans Merci*, but later. It would be an easy parlor game to accumulate poetic references to unquoted or unwritten poems, novelistic allusions to other works of literature, real and imaginary, stage directions that call for wordless communication by the actors or that contain voluminous background information that can never be communicated in the theater. Harold Bloom has built his career on the premise that the meaning of a poem is always another poem: behind the words that you read lie others—usually from *Paradise Lost*—that motivate them and give them their significance. The notions of a poem behind the poem or of a story behind the novel are too common for words.

Such things, however, are not quite unheard melodies. They are iconographic backgrounds, explanations of the surface content of the works. But in music and painting we have been looking at structural patterns that reflect the shape and tone of the work. Aren't the unheard melodies of poems less innocuous and more like the inner movement of the Grecian urn? Their type is the complex interplay of comparisons and negations in Keats's lines. Isn't such a shuttling among similarities, intensities, and contrasts the very essence of the mind's structuring activity, teasing us into thought? Don't we have in those lines a portrait of precisely the kind of thought that I have called the unheard melodies of our existence?[7]

A portrait of thought. A reflection on reflection. You can say what Keats means, but in saying it you have only the surface meaning, the heard melody, the visual transcription. But if you show his meaning, if you perform it, you have created something "more endear'd," of greater value, deeper. That performance is what makes a poem poetic. What makes a poem is not what it says but what it does in saying it. What makes a mind is not what it thinks but that it thinks, not the content but the activity. The reflecting surface is fluid; it breaks up appearances in order to perceive substrates. The meaning of a work is never identical to what it says, or depicts, or sings. Even if it utters truths—and works often do—even then the enacted meaning, the unseen picture, the unheard melody is never the same as the statement. The meaning of a poem can be described in words—that is what we literary critics do for a living—but it cannot be reduced to words. "Ditties of no tone" is a great phrase, for what works of art contain is not a meaning that is uttered but one that is carried by force of example from mind to mind, spirit to spirit, soul to soul.

* * *

I will conclude by mentioning a few poems and citing some utterances by a later and simpler poet than Keats: Stéphane Mallarmé. (For a fine discussion of formalism and expressivism in Mallarmé see McDonald, *Dispositions* 37–69.) Mallarmé is not simpler, of course, in his verbal surface, but he is in what matters more—the directness with which he calls our attention to the organizing thoughts underneath. The very name of Mallarmé, to be sure, popularly evokes an impressionism in which all definite realities dissolve into the shimmering expressive immediacy of pure voice: "Je dis: une fleur! et hors de l'oubli où ma voix relègue aucun contour, en tant que quelque chose d'autre que les calices sus, musicalement se lève, idée même et suave, l'absente de tous bouquets" (I say: a flower! and, beyond the oblivion to which my voice consigns any outline, as something other than known calyxes, musically arises—the suave idea itself—the One absent from all bouquets; *Oeuvres* 368). But you shouldn't read those well-known lines from the end of the essay "Crise de vers" out of context, as is normally done. If you have the whole essay before you, you will have read this, three sentences earlier: "Un désir indéniable à mon temps est de séparer comme en vue d'attributions différentes le double état de la parole, brut ou immédiat ici, là essentiel" (An undeniable desire of my time is to separate as if with an eye to different predications the dual status of the word, raw or immediate here, there essential; 368). The musical flower, the suave idea, is a word after all, not a pure, wordless impression, though indeed it is a deeper, essential, inapparent word, a ditty of no tone. How do we discern that essential word? The immediately preceding paragraph describes as unmistakably as anyone could desire how Mallarmé discerns it, at concerts:

Certainement, je ne m'assieds jamais aux gradins des concerts, sans percevoir parmi l'obscure sublimité telle ébauche de quelqu'un des poëmes immanents à l'humanité ou leur originel état, d'autant plus compréhensible que tu et que pour en déterminer la vaste ligne le compositeur éprouva cette facilité de suspendre jusqu'à la tentation de s'expliquer. . . . Car, ce n'est pas de sonorités élémentaires par les cuivres, les cordes, les bois, indéniablement mais de l'intellectuelle parole à son apogée que doit avec plénitude et évidence, résulter, en tant que l'ensemble des rapports existant dans tout, la Musique.

Certainly, I never take my seat in the tiers of the concert hall, without perceiving amid the dark sublimity some sketch of one of the immanent poems of humanity, or their original state, all the more comprehensible because silenced and because the composer, so as to determine their vast line, felt a readiness to suspend even the temptation to explain himself. . . . For, it is not from elementary sonorities by the brass, the strings, the woodwinds, undeniably but from the intellectual word at its apogee that there should result, in full and demonstrably, as the entirety of the relations existent in everything, Music. (367–68)

Music is, undeniably, relationships and not sounds, the perfection of utterance and not visceral feeling, not the channeling or taming of noise but the intellectual word that manifests the silent pulse of being. The unheard melody resides in shape and pattern, as Mallarmé says two paragraphs earlier: "Tout devient suspens, disposition fragmentaire avec alternance et vis-à-vis, concourant au rythme total, lequel serait le poëme tu, aux blancs" (All becomes suspense, fragmentary arrangement with alteration and juxtapositon, concurring in the total rhythm, which would be the silent poem, in the blanks; 367). Go back to the previous page, and Mallarmé has said it all, in a one-line paragraph setting the topic that these concluding pages have merely been explicating: "Cette visée, je la dis Transposition—Structure, une autre" (This [preceding] aim I call Transposition—Structure [is] something else; 366).[8] Structure, as the something else within expression, is the silent poem, the essential word, the flower absent from all bouquets, the musical idea.

Such is the context for the impressionistic musical disappearance of the contour of the flower. One could hardly dream of a more explicit declaration of the themes concealed within the urn. And so, when Mallarmé, in his poetry, praises the pale reflection of a portrait of Saint Cecilia ("Sainte"), I think there can be no question but that his "Musicienne du silence" (Musician of silence) evokes the perfect organization without which all would be blank to the mind. Or, that the denials of another sonnet ("Une dentelle s'abolit")—the self-canceling lace of the title, the "absence éternelle de lit" (eternal absence of bed) the "unanime blanc conflit / D'une guirlande" (unanimous white conflict of a garland) with its mirror image, and the "musical hollow void" within the mandolin—are likewise all enabling virtualities underneath the world of appearances, making it possible to end the poem not, as one might predict, with nonbeing (n'être), but instead with birth (naître). (Like so much in Mallarmé, the lines "Tristement dort une mandore / Au creux néant musicien" [Sadly sleeps a mandolin / In the hollow musical void] seem to echo Coleridge, specifically the silent music of "The Eolian Harp": "and the mute still air / Is Music slumbering on her instrument.") Another poem opens with the utter silence of dark, formless matter:

> A la nue accablante tu
> Basse de basalte et de laves
> A même les échos esclaves
> Par une trompe sans vertu. . . .
>
> Silent in the overwhelming cloud
> Basalt and lava shoal
> Enslaved even to echoes
> By a horn without force. . . .

But even this beginning opens out into the bright afterglow ("le si blanc cheveu" [the so white hair]) of a submerged musician ("Le flanc enfant d'une sirène" [The childlike side of a siren]). In resisting the chaos of "enslaved echoes" into which our lives are forever falling, art transmits to us the shaping power of the unseen, the unheard, and the unspoken that enables expression to take place.

* * *

Decant, descant, discount. Have I done nothing more in these pages than pour old wine into a new bottle? Aired it, refreshed it, embellished it, yet left it fundamentally untouched, taken it for granted even? Yes, to be sure. And no, by no means. Yes, in that the spirit of Cassirer and Langer rightly lives. Formalist is an epithet to be honored, not blushed at. Without form there is no power of resistance to the immediate, nought but the "enslaved echoes" of an abject consciousness. But no, if it be supposed that the new bottle is as rigid a container as the old one. The glass exists to be broken, the wine of form to be drunk, as in that drunken, distorting mirror of Manet.

> Le vierge, le vivace et le bel aujourd'hui,
> Va-t'il nous déchirer avec un coup d'aile ivre
> Ce lac dur oublié que hante sous le givre
> Le transparent glacier des vols qui n'ont pas fui!

> The virgin, lively and fair today,
> Will it with a drunken blow of its wing
> Tear our hard, forgotten lake haunted beneath the frost
> By the transparent glacier of flights that have not fled!

The icy surface that transmits without reflecting is the form of the dead present, forgotten because closed to its own possible unfolding. Mallarmé resolves to reawaken form, but not by remembering the forgotten surface or capturing the unflown and (in French) thievish flights. The divine parousia is not to be chained in bonds of ice or marble, freeze or frieze. Rather, form becomes the personifying force that liberates today into its unknown possibilities of action and of expression, of remembering and projecting, transcending the inert ideality of the moment and the inert materialism of the thing itself.[9]

By taking my cue from music, I have stacked the cards in favor of a thesis that form is energy, expression, and movement. But in truth that thesis is inscribed in the restiveness to be felt in the most inert or the most mimetic of paintings (see Bryson, "Chardin"),[10] as well as in poetry's recurrent envy of what it is not—of the pictorial balance that a sequential art can never attain, or of the musical pulse beyond the waywardness of natural life (see Paz, "El Ritmo," El Arco y la lira 49–67). Apollo is Dionysus.[11] The noble, intact today is the drunken pugilist of tomorrow and yesterday. I do not know why the critics of Keats, who tend to divide between the Apollonians and the Dionysians, should so seldom have seen this mutuality in the Ode on a Grecian Urn, where it seems so inescapable, let alone in the unseen landscapes of the Ode to a Nightingale or the dreaming wakefulness of the Ode to Psyche. All you need to know, on earth, is that beauty is . . . as truth, and truth . . . as beauty. The one *becomes* the other—how delightfully colloquial are our philosophical puns in English—in the vital round dance that lets form give life and meaning to content, and content give substance and expression to form. Base materialisms and empty formalisms alike may pretend to ignore the unheard call, but they cannot escape their destinies.

Reference Matter

Notes

Overture

1. Need it be observed that a worm in a garden path is an emblem of evil? The circles in *Bleak House* are discussed by J. Hillis Miller (*Charles Dickens* 185–90) and more fully by Robert Newsom (*Dickens* 18–39).

2. In two excellent feminist essays, Mary Jacobus and Margaret Homans describe Eliot's dialectic in analogous terms ("The Question of Language," "Eliot, Wordsworth, and the Scenes of Critical Instruction"). These essays take the sexual problem to be primary; I take it to instance a dialectical position. The feminine, an indispensable concept and quality, is not necessarily coextensive with the female.

3. Stuart M. Tave encloses the first chapter of *Some Words of Jane Austen* with fine discussions of dance as order (1–2, 34–35). "Every savage can dance," however (Darcy, quoted by Tave, 34), and Anne Elliot, the Austen heroine with the greatest mastery over her confused feelings (275), is also the one who "never dances" (262). C. J. Rawson surveys dancing in the eighteenth century and after (*Henry Fielding* 3–44); see esp. p. 29 on the "mincing, ambiguous figure" of the dancing master. See also Derrida and McDonald, "Choreographies" 68.

4. Or does Zola surreptitiously activate the mental sense of "balancer"? What, precisely, does the verb mean when he says of the "toy soldier" lover Zéphyrin, "il ne répondait ni oui ni non, se balançait comme si on l'eût chatouillé, puis s'élargissait d'aise" (he answered neither yes nor no, rocked [hesitated?] as if he had been tickled, then stretched out comfortably; part 5, chap. 1, p. 1168)?

5. The word ἀνατρέπω is not used by Plato to mean "refute," but Aristophanes uses it prominently in his satire of Socratic philosophy, *The Clouds*, which is centrally concerned with exploring turns (the character Strepsiades, the "vortex," etc.). The other locus for ἀνατρέπω in this sense is a late commentator who refers to some of Plato's dialogues as διάλογοι ἀνατρεπτικοί.

6. I have been unable to locate any extended discussion of *aporia* in Plato. The

major commentaries on the *Meno*, for instance, ignore the relevant passages, as if *aporia* belonged only to the interlocutors and not to the Socratic method. The absence of a word for *aporia* in modern languages may have contributed to the impression one gets that *aporia* is neither regarded as a concept nor acknowledged to have a function. Hans-Georg Gadamer at least recognizes the problem: on the one hand, he says that the *aporia* of presentation "fills us with confusion and uncertainty" (*Dialogue and Dialectic* 113) and that "because of the apeiron, human life can never be absolutely successful" (154–55), but on the other hand, he does allow that "this source of all aporia is also the source of the *euporia* which we achieve in discourse" (11). Gadamer's translator, typically, omits *aporia* from the index.

7. A transitional state of the word "revolution" may be found at the end of letter 83 of Goldsmith's *Letters to a Citizen of the World*: "The world is like a vast sea, mankind like a vessel sailing on its temptestuous bosom. Our . . . judgment is the rudder, without this last the vessel is tossed by every billow, and will find shipwreck in every breeze. In a word, obscurity and indigence are the parents of vigilance and œconomy; vigilance and œconomy of riches and honour; riches and honour of pride and luxury; pride and luxury of impurity and idleness, and impurity and idleness again produce indigence and obscurity. Such are the revolutions of life" (*Works* 2: 341). I believe that Blake's line, "And the Male gives a Time & Revolution to her Space" (*Jerusalem*, pl. 69, line 23), offers another transitional example; "revolution" here seems to imply (1) circling, (2) orgasm, and (3) the Fall. Leslie Brisman discusses "revolution" as circling and as violence in Wordsworth (*Romantic Origins* 328–29). Koselleck's *Kritik und Krise* is a brilliant account of the birth in the eighteenth century of a prolific crisis mentality (especially "in the philosophers professing a cyclical view of history," 134) and its degeneration into the hostile dualisms of politicized critique.

8. *Vom Schwindel* is cited from the enlarged 1791 edition, whose preface indicates that the principal changes are in the later, technical parts of the book.

9. For the view that dance teaches order see John C. Meagher, "The Dance." He concedes some of the difficulties of his position on p. 276.

10. Thomas M. Greene's masterful study affirms stability, but I believe that Jonson's works can be reread from the standpoint of his "centrifugal spirit" and of the present essay.

11. Antinous does not render the notion of twins any more stable when he later alludes to Castor and Pollux as "the victorious *twinns* of *Laeda'* and *Jove*" (71), hardly a tactful periphrasis to address to Penelope in the midst of her entanglement with the actions of Leda's other twins.

12. "*Brawles*: the *branle*, a dance distinguished by movement from side to side" (Davies, 369n). Love, that is, teaches a tottering dance.

13. The association of Penelope with mind is fairly consistent. True, st. 11 refers to *Antinous*'s mind. But the context is the power that Penelope's eyes exert

(and that Antinous merely receives) over "the noblesse and the splendour of his mind." In st. 46 Antinous calls music "the soft minds Paradice, the sick minds Leach"; clearly he is siding here with emotion, not with thought.

14. Rousset derives his notion of classicism from the customary misreading of Heinrich Wölfflin, who is discussed later in this volume.

15. Jacques Derrida discusses the turn against turn on 252–63 of the Hegel column of *Glas*: "Essayer de *penser* (mais ce mot déjà retient dans le cercle) un reste de *temps* (mais le temps déjà engage dans le cercle) qui ne serait pas, qui ne relèverait pas d'un présent, d'un mode d'être ou de présence et qui par consé-quent tomberait hors du cercle du *Sa*, n'en tomberait pas comme *son* négatif, tout prêt à reprendre la tangente pour rester collé au cercle et se laisser par lui réentraîner" (252a). Puns make Derrida's prose untranslatable, so that I can only give an approximate rendition: "To try to *think* (but this word already retains in the circle) a remainder of *time* (but time already engages in the circle) that would not be, that would not participate in a present, in a mode of being or of presence and that consequently would fall out of the circle of *absolute knowledge*, would not fall out as *its* negative [as a negative *sound*], quite ready to resume the tangent so as to remain stuck to the circle and to let itself again be swept along with it." While the processes described in *Glas* are most intriguingly bizarre (*anthérection, coupture*, etc.), I believe that my concluding turn toward process is compatible in a general way with Derrida's contention (as in the paragraph on "gl," p. 262b) that we remain indissolubly glued to the ring of difference.

16. Nature, in Harry Berger's beautiful expression, is "*too* perfect" ("The *Mutabilitie Cantos*" 171 n). Patricia A. Parker's entire book is an important treat-ment of my subject; see esp. pp. 54–64 on the *Mutability Cantos* and pp. 16–31 and 64–77 on error in Ariosto and Spenser. Typical of the difficulty in disentan-gling these cantos is William Nelson, *The Poetry of Edmund Spenser* 309, where Boethius is pressed into service in an awkward attempt to distinguish Muta-bility's "perdurability" from genuine "eternity."

17. St. 2 of canto 6 says, "As I have found it registered of old / In Faery Land mongst records permanent." St. 2 of canto 7 says, "for who, but thou alone / That art yborne of heaven and heavenly Sire, / Can tell things doen in heaven so long ygone, / So farre past memory of man that may be knowne?"

18. Angus Fletcher advocates a more hopeful view of Mutability in *The Pro-phetic Moment* 217–28. Arguing that the cantos subsume rebellion under revolu-tion (in the old sense of cycle), he concludes that error is redeemed, or at least "continually reborn" (227), in the anagogical Sabbath vision. How to translate theological truth (Fletcher quotes Tillich to confirm his reading) into sublunary experience remains, of course, the question. I think Fletcher answers it as I do; at least, he returns to the Mutability Cantos at the end of the same chapter ("Error and Experience," 215–57) in a section called "The Fall into History" (253–57).

19. "Poets' verses cannot really be endless; poems end, and, like every other

thing we make, they die." So says Isabel G. MacCaffrey (*Spenser's Allegory* 431), in the course of linking Spenser to Stevens in a more resigned fashion than I am about to do. Indeed, poems stop, even *The Faerie Queene*. But the issue is qualitative potency, not quantitative bulk. See also Altieri, "The Qualities of Action," and Kümmel, *Platon und Hegel*.

20. Commenting on the double meaning of Yeats's question, Paul de Man attributes its ambiguity to the split between the grammatical and the rhetorical functions of language, without remarking on the simpler semantic ambiguity of the expression, "to know from" (*Allegories of Reading* 11–12).

21. Frank Kermode, in a seminal, proto-feminist essay, "The Dancer," discusses the negativity, the faceless, sphinxlike quality of the dancer. I would like to suggest here what is achieved through this negation.

22. Jonathan Goldberg's *Endlesse Worke* puts a historian's question, "Where does *The Faerie Queene* move from its vantage point?" then immediately rephrases it in a categorically deconstructive mode: "Where *can* the text go . . . ?" 166, my emphasis). The answer, in the book's final phrase, must then be this: "into the reality of loss" (174).

23. Donald G. Marshall, "Ideas and History," attacks the still extant notion that an idea has a "true meaning." "On such a model," he writes, "we would have a history of errors and of glimpses of truth with a clear terminus." In view of this dilemma, he expresses "scepticism that 'imagination' in fact has a history" (358). My belief, on the contrary, is that in fact ideas like "imagination" have *only* a history. A valuable history of crisis-consciousness itself has now appeared: Eugene Hollahan, *Crisis-Consciousness and the Novel*.

Chapter 1

1. Weinstein, *Hippolyte Taine* 51. Despite its dated attitudes, however, this is a serious, careful book that remains well worth reading.

2. My quick sketch identifies books by their definitive titles; in several cases the first book publications, whose dates are given, have somewhat different titles. There is some uncertainty in the dates since bibliographies and reference works sometimes differ; in any case, many essays and chapters were published earlier in periodicals (or, in the case of the Mill chapter of the *History of English Literature*, as a separate book).

3. Taine seldom wrote at length about women: a brief essay of 1857 about Mme. de la Fayette; an even briefer late essay (1876) about George Sand; and a somewhat fuller discussion (1866) of Spanish culture and domesticity with reference to Mme. d'Aulnoy. (Giraud's *Essai sur Taine* also excerpts four uncollected reviews of books—including one on contemporary women—by Camille Selden, the pseudonym for Heinrich Heine's *Mouche*, Elise von Krienitz.) The *History of English Literature* mentions a substantial number of women writers but

features none. Given the obsession with the dead father and with surrogate fathers portrayed in *Etienne Mayran*, together with Taine's personal reticence and late marriage, there is evident occasion for a revealing essay concerning sexuality in his writing. While I do not examine the topic further, I use masculine pronouns throughout this essay in order to signal the problem.

4. The only full-scale analysis of Taine in many decades, Jean-Thomas Nordmann's *Taine et la critique scientifique*, presents Taine as my initial paragraphs have sketched him. It is a philosopher's account that puts *De l'intelligence* at the center while intentionally downplaying the more personal travel writings and the French history and that emphasizes structural unity over temporal division and literary character over style. (There are some pages on Taine's own writing, but no mention of his views on style.) Few of the passages I quote even appear in the book, and those that do are evaluated quite differently. Thus, Nordmann regards Taine's striking remark about the history of pants cited in note 32 below as deviant (304–5) and notices the "difficulties of transitional periods" (357) in preference to the achievements that Taine also celebrates. It is an admirably full and clear portrait from an entirely different angle.

5. Michelet's history, Taine complains in the essay devoted to him, is a work of inspired art, but not of thoughtful reflection and science (*Essais* 95). Typically, Taine was more charitable about Michelet when he was focused on assessing the strengths and weaknesses of another writer; see the glowing comparison of Michelet with Victor Cousin in *Les Philosophes classiques* 117–19.

6. Some examples of Taine's reportage of the Revolution: A chapter opening, "Through their carmagnoles there pierces a calculation which they will later acknowledge" (*La Révolution* 2: 137), is the only allusion to these popular orgies. Here is the only mention of regicide, the first clause of a many-headed sentence: "Consequently we have dethroned the king and cut off his head" (3: 90). The Terror gets most of a paragraph, of which the following is the most explicit part: "Indeed, before guillotining Robespierre and consorts for their orthodoxy, [the Convention] guillotined the Girondins, Danton and Hébert, as heretics" (3: 553). Nothing could be further from the magniloquent Greek tragedy constructed for Robespierre by Carlyle (*French Revolution* 6.7).

7. See the materials assembled by Victor Giraud in "Taine et le pessimisme," *Hippolyte Taine* 83–102. Colin Evans's "Conflict and Dualism in Taine" scrutinizes Taine's divided legacy, relying heavily on early manuscripts, some excerpts from which he prints for the first time.

8. Zola, "La Formule critique appliquée au roman," *Le Roman expérimental* 225–30. Taine's hostility to method is one of many British characteristics or tendencies in his writing; see the general account of this (racial?) tendency by David Simpson, *Romanticism, Nationalism, and the Revolt Against Theory*.

9. The preface to *Les Philosophes classiques* is frank and explicit about Taine's calculation as a writer. "I know that these manners are irreverent, and that one

should never call a thing by its name. My excuse is that this book was not made for established persons. I wished to persuade my reader, and my reader should not be more than thirty years old" (iv). The relation of creator to audience is a regular, important, and, indeed, markedly original focus of Taine's criticism as well as a feature of his own writing.

10. Drawing on Claude Bernard's notion of the *milieu intérieur*, on the double meaning of the French *expérience* as (subjective) experience and (objective) experiment, and on the general tendency of his imagination to polarize exterior and interior spaces, Zola's criticism silently converts Taine's three factors into six: nationality and blood line (exterior and interior race), environment and psychology (exterior and interior milieu), public and personal history (exterior and interior moment). He aims not to explain particular convergences so much as to correlate inner and outer truths, as in the oft-repeated naturalist slogan, "a corner of creation seen through a temperament," or in his advocacy of "the ascertainment of the states of external world corresponding to interior states of the personages" ("De la description," *Le Roman expérimental* 232). The resulting system might arguably be clearer and more coherent than Taine's, but it is certainly, at any rate, different.

11. Patrizia Lombardo's "Taine scrittore" finely evokes Taine's dual nature, stressing his vitalism, colorism, and passion for style. It is a corrective to the same author's "Hippolyte Taine Between Art and Science," which casts a harsh light on the Spinozism of the *Essai sur Tite Live*.

12. Bergson was born in 1859 and was a student at the height of Taine's influence. The only significant discussion of connections I have located is Günther Pflug's *Henri Bergson*, where Taine's *De l'intelligence* becomes the constant reference point: "Thus the debate with Taine's thesis is fundamental to 'Matière et mémoire,' even if Taine's name is nowhere mentioned" (139). Pflug stresses the differences—and certainly Bergson rejects the Hegelian and historicist components of Taine's vitalism—but then I will be stressing the internal differences between Taine's own vitalism and the systematics of *De l'intelligence*.

13. Edmund Wilson gives a harsh but just appraisal of Taine's failure of imagination in *Origines*—together with a strongly mixed appraisal of the *History of English Literature*—in *To the Finland Station* 53–64, which should be compared with Remy de Gourmont's almost unqualified praise in his chapter, "La Question Taine: Les Idées et les images," *Le Problème du style* 67–82.

14. Fritz Schalk gives a balanced account of Taine's empiricized Hegelianism in "Zu Taines Theorie und Praxis."

15. On Guizot see the useful pages (240–44) in Lucien Febvre's essay, "*Civilisation*: Evolution of a Word and a Group of Ideas," in "*A New Kind of History*" 219–57. Febvre, however, does not clearly distinguish the concepts of progress *of* (evolving) civilization and of progress *toward* (an ideal of) civilization, a tension that Jean Starobinski ("The Word *Civilization*," *Blessings in Disguise* 1–

35) considers fundamental to the development of the concept. Also relevant is the critique of Febvre by Fernand Braudel in "The History of Civilizations: The Past Explains the Present," *On History* 177–218.

16. Taine here footnotes Darwin, whose *Origin of Species* was published in 1859 and appeared in French in 1862.

17. Thus, in an uncollected 1865 review of a history of Greek literature, Taine writes that "literary style . . . brings to light the sentiments of men whose portrait or history we are making. A great historian said to me: I accumulate, I check and I arrange my materials, as I should do in a Memorial for the Academy of Inscriptions; then, I write my book like a novel" (Giraud, *Essai sur Taine* 236).

18. Yet the *annalistes* often seem rooted in Taine despite themselves. What, after all, are Braudel's triad of *longue durée*, conjuncture, and event—or, as Febvre puts it, "permanent forces" like "the Mediterranean," "stable forces" associated with "the space of time occupied by the reign of Philip II of Spain," and the "chance" of "events"—what are these other than race, milieu, and moment? (See Braudel, "History and the Social Sciences: The *Longue Durée*," *On History* 25–54, esp. 44, and Febvre, "A New Kind of History," *"A New Kind of History"* 37.) To be sure, there is a crucial difference in Taine's resistance to the illusions of scientific permanence. Still, Febvre's repeated denunciations of Taine and his followers in *La Terre* must, in this instance, be acknowledged as a sign of influence and kinship.

19. See also Albert S. Cook's fine analysis (*History/Writing* 119–35) of Michelet's jerky narrative rhythms and "nervous lapses of time" (124), which project the movement of time as a deep or "subterranean" (126) progress only fitfully and unevenly manifest in experience.

20. Taine is careful to specify that Milton's poetic output virtually ceased during the decades of the Puritan Revolution.

21. "Beside the permanent impulse and the given surroundings, there is the acquired momentum" (1: 16/1: xxix). A passage in the *Voyage en Italie* dismisses "vitesse acquise" as mere "inertia" and "dead forces," preferring "active forces . . . continuously renewed by new impulses" (1: 384–85). Despite the shift in vocabulary and in emphasis, the core of vitalism is recognizably the same in both books. Though Wellek correctly reports that after the introduction "Taine never again speaks of acquired speed" (31), the conception is pervasive; see, for instance, the passage quoted in note 33, where the translator has introduced the phrase for a slightly different French phrase.

22. Here are bits of some typical, extended paeans to realism. While quality is routinely praised (as with Donatello's formulaic originality and energy, just below), it is vastly outweighed by the realists' quantitative achievements. "What power! What foreground and background the endless enumeration gives the figure! how well he is known in all his actions and all his parts! how real he becomes! . . . For such is nature: the details are infinite and unravel infinitely"

("Balzac" 20). "By [Titian's] intelligence of real things, the field of art increases tenfold. . . . The infinite diversity of nature . . . opens to him" (*Italie* 2: 353).

23. In *George Sand and Idealism* (35–42) Naomi Schor usefully contrasts the rigidly masculinist Proudhon with Taine (one of whose two essays on women novelists concerns Sand), concentrating on the two books from 1865.

24. There are numerous passages praising realism in the *Voyage en Italie*, and one notable one in the *History of English Literature*, concerning Defoe: "Never was such a sense of the real before or since. Our realists of to-day, painters, anatomists, partisan men of business, are a hundred leagues from this naturalness; art and calculation crop out amidst their too minute descriptions" (2: 192/4: 88–89). Also relevant is the following, in *Notes sur l'Angleterre*: "No painter, nor artist is a pure copyist; he invents, even when he confines himself to translating; for, what nature executes by one system of means and values, he is obliged to render by a different system of values and means.—Such is the error of contemporary English painters; they are faithful, but literally" (354).

25. "Whether you come from the deep sky or rise from the abyss, / O Beauty! your look, infernal and divine, / Pours charity and crime all confused" (*Les Fleurs du mal* 28). On Baudelaire's infatuation with Proudhon around 1848, see T. J. Clark, *The Absolute Bourgeois* 164–69.

26. For a helpful new perspective on the instability of mid-century aesthetics see Pierre Bourdieu, *The Field of Cultural Production*, esp. "Field of Power, Literary Field and Habitus," trans. Claude DuVerlie, 161–75.

27. "A beautiful falsehood is always shocking; better an ugly truth" ("Du style," from Giraud, *Hippolyte Taine* 236). Giraud, a great authority on Taine, prints "Du style" as a companion to a "Lettre sur l'idéal," for which, on stylistic grounds, he rejects a date of 1851 and conjecturally suggests the period of *De l'idéal dans l'art* (i.e., around 1865, or just after the *History of English Literature*). The dating seems untenable. The "Lettre sur l'idéal" lambastes the French classical authors, for whom a series of essays from the late 1850's tries to develop a more sympathetic understanding. "Du style" extols Shakespeare for his realism, the *History of English Literature* for his soaring imagination that did not "confine [it]self to the imitation of nature" but instead "br[oke] loose from the laws of the real world" (1: 412/2: 259). The early book analyzing Livy as an "oratorical historian" already seems to be working free of the hostility to artistry of "Du style."

28. The only essay I have found on Taine's conception of style is Ulrich Schulz-Buschhaus, "Taine und die Historizität des Stils," with well-contextualized praise for Taine's style analyses, a deficient notion of "historicity," and, surprisingly, no discussion of the *History of English Literature*. Jean-François Revel's sensitive introduction to his selection of Taine's art criticism also points to the centrality of style in Taine's thought. And Fredric Jameson at least mentions style in joining Taine to Oswald Spengler as historians who focus on "the total *style* of a

culture" (*Marxism and Form* 324). Yet style is nowhere in evidence in such formative writings as Sainte-Beuve's sympathetic reviews (which fault Taine at length for failing in sympathy, particularly toward Pope, and in passing for his unforgivable sympathy toward Stendhal), Emile Faguet's scowling assault, Giraud's intellectual biography, Louis Juglar's ponderous *Le Style dans les arts* (whose extended and carping critiques of other aspects of Taine's thought perhaps constitute a backhanded acknowledgment that Taine *also* discussed style), or—most surprisingly of all—the *History of French Literature* by Taine's English translator, Henri van Laun.

29. Shakespeare is perhaps another example of absolute pastness: "His style and our style—two languages not to be reconciled" (1: 374 / 2: 192). In Shakespeare's unique case, however, historicity is problematized by absolute genius.

30. Wellek mentions style only in the second half of a paragraph about form, unity, and Taine's "purely emotionalistic point of view" toward modern poetry. He praises Taine's "nontechnical but often acutely observant" comments on style (49). To put Taine in perspective, here is the paltry best I could find in his translator, about Molière's types: "The language which they employ is always natural to them, and is neither too gross nor over-refined. His verse has none of the stiffness of the ordinary French rhyme, and becomes in his hands, as well as his prose, a delightful medium for sparkling sallies, bitter sarcasms, and well-sustained and sprightly conversations" (van Laun, *History of French Literature* 2: 224).

31. Hans Aarsleff's "Taine and Saussure" (*From Locke to Saussure* 356–71) is a learned and persuasive account of Taine's influence. Aarsleff rests with too simple a structural dualism, however, when he calls race and milieu synchronic concepts in contrast to the diachronic moment. Also informative, though less sympathetic to Taine, is Antoine Compagnon, *Troisième république* 174–97.

32. The passage about Burns (which ends book 3 of the history) concludes by shifting from verbal style to dress. "When Roland, being made a minister, presented himself before Louis XVI. in a simple dress-coat and shoes without buckles, the master of the ceremonies raised his hands to heaven, thinking that all was lost. In fact all was changed" (2: 282 / 4: 232). There are parallels in other periods, such as the Elizabethan, when the rapier replaced the shield and two-handed sword, "a little, almost imperceptible fact, yet vast, for it is like the change which, sixty years ago, made us give up the sword at court, to leave us with our arms swinging about in our black coats" (1: 172 / 1: 243). More startling is a moment in the *Voyage en Italie* where Taine says, "since I dare to speak without mincing words and to speak things as I feel them, my decided opinion is that the great change in history is the arrival of pants: all the Northern barbarians already wear them in the statues; they mark the passage from Greek and Roman to modern civilization.—This is not a quip or a paradox; nothing is more difficult than changing a universal and daily habit" (138). Taine protests too

much, of course; the spirit of the age is a habit of mind more than it is a habit of dress. But then, style is precisely the dress of thought.

33. Under the Puritans, to be sure, England did fall into the morass of a revolution that was fashioned "without style" and lived without joy by men whose "style [was] borrowed from the prophets" and who made their "fears of conscience . . . into laws of the state" (1: 484, 561 / 2: 381; 3: 7). But the soil was too fertile, even in Scotland, for "the indistinct forms of gloomy despots, of bilious sectarians, of silent victims" to prevail; and "deliverance, . . . like a checked and flooded stream, . . . with all its natural force and all its acquired momentum [*poids naturel et . . . masse acquise*] carried away the dams" (1: 562 / 3: 9–10).

34. Cf. Bourdieu, the contemporary thinker who seems to me closest to Taine's spirit: "An aesthetic revolution could only occur aesthetically. . . . The revolution of the gaze, and the rupture of the bond between ethics and aesthetics implied by that revolution, effected a total conversion of lifestyle" ("Flaubert's Point of View," *The Field of Cultural Production* 208–9). Or, again: "Struggles over words . . . will consist in . . . putting into action a symbolic revolution which may be at the root of political revolutions" ("Reading, Readers, the Literate, Literature," *In Other Words* 97). Bourdieu's sense of the working of time within consciousness likewise bears comparison with Taine.

35. The chapter on the Romantics expresses unreserved admiration only for *The Excursion*, a taste that I at least can share, provided it remains subject to the precisely evocative image Taine uses, comparing the poem to "the grand and monotonous music of the organ, which in the eventide, at the close of the service, rolls slowly in the twilight of arches and pillars" (2: 337 / 4: 322). The place of music in Taine's thought is discussed below.

36. Van Laun translates "agreement" rather than "accord"; it will be seen how much is lost in that translation.

37. Using the English word, since "there is no French word," Taine says he was "roused" by hearing Beethoven on the piano (*Notes sur Paris* 323).

38. For a more technical statement concerning formalism, expression, and historicity in music, see my review of John Daverio.

39. My formulations concerning style as ethos in the Renaissance are derived from, though not directly found in, the classic studies of Croll, Williamson, and especially Wallerstein (who speaks on p. 91, for instance, of "a half symbolic or allegorical view of style which transforms the idea of decorum").

40. The *Oxford English Dictionary* does not distinguish normative from non-normative uses of "style." In other words, it does not distinguish usages according to whether the implied alternative is a different style, a poor style, or a lack of style. Citations consequently were not selected to illustrate these distinctions; however, they seem to support a date of around 1800 for the semantic development. It was surely part of a general cultural development; for instance, Stephen Orgel's "Shakespeare and the Kinds of Drama" locates a shift from a descriptive

to a normative sense of dramatic genre in roughly the same period. Klaus Dirscherl's "Stillosigkeit als Stil" turns on Marivaux and Rousseau, without recognizing that stylelessness was, seemingly, not conceivable previously. Nor does Hans Ulrich Gumbrecht's richly informative history of the concept of style go beyond shifting categorizations (individual, collective; conventional, invented; etc.) to acknowledge the paradigm shift in the very construction of the categories, when style becomes an optional rather than an obligatory element of expression.

41. See Thomas Pfau, "Immediacy and the Text," for a good account of Schleiermacher's insights into the conflicted nature of style. For general worries about the identity of style see Charles Rosen, *The Classical Style* 19–23. The desultory closing discussion in Thomas Sebeok's symposium, *Style in Language* (420–34), is an object lesson in the frustrations attendant upon single-valued definitions of style; if there is a focus, it is on the tension between descriptive and normative definitions.

42. Barthes: "Whatever its refinement, style always has something ugly about it. . . . Its references are at the level of a biology or a past, not of a History" (*Degré zéro* 14). "Enough will never be said about the ravages of 'style' on our bourgeois stages. Style excuses everything, dispenses with everything, and notably with historical reflection" ("Deux mythes du jeune théâtre," *Mythologies* 110, and cf. in "La Critique ni-ni," p. 146, the critique of the bourgeois "euphoric reference to the writer's 'style' as an eternal value of Literature"). Among nineteenth-century enthusiasts for bad style are Kant (see Jean-Luc Nancy, *Discours de la syncope*) and Hazlitt (see Mary Jacobus, "The Art of Managing Books" 225–31); related in effect is Herbert Spencer's praise for economy, which is tantamount to a disparagement of style for its own sake: "to have a specific style is to be poor in speech" (*Philosophy of Style* 47).

43. Berel Lang's essays on style as uncategorizable expression and intention analyze the force of style (though not its historicity) in ways related to Taine's. Also illuminating is John Guillory, "Canonical and Non-canonical" 517–19, discussing style as "both a mode of apprehension irreducible to reason, and the sign of a cultural capital always unequally distributed" (518–19, not in the rewritten version of this essay in Guillory's book *Cultural Capital*).

44. Even at that, many of Taine's analyses and assessments hold up remarkably well or return to fashion; though Wellek, for instance, scorns Taine's admiration for *Aurora Leigh*, many current readers would share his devotion to Barrett Browning and George Sand.

45. Readers will surely wonder about comparing Taine with the greatest twentieth-century historian of style, Erich Auerbach. Auerbach, indeed, greatly admired Taine's essays on French writers and even cites the social analysis of *L'Ancien régime* with approval (*Scenes* 244). Yet Auerbach was, or at least became, a pessimist who recognized only a limited possibility, or none, for indi-

viduals to shape culture. About Balzac, for instance, he writes, "Balzac's atmospheric realism is a product of his period, is itself a part and a result of an atmosphere" (*Mimesis* 417). In the long section of his Balzac essay concerning Balzac's style, Taine writes more circumspectly that Balzac's "stylistic habits fit our habits of life, and that the author is authorized by the public" (*Nouveaux essais* 41), and the essay moves on toward Balzac's greatest imaginative inventions. While Auerbach's sensitivity to stylistic innovation has never been equaled, it remains for him either "a well-nigh incomprehensible miracle" (*Mimesis* 159, on Dante) or at best a self-confirming accomplishment with no definable agency, as when he writes about a unique and beautiful narration by Antoine de la Sale: "It is apparent that the late-feudal epideictic style is able to produce a visual representation of such a genuinely tragic and genuinely real scene" (*Mimesis* 215, continuing for pages with impersonal and even passive constructions).

Even where Auerbach comes closest to Taine's vision and imagery for cultural emergence, the language of representation supplants the language of agency. Thus, on Baudelaire: "The visionary power of such combinations exerted a crucial influence on later poetry; they seemed the most authentic expression both of the inner anarchy of the age and of a still hidden order that was just beginning to dawn. In an entirely new and consummate style, this poet . . . expressed the naked, concrete existence of an epoch. For his style was not based on his personal situation and his personal needs; it became apparent that his extreme personality embodied a far more universal situation and a far more universal need" (*Scenes* 225; Taine is mentioned with resounding approval in a note to the essay on p. 249). Even though "dawn" sounds Taine-like, the affect for Auerbach lies with light and not with flow. Though Auerbach's early Dante book praises the poet for "preserving the *Evidenz* [clarity, visibility] of appearances" (*Dante* 76), a decisive turning point comes in the 1944 explication of *figura* as a shadow (*umbra*) awaiting revelation (*Scenes* 34, 63, 66). Thus, the last chapter of *Mimesis* ends with a visionary play of lights, in a kind of terrified celebration of the impending end of history. History remains deeply problematic for the later Auerbach (as it was to become for the later Taine), and he contrives to write a discontinuous account of innovations with no concept of emergence. In Taine's terms, to put it bluntly, Auerbach is not a historian at all.

46. As the author of a book entitled *Preromanticism* that has sometimes been reviled for its teleology, I welcome the teleological leanings implied by "early modern," but not the telescoping of history that "emphasiz[es] larger historical divisions at the expense of smaller ones," as Heather Dubrow says in one part of her fine critique of the current fashion (Letter to the Forum 1026, and see also Marcus, "Renaissance / Early Modern Studies" 41–44).

47. On p. 1 of *Learning to Curse*, Greenblatt speaks of his early fascination with "radical uncertainty (what would now be called *aporia*)." For Greenblatt's

use of "dialectic," the conclusion to the Sir Thomas Wyatt chapter of *Renaissance Self-Fashioning* is telling. "His achievement is dialectical," Greenblatt says. But it isn't. "We sense, in short, a continual conflict between diplomatic self-representation . . . and inwardness. . . . Neither triumphs: hence the *suspension* of Wyatt's court lyrics" (156). On p. 1, Greenblatt says that "the early modern . . . structures that govern [!] the generation of identities" arrived in "complex but resolutely dialectical" ways. Yet it remains hard to discern either the resolutions or the resoluteness in Greenblatt's perpetually subtle and (to use one of his favorite words) anamorphic analyses. The essay on *The Tempest* that concludes *Shakespearian Negotiations* illustrates the uses of "circulation" as unproductive circling. An awkward preposition can mark it, indeed, as shuttling: "This complex circulation *between* the social dimension of an aesthetic strategy and the aesthetic dimension of a social strategy" (147, my emphasis). And when "Prospero's magical power and princely authority . . . pass, in a startling display of the circulation of social energy, from the performer onstage to the crowd of spectators," the play turns into "a model of unresolved and unresolvable doubleness" (157–58). "Introduction," "Towards a Poetics of Culture," and "Resonance and Wonder" (*Learning to Curse* 1–15, 146–60, 161–83) argue that the profit from the "negotiation" or "exchange" involved in art is found in a pleasure that cannot readily be analyzed or historicized.

A related evaporation of history tied to a concept of circulation surfaces in Patricia Fumerton's *Cultural Aesthetics*. Fumerton proposes the anthropological cycle of gift exchange as a "more positive" alternative to deconstructive deferral (58), whose "most striking example is Jonathan Goldberg's *Endlesse Worke*" (224). Circulation accomplishes something: it produces "trivia," and more specifically aesthetic articles of consumption. Still, when we find "the self . . . chasing its self-image *endlessly* along an empty corridor of vision between facing mirrors" (129, my emphasis), with a "status" that remains "undecidable" on the last page of the text (206), we may wonder what effect the redescription or "uncanny double" (24) of deconstruction has. Fumerton's polarities are no more mediated than Greenblatt's; in privileging the oblique, the fragmentary, or the trivial over the central, the total, or the "wholly representative" (11, with misleading reference to Taine), her "highly idealizing" view of gifts (William Flesch's critique, *Generosity* 99) functions as a kind of send-up of Theodor Adorno—negative dialectics without the dialectic.

48. *Shakespearean Negotiations* begins with an emotional—and surely in some sense Oedipal—attack on William Wimsatt, the most exact student of style in his generation. I have noted "style" once in *Renaissance Self-Fashioning* as a background term (16–17, offering the alternatives either of referring More's *contemptus mundi* to "the style of late medieval culture" or else of taking stock of its "actual effect in his life and writings"), and once in *Shakespearian Negotiations*, italicized even, but only in a quote from Bourdieu in a note (178–79). While I

have not searched the writings systematically, I suspect these instances are symptomatic.

49. Frank Lentricchia tars Taine with Greenblatt's feather in his acute critique of the latter, "Foucault's Legacy." For another comparison of Taine and Greenblatt see Edmundson, *Literature Against Philosophy* 186–87.

50. Apparently coining a phrase, Catherine Gallagher scrutinizes the "emphasis, . . . in 'oppositional' American criticism, on indeterminante negation" ("Marxism and the New Historicism" 41). In substance Brook Thomas's *The New Historicism* makes the same critique. It shows how both Renaissance and Americanist New Historicists totalize chiasmic polarities. Lacking a concept of limited negation, they relegate art to the unsatisfactory alternatives of reproductive complicity in the real or utopian evasion. Thomas proposes instead a "description of literature as a rhetorical means to question present constructions of rhetoric" (217), which he further concretizes in an essay devoted to what formal logic calls subaltern negation. While it seems natural here to move from rhetoric to style and from Aristotelian limitation to Hegelian determination, Thomas instead falls back on Wolfgang Iser. To my mind, the issues are deflected, not resolved, by Iser's notion of negation as textual blanks and by his focus on the phenomenology of reading. (Iser's fullest discussion of negation and negativity, which Thomas does not cite, is *The Act of Reading* 212–31.)

51. Impersonation: Stephen Greenblatt, "Psychoanalysis and Renaissance Culture" (*Learning to Curse* 131–45). Thomas Greene's "The Flexibility of the Self" is the first scholarly study cited in *Renaissance Self-Fashioning*. Greenblatt misleadingly implies that the essay concerns undirected, fictive selfhoods: "Greene's starting point is the assertion in Pico that man may choose to fashion (*effingere*) himself in whatever shape he prefers" (258). True, but starting from there the essay in fact surveys the specific and differential kinds of self-positioning found in many diverse authors.

52. McGann more characteristically deprecates Hegel (for instance in comparison to Kierkegaard) as a totalizer. And he avoids the term style (except in the technical, typographical sense), preferring less fraught words such as procedure. For the reasons why I nonetheless invoke him here, see "What's in a Text?"

Chapter 2

1. The fullest survey of Wölfflin's milieu is given in Walther Rehm's monograph *Heinrich Wölfflin als Literarhistoriker.*

2. See also the nominalistic critiques of Wölfflin in Walter Bockelmann, *Grundbegriffe*, and Arnold Hauser, *The Philosophy of Art History* 139–66.

3. The early essay on ancient triumphal arches gives no hint of a notion of rebirth; instead, it says that "a playful beginning . . . , a period of classicism . . . ;

finally a period of dissolution . . . where the forms lose sense and meaning . . . , will be observable in every style in art history" (KS 70). Evidently, the notion of continuous historical change, not the notion of cycle, was Wölfflin's starting point.

4. The slogan "Kunstgeschichte ohne Namen" is often quoted but rarely attributed. It comes from the suppressed preface to the first edition of Kunstgeschichtliche Grundbegriffe, which has not been translated into English.

5. "The concepts of multiple unity and unified unity require special treatment here too. It is just in architecture that the concepts attain an unusual lucidity" (PAH 186).

6. See Talcott Parsons, "Value-freedom and Objectivity" (and the discussion following) 27–82. Weber comes closest to Wölfflin in passages concerning the scholar's role in resisting the chaotic movement of history, such as the astonishing conclusion of the essay "Die 'Objektivität' sozialwissenschaftlicher und sozialpolitischer Erkenntnis," 206–14. Hauser compares Wölfflin and Weber in Philosophy of Art History 212–15, and the question of Wölfflin's "objectivity" is well discussed at the end of "Sense and Sensibility" 35–50. A recent, interesting, ideological reading is Martin Warnke, "On Heinrich Wölfflin."

7. The published translation uses the passive "posed" rather than "posing," a slight but revealing instance of the repression of Wölfflin's dynamism.

8. Since I wrote this, Jacques Derrida has expressed himself decisively on this point: "The gesture that has been called deconstructive . . . is accompanied, can be accompanied (in any case, that is how I would always prefer to accompany it) by an affirmation; it is not negative, it is not destructive" ("Table ronde sur l'autobiographie: Réponse de Jacques Derrida," in Lévesque and McDonald, eds., L'Oreille de l'autre 117).

9. The "contrasted handling of . . . right and left" could also describe the great innovation of Wölfflin's classicizing, coolly objective lecture technique: using tandem slide projectors to enable constant comparison of different pictorial modes.

10. Notable polarizing theoreticians—apart from Wölfflin's followers and from Alois Riegl and his disciple Wilhelm Worringer—include the philosopher Johannes Volkelt, Ästhetische Zeitfragen, chap. 4, and System der Ästhetik 3: 300–37; the psychologist Herman Nohl, Stil esp. 7–11; the art historian August Schmarsow, Unser Verhältnis; and the literary historian Ernst Elster, Prinzipien, vol. 2. Elster clearly reveals the Schillerian affiliation through his habit of realigning and subdividing categories; Wölfflin's teacher Volkelt (who was a notoriously indecisive thinker) waffles on the question of a possible synthesis of opposing categories and thus highlights the incisiveness of Wölfflin's logic.

11. See Wind, "Zur Systematik der künstlerischen Probleme" 480–86, and Venturi, History of Art Criticism 288–89. Wölfflin himself concedes that "in every chapter the baroque standpoint has meant a kind of obscuring" (PAH 224).

12. Italian critics have been particularly guilty of assimilating Wölfflin's position to that of Fiedler and Hildebrand: see Benedetto Croce's attack in *Nuovi saggi* 251–57, and the even less discriminating treatments in Lionello Venturi's *History of Art Criticism* 288–89 and in Carlo Ragghianti's essays collected under the title *L'arte e la critica*.

13. Lipps, *Grundzüge der Logik* viii. Lipps's preexistentialist idealism seems to me closer in spirit to Wölfflin than are Wölfflin's actual predecessors, Robert Vischer, Herman Lotze, and Gustav Fechner, who are more empiricist in temperament; see esp. Fechner's *Vorschule* 1: 108–11.

14. "Tiepolo composed a *Last Supper* which, while it cannot be compared with Leonardo as a work of art, stylistically presents the absolute opposite. The figures do not unite in the plane, and that decides" (*PAH* 88).

15. See the conclusion of Jacob Burckhardt, *Force and Freedom* 369–70. Wölfflin's numerous essays on Burckhardt harp on the classicizing, static quality of his presentation and a notation of 1891 is preserved to the effect that "development receives too little emphasis" in Burckhardt's book on Renaissance architecture (*Jacob Burckhardt und Heinrich Wölfflin* 70). Given the intimate personal relations between the two men, it is not surprising that Wölfflin's critique never became more explicit.

16. A letter of January 14, 1889, demonstrating Wölfflin's early and approving familiarity with the school of Taine is printed in Rehm, *Wölfflin als Literarhistoriker* 116.

17. Cf. Burckhardt's judgment, "Baroque architecture speaks the same language as the renaissance, but a barbarian dialect of it" (*Gesammelte Werke* 9: 305). On Goethe, see Wölfflin, "Goethes italienische Reise," *Gedanken* 49–56. On Schiller, see Peter Szondi, "Das Naive ist das Sentimentalische." On Humboldt, see my "Humboldt and the Mediation Between Self and World." In art history, this line is continued by Erwin Panofsky, for instance *Renaissance* 112–13.

18. The whole enterprise of Heidegger's "grant of Being" can be understood as a commentary on the impossible tautology, The classic is the classic. Derrida has warned against the temptations of this introduction to metaphysics that never quite succeeds in being a reintroduction of metaphysics, but even Heidegger himself readily acknowledged the antithetical logic of being toward which this study of Wölfflin has been pointing: "*existasthai,* 'existence,' 'to exist,' meant for the Greeks precisely nonbeing" (Heidegger, *An Introduction to Metaphysics* 64). See also Derrida, "The Supplement of Copula."

19. The spirit of Hegel's logic of existence could have been transmitted to Wölfflin through the epistemological discussions in Conrad Fiedler's 1887 essay, "Über den Ursprung der künstlerischen Thätigkeit," *Schriften* esp. 200–201: "The origin of language does not resemble a process of crystallization in which matter accretes toward a definite form in which it continues to exist; rather the

work is like the bloom, the fruit of a plant; in the bloom, in the fruit the plant develops something from itself which is no longer itself, a metamorphosis begins, but the plant is not destroyed thereby."

20. The example of the Romanesque is based on Paul Frankl, "Der Beginn der Gotik"; the example of the primitives is based on Wölfflin's *Dürer*: "The heads are expressive in the manner of the sixteenth century, to whom the art of earlier times seemed to be a mute art" (158). Apropos of heads that are stylized (formalistic) in background detail and naturalistic (expressive) in principal features, Wölfflin writes: "The essence of greatness is the same at all stages [of history]: it means that an artist recognizes the one feature in the large variety of visible objects which is of essential significance. He need not abandon the other features but only make them subordinate so that the leading voice can be heard distinctly. The subject does not matter; it may be simply a head or a history-piece: this relation of predominant to subordinate parts must be maintained and the eye must be capable of recognizing the essential feature immediately and without difficulty" (*Dürer* 247; modified translation).

21. Henri Meschonnic, *Pour la poétique* 2: 62. Meschonnic's direct critique of Macherey is on 124–29.

22. See Michel Foucault, *The Order of Things*, chap. 1, and John Searle, "*Las Meninas.*" Searle's exposition has been decisively refuted by Joel Snyder and Ted Cohen, "Reflexions on *Las Meninas*"; the refutation confirms one point of my essay, that we are dealing with an ideal of classicism, not with an "objective" view of actually existing classic works. The authoritative Velázquez scholar of Wölfflin's day, Carl Justi, and Wölfflin himself both offer illuminating comments on the visual uncertainties of *Las Meninas*: Justi, *Diego Velázquez* 418, and Wölfflin, *Gedanken* 78.

Chapter 3

1. Crucial to the "postmodern," dialogic forms in McGann's criticism is the closing section (161–75) of "The Poetry of Truth: A Dialogue (on Dialogue)," *BR* 151–75.

2. See, for instance, *SV* 91, where the issue is distilled: "Poetry is obliged, as it were, to present all sides of a question. This includes bringing forth, *within a sympathetic structure*, those details and points of view which are by ordinary measures incommensurate with themselves and with each other. . . . The consequence is a certain kind of nonnormative discourse: not a discourse *without* norms, but one in which we observe the collision of many different and even contradictory norms." I find the generally dialectical tenor hard to reconcile with the sovereign embrace of the phrase that McGann italicizes. On Goethe and Marx, see Marc Shell, "Money and the Mind."

3. "How one decides which parts of the strategic programme need to be emphasized in particular case studies is always a difficult question. I am not even sure that one can theorize these sorts of problem at all" (*BI* 9).

4. *SV* 128–29, my italics. (McGann italicizes "natural" and "Eros.") Since the categorical is, in fact, the determinative (*die Bestimmung*, in post-Kantian usage), the passage ends by rejecting the very emphasis that it began by declaring "fundamental."

5. For an excellent case study, see Peter J. Manning, "The Hone-ing of Byron's Corsair."

6. See the forceful critique of would-be divisions of intrinsic from extrinsic factors in Lee Patterson's essay, "The Logic of Textual Criticism." McGann's basically intelligent reading of Kant's aesthetics as a cardinal instance of the individualist and idealizing "romantic ideology" is a case in point. When he criticizes de Man for "bracket[ing] our attention to the way 'Kant' performs. . . . in his sociohistorical field" (*SV* 104), McGann overlooks both extrinsic and intrinsic factors that would *conjointly* condition his account. Externally, Kant's political and theological reputation was generally radical, at the opposite pole from the later Coleridge. And, textually, McGann's proof passages from early in the "Critique of Aesthetic Judgment" should be registered as a transitional moment of idealism on the way back to the natural science of the "Critique of Teleological Judgment."

7. *Black Riders* analyzes schools of postmodern writing in which verbal meanings are undecipherable and messages are carried chiefly by the physical appearance of the work. Even in these cases, however, there does not appear to be a contradiction between material and verbal meaning. In the still-troubling case of Pound ("The *Cantos* of Ezra Pound, the Truth in Contradiction," *BR* 96–128), McGann does seem to defend Pound by splitting off aura and effect from sense, meaning from saying: "while the face of these texts says one thing, their converse says something very different" (*BR* 107). However, the road to a more adequate and sympathetic understanding comes through closer attention to the text: "Lauber has not *read* the passage" (120); "when readers dismiss writing of this kind they are often merely exposing . . . their failure to read, and to think through their reading" (120); "The *Cantos* is remarkable because when we read it—the whole of it and not simply selected parts," we come to appreciate its "disturbing mode of truth" (125, 128). While many critics these days want to embed texts in contexts outside of them, McGann stands out as one for whom the primary context is what the word primarily means—*the rest of the text.*

8. McGann, "Some Forms of Critical Discourse." The four forms are listed on p. 399, the first two examples are given in the footnote on p. 416, the others are developed in the text.

9. See, for instance, the following: on scientific essays, Charles Bazerman, *Shaping Written Knowledge;* on Euclid, Gilles-Gaston Granger, *Essai d'une philoso-*

phie du style 24-42; on cookbooks, Susan J. Leonardi, "Recipes for Reading" 340–47. With respect to the array form, Hayden White's essay needs to be consulted ("The Value of Narrativity"). McGann says that White narrates what is really a pseudo-progress from nonnarrative to narrative forms. He does not say that White demonstrates how we can actually read annals narratively, thus effectively effacing the distinction that McGann wants to make.

10. *Critical Inquiry* version, 414 (my emphasis). Symptomatically, the dialectic is attenuated in *SV* 149: "Although these three types of critical discourse (array, narrative, dialectic) exhibit the *form* of criticism, that form is no guarantee that the discourse will in fact be critical."

11. See the change from the original uncompromising formulation: "the array and the dialectic offer especially clear contrasts with narrative forms of discourse, both critical and noncritical" (*Critical Inquiry* 400), to the later version: "In this respect the forms of array and dialectic are particularly important, not merely as alternative critical modes, but as forms which cast an important critical light on the structure of narrativized discourse" (*SV* 133).

12. The treasured modernist text is not so pure a conception as McGann's phrasing might seem to imply. For the material complexities—i.e., the social dimension—involved in producing the first edition, see Hugh Kenner, " 'The Most Beautiful Book.' "

13. Verdi repeatedly added, subtracted, and recomposed material (musical and verbal) in response both to his own second thoughts and to aesthetic and political promptings from outside—a fairly normal situation for nineteenth-century opera composers, and not unparalleled in symphonic music (e.g., orchestration in Mahler or Schumann). Some literary authors also have been tinkerers producing uncontrolled textual forms—McGann's immediately preceding essay on *Urizen*, "The Idea of an Indeterminate Text: Blake and Dr. Alexander Geddes," presents a great instance, Philip Gaskell's "*Night and Day*: Development of a Play Text" (*TCLI* 162-79) a minor one, not very interestingly analyzed. Other authors, such as William Dean Howells and Thomas Wolfe, have written in complex collaboration with editors. And manuscript transmission, of course, is prone to unresolvable indeterminacies, such as Dickinson's or Hölderlin's punctuation. (Heidegger's exegesis of Hölderlin depends crucially on an attributed line-end comma ["Des gemeinsamen Geistes Gedanken sind, / Still endend in der Seele des Dichters"] in a poet who characteristically neglected line-end punctuation.)

14. There is a less dismissive reading of "A slumber did my spirit seal" in chapter 6 (*RI* 68-69).

15. For a challenging, unnecessarily difficult, but often profound extension of McGann's impulse into (among other things) the psychological dimension, see Marjorie Levinson, *Keats's Life of Allegory*.

16. More in McGann's spirit is Gerald MacLean's "What Is a Restoration

Poem? Editing a Discourse, Not an Author," which argues that "authors are never entirely in control of their texts" (339) and which brilliantly demonstrates how an unnormalized text can reveal significances hidden by emendation according to principles of authorial meaning.

Chapter 4

1. For a less Byronic view of aporia see the Overture to this book, "Errours Endlesse Traine." In "Displacing Post-Structuralism" 451–74, Tilottama Rajan argues congenially that "displacement" should edge out "aporia," because the latter is misunderstood too often in a romantically demonized way (see esp. notes 4 and 5).

2. "No Apocalypse" 20–31. And see *Memoires: For Paul de Man*, whose topics are "deconstruction in America" (implying that deconstruction, as America knows it, is not in France) and Derrida's Parnell-like concern for finding a path out of the graveyard (132: "it seems to me [not to 'deconstruction in America'] that the experience of the aporia, such as de Man deciphers it, gives or promises [the experience gives to Derrida, but perhaps not to de Man who merely deciphered the experience] the thinking of the path"). Derrida's itinerary in the lectures is from Hegel to Heidegger, allowing him to predicate "nondialectizable opposition" (134) of de Man; de Man's itinerary, biographically, was from Heidegger to Hegel. Only in the early, Sartrean de Man, I believe, is the path beyond death a concern, as in "Hölderlin et Heidegger" (816): "For us, however the pain of mediation is always that of finitude and we can only conceive it in the form of death. . . . The task of the poet then becomes to internalize this death, to think of the death of God." Or even more clearly in "Mallarmé, Yeats, and the Post-Romantic Predicament" 60: "To be conscious of death is to be conscious of the self as *becoming*, to know that it moves us toward an unknown." The later de Man puts death aside through what seems to me a dialectical renaming: "Death is a displaced name for a linguistic predicament" ("Autobiography as De-Facement," *Rhetoric of Romanticism* 81), which does not enlighten death, but makes light of it. The American bravado is moving; equally so, but contrasting, is the European's troubled, meditative response (see *Memoires* 87–88 n. 4).

3. J. Hillis Miller ("The Critic as Host" 230) says cozily that " 'Deconstruction' is ... simply interpretation as such." True, but beware of his "simply," which has the same rhetorical status as Parnell's "surely."

Chapter 5

1. For a fuller discussion of the philosophical and literary revolutions of the 1780's, see my *Preromanticism* 75–81.

2. Hoffmann, *Betrachtungen über Musik* 78. More recent scholarship has invalidated the traditional attribution of this review to E. T. A. Hoffmann; see Hoffmann, *Schriften zur Musik* 402.

3. For an account of the Bagatelles themselves that typifies the negative view of Romantic reverie, see Riccardo Bacchelli, *Rossini* 444–48.

4. Julie Anne Vertrees reviews the Fétis debate in "Mozart's String Quartet K. 465." Mozart's principal defender in the controversy, A. G. Leduc, stressed the intentional harmonic obscurity of the introduction: see "Ueber den Aufsatz des Herrn Fetis" 124.

5. Commentators generally have concentrated on the harmonic chaos of the introduction and have ignored the metrical chaos. Fétis, however, was primarily troubled by the lawlessness of the rhythm in the contrapuntal imitation and would have normalized the piece by means of an alteration in the rhythm alone, delaying the entry of the first violin by a beat.

6. In less technical (and less precise) language, it could be said that C-sharp, which is the second in the normal cycle of sharps, neutralizes the E-flat, which is the second in the normal cycle of flats. The repeated accented sharps of these final bars introduce an unclassical note of dynamism as the reverie works toward clarification; hence, they are ignored in Antoine-Elisée Cherbouliez's otherwise exhaustive analysis, which attempts to assimilate the introduction to canonical classical patterns.

7. It was common practice in the classical period to reinforce a pulsing cello C in this register with an occasional open C string, combining the resonance of the lower octave with the clearer articulation of the higher octave. Examples may be found in Mozart's C-Major Quartet (first movement, bar 72; second movement, beginning), at the opening of Beethoven's C-Minor Quartet, opus 18, no. 4, and elsewhere.

8. See Joseph Kerman's analyses of the introduction to opus 59, no. 3, and of the "La Malinconia" introduction to the last movement of opus 18, no. 6, in *The Beethoven Quartets* 135–37 and 77–80. Slow introductions, while still the exception, are far less rare in other chamber combinations (duo sonatas, trios, quintets) than in string quartets and solo piano sonatas.

9. There is some good analysis of the Fantasia's harmonic ambiguities and descending tendencies in Wilhelm Keller, "Modulationen." At times overly literal, Keller concludes that the movement ends not in C but in F-quintuple-flat (is that also the key of the associated C-Minor Sonata?); he might consider the final three-octave ascending scale as a compensation for the downward harmonic cycling (marked by three enharmonic modulations) and as a movement out of the depths of harmonic confusion and back up to conventional form. The rising gesture is repeated in the arpeggio that opens the sonata.

10. For a differing view, see Lieselotte Theiner, "Das Phänomen der atonikalen Werköffnung," where Mozart appears among the most conventional of

composers. This article stands as an example of the dangers of a purely mechanical study, arbitrarily limited not by genre but by instrument and with no regard to the structural function, weight, or (except in a very limited sense) complexity of the material. So narrow is the definition that the C-Minor Piano Fantasia is not even mentioned! Potentially interesting formal issues are raised by example 45 (p. 157), a third movement introduction used as a transition in a sonata by Johann Ladislaus Dussek.

11. On the significance of the key of C, see Douglas Porter Johnson, *Beethoven's Sketches* 932–39. How far did the C-major phenomenon spread? To Johnson's examples may be added the Symphony no. 33 (1780), subtitled *Il Maniatico*, by the Madrid composer Gaetano Brunetti. This symphony has two introductions: the standard fanfare and then a programmatic introduction, where the wavering pitch of slow trills in the solo cello is used to symbolize mental alienation. Reason (and C major) triumphs over unreason at the end of the piece. For an even earlier example, see Wilhelm Heinse's extraordinary rhapsody (in a letter to J. W. L. Gleim of August 1776) about the great C bell in Erfurt, whose resonant harmonics he compares to the pure Row of time: "*Becoming, being, and decaying, and renewed becoming,* eternally creating and eternally decaying harmony. . . . *The first breath of beauty out of the bosom of night, of the invisible,*" *Werke* 9: 292–94. On the other hand, none of the models for the Piano Fantasia cited by Oskar Sigmund is in C.

12. A typical Mozart-Raphael comparison is Emil Naumann, "Wolfgang Mozart"; a typical Mozart-Goethe (vs. Beethoven-Schiller) comparison is Ludwig Nohl, *Mozart*. The best studies of Mozart's reputation that I have found are Leo Schrade, "Mozart und die Romantiker" and "Vom Nachleben Mozarts." Of course, the revolutionary character of Mozart's libretti is widely recognized: see Jean Starobinski, *1789* 25–30; Rosen, *Classical Style* 321–35; and Angus Fletcher, "On Two Words."

13. This Mozart-as-child tradition is most accessible in Stendhal's brief *Vie de Mozart.* The justly famous literary embodiment is Eduard Mörike's story "Mozart auf der Reise nach Prag," which perfectly fuses all three strains of Mozart's reputation: the naive, the demonic, and the classically pure. It should be added that Ingmar Bergman's *Magic Flute* and *Amadeus* have resuscitated the demonic Mozart since my essay was first published.

Chapter 6

1. I have left the Heidegger translation unmodified because its highly evaluative rhetoric so well illustrates the risks to which historians of philosophy are exposed. As I read Heidegger (2: 167–68 in the German edition), his concern is with a universal philosophical situation, not with improvements made by Descartes. In particular, for "superficially" the German has "von außen her"—from

an outside perspective, not a foolish or ignorant one. For "inappropriately," which also sounds like a condemnation, the German has the more neutral "unangemessen" (not tailored to the occasion); rather than a "contingency" that "threatens" thought it speaks of a "Vorgang" (procedure) to which thought is "exposed" (ausgesetzt). In that context, "Descartes was forced to discourse at the already prevailing level" is more accurately translated, "Descartes was forced to speak from a prior level" (aus der Ebene des Bisherigen zu sprechen)—not particularly a lower level. My essay is intended to make the case that the history of philosophy (like the history of poetry and the arts) is not a progress from lower to higher levels but rather a continuing mutation of language and point of view.

2. Edmund Husserl argues that Descartes mistakes his own transcendental reduction as a merely psychological insight. But while *Die Krisis der europäischen Wissenschaften* persuasively demonstrates what is termed Descartes's "self-misinterpretation" (sect. 18), Husserl does not even ask why Descartes should have made so fundamental a mistake; that is to say, he does not view the problem on Descartes's level. The deficiency lies in Husserl's philology. Though at one point he appeals to "the grammatical sense of the statement *ego cogito*" (*Cartesianische Meditationen* 24), he constantly presumes the "world" and material things as the contents (and grammatical objects) of thought. As I shall show below, *cogito* is a mental construction (judge or imagine), not a mere mental response (mediate or ponder); consequently, the analysis offered by Husserl remained beyond Descartes's horizon. Even if the "self-misrepresentation" belies the logical implications of Descartes's thought, it remains the only interpretation that his language permits.

3. Contending that philosophy concerns the search for eternal verities not dependent on language, Alquié undertakes to demonstrate that "Kant rediscovered the true essence of Cartesianism" (152). This is my argument turned inside out. What it does not explain is why Descartes failed to discover the true essence of his own philosophy and why Kant was so misled by Leibniz that he failed to notice how that essence lay implicit in the earlier philosopher. Jean Ferrari (*Sources françaises* 22–78) decisively refutes Alquié's essay (though he does not cite it) by demonstrating Kant's lifelong disregard for Descartes; he finds Kant's critique of the *cogito* "in flagrant contradiction with the Cartesian text" and concludes, "it is clear that the properly Cartesian meaning of the cogito ergo sum has been completely forgotten" (65, 69).

4. In this chapter, Kant is quoted in Norman Kemp Smith's translation, with modifications. In particular, as with Heidegger's *Nietzsche*, I have again altered the translation of *Satz* to "sentence," replacing Smith's "proposition."

5. Berel Lang's clever account of the genre of the *Meditations* clarifies the priority of the movement of truth over its fixity in this text.

6. Kemp Smith translates "ich bin einfach" adjectivally, as a determinate judgment: "I am simple"—a grammatical possibility that, however, falsifies the con-

tentlessness Kant always attributes to the *cogito*. Likewise, in the preceding sentence, by emending the gender of a relative pronoun, Kemp Smith makes "simplicity . . . involved in every thought," whereas the unemended text says that "the sentence 'I think'" is "involved in every thought."

7. In the *Discourse*, the translation reads, "attente examinans quis essem" and "mens per quam solam sum is qui sum" (6: 558), where Descartes writes, "examinant avec attention ce que i'estois" and "l'Ame par laquelle ie suis ce que ie suis" (6: 32–33); in the *Meditations*, Descartes writes, "Nondum verò satis intelligo, quisnam sim ego ille" (9: 19), where the translation reads "Mais je ne connais pas encore assez clairement ce que je suis" (7: 25) and where the long ensuing discussion similarly drives insistently at "what" (quid) and even "what kind of thing" (qualis res) I am (7: 25–29). Curiously, Gilson's commentary on the *Discourse* does not discuss this discrepancy.

8. *Meditations* 3 (*Oeuvres* 7: 44 Latin = 9: 35 French). The fulfilled type of this image is common in Kant's era, notably in Wordsworth: see my *Preromanticism*, chap. 12.

9. A noteworthy contradiction concerns another famous passage in the *Discourse on Method*: "like a man who walks alone and in the shadows, I resolved to go so slowly, and to use so much circumspection in all things, that, if I advanced but very little, I should keep myself, at least, from falling" (*Oeuvres* 6: 16–17). By translating "circonspection" with "caution," F. E. Sutcliffe's version makes this sound like the reverie of a solitary wanderer who holds back from an encounter with the world. The Latin translator finds a different tonality of genuine attentiveness here: "so diligently looking about at all things" (tam diligenter ad omnia circumspicere; *Oeuvres* 6: 549). By emphasizing alertness, he edges the passage toward Descartes's discussion of method in the *Rules for the Direction of the Spirit*, which warns against shadows: "all those who thus accustom themselves to walk in the shadows so weaken their eyesight in consequence that they can no longer support the light of day" (*Oeuvres* 10: 371).

10. While the notion of Descartes as *bon vivant* certainly does not reflect all of his moods, the parallel with Hume's view of the world theater shows that this translation of the motto is not a philosophical absurdity. It could serve to characterize a Humean great man: Hume writes in the chapter "Of Greatness of Mind" "that a genuine and hearty pride, or self-esteem, if well concealed and well founded, is essential to the character of a man of honour, and that there is no quality of the mind which is more indispensably requisite to procure the esteem and admiration of mankind" (*Treatise* 532). On the personality of the philosopher as reflected in the philosophy, see Henri Gouhier's beautiful book.

11. "M. Descartes . . . arose at once, changed countenance, drew his sword with unforeseen pride, spoke to them in their language with a tone that seized them, and threatened to pierce them through on the spot, if they dared offer him any insult. It was in this encounter that he perceived the impression the bold-

ness of a man can make on a low soul; I mean a boldness rising far above one's forces and power of execution: a boldness which, on other occasions, could pass for pure bravado." Descartes, *Oeuvres philosophiques* 51.

12. Nancy concludes his analysis with the image of a camera; he compares Descartes's convulsive self-assertions to the "brutal shutting of the diaphragm" (*Ego Sum* 152). Abandoning his usual philological caution, he presents his principal piece of evidence in this fashion: "*ego sum* is true 'every time that *I* utter it or that *I* conceive it in my mind' (it is *I* [*moi*] who underline *I* [*je*])" (150). The French text (with which Nancy has taken some slight freedoms) is, however, not Cartesian, and the Latin ("quoties a me profertur, vel mente concipitur"; *Meditations* 2; 7: 25) contains no *I* to be snapshotted, or to misfire. Anachronism is misused here; it can properly illuminate historical difference and direction, but it does not properly support assertions of systematic deficiency.

13. Jaakko Hintikka calls the *cogito* a performative. His plausible account is controversial but, I think, less for the reasons given by his critics than because the notion of a performative suggests the creation of something enduring beyond the performance. The misjudgment concerns Cartesian temporality rather than Cartesian linguistics. From a different perspective, see Nancy's punning discussions of Descartes's *for* (Latin "speech," French "conscience, internal tribunal").

14. There are good overviews of the problem of consciousness in Descartes and after in Francisque Bouillier, chap. 3; Kurt Joachim Grau; Theodor Kehr, chap. 7; and Heinrich Scholz. Vendler gives the most careful account of the *cogito* in the Cartesian system. Etienne Gilson's edition of the *Discours de la Méthode* has been indispensable, although I have risked proposing differing interpretations of the phrases "ego cogito" and "sum, sive existo."

15. On Descartes's confidence see Bouillier, 1: 74. On clarity see the important pages in Gilson, *Etudes* 264–65, contrasting Descartes with the Pantheist Tommaso Campanella. Georges Poulet's brilliant reading of the famous dreams reported by his biographer recuperates even their passages of bizarre terror as experiences of hyperbolic doubt within a framework that anticipates the mature system of the *Meditations*.

16. On Descartes's voyage to construct a worldly self, see the subtle interpretation of the *Discourse* in Gerald L. Bruns, *Inventions* 63–87. Nathan Edelman's more conscientious survey takes similar imagery to reflect a yearning for a solid foundation; though he speaks of insecurity, his findings are not inconsistent with the self-assertiveness claimed by other scholars. William Kerrigan and Gordon Braden (*Idea of the Renaissance* 135–53) suggestively, though not always convincingly, relate Descartes's enterprise to the will to power within Renaissance individualism.

17. In his often subtle study of Descartes's style, Pierre Alain Cahné (*Un Autre Descartes* 49–52) misleadingly limits the formula "is or exists" to God—which is

true of the French text of the *Discourse*, but not of the Latin text, nor of other occurrences of the doublet—and regards *exists* as an "intensifier" of *is*: "The coordination with 'or' signifies perhaps that the second term corrects the first, or *rather* erases it" (52). But the Latin *sive* that renders *ou* means "in other words" not "or rather"; in the *Meditations*, *sive* is regularly rendered *c'est-à-dire*.

18. Semantically, *cogito* approximates "deliberate," as opposed to "contemplate." Hence in the Vulgate it often renders λογίζομαι. Only one citation in the entire *Thesaurus Linguae Latinae* resembles the Kantian misreading of Descartes's *cogito* as an intransitive verb, and it is the exception that proves the rule. It is the very first example, s.v. *cogito*: "sed cum cogito, equidem certo idem sum qui semper fui." This comes from Plautus's *Amphitryon*, line 447. Comparing himself with his double (Mercury in disguise), Sosias is baffled in the attempt to construct a self-intuition. This apparent approximation of "cogito, ergo sum" is thus a mark of delusion, or even madness. In all other recorded examples of *cogito* used absolutely, the sentence is clearly elliptical, with a judgment as the implied object. Vendler appears to be alone in recognizing that *cogito*, in Descartes, "is a propositional verb" ("Descartes' 'Res Cogitans' " 198), yet demonstrably wrong in declaring "that the verb *cogitare*, unlike its kin *putare*, is not a propositional verb in Latin" (199).

19. Gerhart Schmidt, *Aufklärung und Metaphysik* 169. To refer to thought stripped of all its objects, Schmidt uses the Kantian word "bloß," which literally means "nakedly." The equivalent French and Latin phrases mean "thought alone" and would not connote empty thought. Similar claims are widespread. The most extreme formulation is that of G. E. Barié: "thought alone is concrete without the aid of anything else, for it has, by its very nature as thinking activity, its first object in itself: *ego cogito me*" (225). Related misconstructions of Descartes's *cogito* include Dalia Judovitz, *Subjectivity and Representation* 116 ("The *cogito* is presented here as a primitive act of knowledge, one based on a *simple act of mental vision*—in other words, *intuition*"—her emphases), Roger Lefèvre, *Pensée existentielle* 31 ("The Cogito [takes place] in a limpid intuition where the subject and the object form a single certainty. The essence [*propre*] of the thinking being is for it to think its very self [*de se penser soi-même*], I can never think without being"), and, in a more general context, A. Carlini "Grundeigenschaften des Geistesaktes" 356 ("Thinking here means: *thinking oneself* [*Sich-Denken*]," his emphasis). Hintikka, " 'Cogito, Ergo Sum' " 117–18, recognizes correctly that the *cogito* is "a conceptual operation" but accuses Descartes in consequence of "shortcomings" and "ambiguity."

20. Andreas Kemmerling has argued, with considerable finesse, that the *cogito* must logically be reflexive. Its proper formulation, he deduces, is, "The thinker of this thought-occurrence exists" ("Reflexive Deutung" 165), a formulation in which "the 'cogito' inheres in the subject, the 'sum' in the predicate, and the 'ergo' in the origin" (166). But an "Entstehungsgeschichte"—a notably difficult

word to translate—presupposes a temporal continuity and a substratum enduring through time; in other words, it gives an ongoing life to "thought-occur-
rences." The point, as I shall be arguing more fully, is that Descartes has no
language for such subsistence and consequently no way to conceive it. Kemmerling's conclusion adroitly recognizes that his reconstruction, however necessary,
may be impossible. "Cogito Ergo Sum [is] a thought revolving in itself. [But it
isn't a "thought"; it's a statement, in a language.] The I that it concerns is
possibly very ephemeral. . . . Whether all that speaks against the above interpretation or against its object is one of the many difficult questions that I here
leave aside" (166). If only philosophy were a matter of logic!

21. See *Principia* 1.66–71, where it becomes evident that it is indeed difficult to
arrive at clear and distinct ideas of our sensations—and hence to take sensation
as a first principle—yet, apparently, it is not logically impossible.

22. See my *Preromanticism*, chap. 4.

23. Intuition, for Descartes, is yet another form of judgment, as he describes at
length in the third of the *Rules for the Direction of Spirit* (*Oeuvres* 10: 368). So too, I
think, is perception. In the *Meditations*, at any rate, *percipio* and *perceptio* are
regularly rendered with *connaître* and *connaissance* (last paragraph of *Meditations* 2; 7: 34 = 9: 26; *Meditations* 3; 7: 35 = 9: 27; *Meditations* 5; 7: 65 = 9: 52;
Meditations 5; 7: 71 = 9: 55 [*reconnaître*]). Particularly interesting is a phrase in the
preface: "ex eo quod mens humana in se conversa non *percipiat* aliud se esse
quam rem cogitantem" (de ce que l'esprit humain, faisant réflexion sur soi-
même, ne se *connaît* être autre chose qu'une chose qui pense; *Oeuvres* 7: 7–8 =
Meditations, ed. Rodis-Lewis, 6–7, my emphases in both quotes). The passage
does not appear in the original translation and was not reviewed by Descartes.
Still, the seventeenth-century translator seems to be in conformity with the rest
of the work when he takes *percipiat* as a stylistic variant for *cognoscat*. Even the
mind turned in upon itself is reflecting, not intuiting in the modern sense. In a
letter written in French concerning the Fifth Objections to the *Meditations* (9:
208), Descartes equates (true) perception with both knowledge and thought, but
not with judgments, which come after. By "judgments" here he appears to mean
inferences or conclusions; he is not denying propositional form to the "perception or thought" (his phrase) preceding the judgment.

24. Cahné (*Un Autre Descartes* 43–44) quotes the following decisive passage
from Augustine's *Confessions* 10.18, though he uses it for other purposes: "Cogenda rursus, ut sciri possint, id est uelut ex quadam dispersione colligenda,
unde dictum est cogitare. Nam cogo et cogito sic est, ut ago et agito, facio et
factito" (They are to be brought together [*cogenda*] so as to be known; that is,
collected as if from a state of dispersion, whence this is called *cogitare*. For *cogo* is
to *cogito* as *ago* to *agito*, *facio* to *factito*). The issue here is one of linguistic resonance, not of doctrine. Consequently, Augustine's testimony is powerful even
though Descartes had little interest in or knowledge of his writings.

25. Scholz discusses fully the iterative adverbs that regularly accompany Descartes's reasoning, though without signaling the iterative character of thought itself. See also Hintikka, " 'Cogito, Ergo Sum' " 113: "Descartes's insight emerges from his own descriptions as a curiously *momentary* affair. It is a consequence of the performatoriness of his insight. Since the certainty of my existence results from my thinking of it in a sense not unlike that in which light results from the presence of a source of light, it is natural to assume (rightly or wrongly) that I can be really sure of my existence only as long as I actively contemplate it." "Momentary" is right, but from Descartes's perspective the momentariness is inevitable not curious. And the example is wrong: it is durative where Cartesian thought is iterative. To be sure, Descartes sometimes uses the durative conjunction *quamdiu* in *Meditations* 2: "for he will never cause me to be nothing so long as I think myself something"; "I am, I exist; that is certain. But for how long? For so long as I think" (7: 25, 27). But these durations remain composed of particles: "every time I utter it," "every time I consider myself to be something" (7: 25, 26).

26. "Semper" gives the translator difficulties. In French it becomes "actuelle et éternelle" (9: 52). The doublet recaptures (in reverse order) the two faces of "est ou existe": action and subsistence. Descartes emphatically calls this conception of God clear and distinct, suggesting that he had less difficulty than his translator with the notion of a worldly, iterative eternity.

27. On error in Descartes, see the speculative essay by Ralph Flores. More generally, see the chapter "Substance at Risk" in Grene, *Descartes* 88–109, which concludes as follows: "It is the real distinction and the concomitant double reduction of mind to thought and nature to machinery that have plagued our thinking. . . . The bare unstable Cartesian world does indeed demand a foundation and must indeed fail to find it" (108). The central argument of the book is that Descartes neglected "the category of life" (21). That is, in substance, exactly my conclusion, which I have formulated as the absence from Descartes's texts of a certain (vitalist) temporality. However, I do not regard the absence as a failure, but rather as a linguistic-conceptual gap that only Descartes's conceptual and stylistic rigor could render visible, and then only to or through subsequent writers such as Kant.

28. Jean Wahl's booklet *Du rôle de l'idée de l'instant* celebrates Descartes's "actualism." Yet the features that he singles out are largely negations (the infinitesimal and history that "becomes the negation of the importance of history," 43) or insubstantial images (fire and light). Such achievements are prone to melt away, like wax.

29. "Pars itaque temporis quaelibet est tempus, et, quae sunt in tempore, simplicia, nempe *momenta*, non sunt partes illius, sed *termini*, quos interiacet tempus." In a note to *Le Monde* (*Oeuvres philosophiques* 347), Alquié says, "space is the a priori condition of all external representation. The Cartesian affirmation is quite close to that of Kant's *Transcendental Aesthetic*." But Descartes at this point is talking about matter and not, as Kant would, about space.

30. Cahné (*Un Autre Descartes* 142–43) attributes to Descartes imagery of dark labyrinths, but his only textual citation (from *Regulae* 5; 10: 379–80) concerns finding one's way through a labyrinth. Asserted parallels from Bacon and Leibniz do not consolidate the case. Nor do Cahné's examples make the phonetic linkage of *Icarus* and *cera* plausible. Edelman's essay is a helpful account of some of the relevant imagery. Gouhier, *Essais sur Descartes*, chap. 2 (esp. pp. 78–79 and 98–102) explains Descartes's apparent prudence in withholding *Le Monde*.

Chapter 7

1. *Watchman* 2: 68–70.

2. Derrida relates the problematics of "natural" language to the image of the sun in "White Mythology." See esp. 53: "With every metaphor, there is no doubt somewhere a sun; but each time that there is the sun, metaphor has begun. If the sun is already and always metaphorical, it is not completely natural. It is already and always a lustre: one might call it an *artificial* construction if this could have meaning in the absence of nature." Notice that Coleridge adds the metaphorical sun ("the eye of Day"), which is not mentioned in the Latin.

3. The first edition of the odes, in three books, was published in 1625; the first complete edition of the odes and epodes appeared in 1634, and there were some two dozen before 1800. Volume 1 of *The Happy Man* by Maren-Sofie Røstvig discusses Sarbiewski's influence in England at length, generally without considering the differences between Latin and English versions, though there is a useful contrast of Vaughan and Sarbiewski on 272. To my knowledge, the only good introduction to Sarbiewski in the neo-Latin context is Gerald Fitzgerald's "*Cenodoxus* and Baroque Latin": see esp. 10–12 and 130–31 (on "momentalism") and 44–46 and 69 (on strange sonorities and linguistic excesses). Leonard Forster's inaugural lecture, *The Temper of Seventeenth-Century German Literature*, surveys problems of baroque temporality with emphasis on northern Europe. On baroque opulence and its relation to sonority and the rhetorical voice, see Angus Fletcher, *The Transcendental Masque*, chap. 1.

4. Compare, for example, Horace's very supple use of the rare Ionic *a minore* (‿‿‒‒) in his *Odes* 3.12 with Sarbiewski's leaden succession of two- and four-syllable words in his *Od.* 2.28.

5. *Od.* 2.4.13–14: "Multi magna loqui possumus: ardua / Raros ausa vocant." Cf. also *Od.* 4.3.33–36: "Ad prima si quis vulnera non gemit, / Solo peregit bella silentio; / Celare qui novit sinistros, / Ille potest bene ferre casus," and *Od.* 4.11.13–16: "Vera laus sciri fugit. Ipse pulcher / Se suâ Titan prohibet videri / Luce: qui totus potuit latere, / Major habetur."

6. *Od.* 1.6.29–34: "Frustra Novembres dicimus ad focos / Pugnata Rhaetis bella sub Alpibus: / Frustra renarramus Gelonum / Versa retro retulisse signa: / Si non & ipsi stringere Noricos / Audemus enses." Observe the characteristic accumulation of "re-" prefixes.

7. The ode just cited continues (lines 45–46): "To him Tempe, bought with much blood, will afford recreation" (Hunc empta multo sanguine recreent / Tempe). The opposition of martial iron and degenerate gold appears in lines 14–15: "Ferro, Quirites, si lubet, abditum / Mercemur aurum."

8. When Sarbiewski attempts the description of nature in movement, the result is liable to be as absurd as the following, from the very first ode: "The hills moo, and breathless the wood from the tired calves. In peace the ridges spring up, in peace the foul rocks smile" (lines 31–34: "Mugiunt colles, & anhela fessis / Silva juvencis. / Pace subsultant juga, pace rident / Tetricae rupes").

9. Od. 4.8.29–30: "Humana quidquid composuit manus, / Humana rursus disjiciet." Od. 2.6.33–36: "Et qui conspicuus tot populis heri / Spectabar tacito non sine gaudio; / Ridens e mediâ plebe vicariam / Cras spectabo Tragoediam." Cf. the phrase "taciti . . . Dies" in Od. 1.7.36, an otherwise more conventional poem about natural mutability. Contrast the well-known sonnet 3.8 of Andreas Gryphius ("Du siehst, wohin du siehst, nur eitelkeit auf erden"), which describes nature's noisy destruction of human vanity. The contrast is apposite because Sarbiewski translated Gryphius's sonnet 3.7. On Gryphius's translations from Biedermann and Sarbiewski, see Fitzgerald 96–100 and 116–18.

10. Od. 3.23.5–7: "Mitte sectari, quis amoena praeter / Prata non parco fluit amnis auro. / Sit satis Virtus." Od. 1.23.21–28: "Numquam . . . / Auri deciduis vestierat jubis / Graium pellis Iasona; / Si non difficiles imperii boves / Egisset dominâ vertere dexterâ / Ferratis Chalybum saucia dentibus / Colchi litora Phasidis." Cf. also Od. 44.26.18–20: "In arma ferrum / Sit satis. Rapto malè pugnat olim / Miles in auro."

11. Od. 4.19.9–12: "At te quae tacitis distinet otiis, / o JESU, regio? quis mihi te locus / Caecis invidet umbris, / Aut spissâ nemorum comâ?"

12. Od. 2.12.33–41. I call the sound effects false because (1) they are unclassical, (2) they ignore etymology ("ite . . . iterate . . . te"), and (3) they apparently ignore vowel quanity ("culmis . . . orbis").

13. Observe that the problems of time and space are fundamentally inseparable. On the relation of vision as sight to vision as prophetic foresight see Bishop Berkeley's New Theory of Vision, § 148, and Meyer H. Abrams, Natural Supernaturalism 373–84.

14. Od. 1.7.41–44: "Et sunt quae, Lyce, cernimus? / An peccant fatuis lumina palpebris, / Et mendax oculi vitrum? / An longi trahitur fabula somnii?"

15. There are no epiphanic formulae in Horace either; their origins in English poetry need to be investigated. On the use of "ecce," see Erich Auerbach, Mimesis 157.

16. Silviludia 4.6: "En pictis foliorum / Multicolor labellis / Flos tacitus divinos / Eloquitur honores" (my italics). "En" in Epodes 3.37 is also not original with Sarbiewski but derives from the same source as Silv. 4. On the attribution

of the *Silviludia*, which were regularly printed with the *Odes* and translated as Sarbiewski's by R. C. Core in 1848 under the title *Wood-Notes*, see John Sparrow, "Sarbiewski's *Silviludia*."

17. Thus the epitaph in *Od*. 2.5.56–57 ("Cum populo jacet hic et ipso / Cum rege regnum") is one-and-a-half lines in the Latin spanning a stanza break, one line in G. Hils, two full lines (though of differing lengths) in John Hughes's "The Ecstasy." There is similarly a strong tendency to force anaphoric repetition into a uniform position at the beginning of the line; examples can readily be found in the Oxford *Miscellany* translations and on almost any page of Hils's bilingual edition. It should be noted that there is no alternative principle of formal balance in Sarbiewski, such as could be achieved, for example, by a careful management of clause lengths. Even where isocolon is found, the effect in context is not so much balance as urgency (as in the lines, "Integram nobis sine labe vitam, / Prosperam nobis sine clade mortem," found in *Od*. 4.24.13–14 and again in *Ep*. 9.33–34).

18. Examples of punning translations based on sound rather than sense are "regent" for "regina," "sublimes and takes me" for "me eripit sublimem," and "oh what a *longing*, Jesu, thus / With thy delay thou mak'st in us?" for "*Longam ducis*, JESU, / In desideriis moram" (Hils 91, 63, 79; my italics). The last pun, not noticed in the *Oxford English Dictionary*, is also found in Donne, e.g., *Metempsychosis*, lines 63–64, and *The Litanie*, line 83.

19. Sarbiewski, *Od*. 4.28 ("Cum novi e Germania, Gallia, Italiaque motus bellici nuntiarentur"): "Punctum est, sors avidis quod secat ensibus / Inter tot populos." Vaughan, lines 17–20: "It [the world] is a *ball* / Which *Fate* and *force* divide 'twixt all / The *sons* of *Men*."

20. We can see the process of compensation at work in the translations of *Od*. 2.5. First, Cowley in "The Exstasie" replaced figures from the Trojan War with Galileo and with St. Paul, who, in turn, being insufficiently modern, gives way to Columbus ("Not *Paul*, who first did thither pass, / And this great *Worlds Columbus* was," st. 6). Then Hughes, in his version of "The Ecstasy," substitutes Newton for Paul and directly compares the modern figures to their outmoded classical prototypes: " 'Tis he—as I approach more near / The great Columbus of the skies I know, / 'Tis Newton's soul! that daily travels here / In search of knowledge for mankind below. / O stay, thou happy Spirit! stay, / And lead me on thro' all th'unbeaten wilds of day; / As when the Sybil did Rome's father guide" (lines 175–81).

21. Hans-Georg Gadamer's *Wahrheit und Methode* generalizes the principle by arguing that any creative inheritance of a tradition is in fact a translation, involving such a re-placement and redefinition of style. For an elegant literary demonstration of the principle, see Emil Staiger, "Entstellte Zitate."

22. "The Celebrated Victory . . . ," Watts, *Horae Lyricae*, No. 204. Watts's monosyllabic strong verbs (hung, fell, fled, spread) sound like participles or adjectives

and thus manage to combine the monumentality of the Latin with the vivid animation of true narrative.

23. Cf. Paul de Man, "Intentional Structure of the Romantic Image," *Rhetoric of Romanticism* 5: "Strictly speaking, an epiphany cannot be a beginning, since it reveals and unveils what, by definition, could never have ceased to be there." The sentence which follows seems less appropriate to the optimistic early English romantics than to de Man's immediate subject, Hölderlin: "Rather, it is the rediscovery of a permanent presence which has chosen to hide itself from us—unless it is we who have the power to hide from it."

24. G. Wilson Knight's *The Starlit Dome* contains a fine study of illumination in Coleridge. The key sentence is on 119: "We have disentangled a progress from normal sexuality . . . towards the specifically artistic consciousness, which is, however, generally entwined with some literary or musical feminine figure; while the whole progress is, as it were, *lighted* by a nostalgic memory of youthful love, felt as a still existing, but somehow mislaid, experience" (Knight's italics).

25. "Everything seems to stream in on us because we do not stream out. We are negative because we want to be—the more positive we become, the more negative the world around us becomes—until at last there will be no more negation, but we are all in all. *God wants gods*" (Novalis's italics), *Schriften* 2: 584.

26. "The Extasie," stanza 2. Willis, too, springs an epiphany in mid-ascent: "Go, go, my Muse, the winged horse prepare; / I purpose now to take the Air / Take solid Judgement for the Bit, / And put on the rich Ornaments of Wit; / Where sense does shine like Dawn of Morn, / (Not dazzled by the thick, / And gaudy Flowers of Rhet'rick;) / Thro' Interspaces which the work adorn; / Lo! now I mount and (lo!) I take my flight," and so on (*Miscellany Poems* 27).

27. Wordsworth, *Prelude* (1805) 6:534, 525. As here, so too in Hughes and Coleridge (see the discussion below), "past and future overtake the present," as Hartman says (*Wordsworth's Poetry* 46).

28. "Hermeneutic wedge" is Hartman's phrase in "The Voice of the Shuttle," *Beyond Formalism* 351. Cleanth Brooks's search for ironies is a privileged mode, but not the only mode of hermeneutic inquiry.

29. Two roughly contemporary translations of 4.23 attempt this effect, but achieve only a sense of reciprocal directionality, rather than Coleridge's diffusion of directionality. For "Et te voce, *Cicada*, / Et mutum recreas nemus" (lines 3–4), Joseph Hucks has "lull the listening grove" (83) and Götz has "den horchenden Hain" (2: 16).

30. On the ambiguities of the light and the air cf. the following sequence in *Notebooks* 2936: "—like a lake beneath the Sun seemed to possess in its own right & prodigally give the fiery Light, which by not receiving it flashed forth"; 2937: "Aeolian Harp motive for opening the Sash; & at once lets in music & sweet air," and so on. On the harp and the light see also 2435.

31. This is apparently a common and spontaneous ambiguity; see *Oxford English Dictionary*, "lour."

32. Empson, *Structure*, chap. 1. See chap. 4 ("'All' in Milton") for Empson's analysis of a purely emotive word. For an argument that words are inherently simple though not "natural," see Emile Benveniste, "Nature du signe linguistique." Martin Price has some interesting comments on Blake's avoidance of irony in the *Songs of Innocence*; see *To the Palace of Wisdom* 390–97.

33. Among the many relevant commentaries on Wordsworth's poem, see in particular that by Paul de Man in "The Rhetoric of Temporality" 204–6.

34. The association of glitter (also glimmer and gleam) with water is peculiar to the early Coleridge (before about 1805). Wordsworth's glitter, by contrast, is dry, as in "A Farewell," lines 53–54: "The steep rock's breast / Glittered at evening like a starry sky." Wordsworth's usage eventually impinged on Coleridge, as in the second paragraph of *Biographia Literaria*. See also Josephine Miles, "Wordsworth and Glitter."

35. It would take another essay to trace the implications of the imagery linking water-eyes-illumination-expansion-animation (one life)-Aeolian harp. Some key passages are "Dejection," lines 73–75; "Hymn before Sunrise in the Vale of Chamouni," lines 23–25 and 70–85; and "The Night-Scene," lines 42–45. Ecstasy, not epiphany, is the proper term for the poetical "lo!"—it is more descriptive and more accurate historically. See, for instance, the odes entitled "The Ecstasy," cited above, and also the analysis in Heidegger, *Sein und Zeit*, § 65.

36. Gustave Guillaume's discussion of perfects compounded with "to be" (*être*) could be applied *in toto* to Coleridge's poem. The so-called "Passé composé intégrant," according to Guillaume, is characterized by a passive agent, by the absence of a strong distinction between subject and object, and by a conception of event as a participatory, continuous totality. See "Existe-t-il un déponent en français?"

37. I choose the term "self-projection" not because Heidegger later adopted it to describe the "transcendent" unity of subject and object but rather because it is used by the Romantic philosophers. See, for instance, the page on "Entwerfen" beginning, "Wer bin Ich? Subjekt und Objekt in Einem," in Johann Gottlieb Fichte's *Bestimmung des Menschen* (*Sämmtliche Werke* 250). Heidegger, however, is more lucid; see *Sein und Zeit*, § 31 (definition of "der Entwurf"), and §§ 63, 64, and 69 (on transcendent unity). It is worth remembering the characteristic seventeenth-century rejection of anticipation in George Herbert. Prudence (pro-videntia) belongs to divine providence, not to men, who should live in the present and whose only future is death. "Men and the present fit: if he provide / He breaks the square. / This houre is mine: if for the next I care, / I grow too wide, / And do encroach upon deaths side" ("The Discharge," lines 31–35).

38. Cf. also *Notebooks* 2439: "patiendo agam . . . et agendo patiar." Hegel's *Science of Logic* contains the most searching philosophical analysis of the fusion of action and passion into what is called "determinate simplicity"; see the concluding sections of vol. 1: "Action and Reaction" and "Reciprocity."

39. Before Coleridge, Hume had already seen the "indolent belief in the general maxims of the world" (and later "indolence and pleasure") as the remedy for "philosophical melancholy and delirium" (*A Treatise of Human Nature* 1.4.7). In the preceding section of the *Treatise* Hume describes the spectacle of perception in a way that is relevant to—and indeed answered by—Coleridge's "simple" style: "The mind is a kind of theatre, where several perceptions successively make their appearance; pass, repass, glide away, and mingle in an infinite variety of postures and situations. There is properly no *simplicity* in it at one time, nor *identity* in different, whatever natural propension we may have to imagine that simplicity and identity" (Hume's italics). The topic is well surveyed in Spiegelman, *Majestic Indolence*.

40. Coleridge's comment to Mrs. Barbauld concerning the moral of the "Ancient Mariner" is well known. Richard Haven traces the problem of Coleridge's moralizing conclusions in chap. 2 of *Patterns of Consciousness*.

41. See Maurice Blanchot, *Le Livre à venir* 9–19 (part of the essay, "Le Chant des sirènes"). Mallarmé's closest approach to the Aeolian harp—a relatively recent invention first described by Athanasius Kircher in his *Musurgia universalis* of 1650—is an obsolete instrument hanging in an enclosed showcase, "musicienne du silence" ("A la fenêtre recelant").

42. Contemporary with Coleridge and closely allied to him in spirit is the French aphorist Joubert (1754–1824); see Blanchot's eloquent essay "Joubert et l'espace," *Le Livre à venir* 75–98, where (in the section entitled "Une première version de Mallarmé") the following is quoted: "I am an Aeolian harp. No wind has blown over me" (94).

43. "The Double Session," *Dissemination* 220–22, apropos of the word *entre*. Cf. also 262–64 and Philippe Sollers, "Littérature et totalité," esp. 78–82. After Mallarmé the self-sufficiency or "littéralité" (Sollers, 81) again perhaps declines; see, for instance, J. Hillis Miller's analysis of Wallace Stevens's revision of the Arab dream passage in the *Prelude*: *Linguistic Moment* 390–422.

44. "Le Livre, instrument spirituel." The fundamental study of the effervescence of Mallarmé's imagery is Jean-Pierre Richard, *L'Univers imaginaire de Mallarmé*, esp. 377–409.

45. Northrop Frye, "The Drunken Boat" 200–217, and also *Fearful Symmetry* 138–39.

Chapter 9

1. Roland Barthes, "La Musique, la voix, la langue" and "Le Chant romantique" in *L'Obvie et l'obtus* 247 and 253. See further the useful survey by Françoise Escal, "Roland Barthes: Fragments d'un discours."

2. An exception to the word-envy of musical semiotics is Theodor Adorno's essay, "Fragment über Musik und Sprache." Most prominent among the exam-

ples of the yearning to assimilate music to language is perhaps Jean-Jacques Nattiez, *Fondements*, esp. 76–82. More extreme is B. M. Gasparov, "Nekotorye deskriptivnye problemy muzykalnoi semantiki." More attuned to the specificity of music is Vladimir Karbusicky; see, for instance, his "Zeichen und Musik," though even here we read: "Since musical symbols are more nearly [iconic] characterizations than arbitrary encodings [eher Charakteristika als willkürliche Chiffren] they point toward early stages in the development of language" (240). In "Das Verstehen der verbalen Sprache und das 'Verstehen der Musik,'" Adam Schaff says that music has phonemes but not words. In consequence, he argues, whereas language communicates meaning, music communicates only feelings. The reduction is like that of Barthes or, before him, of Suzanne Langer. Schaff's essay is part of a collection containing numerous valuable essays of a general nature that are relevant to the present discussion.

3. My semiotic account applies to musical texts, not to performance. Indeed, it has been argued that no formal semiotic analysis is possible of music as actually realized: see François Delalande, "L'Analyse." The objection is true, but not relevant, since the same objection would apply to plays as performed or to poems—or even novels—as read aloud.

4. Harold Krebs discusses examples of wandering tonality in Schubert songs and in Chopin in "Alternatives to Monotonality." In some cases, he argues, Schenkerian analysis reveals the initial sonority to be a false tonic; in the others the harmonic movement is genuine and is textually motivated. The key relation between beginning and end in the latter cases is always a third. Even rarer are the works (always songs or programmatic character pieces) that end on a suspension; see the list in Vladimir Jankélévitch, *Fauré* 26. One domain where the law of tonal consistency does not regularly apply is opera, particularly in the *bel canto* tradition and in Wagner.

5. Drawing on Peter Brooks's book *Reading for the Plot*, Anthony Newcomb's "Narrative Archetypes" illustrates the origin of a modernist sense of closure in Mahler's Ninth Symphony. For another interesting modernist account that regards closure as a repression, see D. A. Miller, *Narrative and Its Discontents*. I have criticized this approach on other grounds in "Plan vs. Plot."

6. Cf. Jérôme J. de Momigny, *Cours complet d'harmonie et de composition*, cited in Leonard Ratner, *Classic Music* 146: "the general plan is established by these instruments [the strings] and the wind instruments, when they are not assigned a leading part, only serve to reinforce the plan with a clearer or more decisive color."

7. So, in connection with the "antinomy that everything should be at once understandable and striking [verständlich und apart]," Adorno writes even of so complex a work as *Tristan* that "the socially conformist demand of comprehensibility and the artistic one of plasticity split asunder," "Versuch über Wagner" 51.

8. Arnold Schoenberg, "Symphonien aus Volkslierdern," *Gesammelte Schriften* 134. I have retranslated this from Schoenberg's German version, which is a little more colorful than the original English, found in "Folkloristic Symphonies," *Style and Idea* 161.

9. The remainder of Chekhov's conclusion reads: "He descended in exhaustion into the shop and, with hot tears, greeted the new, unknown life which was now beginning for him. . . . How was this life to be?" (Chekhov's suspension points). The pun on "ravnodushno" (indifferently) and "ravnina" (plain) appears on 261, in the first chapter. For a more extended analysis, see the brilliant essay by Michael Finke, "Chekhov's 'Steppe': A Metapoetic Journey," 79–120, where the "irreconcilable, disharmonious directions" of the anticlimactic plot (91) are shown to be resolved in a "drama of motifs" and a musicality of structure (107–12) in which "words more than characters are the story's actors" (102).

10. The emergence of modernist features in Debussy's style is well traced in Arthur B. Wenk, *Claude Debussy*. There is a nice comparison of temporality in Debussy's *Canope* and in Proust in Claudia Zenck-Maurer, *Versuch über die wahre Art, Debussy zu interpretieren*.

11. Jankélévitch, *La Vie et la mort dans la musique de Debussy* 93: "The voice of things is captured as closely as possible, and by so immediate an intuition that the human voice, that human presence, that the human person are finally effaced." This book also contains a sensitive appreciation of Debussy's temporality.

12. Gérard Genette, *Mimologiques* 257–314, gives a fine account of the turn toward embodiment in both linguistics and poetics (Mallarmé, Valéry, Sartre, and Jakobson). See esp. pp. 286–88 on the musicalization of language and pp. 298–99 on "signification that has 'fallen into immanence,' [and] 'become a thing.'"

13. A similar programmatic fragmentation is enacted in Luigi Pirandello's novel *Uno, nessuno e centomila*; see the analysis in Gregory Lucente, *Beautiful Fables* 116–55.

14. Shoshana Felman, "Turning the Screws of Interpretation"; Christine Brooke-Rose, "The Squirm of the True." Christopher Lewis speaks of "a general trend in the arts away from a linear perception toward the idea of a multidimensional network of implications and cross-relations in all directions" ("Mirrors and Metaphor"). The term "trend," however, does not adequately capture the conflict between opposing modes reenacted so often in works of the period and well illustrated by the article's own examples of interference between Schenkerian monotonality and post-Wagnerian dual tonality.

15. In Schoenberg's atonality, as Carl Dahlhaus well expresses in the essay "Emanzipation der Dissonanz," "consequentiality is taken away from the chord, but not comprehensibility"; see Dahlhaus, *Schönberg und andere* 148.

16. There is an excellent, nuanced description of the disjunction between style and form in Charles Rosen, *Schoenberg* 79–116. He characterizes the aims as "a

move to resurrect an old classicism" (82) and "as much a defiant proclamation of freedom as an exercise in nostalgia" (103), but the attribution of a mood is risky at best. Along similar lines, see the precise and eloquent analysis of musical structures in Thomas Mann's *Doktor Faustus* in Harry Redner, *In the Beginning Was the Deed* 216–41, though Redner appears to understand Schoenberg differently (236–37).

17. In Schoenberg's *Pierrot Lunaire*, for instance, consonances (never comfortably scored and in root position) always allude to the lost past. They appear at the opening of No. 4, "Eine blasse Wäscherin" (A Pale Washerwoman), in the nostalgic postlude of No. 5, "Valse de Chopin," and on occasion in the last song (No. 21) in connection with the text "O alter Duft aus Märchenzeit" (Old aroma from fairy tales of yore).

18. Letter to Grant Richards, March 13, 1906, *Letters of James Joyce* 2: 134. By "meanness" Joyce presumably understands parsimoniousness but with an unpleasant affect, as in "A Little Cloud," *Dubliners* 83 ("He found something mean in the pretty furniture which he had bought for his house on the hire system"), and "A Painful Case" 107 ("He found all the other suburbs of Dublin mean, modern and pretentious").

19. Theodor Lipps, "Das Wesen der musikalischen Konsonanz und Dissonanz" 195. The key word is equilibrium, in contrast to the modernist sense of an ending that is illustrated in D. A. Miller's *Narrative and Its Discontents*. Or, similarly, contrast the "resting place" in "The C Major of this life" at the end of Robert Browning's *Abt Vogler* with the conclusion of Thomas Pynchon's story, "Entropy": "[Aubade] turned to . . . wait with him until . . . the hovering, curious dominant of their separate lives should resolve into a tonic of darkness and the final absence of all motion" (*Slow Learner* 98).

Finale

1. My invocation of "action" and the pun on "void" allude to Kenneth Burke's excremental reading of Keats's ode, "Symbolic Action." What that essay refused to say, "Body is turd, turd body," finally came out elsewhere, still not verbally, but with sufficiently explicit hints: *Rhetoric* 204.

2. The Platonic and the Heideggerian Keats have come under attack lately. Yet they revive, for this poem at least, if we recognize "The Deserted Village" as an intertext. (Keats gave his sister a collection of Goldsmith's works in February 1819, about three months before the ode was composed.) Keats's "sylvan historian" replaces the figure in Goldsmith's frontispiece, "The sad historian of the pensive plain" (136). His "flowery tale" replaces the village garden: "Near yonder copse, where once the garden smiled, / And still where many a garden flower grows wild" (137–38). His reiterated "sweet" is even more emphatic in Goldsmith; his lovers' chase, his empty town, his wasted generation, all

likewise sublimate more realistic motifs in Goldsmith; and the urn's valedictory replaces that of Goldsmith's "loveliest maid" (407), Poetry, whose voice can "Aid slighted truth" (423). Readers who willingly suspend disbelief will enjoy seeing in the "broken teacups" on display in Auburn (235) a type of the Grecian Urn.

3. See further Geraldine Friedman's "Erotics of Interpretation" for penetrating observations on the gender trouble wrought by (among other things) the poem's acoustics: "bride of quietness," lowing heifer, silent town, and so forth.

4. Charles Rosen has recently discussed the "inner voice" in Schumann's *Humoresque* in nearly identical terms; see *The Romantic Generation* 7–9.

5. I feel that a sketch of the interpretive support is more necessary here than with my other musical examples. Characteristic of Strauss's scores following the Ovidian death-music of the wartime *Metamorphoses* is a revival of the Romantic past: the unending triads of the Second Horn Concerto, or the melodic lyricism of the Oboe Concerto (redeeming for Romanticism an instrument that had not had a distinguished solo piece since the era of the baroque concerto grosso—a form recently renewed by the likes of Stravinsky and Manuel de Falla). Characteristic of the *Four Last Songs* are (1) prosopopoeia (such as flute trills where the text mentions birds, low tessitura at the word "tief" [low] in *Beim Schlafengehen*, and a quotation from Strauss's own *Death and Transfiguration* at the word "Tod" [death] in *Im Abendrot*); (2) controlled, calm lushness, over a firm, steady bass line; (3) a preference for pure instrumental colors (little wind doubling or foreground mixing of wind timbres); (4) a sparing use of the horn, which is, however, featured as the sonority of peaceful repose at the end of the second and third songs, *September* and *Beim Schlafengehen*, to modern poems by Hesse. It is in this context that I take the final fade-out of the horns in the only song with a Romantic text to signify a loosening of all the links so lovingly forged by the songs—of text with music, sound with meaning, and present with past. A closely related effect is the absence of the English horn from the final chord of Wagner's *Tristan und Isolde*.

6. David Epstein, *Beyond Orpheus* 128–29, discusses the unusual spacing of Beethoven's opening chords, which, he observes, if one stray clarinet note is discounted, "spells out" the opening theme. Unlike the clearly audible effects I have discussed in this symphony, or the guidance to expression given by those in the other works I have discussed, Epstein's effect is an inaudible abstraction. This mapping of the axis of succession onto the axis of simultaneity is persuasive, if at all, as an indicator of the will to spatial form that motivates the effects I have discussed. On pp. 133–34, there are some excellent comments about the structural function of repeated notes in the symphony, including a number of passages that my limited remarks omit and of a more technical nature than is appropriate for a literary audience.

7. Frank Kermode's brief reflections on the poem (*The Art of Telling* 134–35

and 154) are particularly suggestive on its imitation of mental action. In the phrase I have echoed, Kermode says, "I've been teasing Keats's poem into thought," but three sentences later he reverses the direction of flow: "Of course the poem encourages us to do these things" (135). Different in rhetoric yet allied in spirit is Barthes's discussion of "The Pensive Text" at the end of S/Z (216–17), in conjunction with his notions of "structuration without structure" (5) and with what might be called the supplement of deficiency (24, 143, 175).

8. Leo Bersani sees Mallarmé's essay as floating among disparate positions, and he drives a wedge between the two poles that my chapter seeks to reconcile: the structural, where "the author is omitted by his structure," and the musical, "conveying the opposite message," which embraces "not only . . . a view of poetry as the music of individual souls, but also . . . other (non-structural *and* non-psychological) notions of art" (*Death* 39, Bersani's italics). In the following later summary, I emphasize the terms at issue: "In . . . the speculative turbulence of the essay 'Crise de vers,' Mallarmé seems to be proposing a view of literature as an unlocatable—perhaps even *unheard* and unseen—*performance* devoid of any semiotic or epistemological authority. And yet it is in the erasing of his own capacity for making authoritative statements—indeed, in his apparent unlearning of the very technique by which what we call statements are *formed*—that Mallarmé sought to define the historical, even the political interest of his career" (Bersani, *The Freudian Body* 25; the words from "unlocatable" to "authority" also appear in *Death* 45, except that "performance" is there "activity"). The gaps in this reading that my chapter addresses are, first, the unspecified location where "interest" inheres (the "in" of "in the erasing") and, second, the undefined dialectic that generates definition out of the negations "erasing" and "unlearning."

9. Marjorie Levinson explores and deconstructs the pun on frieze-freeze-frees in order to bring Keats's depths to the surface and to remake his "Ideas" into "a conceptual physics" (*Keats's Life of Allegory* 105–6, and see also 130, 133, 140, and 175 on ideas and Ideas). Ultimately, I suggest, her materialism cannot be distinguished from a properly dynamic formalism, such as her title word "allegory" designates.

10. Bryson's book, *Looking at the Overlooked*, considers at length the implications of a kind of painting that suppresses narrative (see especially 60–95) and also contains a section (145–55) on some still life paintings with hazy scriptural scenes in the background, where "transcendental truth does not belong to the realm of the visible" (150).

11. "Le différend, la *différance* entre Dionysos et Apollon, entre l'élan et la structure, ne s'efface pas dans l'histoire car elle n'est pas *dans* l'histoire. Elle est aussi, en un sens insolite, une structure originaire: l'ouverture de l'histoire, l'historicité elle-même" (The dispute, the *differance* between Dionysus and Apollo, between thrust and structure, is not erased in history because it isn't *in* history. It too is, in

an unaccustomed sense, an originary structure: the opening of history, historicity itself; Derrida, "Force et signification" 47). Missing from Hegel's accounts of form and force—particularly the relatively accessible, but highly segmented presentation in the *Enzyklopädie*, sections 131–38—is the history-begetting thrust that inspires Keats and Derrida.

Works Cited

Aarsleff, Hans. *From Locke to Saussure: Essays on the Study of Language and Intellectual History*. Minneapolis: University of Minneapolis Press, 1982.

Abert, Hermann. *W. A. Mozart*. 3 vols. Leipzig: Breitkopf und Härtel, 1956.

Abrams, Meyer H. *The Mirror and the Lamp: Romantic Theory and the Critical Tradition*. New York: Oxford University Press, 1953.

———. *Natural Supernaturalism*. New York: Norton, 1971.

Adorno, Theodor. "Fragment über Musik und Sprache." In *Gesammelte Schriften*. Ed. Gretel Adorno and Rolf Tiedemann. Vol. 16. Frankfurt am Main: Suhrkamp, 1978. 251–56.

———. "Versuch über Wagner." In *Die musikalischen Monographien. Gesammelte Schriften*. Ed. Gretel Adorno and Rolf Tiedemann. Vol. 13. Frankfurt am Main: Suhrkamp, 1971. 7–148.

Adorno, Theodor, and Max Horkheimer. *Dialectic of Enlightenment*. Trans. John Cumming. New York: Seabury, 1972.

Alquié, Ferdinand. "Une Lecture cartésienne de la Critique de la raison pure est-elle possible?" *Revue de métaphysique et de morale* 80 (1975): 145–55.

Altieri, Charles. "The Qualities of Action: A Theory of Middles in Literature." *Boundary 2* 5 (1976–77): 323–50, 899–917.

Anderson, Benedict. *Imagined Communities*. London: Verso, 1991.

Antal, Frederick. "Remarks on the Method of Art History." *Burlington Magazine* 91 (1949): 49–52, 73–75.

Arendt, Hannah. *On Revolution*. New York: Viking, 1963.

Aubin, Robert A. *Topographical Poetry in XVIII-Century England*. New York: Modern Language Association of America, 1936.

Auerbach, Erich. *Dante als Dichter der irdischen Welt*. Berlin: de Gruyter, 1929.

———. *Mimesis: The Representation of Reality in Western Literature*. Trans. Willard Trask. Garden City, N.Y.: Doubleday, 1957.

———. *Scenes from the Drama of European Literature*. Trans. Ralph Manheim and Catherine Garvin. New York: Meridian, 1959.

Austen, Jane. *Pride and Prejudice.* Vol. 2 of *The Novels of Jane Austen.* Ed. R. W. Chapman. London: Oxford University Press, 1933.

Bacchelli, Riccardo. *Rossini e saggi musicali.* Milan: Mondadori, 1968.

Banfield, Ann. *Unspeakable Sentences: Narration and Representation in the Language of Fiction.* Boston: Routledge and Kegan Paul, 1982.

Barié, G. E. "Du 'cogito' cartésien au moi transcendental." *Revue philosophique de la France et de l'étranger* 141 (1951): 211–27.

Barnouw, Jeffrey. "Erziehung des Menschengeschlechts: Die Formierung bürgerlichen Bewußtseins (Voltaire, Johnson, Lessing)." In *Propyläen Geschichte der Literatur.* Ed. Erika Wischer. 6 vols. Berlin: Propyläen, 1981–84. 4: 11–39.

Barthes, Roland. *Le Degré zéro de l'écriture, suivi de: Elements de sémiologie.* Paris: Gonthier, 1969.

———. *Mythologies.* Paris: Seuil, 1970.

———. *L'Obvie et l'obtus.* Paris: Seuil, 1982.

———. *S/Z: An Essay.* Trans. Richard Miller. New York: Hill and Wang, 1974.

Bass, Bernard, and Armand Zaloszyc. *Descartes et les fondements de la psychanalyse.* [Paris]: Navarin-Osiris, 1988.

Baudelaire, Charles. *Les Fleurs du mal.* Ed. Antoine Adam. Paris: Garnier, 1961.

Bazerman, Charles. *Shaping Written Knowledge: Essays in the Growth, Form, Function, and Implications of the Scientific Article.* Madison: University of Wisconsin Press, 1988.

Béguin, Albert. *L'Ame romantique et le rêve.* 2 vols. Marseilles: Cahiers du sud, 1937.

Behler, Ernst. "Die Auffassung der Revolution in der deutschen Romantik." In *Studien zur Romantik und zur idealistischen Philosophie.* Paderborn: Schöningh, 1988. 66–85.

Benveniste, Emile. "Nature du signe linguistique." In *Problèmes de linguistique générale.* Paris: Gallimard, 1966. 49–55.

Berger, Harry, Jr. "The *Mutabilitie Cantos*: Archaism and Evolution in Retrospect." In *Revisionary Play: Studies in the Spenserian Dynamics.* Berkeley: University of California Press, 1988. 243–73.

Bersani, Leo. *The Death of Stéphane Mallarmé.* Cambridge: Cambridge University Press, 1982.

———. *The Freudian Body.* New York: Columbia University Press, 1986.

Besset, Maurice. *Novalis et la pensée mystique.* Paris: Aubier, 1947.

Blanchot, Maurice. *Le Livre à venir.* Paris: Gallimard, 1971.

———. "The Main Impropriety." Trans. June Guicharnaud. In *Literature and Revolution.* Ed. Jacques Ehrmann. Boston: Beacon, 1970. 50–63.

Bloomfield, Robert. *Remains.* Ed. J. Weston. 2 vols. London: Baldwin, Cradock, and Joy, 1824.

Bockelmann, Walter. *Die Grundbegriffe der Kunstbetrachtung bei Wölfflin und Dvořák.* Dresden: Baensch Stiftung, 1938.

Bouillier, Francisque. *Histoire de la philosophie cartésienne*. 2 vols. Paris: Delgrave, 1868.

Bourdieu, Pierre. *The Field of Cultural Production: Essays on Art and Literature*. Ed. Randal Johnson. New York: Columbia University Press, 1993.

———. *In Other Words: Essays Towards a Reflexive Sociology*. Trans. Matthew Adamson. Stanford: Stanford University Press, 1990.

Brands, Hartmut. *"Cogito ergo sum": Interpretation von Kant bis Nietzsche*. Freiburg: Alber, 1982.

Braudel, Fernand. *On History*. Trans. Sarah Matthews. Chicago: University of Chicago Press, 1980.

Brisman, Leslie. *Milton's Poetry of Choice and Its Romantic Heirs*. Ithaca: Cornell University Press, 1973.

———. *Romantic Origins*. Ithaca: Cornell University Press, 1978.

Brooke-Rose, Christine. "The Squirm of the True: An Essay in Non-Methodology," "The Squirm of the True: A Structural Analysis of Henry James's *The Turn of the Screw*," and "Surface Structure in Narrative: The Squirm of the True, Part III." *PTL: A Journal for Descriptive Poetics and Theory* 1 (1976): 265–94, 513–46, and 2 (1977): 517–62.

Brown, Marshall. "Humboldt and the Mediation Between Self and World." *Genre* 6 (1973): 121–41.

———. "Plan vs. Plot: Chapter Symmetries and the Mission of Form." *Stanford Literature Review* 4 (1987): 103–36.

———. *Preromanticism*. Stanford: Stanford University Press, 1991.

———. Review of John Daverio, *Nineteenth-Century Music and the German Romantic Ideology*. In *Nineteenth-Century Music* 18 (1995): 290–303.

Brown, Norman O. *Life Against Death*. Middletown, Conn.: Wesleyan University Press, 1959.

Bruns, Gerald L. *Inventions: Writing, Textuality, and Understanding in Literary History*. New Haven: Yale University Press, 1982.

Bryson, Norman. "Chardin and the Text of Still Life." *Critical Inquiry* 15 (1989): 227–52.

———. *Looking at the Overlooked: Four Essays on Still Life Painting*. Cambridge, Mass.: Harvard University Press, 1990.

Buffon [Georges-Louis le Clerc]. *Oeuvres philosophiques*. Ed. Jean Piveteau. Paris: Presses universitaires de France, 1954.

Burckhardt, Jacob. *Force and Freedom: Reflections on History*. Trans. James Hastings Nicols. New York: Pantheon, 1943.

———. *Gesammelte Werke*. 10 vols. Basel: B. Schwabe, 1955–59.

———. *Jacob Burckhardt und Heinrich Wölfflin: Briefwechsel und andere Dokumente ihrer Begegnung*. Ed. Joseph Gantner. Basel: B. Schwabe, 1948.

Burger, André. "Phonématique et diachronie: A propos de la palatalisation des

consonnes romanes." In *A Geneva School Reader in Linguistics*. Ed. Robert Go-
del. Bloomington: Indiana University Press, 1969. 218–31.
Burke, Kenneth. *A Rhetoric of Motives*. Berkeley: University of California Press,
1969.
——. "Symbolic Action in a Poem by Keats." In *A Grammar of Motives*. New
York: George Braziller, 1955. 447–64.
Butler, Marilyn. *Romantics, Rebels and Reactionaries: English Literature and Its Back-
ground, 1760–1830*. Oxford: Oxford University Press, 1981.
Butor, Michel. "Claude Monet ou le monde renversé." *Art de France* 3 (1963):
277–301.
Cage, John. *Silence*. Middletown: Wesleyan University Press, 1961.
Cahné, Pierre Alain. *Un Autre Descartes: Le Philosophe et son langage*. Paris: Vrin,
1980.
Carlini, A. "Grundeigenschaften des Geistesaktes als Selbstbewußtseins über-
haupt." *Logos* 20 (1931): 352–62.
Carlyle, Thomas. *The French Revolution: A History*. New York: Modern Library,
1934.
Cavell, Stanley. "Naughty Orators: Negation of Voice in *Gaslight*." In *Languages
of the Unsayable*. Ed. Sanford Budick and Wolfgang Iser. New York: Columbia
University Press, 1989. 340–77.
Champigny, Robert. "The Theatrical Aspect of the Cogito." *Review of Meta-
physics* 12 (1959): 370–79.
Chekhov, A. P. *Izbrannye sochinenia*. 2 vols. Moscow: Khudozhestvennaya Lite-
ratura, 1979.
Cherbouliez, Antoine-Elisée. "Zur harmonischen Analyse der Einleitung von
Mozarts C-Dur Streichquartett (K.V. 465)." In *Bericht über die musikwissen-
schaftliche Tagung der Internationalen Stiftung Mozarteum in Salzburg*. Ed. Erich
Schenk. Leipzig: Breitkopf und Härtel, 1932. 102–11.
Christensen, Jerome. "'Like a Guilty Thing Surprised': Deconstruction, Cole-
ridge, and the Apostasy of Criticism." *Critical Inquiry* 12 (1986): 769–87.
Clark, T. J. *The Absolute Bourgeois: Artists and Politics in France, 1848–51*. Prince-
ton: Princeton University Press, 1982.
——. *The Painting of Modern Life: Paris in the Art of Manet and His Followers*. New
York: Knopf, 1985.
Coleridge, Samuel Taylor. *Biographia Literaria*. Ed. George Watson. New York:
Dutton, 1956.
——. *Complete Works*. Ed. William Greenough Thayer Shedd. 7 vols. New York:
Harper and Brothers, 1854–56.
——. *Notebooks*. Vols. 1–2. Ed. Kathleen Coburn. New York: Pantheon, 1957.
——. *Poems*. Ed. E. H. Coleridge. London: Oxford University Press, 1935.
——. *The Statesman's Manual*. In *Lay Sermons*. Ed. R. J. White. Princeton: Prince-
ton University Press, 1972.

———. *The Watchman*. Ed. Lewis Patton. Princeton: Princeton University Press, 1970.

Collingwood, R. G. *The Idea of History*. Ed. T. M. Knox. London: Oxford University Press, 1956.

Compagnon, Antoine. *La Troisième république des lettres, de Flaubert à Proust*. Paris: Seuil, 1983.

Cone, Edward T. *The Composer's Voice*. Berkeley: University of California Press, 1974.

———. "Three Ways of Reading a Detective Story—or a Brahms Intermezzo." *Georgia Review* 31 (1977): 554–75.

Congreve, William. *Comedies*. Ed. Bonamy Dobrée. London: Oxford University Press, 1969.

Conrad, Joseph. *The Secret Sharer*. In *'Twixt Land and Sea*. Vol. 19 of his *Complete Works*. New York: Doubleday, 1924. 91–145.

Cook, Albert S. *History/Writing: The Theory and Practice of History in Antiquity and in Modern Times*. Cambridge: Cambridge University Press, 1988.

———. "The Wilderness of Mirrors." In *Dimensions of the Sign in Art*. Hanover, N.H.: Brown University Press / University Press of New England, 1989. 62–83.

Cowley, Abraham. *Poems*. Ed. Alfred Rayney Waller. Cambridge: Cambridge University Press, 1905.

Croce, Benedetto. *Nuovi saggi di estetica*. Bari: Laterza, 1948.

Croll, Morris W. *"Attic" and "Baroque" Prose Style*. Ed. J. Max Patrick and Robert O. Evans. Princeton: Princeton University Press, 1966.

Culler, Jonathan. "The Uses of *Madame Bovary*." *Diacritics* 11.3 (1981): 74–81.

Curran, Stuart. *Shelley's Annus Mirabilis: The Maturing of an Epic Vision*. San Marino, Cal.: Huntington Library, 1975.

Dalhaus, Carl. "Emanzipation der Dissonanz." In *Schönberg und andere*. Mainz: Schott, 1978. 146–53.

———. *Nineteenth-Century Music*. Trans. J. Bradford Robinson. Berkeley: University of California Press, 1989.

Davies, Sir John. *The Poems of Sir John Davies*. Ed. Robert Krueger. Oxford: Clarendon Press, 1975. 87–126.

Delalande, François. "L'Analyse des conduites musicales: Une Étape de programme sémiologique." *Semiotica* 66 (1987): 99–107.

de Man, Paul. *Allegories of Reading*. New Haven: Yale University Press, 1979.

———. "Hölderlin et Heidegger." *Critique* no. 100–101 (Sept.–Oct. 1955): 800–19.

———. "Mallarmé, Yeats, and the Post-Romantic Predicament." Harvard diss., 1960.

———. *The Rhetoric of Romanticism*. New York: Columbia University Press, 1984.

———. "The Rhetoric of Temporality." In *Interpretation: Theory and Practice*. Ed.

Charles S. Singleton. Baltimore: Johns Hopkins University Press, 1969. 173–209.

Derrida, Jacques. "Cogito et histoire de la folie." In *L'Ecriture et la différence.* Paris: Seuil, 1967. 51–97.

——. *Dissemination.* Trans. Barbara Johnson. Chicago: University of Chicago Press, 1981.

——. "Le Facteur de la vérité." *Poétique* 21 (1975): 96–147.

——. "Force et signification." In *L'Ecriture et la différence.* Paris: Seuil, 1979. 9–49.

——. *Glas.* Paris: Galilée, 1974.

——. "Living On: Border Lines." In *Deconstruction and Criticism.* Ed. Harold Bloom, et al. New York: Continuum, 1984. 75–176.

——. *Memoires: For Paul de Man.* Trans. Cecile Lindsay, Jonathan Culler, and Eduardo Cadava. New York: Columbia University Press, 1986.

——. "No Apocalypse, Not Now (full speed ahead, seven missiles, seven missives)." Trans. Catherine Porter and Philip Lewis. *Diacritics* 14.2 (Summer, 1984): 20–31.

——. "The Supplement of Copula: Philosophy *Before* Linguistics." Trans. James Creech and Josué Harari. *Georgia Review* 30 (1976): 527–64.

——. "Tympan." In *Marges de la philosophie.* Paris: Minuit, 1972. i–xxv.

——. *La Voix et le phénomène.* Paris: Presses Universitaires de France, 1972.

——. "White Mythology." Trans. F. C. T. Moore. *New Literary History* 6 (1974): 3–74.

Derrida, Jacques, and Christie V. McDonald. "Choreographies." *Diacritics* 12.2 (Summer, 1982): 66–76.

Descartes, René. *Correspondance.* Ed. C. Adam and B. Milhaud. 8 vols. Paris: Alcan, 1936–63.

——. *Discours de la Méthode: Texte et commentaire.* Ed. Etienne Gilson. Paris: J. Vrin, 1947.

——. *Discourse on Method and Other Writings.* Trans. F. E. Sutcliffe. Baltimore: Penguin, 1968.

——. *Meditationes de prima philosophia. Méditations métaphysiques.* Ed. Geneviève Rodis-Lewis. Paris: Vrin, 1978.

——. *Oeuvres.* Ed. Charles Adam and Paul Tannery. 13 vols. Paris: Cerf, 1897–1913.

——. *Oeuvres philosophiques.* Ed. Ferdinand Alquié. 3 vols. Paris: Garnier, 1963–73.

Dickens, Charles. *Bleak House.* Ed. George Ford and Sylvère Monod. New York: Norton, 1977.

Dirscherl, Klaus. "Stillosigkeit als Stil: Du Bos, Marivaux und Rousseau auf dem Weg zu einer empfindsamen Poetik." In *Stil: Geschichten und Funktionen eines kulturwissenschaftlichen Diskurselements.* Ed. Hans Ulrich Gumbrecht. Frankfurt am Main: Suhrkamp, 1986. 144–54.

Donington, Robert. *Wagner's "Ring" and Its Symbols*. London: Faber and Faber, 1963.

Dryden, John. *Oedipus*. In *The Works of John Dryden*. Ed. Walter Scott. London: William Miller, 1808. 6: 117–225.

——. *The Works of John Dryden*. Ed. Edward Niles Hooker and H. T. Swedenberg, Jr. 18 vols. to date. Berkeley: University of California Press, 1956–.

Dubrow, Heather. Letter to the Forum. *PMLA* 109 (1994): 1025–26.

Edelman, Nathan. "The Mixed Metaphor in Descartes." *Romantic Review* 41 (1950): 167–78.

Edmundson, Mark. *Literature Against Philosophy: A Defence of Poetry*. Cambridge, Eng.: Cambridge University Press, 1995.

Eliot, George. *The Mill on the Floss*. Boston: Estes and Lauriat, n.d.

Elster, Ernst. *Prinzipien der Litteraturwissenschaft*. 2 vols. Halle an der Saale: Niemeyer, 1897–1911.

Empson, William. *The Structure of Complex Words*. Ann Arbor: University of Michigan Press, 1967.

Epstein, David. *Beyond Orpheus: Studies in Musical Structure*. Cambridge, Mass.: MIT Press, 1979.

Escal, Françoise. "Roland Barthes: Fragments d'un discours sur la musique." *Semiotica* 66 (1987): 57–68.

Evans, Colin H. "Conflict and Dualism in Taine and Taine Criticism." In *Gallica*: *Essays Presented to J. Heywood Thomas*. Cardiff: University of Wales Press, 1969. 165–81.

Faguet, Emile. "Taine." In *Politiques et moralistes du dix-neuvième siècle*. Vol. 3. Paris: Société française d'imprimerie et de librairie, n.d. 237–314.

Febvre, Lucien. *"A New Kind of History" and Other Essays*. Ed. Peter Burke. Trans. K. Folca. New York: Harper and Row, 1973.

——. *La Terre et l'évolution humaine: Introduction géographique à l'histoire*. 1922; Paris: Albin Michel, 1970.

Fechner, Gustav. *Vorschule der Ästhetik*. 2 vols. Leipzig: Breitkopf und Härtel, 1876.

Felman, Shoshana. "Turning the Screws of Interpretation." *Yale French Studies*, no. 55 / 56 (1977): 94–207.

Ferrari, Jean. *Les Sources françaises de la philosophie de Kant*. Paris: Klincksieck, 1979.

Fichte, Johann Gottlieb. *Die Bestimmung des Menschen*. In *Sämmtliche Werke*. 8 vols. Ed. Immanuel Hermann Fichte. Berlin: Veit, 1845–46. 2: 167–319.

Fiedler, Conrad. *Schriften über Kunst*. Ed. Hans Marbach. Leipzig: S. Hirzel, 1896.

Finke, Michael. "Chekhov's 'Steppe': A Metapoetic Journey." *Russian Language Journal* 39 (1985): 79–120.

Fish, Stanley. "Consequences." *Critical Inquiry* 11 (1985): 433–58.

Fitzgerald, Gerald. "*Cenodoxus* and Baroque Latin." Harvard diss., 1963.

Flesch, William. *Generosity and the Limits of Authority: Shakespeare, Herbert, Milton*. Ithaca: Cornell University Press, 1992.

Fletcher, Angus. "On Two Words in the Libretto of *The Magic Flute*." *Georgia Review* 29 (1975): 128–53.

———. *The Prophetic Moment: An Essay on Spenser*. Chicago: University of Chicago Press, 1971.

———. *The Transcendental Masque*. Ithaca: Cornell University Press, 1971.

Flores, Ralph. "Cartesian Strip-Tease." In *The Rhetoric of Doubtful Authority: Deconstructive Readings of Self-Questioning Narratives, St. Augustine to Faulkner*. Ithaca: Cornell University Press, 1984. 66–87.

Forster, Leonard. *The Temper of Seventeenth-Century German Literature*. London: H. K. Lewis, 1952.

Foucault, Michel. *The Archaeology of Knowledge*. Trans. A. M. Sheridan Smith. New York: Random House, 1972.

———. *The Order of Things*. New York: Pantheon, 1973.

Frankl, Paul. "Der Beginn der Gotik und das allgemeine Problem des Stilbeginnes." In *Festschrift Heinrich Wölfflin*. Munich: H. Schmidt, 1924. 107–25.

Fried, Michael. *Absorption and Theatricality: Painting and Beholder in the Age of Diderot*. Berkeley: University of California Press, 1980.

———. *Three American Painters*. Cambridge, Mass.: Fogg Art Museum, Harvard University, 1965.

Friedman, Geraldine. "The Erotics of Interpretation in Keats's 'Ode on a Grecian Urn': Pursuing the Feminine." *Studies in Romanticism* 32 (1993): 225–43.

Friedrich, Hugo. *Die Struktur der modernen Lyrik: Von Baudelaire bis zur Gegenwart*. Hamburg: Rowohlt, 1956.

Fry, Paul. "History, Existence, and 'To Autumn.'" *Studies in Romanticism* 25 (1986): 211–19.

Frye, Northrop. "The Drunken Boat." In *The Stubborn Structure*. Ithaca: Cornell University Press, 1970. 200–17.

———. *Fearful Symmetry*. Princeton: Princeton University Press, 1969.

Fumerton, Patricia. *Cultural Aesthetics: Renaissance Literature and the Practice of Social Ornament*. Chicago: University of Chicago Press, 1991.

Gadamer, Hans-Georg. *Dialogue and Dialectic*. Trans. P. Christopher Smith. New Haven: Yale University Press, 1980.

———. *Wahrheit und Methode: Grundzüge einer philosophischen Hermeneutik*. Tübingen: Mohr, 1960.

Gallagher, Catherine. "Marxism and the New Historicism." In *The New Historicism*. Ed. H. Aram Veeser. New York: Routledge, 1989. 37–48.

Gaskell, Philip. "*Night and Day*: Development of a Play Text." In *Textual Criticism and Literary Interpretation*. Ed. Jerome J. McGann. 162–79.

Gasparov, B. M. "Nekotorye deskriptivnye problemy muzykalnoi semantiki." *Trudy po znakovym sistemam* 8 (1977): 120–37.

Genette, Gérard. *Mimologiques*. Paris: Seuil, 1976.

Gilson, Etienne. *Etudes sur le rôle de la pensée médiévale dans la formation du système cartésien*. Paris: Vrin, 1951.

Giraud, Victor. *Essai sur Taine: Son oeuvre et son influence*. Paris: Hachette, 1932.

———. *Hippolyte Taine: Etudes et documents*. Paris: Vrin, 1928.

Goethe, Johann Wolfgang. *Faust*. Trans. Walter Arndt. New York: Norton, 1976.

———. *Neue Gesamtausgabe der Werke und Schriften*. 22 vols. Stuttgart: Cotta, 1950–68.

Goldberg, Jonathan. *Endlesse Worke: Spenser and the Structures of Discourse*. Baltimore: Johns Hopkins University Press, 1981.

———. *James I and the Politics of Literature: Jonson, Shakespeare, Donne, and Their Contemporaries*. Stanford: Stanford University Press, 1989.

Goldsmith, Oliver. *The Collected Works of Oliver Goldsmith*. 5 vols. Ed. Arthur Friedman. Oxford: Clarendon Press. 1966.

Gombrich, E. H. *Norm and Form: Studies in the Art of the Renaissance*. London: Phaidon, 1966.

Götz, Johann Nikolaus. *Vermischte Gedichte*. Ed. Karl Wilhelm Ramler. 3 vols. Mannheim: Schwan, 1785.

Gouhier, Henri. *Essais sur Descartes*. Paris: Vrin, 1949.

Gourmont, Remy de. *Le Problème du style*. Paris: Mercure de France, n.d.

Granger, Gilles-Gaston. *Essai d'une philosophie du style*. Paris: Odile Jacob, 1988.

Grau, Kurt Joachim. *Die Entwicklung des Bewusstseinsbegriffes im XVII. und XVIII. Jahrhundert*. Halle: Niemeyer, 1916.

Greenblatt, Stephen. *Learning to Curse: Essays in Early Modern Culture*. New York: Routledge, 1990.

———. "Loudun and London." *Critical Inquiry* 12 (1986): 326–46.

———. *Renaissance Self-Fashioning: From More to Shakespeare*. Chicago: University of Chicago Press, 1980.

———. *Shakespearian Negotiations: The Circulation of Social Energy in Renaissance England*. Berkeley: University of California Press, 1988.

Greene, Thomas. "Ben Jonson and the Centered Self." *Studies in English Literature* 10 (1970): 325–48.

———. "The Flexibility of the Self in Renaissance Literature." In *The Disciplines of Criticism*. Ed. Peter Demetz, Thomas Greene, and Lowry Nelson. New Haven: Yale University Press, 1968. 241–64.

Grene, Marjorie. *Descartes*. Brighton: Harvester, 1985.

Griffin, Robert J. "Wordsworth's Pope: The Language of His Former Heart." *ELH* 54 (1987): 695–715.

Gryphius, Andreas. *Werke*. 3 vols. Ed. Hermann Palm. Darmstadt: Wissenschaftliche Buchgesellschaft, 1961.

Guillaume, Gustave. "Existe-t-il un déponent en français?" In *Langage et science du langage*. Paris: Nizet, 1964. 127–42.

Guillory, John. "Canonical and Non-Canonical: A Critique of the Current Debate." *ELH* 54 (1987): 483–517.

Guizot, [François]. *Cours d'histoire moderne*. No publication information.

Gumbrecht, Hans Ulrich. "Schwindende Stabilität der Wirklichkeit: Eine Geschichte des Stilbegriffs." In *Stil: Geschichten und Funktionen eines kulturwissenschaftlichen Diskurselements*. Ed. H. U. Gumbrecht. Frankfurt am Main: Suhrkamp, 1986. 726–88.

Gusdorf, Georges. *Les Principes de la pensée au siècle des lumières*. Paris: Payot, 1971.

Halpern, Richard. *The Poetics of Primitive Accumulation: English Renaissance Culture and the Genealogy of Capital*. Ithaca: Cornell University Press, 1991.

Hardy, Thomas. *An Autobiography*. Ed. Michael Sadleir. London: Oxford University Press, 1953.

———. *The Life and Work of Thomas Hardy*. Ed. Michael Millgate. Athens: University of Georgia Press, 1985.

———. *Tess of the D'Urbervilles*. Ed. Scott Elledge. New York: Norton, 1965.

Hartman, Geoffrey H. "The Voice of the Shuttle: Language from the Point of View of Literature." In *Beyond Formalism*. New Haven: Yale University Press, 1970. 337–55.

———. *Wordsworth's Poetry*. New Haven: Yale University Press, 1964.

Hauser, Arnold. *The Philosophy of Art History*. New York: Knopf, 1959.

Haven, Richard. *Patterns of Consciousness*. Amherst: University of Massachusetts Press, 1969.

Hegel, Georg Wilhelm Friedrich. *Enzyklopädie der philosophischen Wissenschaften, 1830*. Ed. Friedhelm Nicolin and Otto Pöggeler. Hamburg: Meiner, 1959.

———. *Phänomenologie des Geistes*. Ed. Johannes Hoffmeister. Hamburg: Meiner, 1952.

———. *Science of Logic*. Trans. A. V. Miller. London: Allen and Unwin, 1969.

———. *Werke*. Ed. Eva Moldenhauer and Karl Markus Michel. 20 vols. Frankfurt am Main: Suhrkamp, 1969–79.

Heidegger, Martin. *An Introduction to Metaphysics*. Trans. Ralph Manheim. New Haven: Yale University Press, 1959.

———. *Nietzsche*. 2 vols. Pfullingen: Neske, 1981.

———. *Nietzsche*. Trans. Frank A. Capuzzi, David Farrell Krell, and Joan Stambaugh. 4 vols. San Francisco: Harper and Row, 1979–87.

Heinse, Wilhelm. *Sämmtliche Werke*. Ed. Carl Schüddekopf. 15 vols. Leipzig: Insel, 1904.

Helgerson, Richard. *Forms of Nationhood: The Elizabethan Writing of England*. Chicago: University of Chicago Press, 1992.

Herder, Johann Gottfried. *Werke*. Ed. Heinrich Düntzer. 24 vols. Berlin: Gustav Hempel, n.d.

Herz, Marcus. *Versuch über den Schwindel*. Berlin: Vossische Buchhandlung, 1791.

Hildebrand, Adolf von. "Über das Vorstellen und das Körpergefühl in der Kunst." In *Gesammelte Schriften zur Kunst.* Ed. Henning Bock. Cologne: Westdeutscher Verlag, 1969. 358–61.

Hill, Aaron. *Works.* 4 vols. London, 1754.

Hils, G. *The Odes of Casimire.* 1646; Rpt. without Hils's introduction. Ed. Maren-Sofie Røstvig. Los Angeles: Augustan Reprint Society, 1953.

Hintikka, Jaakko. "'Cogito, Ergo Sum': Inference or Performance?" In *Knowledge and the Known: Historical Perspectives in Epistemology.* Dordrecht: Reidel, 1974. 98–125.

Hoffmann, E. T. A. *Betrachtungen über Musik.* Ed. Walter Florian. Stuttgart: P. O. Rohm, 1947.

———. *Schriften zur Musik.* Ed. Friedrich Schnapp. Munich: Winkler, 1963.

Hofmannsthal, Hugo von. *Ausgewählte Werke.* 2 vols. Ed. Rudolf Hirsch. Frankfurt am Main: Fischer, 1957.

Hollahan, Eugene. *Crisis-Consciousness and the Novel.* Newark: University of Delaware Press, 1992.

Holly, Michael Ann. "Wölfflin and the Imagining of the Baroque." In *Visual Culture: Images and Interpretations.* Ed. Norman Bryson, Michael Ann Holly, and Keith Moxey. Hanover, N.H.: Wesleyan University Press, 1994. 347–64.

Homans, Margaret. "Eliot, Wordsworth, and the Scenes of Critical Instruction." *Critical Inquiry* 8 (1981): 223–41.

Howarth, Herbert. *The Tiger's Heart.* New York: Oxford University Press, 1970.

Hucks, Joseph. *Poems.* Cambridge: Deighton, 1798.

Hughes, John. *Poetical Works.* 2 vols. Edinburgh: Apollo, 1779.

Hume, David. *A Treatise of Human Nature.* Garden City, N.Y.: Doubleday, 1961.

Hungerford, E. B. *Shores of Darkness.* New York: Columbia University Press, 1941.

Husserl, Edmund. *Cartesianische Meditationen.* Ed. Elisabeth Ströker. Hamburg: Meiner, 1987.

———. *Die Krisis der europäischen Wissenschaften und die transzendentale Phänomenologie.* Ed. Elisabeth Ströker. Hamburg: Meiner, 1982.

Iser, Wolfgang. *The Act of Reading: A Theory of Aesthetic Response.* Trans. David Henry Wilson. Baltimore: Johns Hopkins University Press, 1978.

Jacobus, Mary. "The Art of Managing Books: Romantic Prose and the Writing of the Past." In *Romanticism and Language.* Ed. Arden Reed. Ithaca: Cornell University Press, 1984. 205–46.

———. "The Question of Language: Men of Maxims and *The Mill on the Floss.*" *Critical Inquiry* 8 (1981): 207–22.

James, Henry. *Partial Portraits.* Westport, Conn.: Greenwood, 1970.

———. *The Turn of the Screw.* In *The Complete Tales of Henry James.* Ed. Leon Edel.

Philadelphia: Lippincott, 1961–64. 10: 15–138.

Jameson, Fredric. *Fables of Aggression: Wyndham Lewis, the Modernist as Fascist.* Berkeley: University of California Press, 1979.

———. *Marxism and Form: Twentieth-Century Dialectical Theories of Literature.* Princeton: Princeton University Press, 1971.

———. *The Political Unconscious.* Ithaca: Cornell University Press, 1981.

———. *Sartre: The Origins of a Style.* New Haven: Yale University Press, 1961.

Jankélévitch, Vladimir. *Fauré et l'inexprimable.* Paris: Plon, 1974.

———. *La Vie et la mort dans la musique de Debussy.* Neuchâtel: La Baconnière, 1968.

Johnson, Douglas Porter. *Beethoven's Sketches in the "Fischhof Miscellany," Berlin Autograph 28.* 2 vols. Ann Arbor, Mich.: UMI Research Press, 1980.

Jonson, Ben. *The Complete Masques.* Ed. Stephen Orgel. Vol. 4 of *The Yale Ben Jonson.* New Haven: Yale University Press, 1969.

Joyce, James. *Dubliners.* Ed. Robert Scholes and A. Walton Litz. New York: Viking, 1969.

———. *Exiles.* New York: Viking, 1961.

———. *Letters of James Joyce.* Ed. Richard Ellmann. Vol. 2. London: Faber and Faber, 1966.

Judovitz, Dalia. *Subjectivity and Representation in Descartes: The Origins of Modernity.* Cambridge: Cambridge University Press, 1988.

Juglar, Louis. *Le Style dans les arts et sa signification historique.* Paris: Hachette, 1901.

Justi, Carl. *Diego Velázquez and His Times.* Trans. A. H. Keane. London: Grevel, 1889.

Kant, Immanuel. *Briefwechsel.* Vol. 10 of *Kants gesammelte Schriften.* Berlin: Walter de Gruyter, 1922.

———. *Critique of Pure Reason.* Trans. Norman Kemp Smith. London: Macmillan, 1929.

———. *Gesammelte Schriften.* 29 vols. Berlin: G. Reimer, 1910–70.

———. *Werke.* 6 vols. Ed. Wilhelm Weischedel. Wiesbaden: Insel, 1956–64.

Karbusicky, Vladimir. "Zeichen und Musik." *Zeitschrift für Musik* 9 (1987): 227–49.

Kayser, Wolfgang. "Der Stilbegriff der Literaturwissenschaft." In *Die Vortragsreise.* Berne: Francke, 1958. 71–81.

Keats, John. *The Poems of John Keats.* Ed. Jack Stillinger. Cambridge, Mass.: Harvard University Press, 1978.

Kehr, Theodor. *Das Bewusstseinsproblem.* Tübingen: Mohr, 1916.

Keller, Wilhelm. "Die Modulationen in Mozarts Fantasie KV 475." In *Festschrift Erich Valentin.* Ed. Gunther Weiss. Regensburg: G. Bosse, 1976. 79–88.

Kemmerling, Andreas. "Eine reflexive Deutung des Cogito." In *Theorie der Subjektivität.* Ed. Konrad Cramer, et al. Frankfurt am Main: Suhrkamp, 1987.

Kenner, Hugh. "The Most Beautiful Book." *ELH* 48 (1981): 594–605.

Kerman, Joseph. *The Beethoven Quartets.* New York: Knopf, 1967.

Kermode, Frank. *The Art of Telling: Essays on Fiction.* Cambridge, Mass.: Harvard University Press, 1983.

———. "The Dancer." In *The Romantic Image.* London: Collins, 1971. 62–106.

Kerrigan, William, and Gordon Braden. *The Idea of the Renaissance.* Baltimore: Johns Hopkins University Press, 1989.

Kleinbauer, W. Eugene. *Modern Perspectives in Art History.* New York: Holt, Rinehart and Winston, 1971.

Kleist, Heinrich von. *Sämtliche Werke und Briefe.* Ed. Helmut Sembdner. 2 vols. Munich: Hanser, 1984.

Knight, G. Wilson. *The Starlit Dome: Studies in the Poetry of Vision.* London: Oxford University Press, 1971.

Koselleck, Reinhart. *Futures Past.* Trans. Keith Tribe. Cambridge, Mass.: MIT Press, 1985.

———. *Kritik und Krise: Eine Studie zur Pathogenese der bürgerlichen Welt.* Frankfurt am Main: Suhrkamp, 1973.

Krebs, Harold. "Alternatives to Monotonality in Early Nineteenth-Century Music." *Journal of Music Theory* 25 (1981): 1–15.

Kronik, John. "The Web, the Hive, and the Looking Glass: Self-Consciousness in Hispanic Literature." Mid-America Conference on Hispanic Literature. University of Colorado, Boulder, October 3, 1986.

Kümmel, Friedrich. *Platon und Hegel: Zur ontologischen Begründung des Zirkels in der Erkenntnis.* Tübingen: Niemeyer, 1968.

Lamb, Charles. *The Works of Charles and Mary Lamb.* Ed. E. V. Lucas. 1903; New York: AMS Press, 1968.

Lang, Berel. "Descartes and the Art of Meditation." *Philosophy and Rhetoric* 21 (1988): 19–37.

———. "Looking for the Styleme." *Critical Inquiry* 9 (1982): 405–13.

———. "Style as Instrument, Style as Person." *Critical Inquiry* 4 (1978): 715–39.

Lasky, Melvin J. *Utopia and Revolution.* Chicago: University of Chicago Press, 1976.

Leduc, A. G. "Ueber den Aufsatz des Herrn Fetis." *Allegemeine musikalische Zeitung* 32 (1830): 117–32.

Lefèvre, Roger. *La Pensée existentielle de Descartes.* N.p.: Bordas, 1965.

Lentricchia, Frank. "Foucault's Legacy: A New Historicism?" In *The New Historicism.* Ed. H. Aram Veeser. New York: Routledge, 1989. 231–42.

Leonardi, Susan J. "Recipes for Reading: Summer Pasta, Lobster à la Riseholme, and Key Lime Pie." *PMLA* 104 (1989): 340–47.

Lévesque, Claude, and Christie V. McDonald, eds. *L'Oreille de l'autre: Textes et débats avec Jacques Derrida.* Montreal: VLB, 1982.

Levinson, Marjorie. *Keats's Life of Allegory: The Origins of a Style.* Oxford: Blackwell, 1988.

———. *Wordsworth's Great Period Poems.* Cambridge: Cambridge University Press, 1986.

Lévi-Strauss, Claude. "Introduction: History and Anthropology." In *Structural Anthropology*. Trans. Claire Jacobson and Brooke Grundfest Schoepf. Garden City, N.Y.: Anchor, 1967. 1–28.

——. *The Savage Mind*. Chicago: University of Chicago Press, 1966.

Lewis, Christopher. "Mirrors and Metaphor: Reflections on Schoenberg and Nineteenth-Century Tonality." *Nineteenth-Century Music* 10 (1987): 229–42.

Lipps, Theodor. *Grundzüge der Logik*. Hamburg: Voss, 1893.

——. "Das Wesen der musikalischen Konsonanz und Dissonanz." In *Psychologische Studien*. Leipzig: Dürr, 1905. 115–230.

Liu, Alan. "The Power of Formalism: The New Historicism." *ELH* 56 (1989): 721–71.

Locke, John. *An Essay Concerning Human Understanding*. Ed. Alexander Campbell Fraser. 2 vols. New York: Dover, 1959.

Lockwood, Thomas. *Post-Augustan Satire: Charles Churchill and Satirical Poetry, 1750–1800*. Seattle: University of Washington Press, 1979.

Lombardo, Patrizia. "Hippolyte Taine Between Art and Science." *Yale French Studies* no. 77 (1990): 117–33.

——. "Taine scrittore." In Hippolyte Taine, *Etienne Mayran*. Ed. Patrizia Lombardo. Milan: Adelphi, 1988. 143–78.

Lovejoy, Arthur O. "On the Discrimination of Romanticisms." In *Essays in the History of Ideas*. New York: Putnam, 1960. 228–53.

Lucente, Gregory. *Beautiful Fables: Self-Consciousness in Italian Narrative from Manzoni to Calvino*. Baltimore: Johns Hopkins University Press, 1986.

Macaulay, Thomas Babington. *Critical and Historical Essays*. 5 vols. Leipzig: Bernhard Tauchnitz, 1850.

MacCaffrey, Isabel G. *Spenser's Allegory: The Anatomy of Imagination*. Princeton: Princeton University Press, 1976.

Macherey, Pierre. *Pour une théorie de la production littéraire*. Paris: Maspero, 1966.

MacLean, Gerald. "What Is a Restoration Poem? Editing a Discourse, Not an Author." *Text* 3 (1986): 319–46.

Major, John M. "The Moralization of the Dance in Elyot's *Governour*." *Studies in the Renaissance* 5 (1958): 27–36.

Mallarmé, Stéphane. *Oeuvres complètes*. Ed. Henri Mondor and G. Jean-Aubry. Paris: Gallimard, 1961.

Manning, Peter J. "The Hone-ing of Byron's Corsair." In *Textual Criticism and Literary Interpretation*. Ed. Jerome J. McGann. 107–26.

Marcus, Leah S. "Renaissance / Early Modern Studies." In *Redrawing the Boundaries: The Transformation of English and American Literary Studies*. New York: The Modern Language Association of America, 1992. 41–63.

Marshall, Donald G. "Ideas and History: The Case of 'Imagination.'" *Boundary 2* 10 (1982): 343–59.

McCorkel, Christine. "Sense and Sensibility: An Epistemological Approach to the Philosophy of Art History." *Journal of Aesthetics and Art Criticism* 34 (1975): 35–50.

McDonald, Christie V. *Dispositions: Quatre essais sur les écrits de Jean-Jacques Rousseau, Stéphane Mallarmé, Marcel Proust et Jacques Derrida.* Québec: Hurtubise, 1986.

McFarland, Thomas. *Coleridge and the Pantheist Tradition.* Oxford: Clarendon Press, 1969.

McGann, Jerome J. *The Beauty of Inflections: Literary Investigations in Historical Method and Theory.* Oxford: Clarendon Press, 1985.

———. *Black Riders: The Visible Language of Modernism.* Princeton: Princeton University Press, 1993.

———. *A Critique of Modern Textual Criticism.* Chicago: University of Chicago Press, 1983.

———. *Fiery Dust: A Study of Byron's Poetic Development.* Chicago: University of Chicago Press, 1968.

———. [Anne Mack, J. J. Rome, and George Mannejc, pseud.] "Literary History, Romanticism, and Felicia Hemans." *Modern Language Quarterly* 54 (1993): 215–35.

———. *The Romantic Ideology: A Critical Investigation.* Chicago: University of Chicago Press, 1983.

———. *Social Values and Poetic Acts: The Historical Judgment of Literary Work.* Cambridge, Mass.: Harvard University Press, 1988.

———. "Some Forms of Critical Discourse." *Critical Inquiry* 11 (1985): 399–417.

———. *Towards a Literature of Knowledge.* Chicago: University of Chicago Press, 1989.

———, ed. *Textual Criticism and Literary Interpretation.* Chicago: University of Chicago Press, 1985.

Meagher, John C. "The Dance and the Masques of Ben Jonson." *Journal of the Warburg and Courtauld Institutes* 25 (1962): 258–77.

Mehrotra, K. K. *Horace Walpole and the English Novel: A Study of the Influence of "The Castle of Otranto," 1764–1820.* Oxford: Basil Blackwell, 1934.

Meinecke, Friedrich. *Historism: The Rise of a New Historical Outlook.* Trans. J. E. Anderson. New York: Herder and Herder, 1972.

Mellor, Anne K. *Romanticism and Gender.* New York: Routledge, 1993.

Meschonnic, Henri. *Pour la poétique.* 5 vols. Paris: Gallimard, 1970–78.

Miles, Josephine. "Wordsworth and Glitter." *Studies in Philology* 40 (1943): 552–59.

Miller, D. A. *Narrative and Its Discontents: Problems of Closure in the Traditional Novel.* Princeton: Princeton University Press, 1981.

Miller, J. Hillis. *Charles Dickens: The World of His Novels.* Bloomington: Indiana University Press, 1969.

——. "The Critic as Host." In *Deconstruction and Criticism*. Ed. Harold Bloom, et al. New York: Continuum, 1979. 217–53.

——. *The Linguistic Moment: From Wordsworth to Stevens*. Princeton: Princeton University Press, 1985.

Miscellany Poems and Translations by Oxford Hands. London: Anthony Stephens, 1685.

Monglond, Henri. *Le Préromantisme français*. 2 vols. Grenoble: Arthaud, 1930.

Murry, J. Middleton. *The Problem of Style*. London: Humphry Milford / Oxford University Press, 1925.

Nancy, Jean-Luc. *Discours de la Syncope*. Vol. 1: *Logodaedalus*. Paris: Flammarion, 1976.

——. *Ego Sum*. Paris: Flammarion, 1979.

Nattiez, Jean-Jacques. *Fondements d'une sémiologie de la musique*. Paris: Union générale d'éditions, 1975.

Naumann, Emil. "Wolfgang Mozart." In *Sammlung Musikalischer Vorträge*. Ed. Paul Graf Waldersee. 6 vols. in 5. Leipzig: Breitkopf und Härtel, 1879–98. 1: 193–211.

Nelson, William. *The Poetry of Edmund Spenser: A Study*. New York: Columbia University Press, 1963.

Nemoianu, Virgil. *The Taming of Romanticism: European Literature and the Age of Biedermeier*. Cambridge, Mass.: Harvard University Press, 1984.

Newcomb, Anthony. "Narrative Archetypes and Mahler's Ninth Symphony." In *Music and Text: Critical Inquiries*. Ed. Steven Paul Scher. Cambridge: Cambridge University Press, 1992. 118–36.

Newsom, Robert. *Dickens on the Romantic Side of Familiar Things*. New York: Columbia University Press, 1977.

Nietzsche, Friedrich Wilhelm. *Also Sprach Zarathustra*. In his *Werke in drei Bänden*. 3 vols. Ed. Karl Schlechta. Munich: Hanser, 1969. 2: 275–561.

Nohl, Herman. *Stil und Weltanschauung*. Jena: Diederichs, 1920.

Nohl, Ludwig. *Mozart: Ein Beitrag zur Aesthetik der Tonkunst*. Heidelberg: Bangel und Schmidt, 1860.

Nordmann, Jean-Thomas. *Taine et la critique scientifique*. Paris: Presses Universitaires de France, 1992.

Norris, John. *A Collection of Miscellanies*. London: E. Parker, 1730.

Novalis [Friedrich von Hardenberg]. *Schriften*. 5 vols. Ed. Paul Kluckhohn, Richard Samuel, and Hans-Joachim Mähl. Stuttgart: Kohlhammer, 1960–75.

Orgel, Stephen. "Shakespeare and the Kinds of Drama." *Critical Inquiry* 6 (1979): 107–23.

Panofsky, Erwin. *Renaissance and Renascences in Western Art*. 2 vols. Stockholm: Almkvist and Wiksell, 1960.

Parker, Patricia A. *Inescapable Romance: Studies in the Poetics of a Mode*. Princeton: Princeton University Press, 1979.

Parnell, Thomas. *Collected Poems*. Ed. Claude Rawson and F. P. Lock. Newark: University of Delaware Press, 1989.

Parsons, Talcott. "Value-Freedom and Objectivity." In *Max Weber and Sociology Today*. Ed. Otto Stammer. Trans. Kathleen Morris. New York: Harper and Row, 1971. 27–82.

Pater, Walter. *Appreciations, with an Essay on Style*. New York: Macmillan, 1905.

Patten, Steven C. "Kant's Cogito." *Kant-Studien* 66 (1975): 331–41.

Patterson, Lee. "The Logic of Textual Criticism and the Way of Genius." In *Textual Criticism and Literary Interpretation*. Ed. Jerome J. McGann. 55–91.

Paz, Octavio. *El Arco y la lira*. Mexico City: Fondo de Cultura Económica, 1967.

Peckham, Morse. *The Triumph of Romanticism*. Columbia: University of South Carolina Press, 1970.

Pfau, Thomas. "Immediacy and the Text: Friedrich Schleiermacher's Theory of Style and Interpretation." *Journal of the History of Ideas* (1990): 51–73.

Pflug, Günther. *Henri Bergson: Quellen und Konsequenzen einer induktiven Metaphysik*. Berlin: de Gruyter, 1959.

Piaget, Jean. *Structuralism*. Ed. and trans. Chaninah Maschler. London: Routledge and Kegan Paul, 1971.

Plato. *Platonis Opera*. Ed. Ioannes Burnet. 5 vols. Oxford: Clarendon Press, 1900–07.

Pope, Alexander. *Poems*. Ed. John Butt. New Haven: Yale University Press, 1963.

Porter, Andrew. *Music of Three Seasons: 1974–77*. New York: Farrar, 1978.

Poulet, Georges. "The Dream of Descartes." In *Studies in Human Time*. Trans. Elliott Coleman. New York: Harper, 1956. 50–73.

———. *Mesure de l'instant*. Paris: Plon, 1968.

Price, Martin. *To the Palace of Wisdom*. Garden City, N.Y.: Doubleday, 1965.

Propp, Vladimir. *Morphology of the Folktale*. Trans. Laurence Scott. Austin: University of Texas Press, 1968.

Proudhon, Pierre-Joseph. *Les Carnets de P.-J. Proudhon*. Ed. Suzanne Henneguy and Jeanne Fauré-Fremelet. Vol. 2. Paris: M. Rivière, 1961.

———. *Correspondance de P.-J. Proudhon*. 14 vols. Paris: A. Lacroix, 1875.

———. *De la justice dans la Révolution et dans l'Eglise*. Ed. C. Bouglé and J.-L. Puech. 4 vols. Paris: M. Rivière, 1935.

———. *Du principe de l'art et de sa destination sociale*. Paris: Garnier, 1865.

———. *Les Majorats littéraires*. Paris: E. Dantu, 1863.

———. *Philosophie du progrès*. Brussels: A. Lebègue, 1853.

Proust, Marcel. *A la recherche du temps perdu*. Ed. Pierre Clarac and André Ferré. 3 vols. Paris: Gallimard, 1954.

Pynchon, Thomas. *Slow Learner: Early Stories*. London: Little, Brown, 1985.

Quintero, Vicente. "El 'Cogito' cartesiano en la 'Crítica de la razón pura' de Kant." In *Homenaje a Descartes en el tercer centenario del "Discurso del Método."*

Ed. Luís Juan Guerrero. Buenos Aires: Imprenta de la Universidad, 1937. 2: 335–39.

Ragghianti, Carlo. *L'arte e la critica*. In *Critica d'arte* 45 (Jan.–June 1980).

Rajan, Tilottama. "Displacing Post-Structuralism: Romantic Studies After Paul de Man." *Studies in Romanticism* 24 (1985): 451–74.

Ratner, Leonard. *Classic Music: Expression, Form, and Style*. New York: Schirmer, 1980.

Rawson, C. J. *Henry Fielding and the Augustan Ideal Under Stress*. London: Routledge, 1972.

Redner, Harry. *In the Beginning Was the Deed: Reflections on the Passage of Faust*. Berkeley: University of California Press, 1982.

Rehm, Walther. *Heinrich Wölfflin als Literarhistoriker*. Munich: Bayerische Akademie der Wissenschaften, 1960.

Revel, Jean-François. "Introduction." In Hippolyte Taine, *Philosophie de l'art*. Ed. Jean-François Revel. Paris: Hermann, 1964. 9–19.

Richard, Jean-Pierre. *L'Univers imaginaire de Mallarmé*. Paris: Seuil, 1961.

Romanowski, Sylvie. *L'Illusion chez Descartes*. Paris: Klincksieck, 1974.

Rosen, Charles. *The Classical Style: Haydn, Mozart, Beethoven*. New York: Norton, 1972.

———. *The Romantic Generation*. Cambridge, Mass.: Harvard University Press, 1995.

———. *Schoenberg*. London: Fontana, 1976.

———. *Sonata Forms*. New York: Norton, 1980.

Røstvig, Maren-Sofie. *The Happy Man*. 2 vols. Oslo: Akademisk Vorlag, 1954.

Rouges, Alberto. "La Refutación kantiana del Idealismo problemático: El realismo empírico." In *Homenaje a Descartes en el tercer centenario del "Discurso del Método."* Ed. Luís Juan Guerrero. Buenos Aires: Imprenta de la Universidad, 1937. 3: 161–70.

Rousseau, Jean-Jacques. *Oeuvres complètes*. Ed. Bernard Gagnebin, Robert Osmont, and Marcel Raymond. Vol. 1. Paris: Gallimard, 1959.

Rousset, Jean. *La Littérature de l'âge baroque en France: Circé et le paon*. Paris: José Corti, 1954.

Sainte-Beuve, Charles-Augustin. "Divers écrits de M. Taine." In *Causeries du lundi*. Paris: Garnier, 1926. 13: 249–84.

———. "Histoire de la littérature anglaise, par M. Taine." In *Nouveaux lundis*. Paris: Calmann-Lévy, n.d. 66–137.

Sarbiewski, Matthias Casimirus [Maciej Kazimierz]. *Matthiae Casimiri Sarbievii Carmina*. Argentoratum [=Strasbourg]: Societas Bipontina, Anno XI [=1803].

Saussure, Ferdinand de. *Course in General Linguistics*. Ed. Charles Bally and Albert Sechehaye. Trans. Wade Baskin. New York: McGraw-Hill, 1959.

Schaff, Adam. "Das Verstehen der verbalen Sprache und das 'Verstehen der Musik.'" In *Musik und Verstehen: Aufsätze zur semiotischen Theorie, Ästhetik und*

Soziologie der musikalischen Rezeption. Ed. Peter Faltin and Hans-Peter Reinecke. Cologne: Volk, 1973. 276–88.

Schalk, Fritz. "Zu Taines Theorie und Praxis." In *Beiträge zur Theorie der Künste im 19. Jahrhundert*. Ed. Helmut Koopmann and J. Adolf Schmoll gen. Eisenwerth. 2 vols. Frankfurt am Main: Klostermann, 1971. 1: 352–59.

Schmarsow, August. *Unser Verhältnis zu den bildenden Künsten: Sechs Vorträge über Kunst und Erziehung*. Leipzig: Teubner, 1903.

Schmidt, Gerhart. *Aufklärung und Metaphysik: Die Neubegründung des Wissens durch Descartes*. Tübingen: Niemeyer, 1965.

Schoenberg, Arnold. *Gesammelte Schriften*. Ed. Ivan Vojtech. Frankfurt am Main: Fischer, 1976.

———. *Style and Idea*. Ed. Leonard Stein. New York: St. Martins, 1975.

Scholz, Heinrich. "Über das Cogito, ero sum." *Kant-Studien* 36 (1931): 126–47.

Schor, Naomi. *George Sand and Idealism*. New York: Columbia University Press, 1993.

Schrade, Leo. "Mozart und die Romantiker." In *De Scientia Musicae Studia atque Orationes*. Ed. Ernst Lichtenhahn. Berne: Haupt, 1967. 519–36.

Schulz-Buschhaus, Ulrich. "Taine und die Historizität des Stils." In *Stil: Geschichten und Funktionen eines kulturwissenschaftlichen Diskurselements*. Ed. Hans Ulrich Gumbrecht. Frankfurt am Main: Suhrkamp, 1986. 189–99.

Searle, John. "*Las Meninas* and the Paradoxes of Pictorial Representation." *Critical Inquiry* 6 (1980): 477–88.

Sebeok, Thomas, ed. *Style in Language*. New York: John Wiley and Sons, 1960.

Shell, Marc. "Money and the Mind: The Economics of Translation in Goethe's *Faust*." *Modern Language Notes* 94 (1980): 516–62.

Shelley, Percy Bysshe. *Shelley's Poetry and Prose*. Ed. Donald H. Reiman and Sharon Powers. New York: Norton, 1977.

Sigmund, Oskar. "Mozarts Phantasie in c-Moll, KV 475." In *Gustav Becking zum Gedächtnis: Eine Auswahl seiner Schriften und Beiträge seiner Schüler*. Ed. Walter Kramolisch. Tutzing: Schneider, 1975. 483–94.

Simpson, David. *Romanticism, Nationalism, and the Revolt Against Theory*. Chicago: University of Chicago Press, 1993.

Snyder, Joel, and Ted Cohen. "Reflexions on *Las Meninas*: Paradox Lost." *Critical Inquiry* 7 (1980): 429–47.

Solie, Ruth. "Whose Life? The Gendered Self in Schumann's *Frauenliebe* Songs." In *Music and Text: Critical Inquiries*. Ed. Steven Paul Scher. Cambridge: Cambridge University Press, 1992. 219–40.

Sollers, Philippe. "Littérature et totalité." In *L'Ecriture et l'expérience des limites*. Paris: Seuil, 1971. 67–87.

Sparrow, John. "Sarbiewski's *Silviludia* and Their Italian Source." *Oxford Slavonic Papers* 8 (1958): 1–48.

Spencer, Herbert. *Philosophy of Style: An Essay*. New York: D. Appleton, 1897.

Spenser, Edmund. *The Faerie Queene*. Ed. J. C. Smith. Oxford: Clarendon, 1909.

Spiegelman, Willard. *Majestic Indolence: English Romantic Poetry and the Work of Art*. New York: Oxford University Press, 1995.

Spinoza, Benedict de. *Chief Works*. Trans. R. H. M. Elwes. 2 vols. London: George Bell and Sons, 1901.

Staiger, Emil. "Entstellte Zitate." In *Die Kunst der Interpretation*. Munich: Deutscher Taschenbuch-Verlag, 1971. 138–54.

Starobinski, Jean. *Blessings in Disguise: Or, the Morality of Evil*. Trans. Arthur Goldhammer. Cambridge, Mass.: Harvard University Press, 1993.

——. *1789: Les Emblèmes de la raison*. Paris: Flammarion, 1973.

Sternberg, Meir. *Temporal Modes and Expositional Ordering in Fiction*. Baltimore: Johns Hopkins University Press, 1978.

Sterne, Laurence. *Tristram Shandy*. Ed. James A. Work. New York: Odyssey, 1940.

Stevens, Wallace. "Adagia." In *Opus Posthumous*. Ed. Samuel French Morse. New York: Random House, 1982. 157–80.

——. *Collected Poems*. New York: Knopf, 1959.

Stevenson, Robert Louis. *The Complete Short Stories*. Ed. Charles Neider. Garden City, N.Y.: Doubleday, 1969.

Stewart, Garrett. *Reading Voices: Literature and the Phonotext*. Berkeley: University of California Press, 1990.

Strauss, Leo. *Natural Right and History*. Chicago: University of Chicago Press, 1953.

Strich, Fritz. *Zu Heinrich Wölfflin's Gedächtnis*. Berne: Francke, 1956.

Svevo, Italo. *La Coscienza di Zeno*. Milan: Dall' Oglio, 1969.

Szondi, Peter. "Das Naive ist das Sentimentalische: Zur Begriffsdialektik in Schillers Abhandlung." In *Schriften*. Ed. Jean Bollack. 2 vols. Frankfurt: Suhrkamp, 1978. 2: 59–105.

Taine, Hippolyte. *L'Ancien régime* (part 1 of *Les Origines de la France contemporaine*). 2 vols. Paris: Hachette, 1899.

——. *De l'intelligence*. 2 vols. Paris: Hachette, 1923.

——. *Derniers essais de critique et d'histoire*. Paris: Hachette, 1923.

——. *Essai sur Tite Live*. Paris: Hachette, 1923.

——. *Esssais de critique et d'histoire*. Paris: Hachette, 1923.

——. *Etienne Mayran: Fragments*. Ed. Paul Bourget. Paris: Hachette, 1910.

——. *Histoire de la littérature anglaise*. 5 vols. Paris: Hachette, 1877 (vols. 1–4), 1873 (vol. 5).

——. *History of English Literature*. Trans. Henri van Laun. 2 vols. New York: A. L. Burt, n.d.

——. *La Fontaine et ses fables*. Paris: Hachette, 1907.

——. *Notes sur l'Angleterre*. Paris: Hachette, 1923.

——. *Notes sur Paris: Vie et opinions de M. Frédéric-Thomas Graindorge*. Paris: Hachette, 1921.

——. *Nouveaux essais de critique et d'histoire.* Paris: Hachette, 1923.

——. *Les Philosophes classiques du XIXe siècle en France.* Paris: Hachette, 1895.

——. *Philosophie de l'art.* Ed. Stéphane Douailler. N.p.: Fayard, 1985.

——. *La Révolution* (part 2 of *Les Origines de la France contemporaine*). 3 vols. Paris: Hachette, 1881–85.

——. *Voyage aux Pyrénées.* Paris: Hachette, 1920.

——. *Voyage en Italie.* 2 vols. Paris: Hachette, 1907.

Tave, Stuart M. *Some Words of Jane Austen.* Chicago: University of Chicago Press, 1973.

Theiner, Lieselotte. "Das Phänomen der atonikalen Werköffnung in der Klaviermusik von Ph. E. Bach bis R. Schumann." *Studien zur Musikwissenschaft* 28 (1977): 115–69.

Thesiger, Sarah. "The *Orchestra* of Sir John Davies and the Image of the Dance." *Journal of the Warburg and Courtauld Institutes* 36 (1973): 277–304.

Thomas, Brook. *The New Historicism and Other Old-Fashioned Topics.* Princeton: Princeton University Press, 1991.

——. "Parts Related to Wholes and the Nature of Subaltern Opposition." *Modern Language Quarterly* 55 (1994): 79–106.

Tillotson, Geoffrey. "The Manner of Proceeding in Certain Eighteenth- and Early Nineteenth-Century Poems." In *Augustan Studies.* London: Athlone Press, 1961. 111–46.

Tillyard, E. M. *Five Poems.* London: Chatto and Windus, 1948.

Trollope, Anthony. *An Autobiography.* Ed. Michael Sadleir. London: Oxford University Press, 1953.

——. *Can You Forgive Her?* Ed. Michael Sadleir and Frederick Page. London: Oxford University Press, 1948.

Valéry, Paul. *Oeuvres.* 2 vols. Ed. Jean Hytier. Paris: Gallimard, 1957–60.

van Laun, Henri. *History of French Literature.* 3 vols. London: Chatto and Windus, 1883.

Vaughan, Henry. *Complete Poetry.* Ed. French Fogle. New York: Norton, 1969.

Vendler, Zeno. "Descartes' Res Cogitans." In *Res Cogitans: An Essay in Rational Psychology.* Ithaca: Cornell University Press, 1972. 144–205.

Venturi, Lionello. *History of Art Criticism.* Trans. Charles Marriott. New York: Dutton, 1964.

Verga, Giovanni. *Tutte le novelle.* 2 vols. Milan: Mondadori, 1961.

Vertrees, Julie Anne. "Mozart's String Quartet K. 465: The History of a Controversy." *Current Musicology* 17 (1974): 96–114.

Volkelt, Johannes. *Ästhetische Zeitfragen.* Munich: Beck, 1895.

——. *System der Ästhetik.* 3 vols. Munich: Beck, 1905–14.

Wagner, Richard. *Sämtliche Schriften und Dichtungen.* 16 vols. Leipzig: Breitkopf und Härtel, 1911.

Wahl, Jean. *Du rôle de l'idée de l'instant dans la philosophie de Descartes.* Paris: Vrin, 1953.

Wallerstein, Ruth. *Studies in Seventeenth-Century Poetic.* Madison: University of Wisconsin Press, 1965.

Ward, Aileen. "The Forging of Orc: Blake and the Idea of Revolution." *Tri-Quarterly* no. 23–24 (1972): 204–27.

Warnke, Martin. "On Heinrich Wölfflin." *Representations* no. 27 (Summer 1989): 172–87.

Watts, Isaac. *Horae Lyricae.* London: J. Clark and R. Hett, 1727.

Weber, Max. "Die 'Objektivität' sozialwissenschaftlicher und sozialpolitischer Erkenntnis." In *Gesammelte Aufsätze zur Wissenschaftslehre.* Ed. Johannes Winckelmann. Tübingen: Mohr, 1951. 206–14.

Weinbrot, Howard. *The Formal Strain: Studies in Augustan Imitation and Satire.* Chicago: University of Chicago Press, 1969.

Weinstein, Leo. *Hippolyte Taine.* New York: Twayne, 1972.

Wellek, René. "Hippolyte Taine." In *A History of Modern Criticism: 1750–1950.* Vol. 4: *The Later Nineteenth Century.* New Haven: Yale University Press, 1965. 27–52.

Wenk, Arthur B. *Claude Debussy and Twentieth-Century Music.* Boston: Twayne, 1983.

White, Hayden. "The Value of Narrativity in the Representaton of Reality." *Critical Inquiry* 7 (1980): 5–27.

Wilkes, G. A. "The Poetry of Sir John Davies." *Huntington Library Quarterly* 25 (1962): 283–98.

Williams, Bernard. *Descartes: The Project of Pure Enquiry.* Atlantic Highlands, N.J.: Humanities Press, 1978.

Williamson, George. *The Senecan Amble: A Study in Prose Form from Bacon to Collier.* Chicago: University of Chicago Press, 1951.

Wilson, Edmund. *To the Finland Station: A Study in the Writing and Acting of History.* New York: Farrar, Straus and Giroux, 1972.

Wimsatt, William. *The Prose Style of Samuel Johnson.* New Haven: Yale University Press, 1941.

Wind, Edgar. "Zur Systematik der künstlerischen Probleme." *Zeitschrift für Ästhetik und allgemeine Kunstwissenschaft* 18 (1925): 480–86.

Wölfflin, Heinrich. *The Art of Albrecht Dürer.* Trans. Alastair Grieve and Heide Grieve. 1905; New York: Phaidon, 1971.

———. *Classic Art: An Introduction to the Italian Renaissance.* Trans. Peter Murray and Linda Murray. 1898; London: Phaidon, 1952.

———. *Gedanken zur Kuntsgeschichte.* Basel: Benno Schwabe, 1941.

———. *Kleine Schriften.* Ed. Joseph Gantner. Basel: Benno Schwabe, 1946.

———. *Principles of Art History: The Problem of the Development of Style in Later Art.* Trans. M. C. Hottinger. 1915; New York: Dover, 1950.

——. *Renaissance and Baroque.* Trans. Kathrin Simon. 1888; Ithaca: Cornell University Press, 1966.

——. Review of Alois Riegl, *Die Enstehung der Barockkunst in Rom.* In *Repertorium für Kunstwissenschaft* 31 (1908): 356–57.

——. *The Sense of Form in Art: A Comparative Psychological Study.* Trans. Alice Muehsam and Norma A. Shatan. New York: Chelsea, 1958.

Wolfson, Susan. "The Language of Interpretation in Romantic Poetry: 'A Strong Working of the Mind.'" In *Romanticism and Language.* Ed. Arden Reed. Ithaca: Cornell University Press, 1984. 22–49.

Wood, Allen W. *Kant's Rational Theology.* Ithaca: Cornell University Press, 1978.

Wordsworth, William. *Poetical Works.* 5 vols. Ed. E. de Selincourt and Helen Darbishire. Oxford: Clarendon Press, 1940–49.

Yeats, William Butler. *Collected Poems.* New York: Macmillan, 1956.

Young, Edward. *Works in Prose.* London: P. Brown, H. Hill, and S. Payne, 1765.

Zenck-Maurer, Claudia. *Versuch über die wahre Art, Debussy zu analysieren.* Munich: Emil Katzbichler, 1974.

Zola, Emile. *Une Page d'amour.* In his *Oeuvres complètes.* 15 vols. Ed. Henri Mitterand. Paris: Cercle du livre français, 1966–69. 3: 959–1209.

——. *Le Roman expérimental.* Ed. Aimé Guedj. Paris: Garnier-Flammarion, 1971.

Index

In this index an "f" after a number indicates a separate reference on the next page, and an "ff" indicates separate references on the next two pages. A continuous discussion over two or more pages is indicated by a span of page numbers, e.g., "57–59." *Passim* is used for a cluster of references in close but not consecutive sequence.